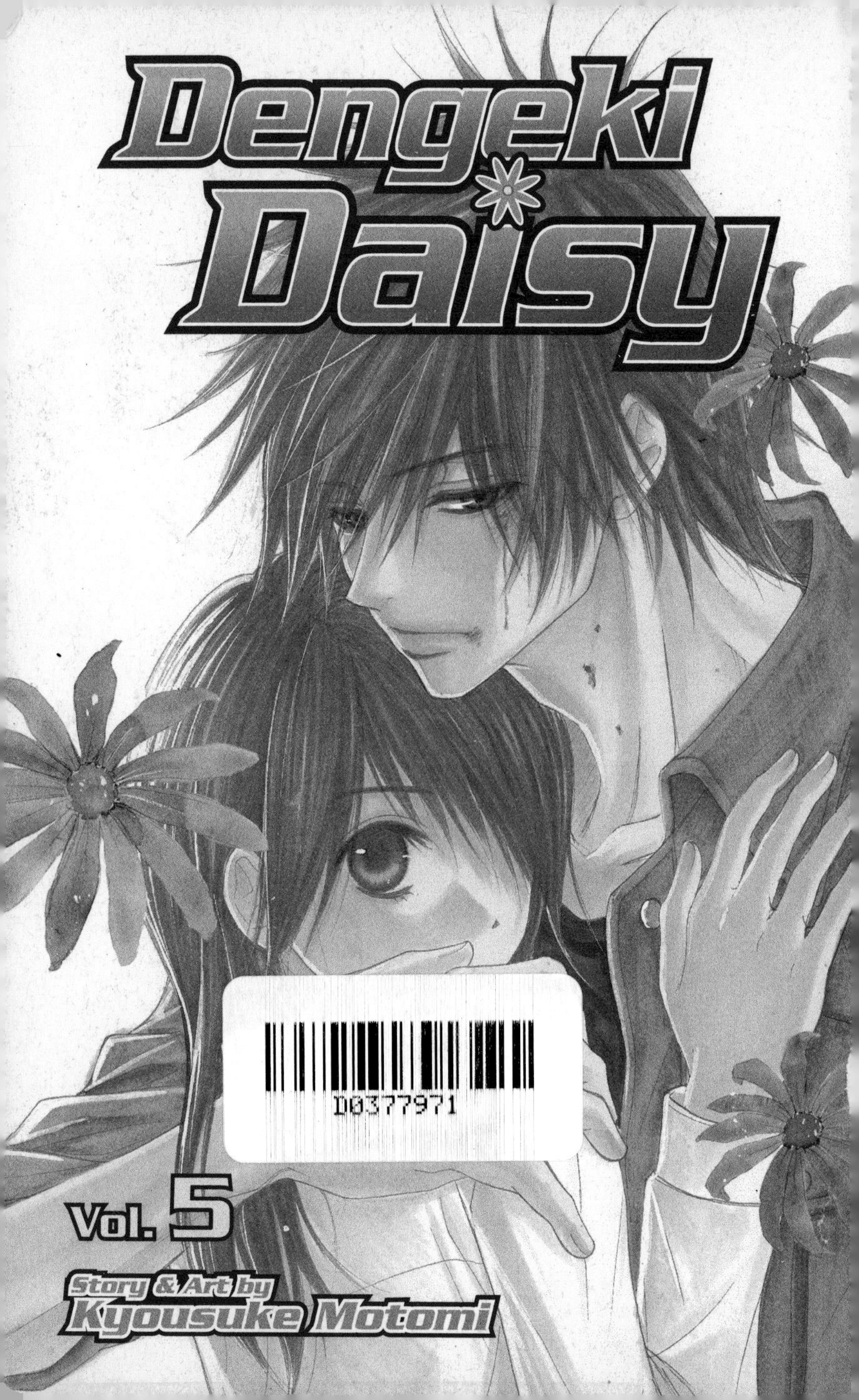
Dengeki Daisy
Vol. 5
Story & Art by
Kyousuke Motomi

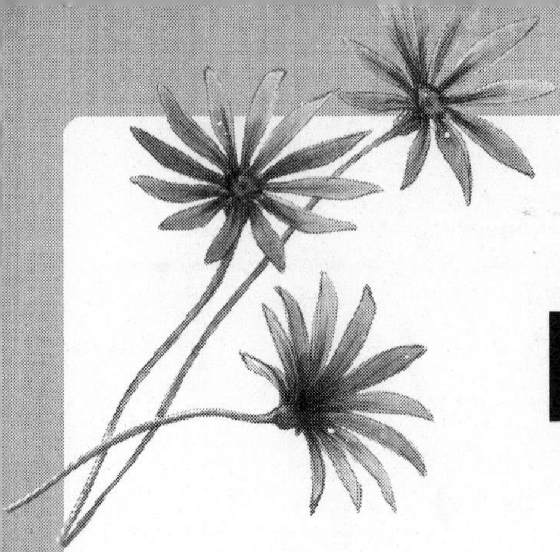

Dengeki Daisy

Volume 5 CONTENTS

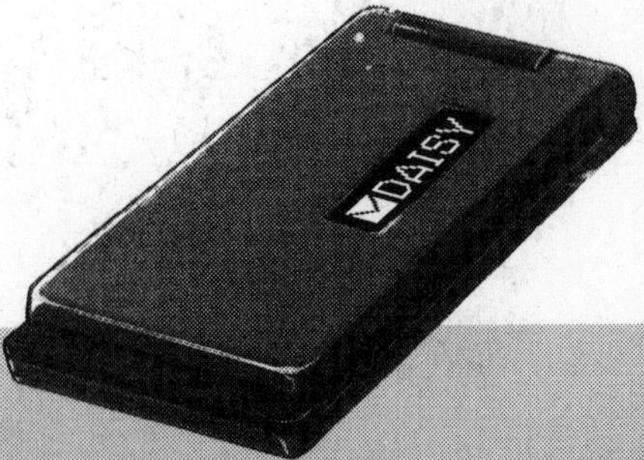
DAISY

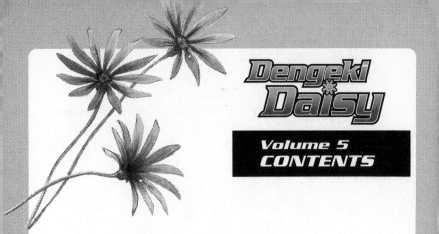

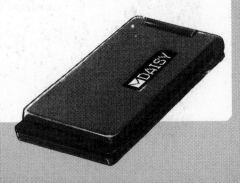

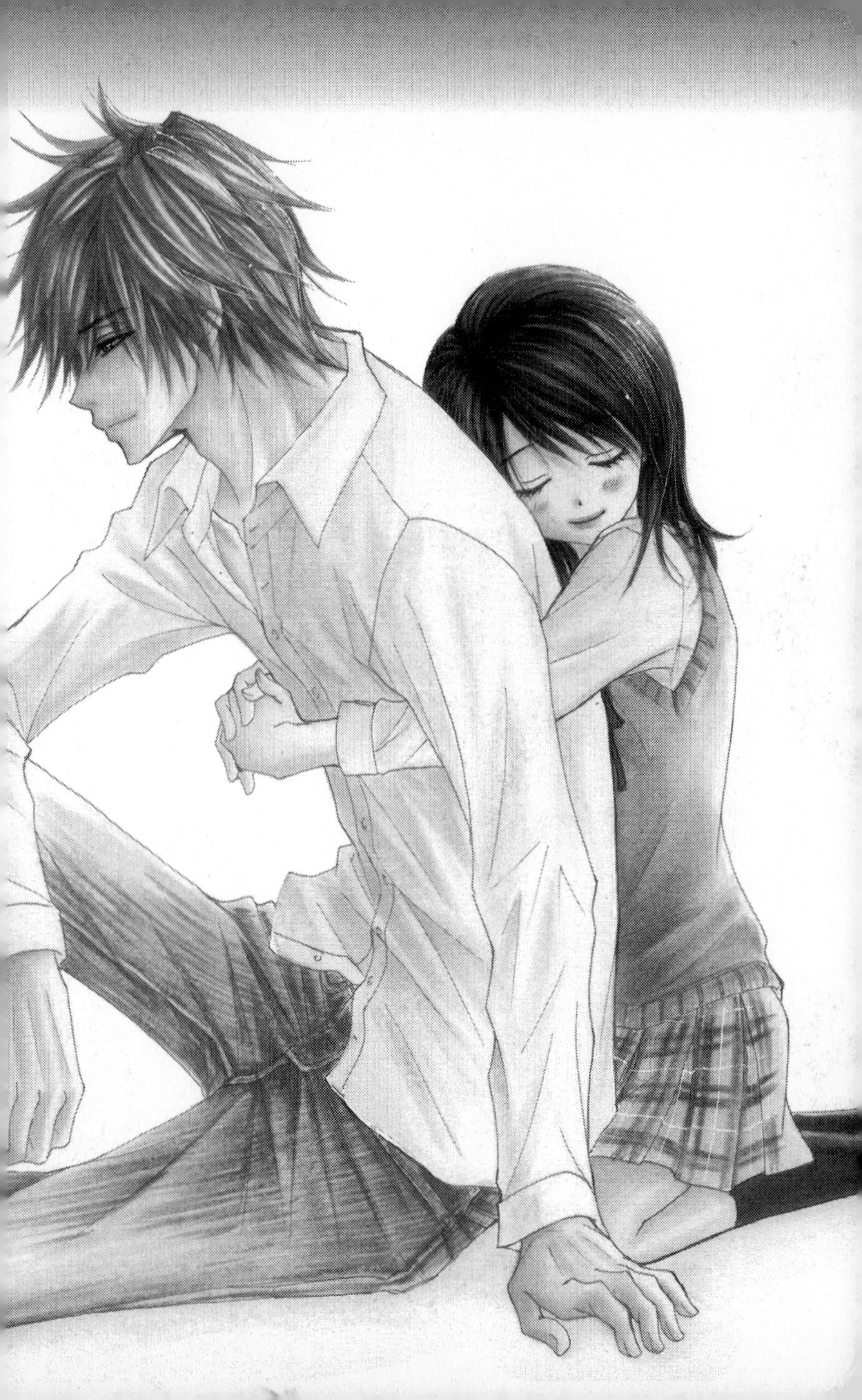

CHAPTER 20: TO THE ONE I LOVE DEARLY

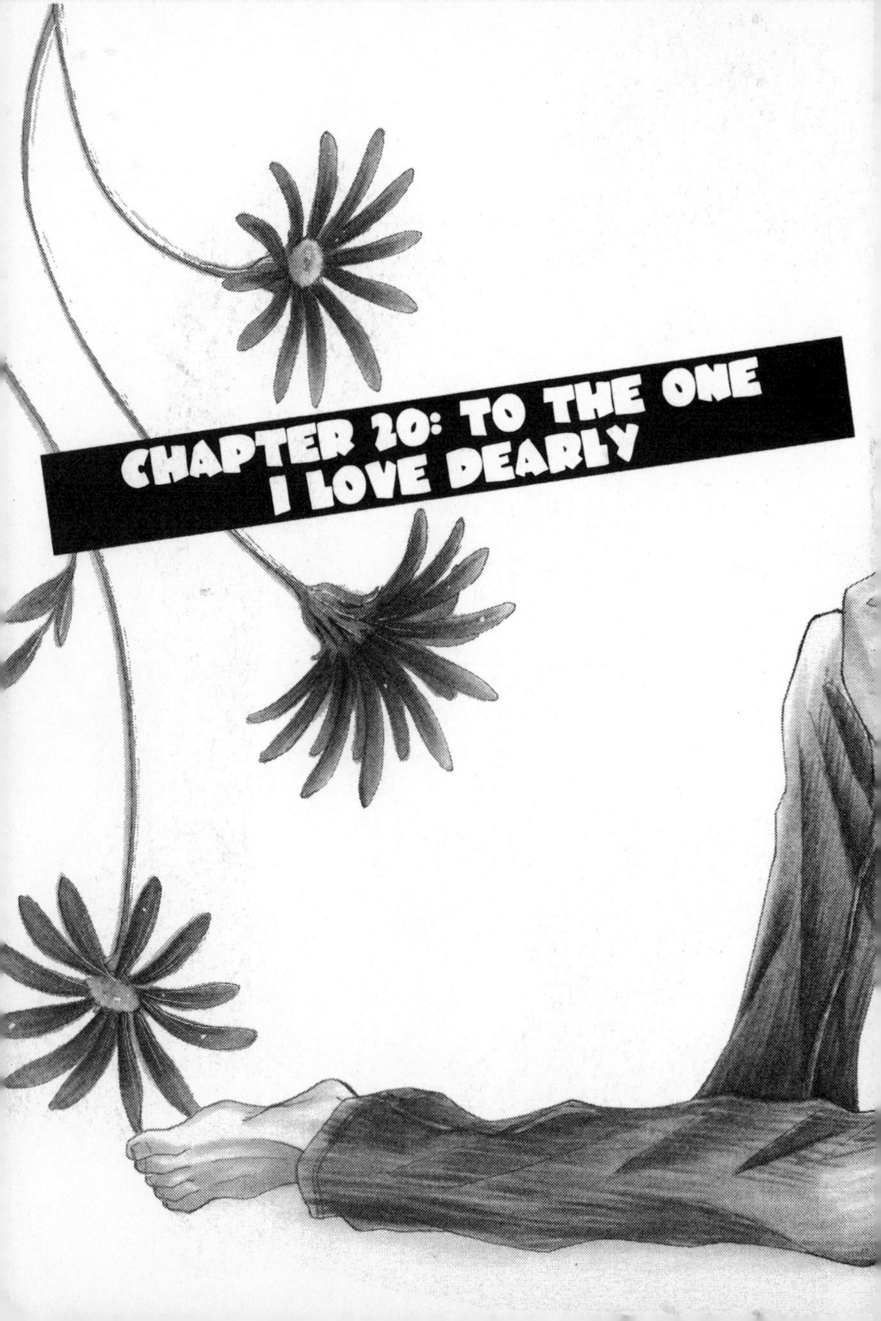

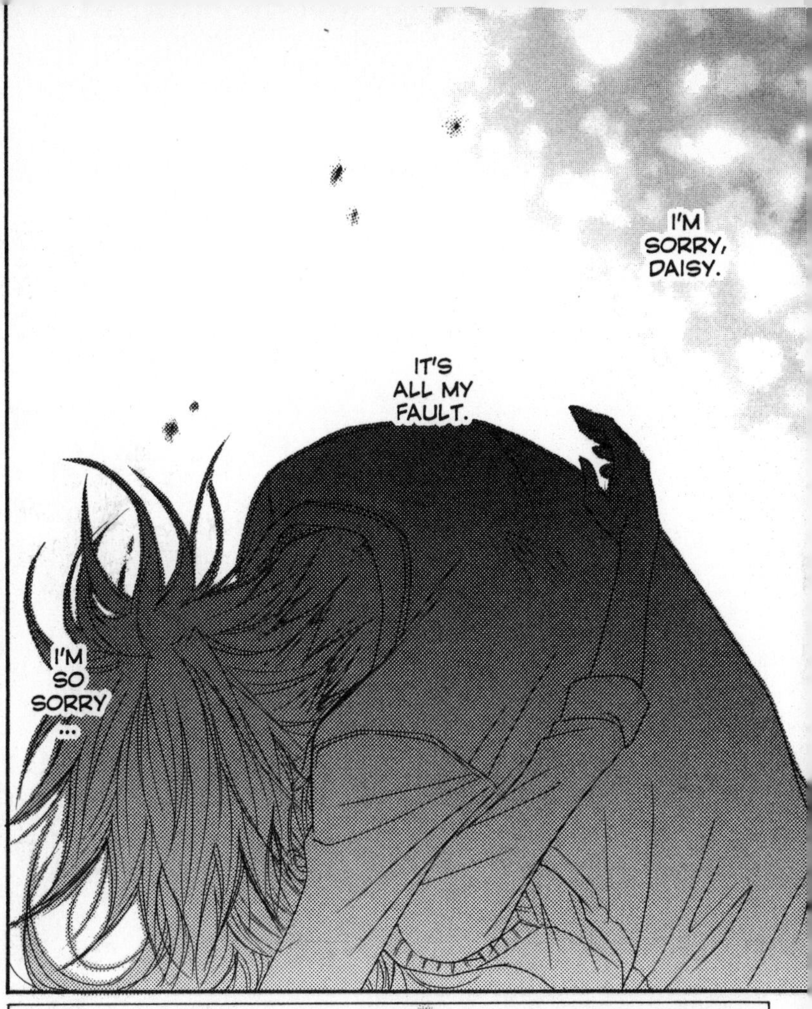
I'M SORRY, DAISY.
IT'S ALL MY FAULT.
I'M SO SORRY...

HELLO, EVERYONE!
IT'S KYOUSUKE MOTOMI.

THIS IS VOLUME 5 OF *DENGEKI DAISY*.

THANKS TO ALL OF YOU, I'VE MADE IT THIS FAR DESPITE MY STRUGGLES. THANK YOU SO MUCH!

WELL, IF THIS GIVES YOU EVEN A BIT OF ENJOYMENT, I'D BE HAPPY.

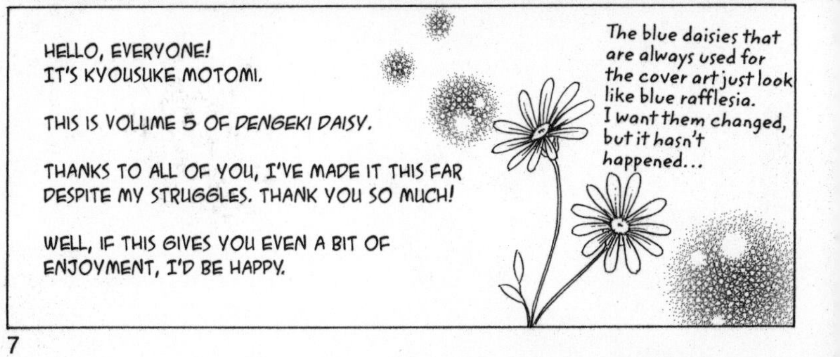

The blue daisies that are always used for the cover art just look like blue rafflesia. I want them changed, but it hasn't happened...

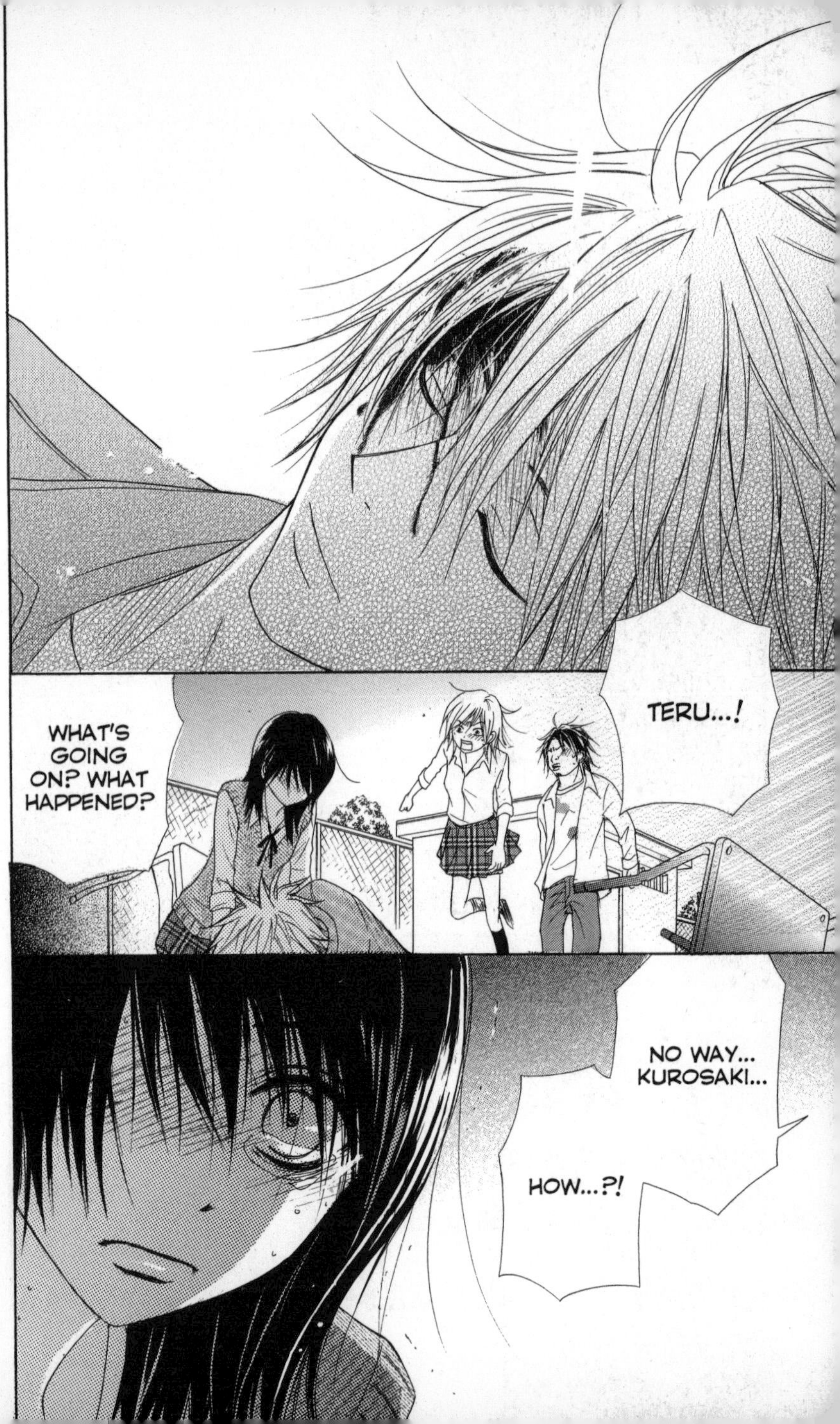
TERU...!
WHAT'S GOING ON? WHAT HAPPENED?
NO WAY... KUROSAKI...
HOW...?!

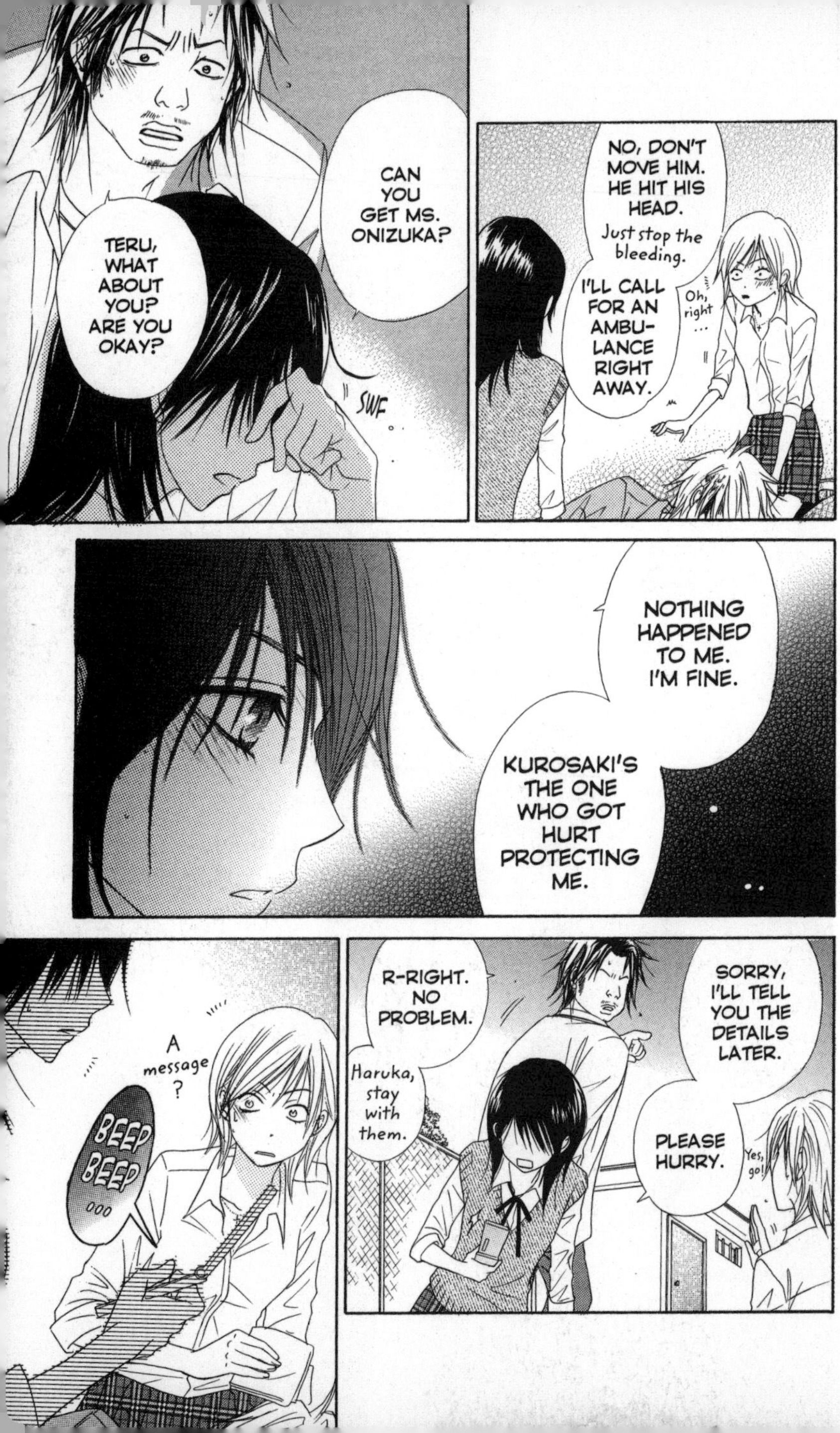
NO, DON'T MOVE HIM. HE HIT HIS HEAD.
Just stop the bleeding.
Oh, right...
I'LL CALL FOR AN AMBULANCE RIGHT AWAY.
CAN YOU GET MS. ONIZUKA?
TERU, WHAT ABOUT YOU? ARE YOU OKAY?
SWF
NOTHING HAPPENED TO ME. I'M FINE.
KUROSAKI'S THE ONE WHO GOT HURT PROTECTING ME.
SORRY, I'LL TELL YOU THE DETAILS LATER.
R-RIGHT. NO PROBLEM.
Haruka, stay with them.
PLEASE HURRY.
Yes, go!
A message?
BEEP BEEP
ooo

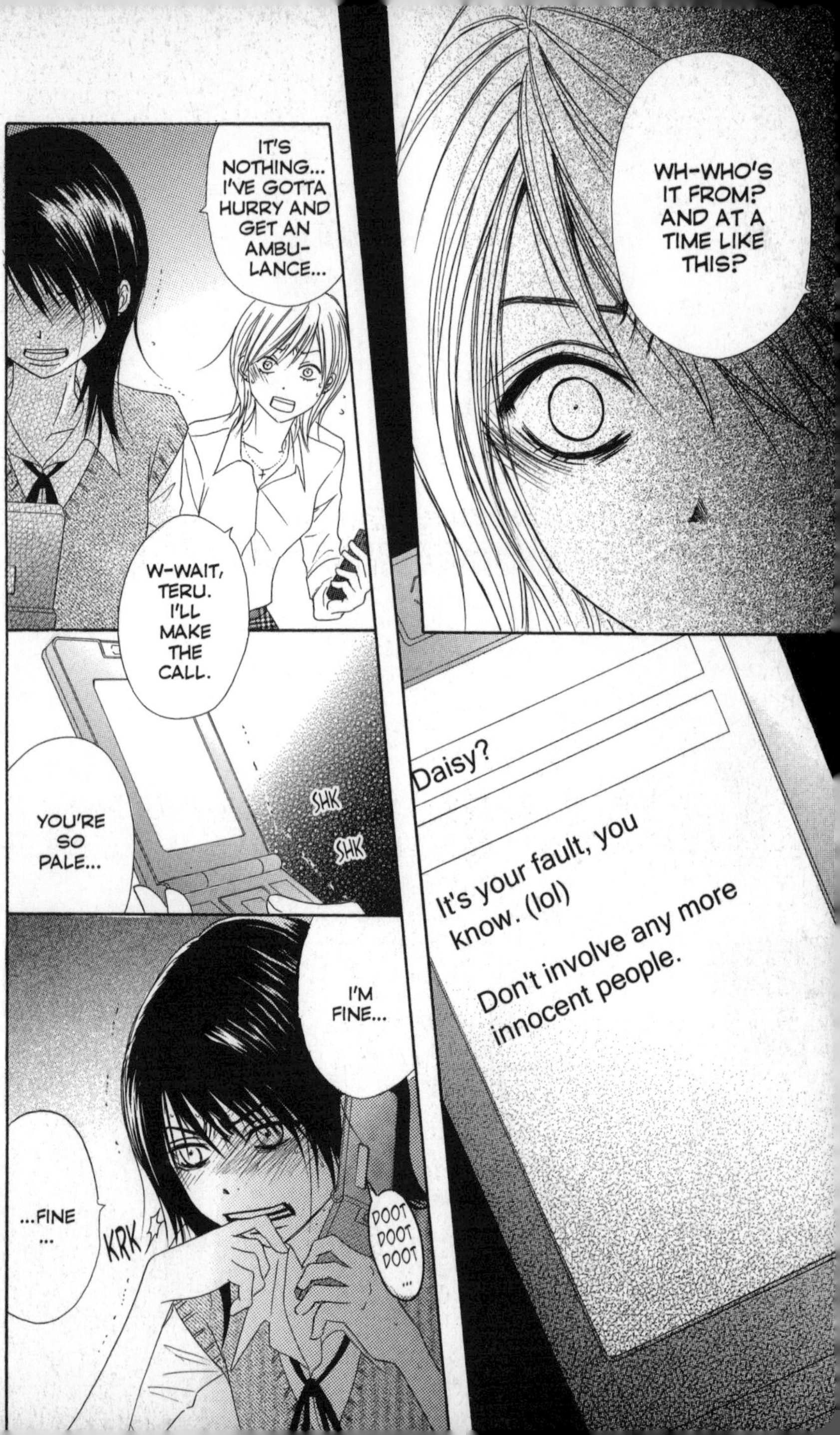
WH-WHO'S IT FROM? AND AT A TIME LIKE THIS?
IT'S NOTHING... I'VE GOTTA HURRY AND GET AN AMBU-LANCE...
W-WAIT, TERU. I'LL MAKE THE CALL.
Daisy?
It's your fault, you know. (lol)
Don't involve any more innocent people.
SHK
SHK
YOU'RE SO PALE...
I'M FINE...
...FINE ...
KRK
DOOT DOOT DOOT DOOT ...

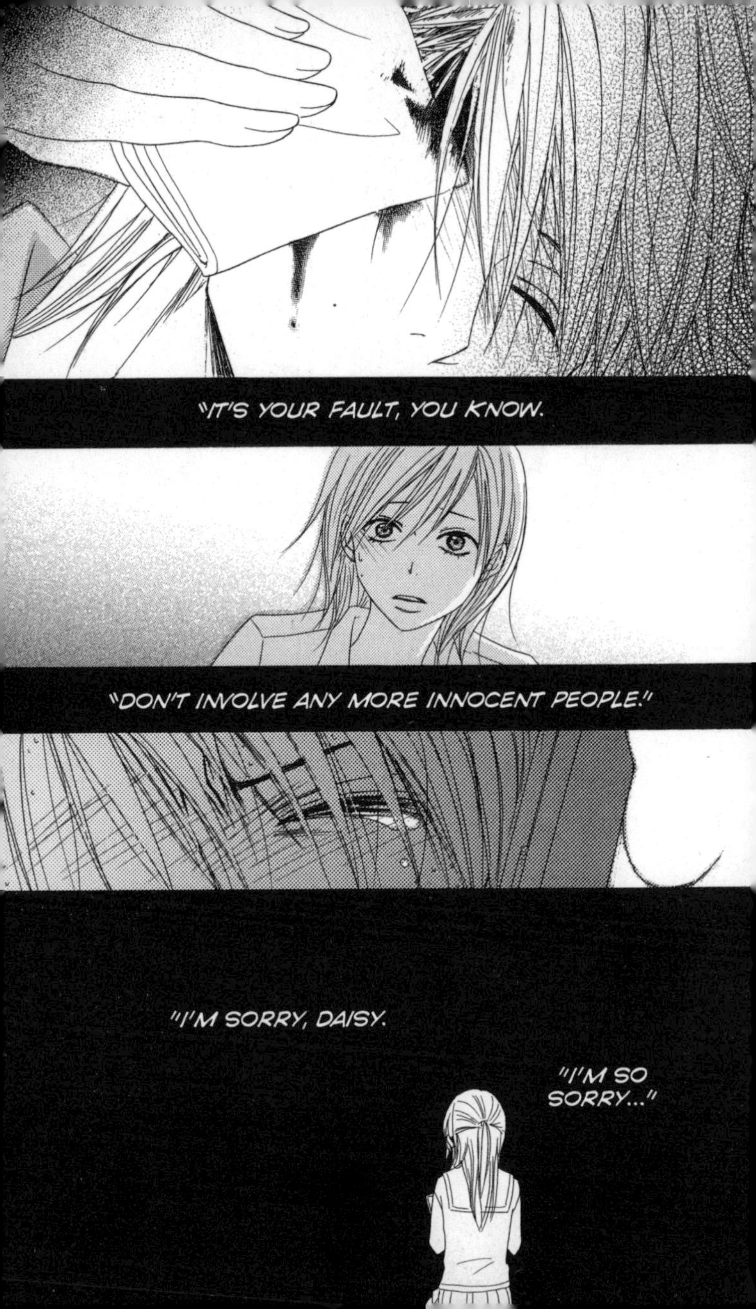
"IT'S YOUR FAULT, YOU KNOW.
"DON'T INVOLVE ANY MORE INNOCENT PEOPLE."
"I'M SORRY, DAISY.
"I'M SO SORRY..."

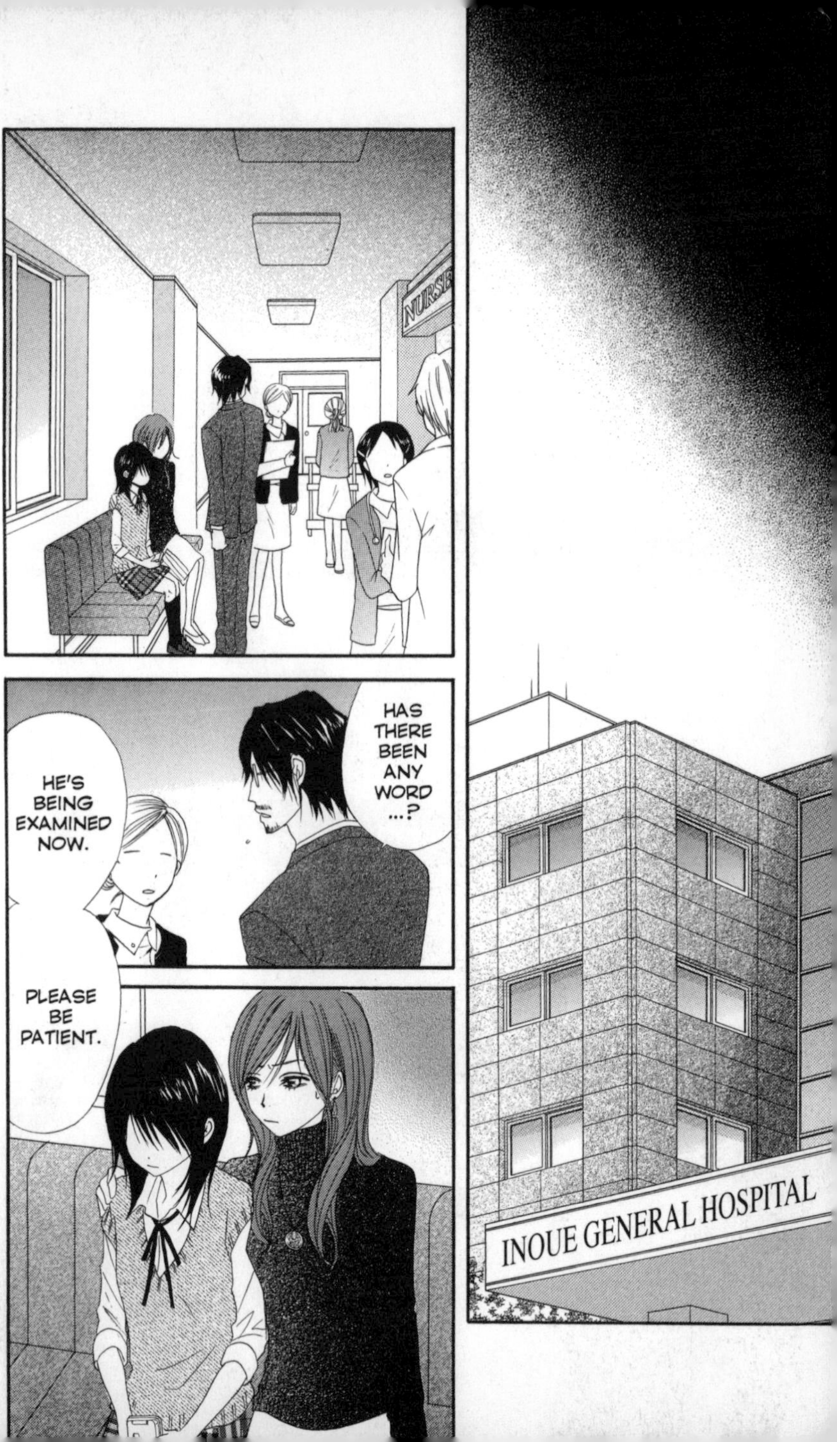
INOUE GENERAL HOSPITAL
NURSE
HAS THERE BEEN ANY WORD ...?
HE'S BEING EXAMINED NOW.
PLEASE BE PATIENT.

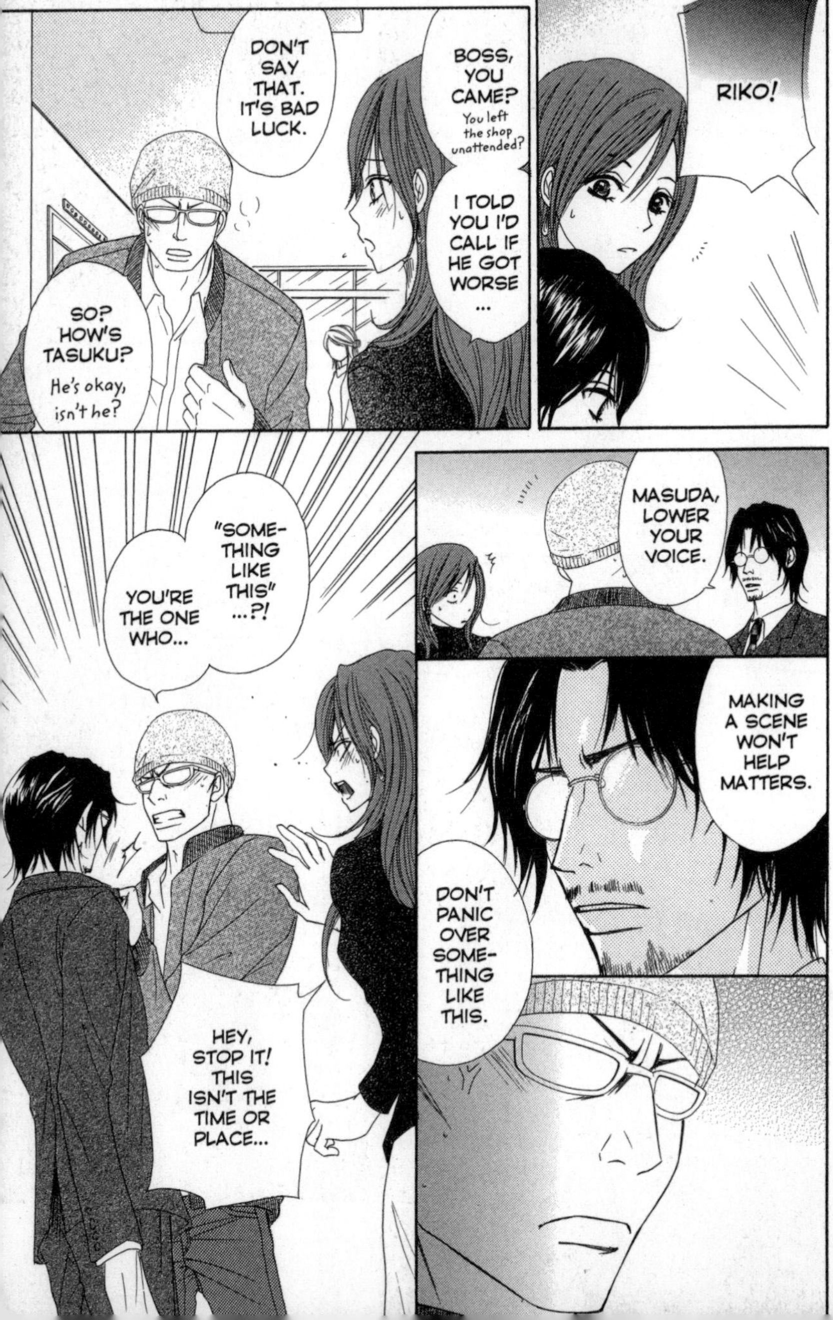
RIKO!
BOSS, YOU CAME? You left the shop unattended?
DON'T SAY THAT. IT'S BAD LUCK.
I TOLD YOU I'D CALL IF HE GOT WORSE ...
SO? HOW'S TASUKU? He's okay, isn't he?
MASUDA, LOWER YOUR VOICE.
MAKING A SCENE WON'T HELP MATTERS.
DON'T PANIC OVER SOME-THING LIKE THIS.
"SOME-THING LIKE THIS" ...?!
YOU'RE THE ONE WHO...
HEY, STOP IT! THIS ISN'T THE TIME OR PLACE...

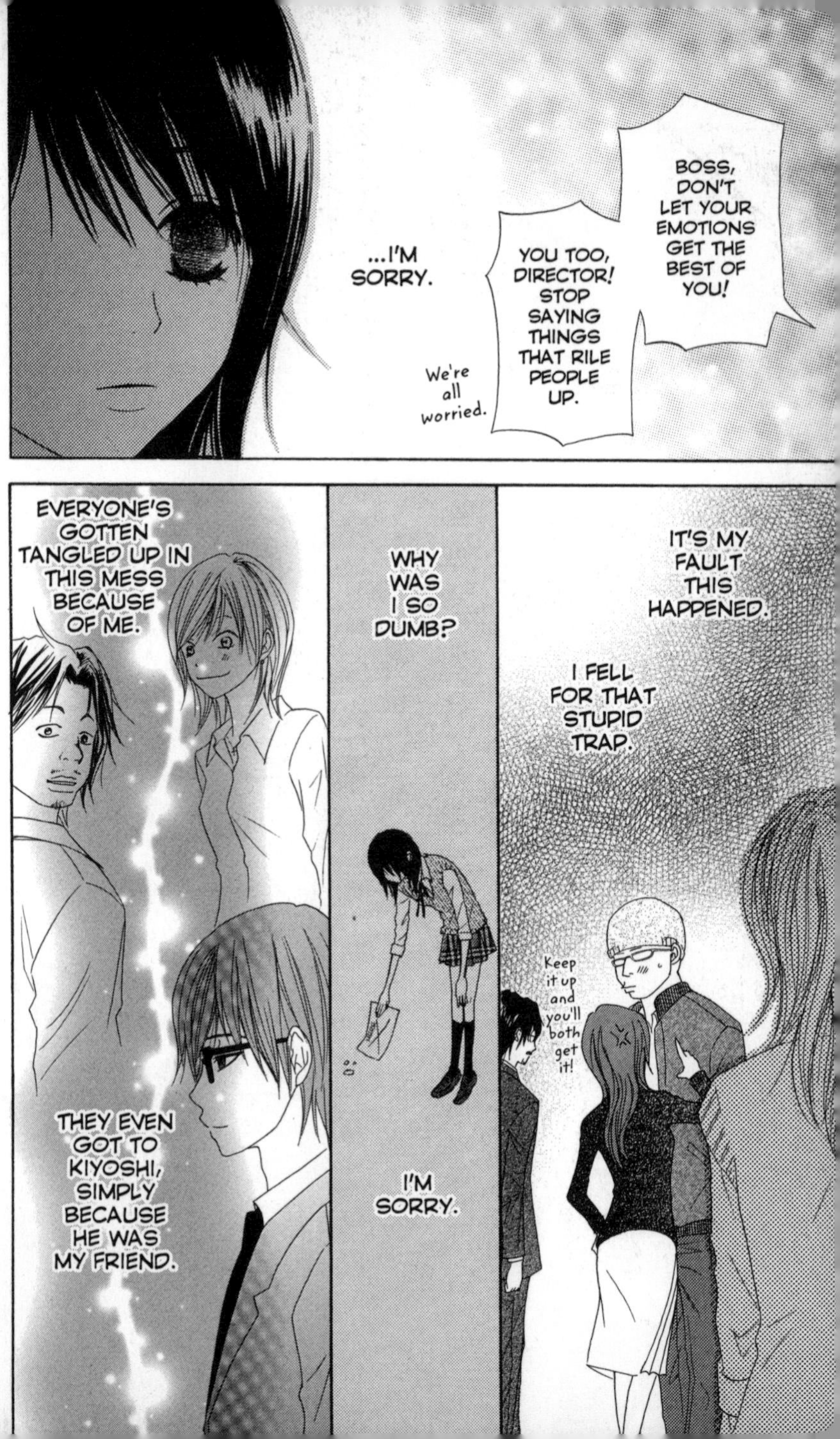
BOSS, DON'T LET YOUR EMOTIONS GET THE BEST OF YOU!
YOU TOO, DIRECTOR! STOP SAYING THINGS THAT RILE PEOPLE UP.
We're all worried.
...I'M SORRY.
IT'S MY FAULT THIS HAPPENED.
I FELL FOR THAT STUPID TRAP.
Keep it up and you'll both get it!
WHY WAS I SO DUMB?
I'M SORRY.
EVERYONE'S GOTTEN TANGLED UP IN THIS MESS BECAUSE OF ME.
THEY EVEN GOT TO KIYOSHI, SIMPLY BECAUSE HE WAS MY FRIEND.

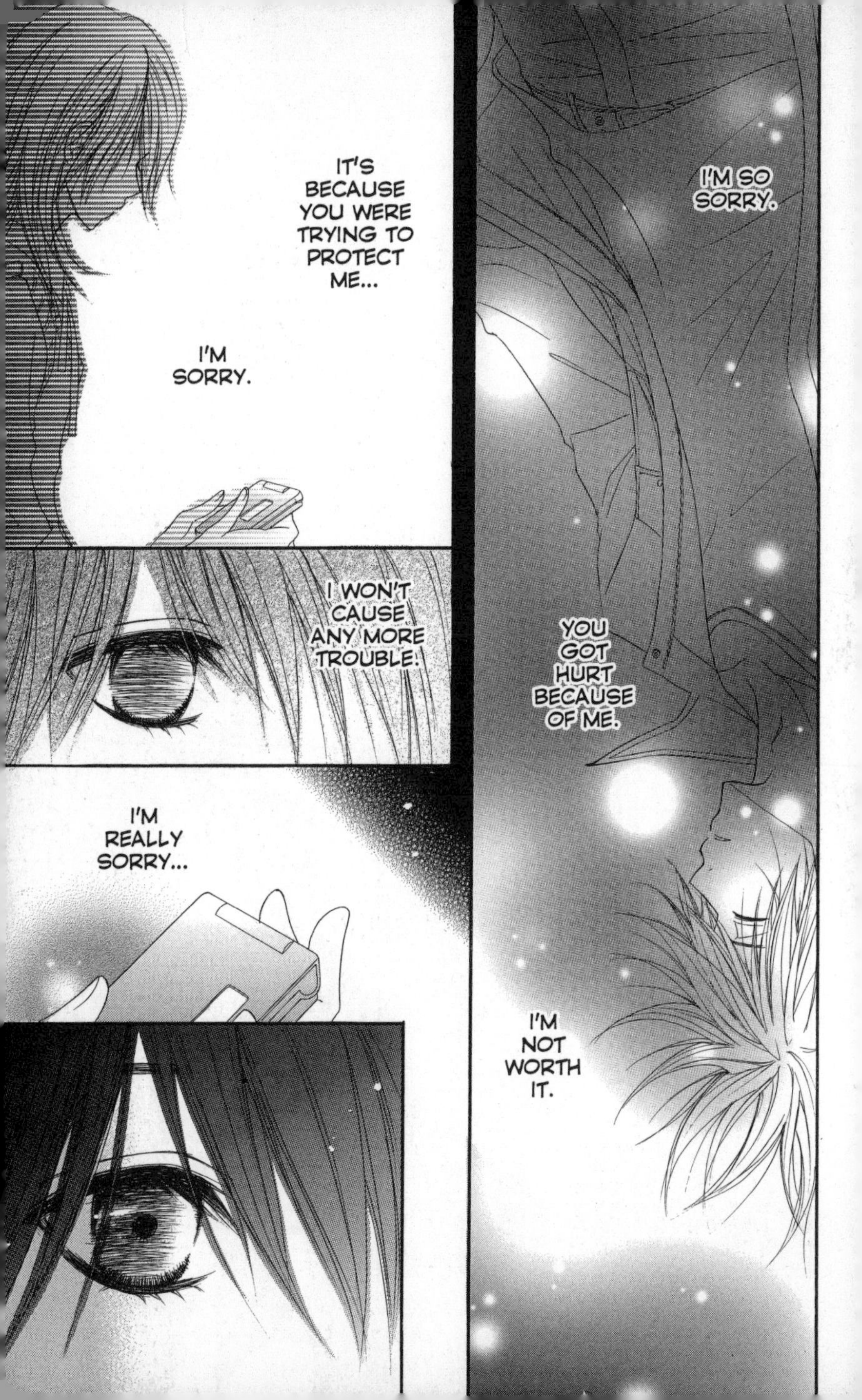
I'M SO SORRY.
YOU GOT HURT BECAUSE OF ME.
I'M NOT WORTH IT.
IT'S BECAUSE YOU WERE TRYING TO PROTECT ME...
I'M SORRY.
I WON'T CAUSE ANY MORE TROUBLE.
I'M REALLY SORRY...

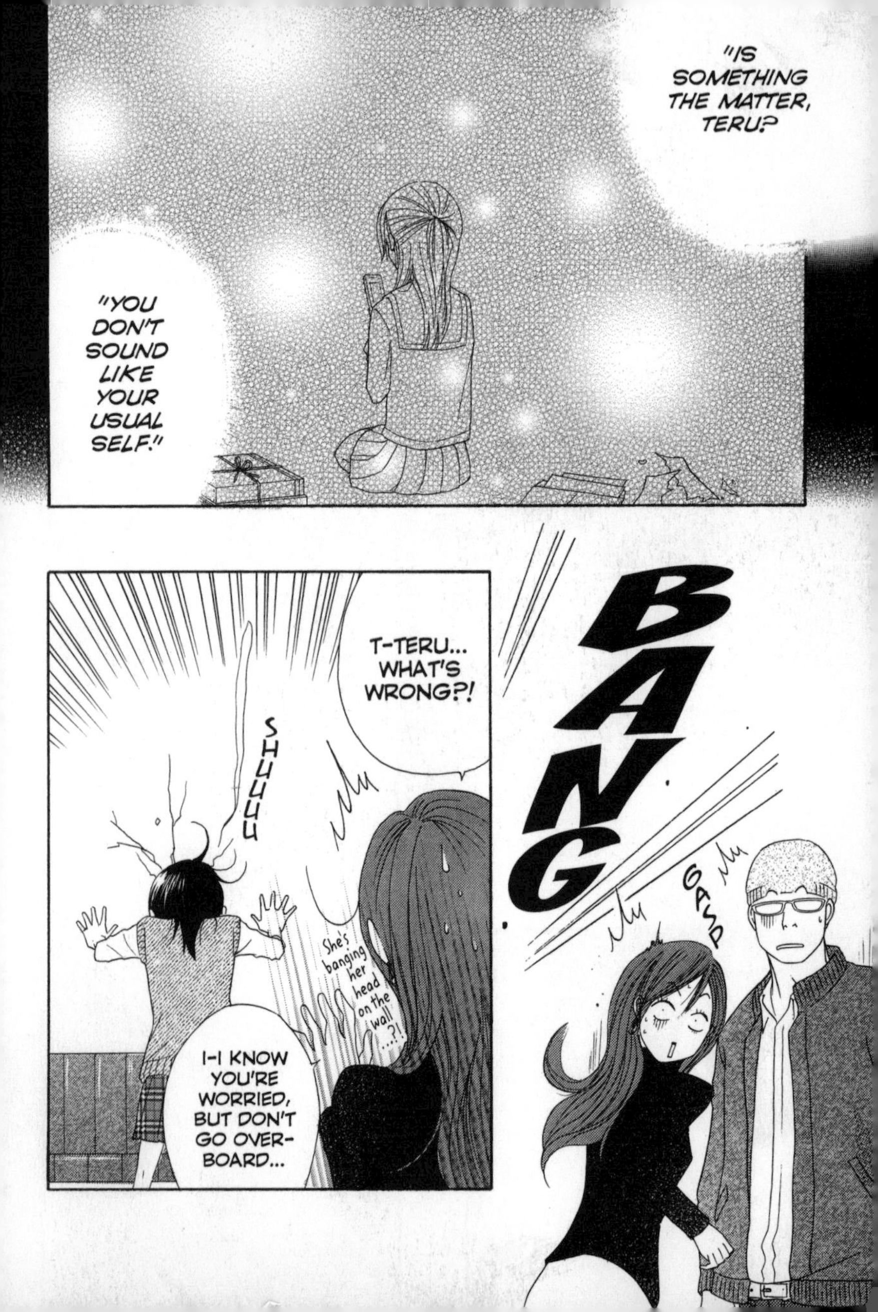
"IS SOMETHING THE MATTER, TERU?
"YOU DON'T SOUND LIKE YOUR USUAL SELF."
BANG
GASP
T-TERU... WHAT'S WRONG?!
SHUUUU
She's banging her head on the wall ...?!
I-I KNOW YOU'RE WORRIED, BUT DON'T GO OVER-BOARD...

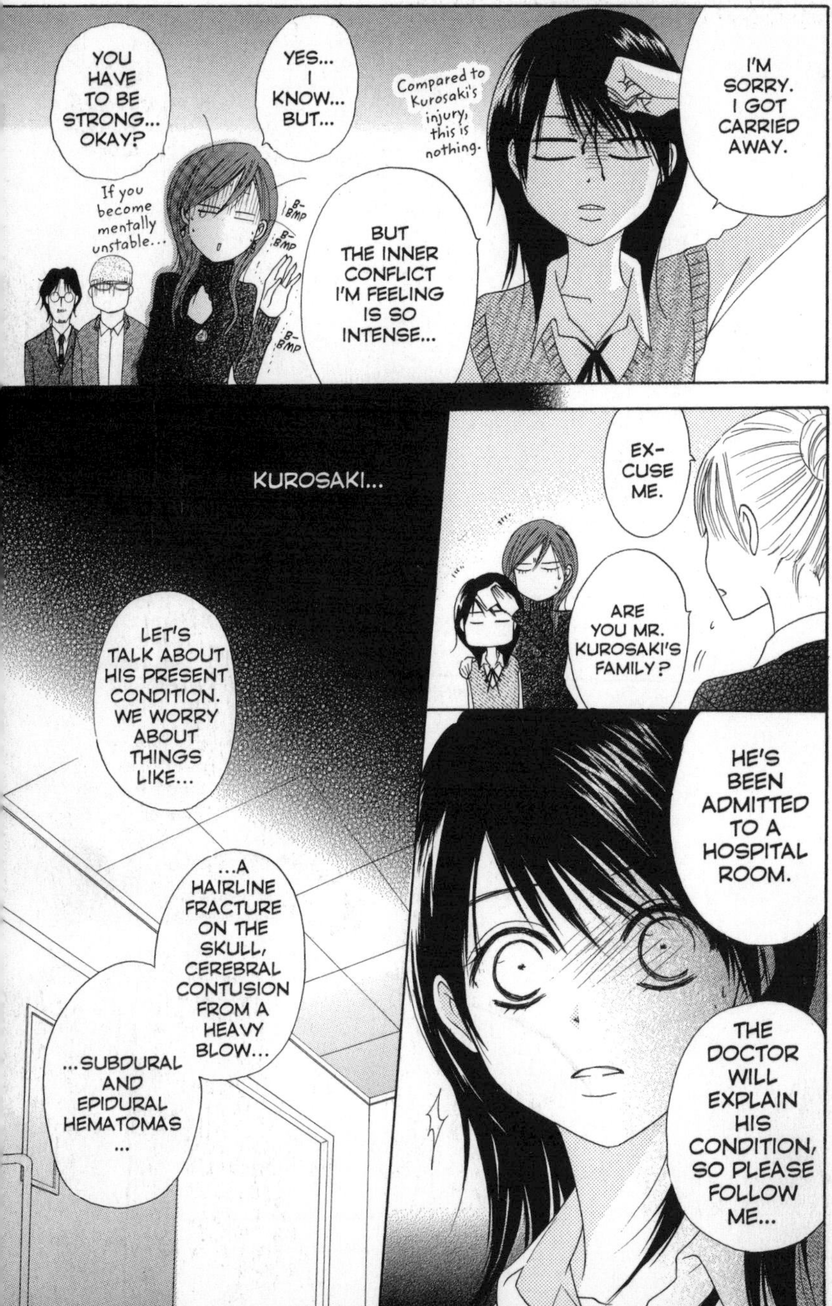
I'M SORRY. I GOT CARRIED AWAY.
Compared to Kurosaki's injury, this is nothing.
BUT THE INNER CONFLICT I'M FEELING IS SO INTENSE...
YES... I KNOW... BUT...
B-BMP
B-BMP
B-BMP
YOU HAVE TO BE STRONG... OKAY?
If you become mentally unstable...
EX-CUSE ME.
ARE YOU MR. KUROSAKI'S FAMILY?
HE'S BEEN ADMITTED TO A HOSPITAL ROOM.
THE DOCTOR WILL EXPLAIN HIS CONDITION, SO PLEASE FOLLOW ME...
KUROSAKI...
LET'S TALK ABOUT HIS PRESENT CONDITION. WE WORRY ABOUT THINGS LIKE...
...A HAIRLINE FRACTURE ON THE SKULL, CEREBRAL CONTUSION FROM A HEAVY BLOW...
...SUBDURAL AND EPIDURAL HEMATOMAS ...

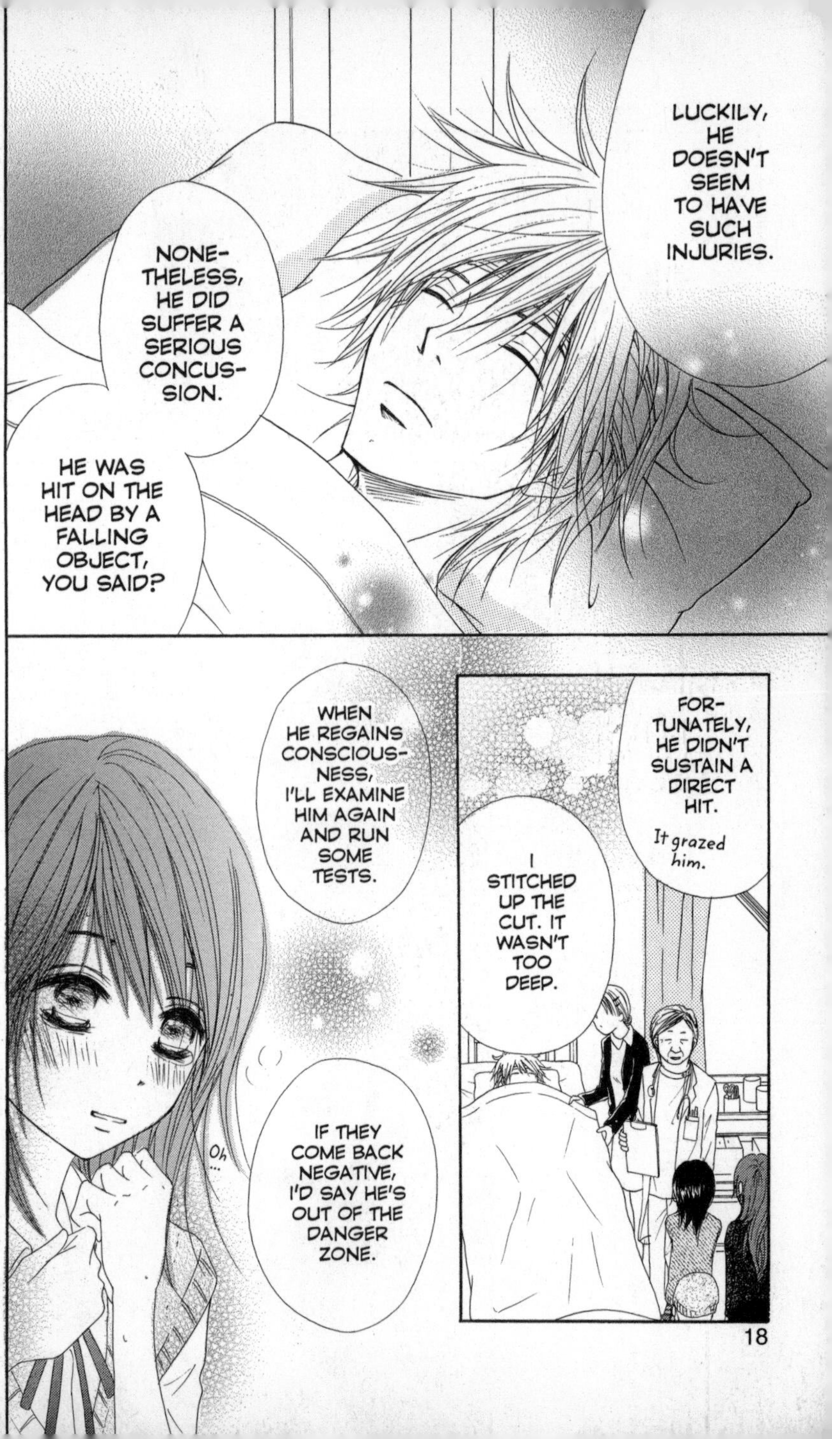
LUCKILY, HE DOESN'T SEEM TO HAVE SUCH INJURIES.
NONE-THELESS, HE DID SUFFER A SERIOUS CONCUS-SION.
HE WAS HIT ON THE HEAD BY A FALLING OBJECT, YOU SAID?
FOR-TUNATELY, HE DIDN'T SUSTAIN A DIRECT HIT.
It grazed him.
I STITCHED UP THE CUT. IT WASN'T TOO DEEP.
WHEN HE REGAINS CONSCIOUS-NESS, I'LL EXAMINE HIM AGAIN AND RUN SOME TESTS.
IF THEY COME BACK NEGATIVE, I'D SAY HE'S OUT OF THE DANGER ZONE.
Oh...

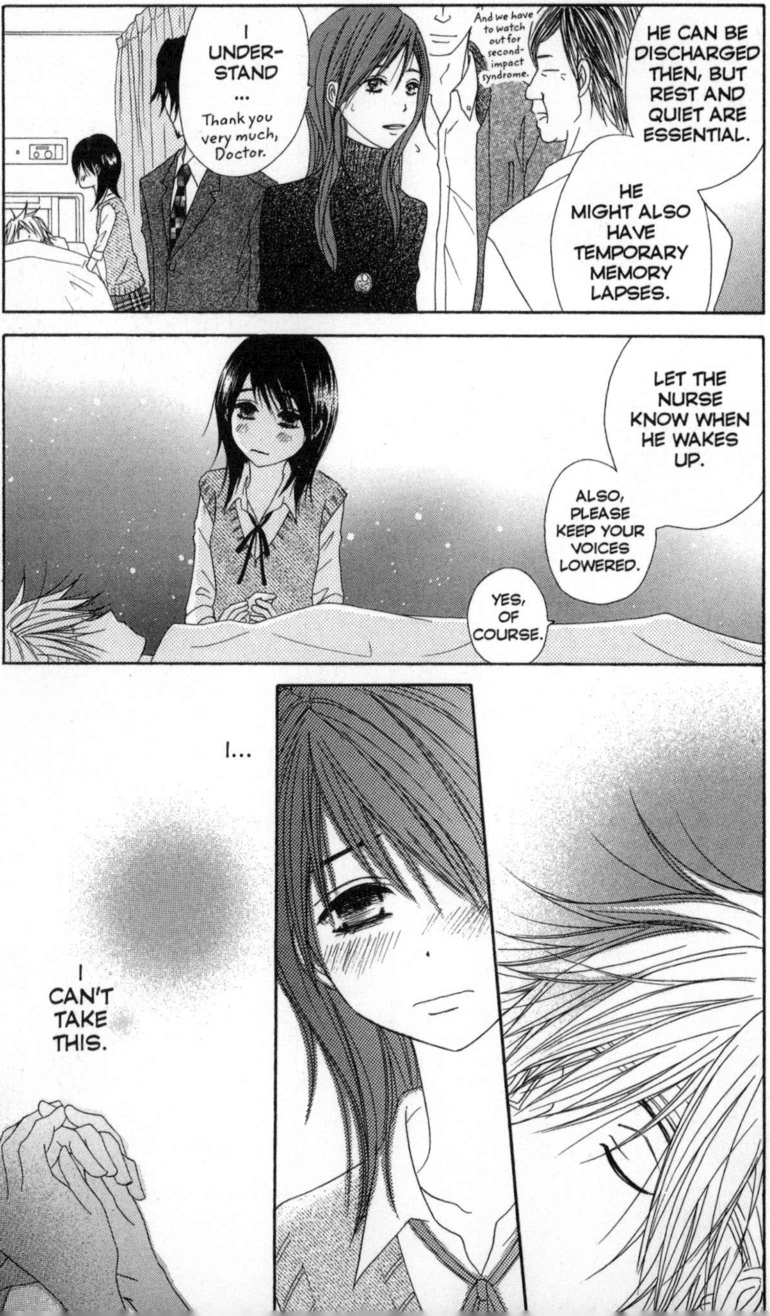
HE CAN BE DISCHARGED THEN, BUT REST AND QUIET ARE ESSENTIAL.
HE MIGHT ALSO HAVE TEMPORARY MEMORY LAPSES.
And we have to watch out for second-impact syndrome.
I UNDER-STAND ...
Thank you very much, Doctor.
LET THE NURSE KNOW WHEN HE WAKES UP.
ALSO, PLEASE KEEP YOUR VOICES LOWERED.
YES, OF COURSE.
I...
I CAN'T TAKE THIS.

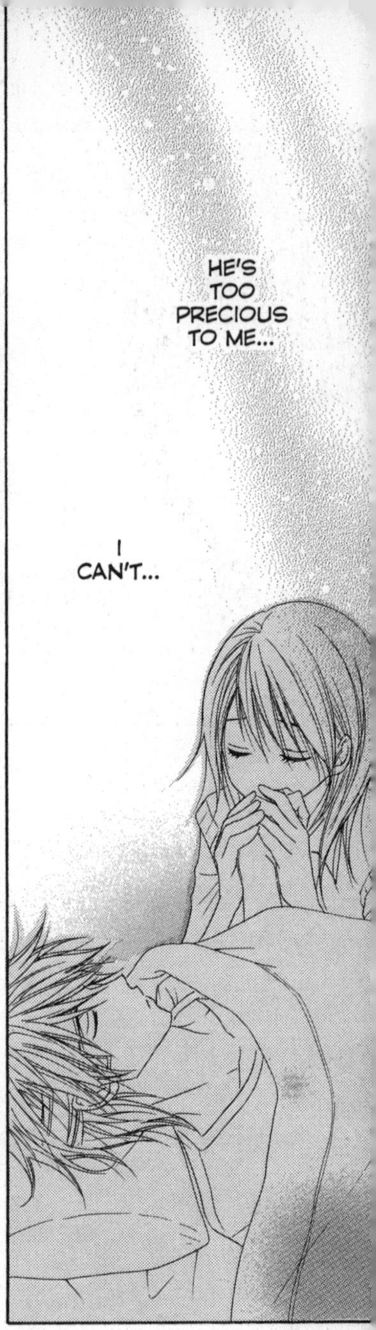
HE'S TOO PRECIOUS TO ME...
I CAN'T...

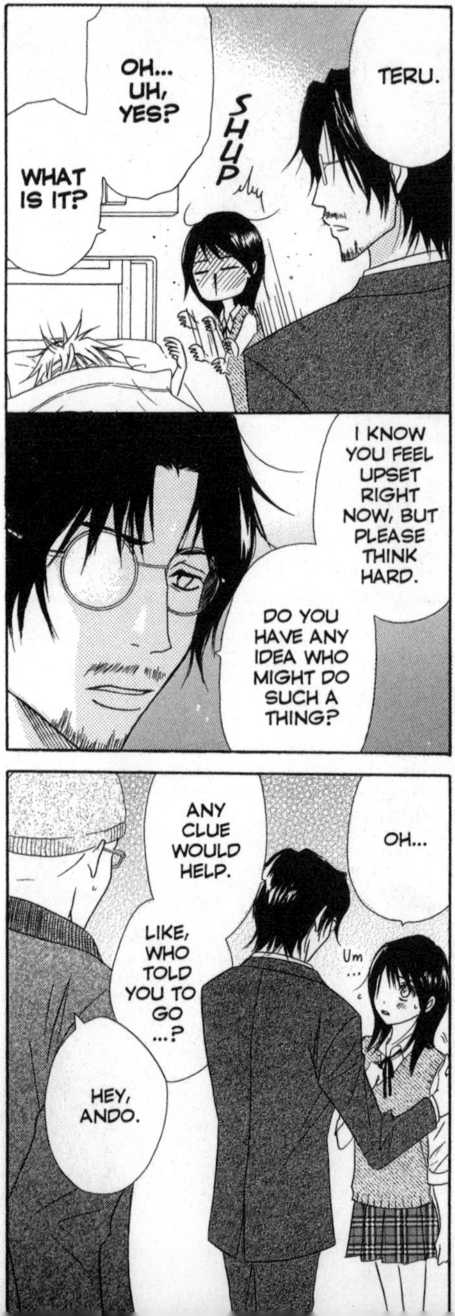
TERU.
SHUP
OH... UH, YES?
WHAT IS IT?
I KNOW YOU FEEL UPSET RIGHT NOW, BUT PLEASE THINK HARD.
DO YOU HAVE ANY IDEA WHO MIGHT DO SUCH A THING?
OH...
ANY CLUE WOULD HELP.
Um...
LIKE, WHO TOLD YOU TO GO ...?
HEY, ANDO.

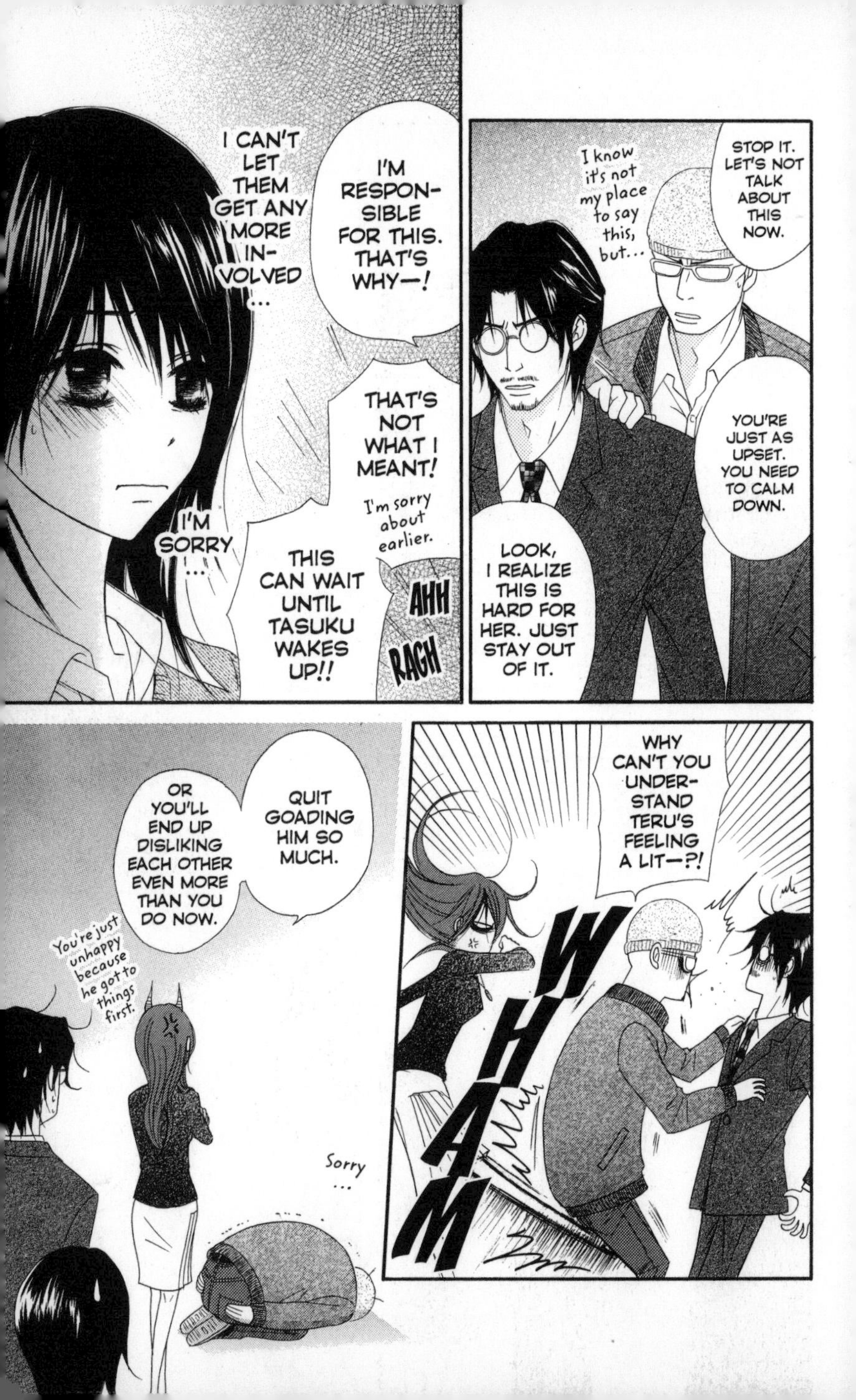
STOP IT. LET'S NOT TALK ABOUT THIS NOW.
I know it's not my place to say this, but...
YOU'RE JUST AS UPSET. YOU NEED TO CALM DOWN.
LOOK, I REALIZE THIS IS HARD FOR HER. JUST STAY OUT OF IT.
I'M RESPONSIBLE FOR THIS. THAT'S WHY—!
I CAN'T LET THEM GET ANY MORE INVOLVED...
THAT'S NOT WHAT I MEANT!
I'm sorry about earlier.
AHH
RAGH
THIS CAN WAIT UNTIL TASUKU WAKES UP!!
I'M SORRY...
WHY CAN'T YOU UNDERSTAND TERU'S FEELING A LIT—?!
WHAM
QUIT GOADING HIM SO MUCH.
OR YOU'LL END UP DISLIKING EACH OTHER EVEN MORE THAN YOU DO NOW.
You're just unhappy because he got to things first.
Sorry...

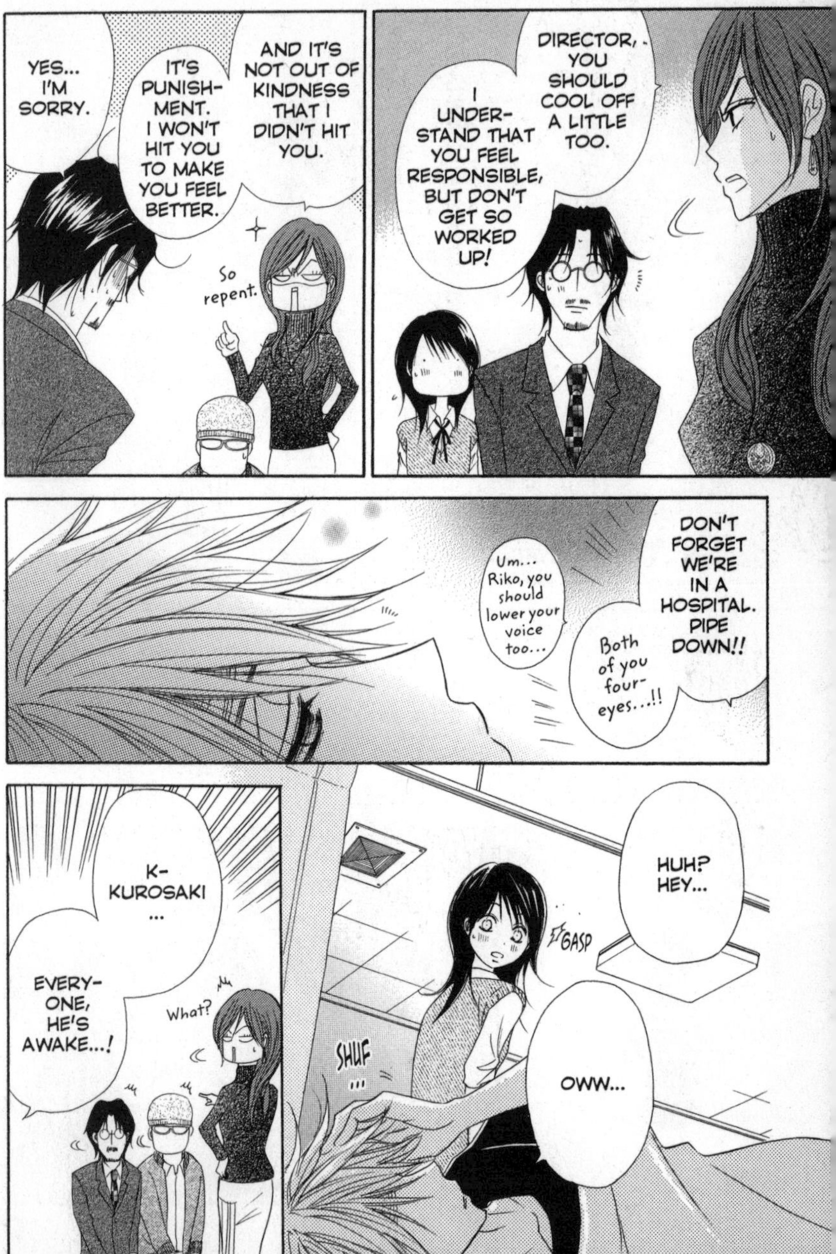
DIRECTOR, YOU SHOULD COOL OFF A LITTLE TOO.
I UNDERSTAND THAT YOU FEEL RESPONSIBLE, BUT DON'T GET SO WORKED UP!
AND IT'S NOT OUT OF KINDNESS THAT I DIDN'T HIT YOU.
IT'S PUNISHMENT. I WON'T HIT YOU TO MAKE YOU FEEL BETTER.
YES... I'M SORRY.
So repent.
DON'T FORGET WE'RE IN A HOSPITAL. PIPE DOWN!!
Both of you four-eyes...!!
Um... Riko, you should lower your voice too...
HUH? HEY...
GASP
OWW...
SHUF...
K-KUROSAKI...
EVERYONE, HE'S AWAKE...!
What?

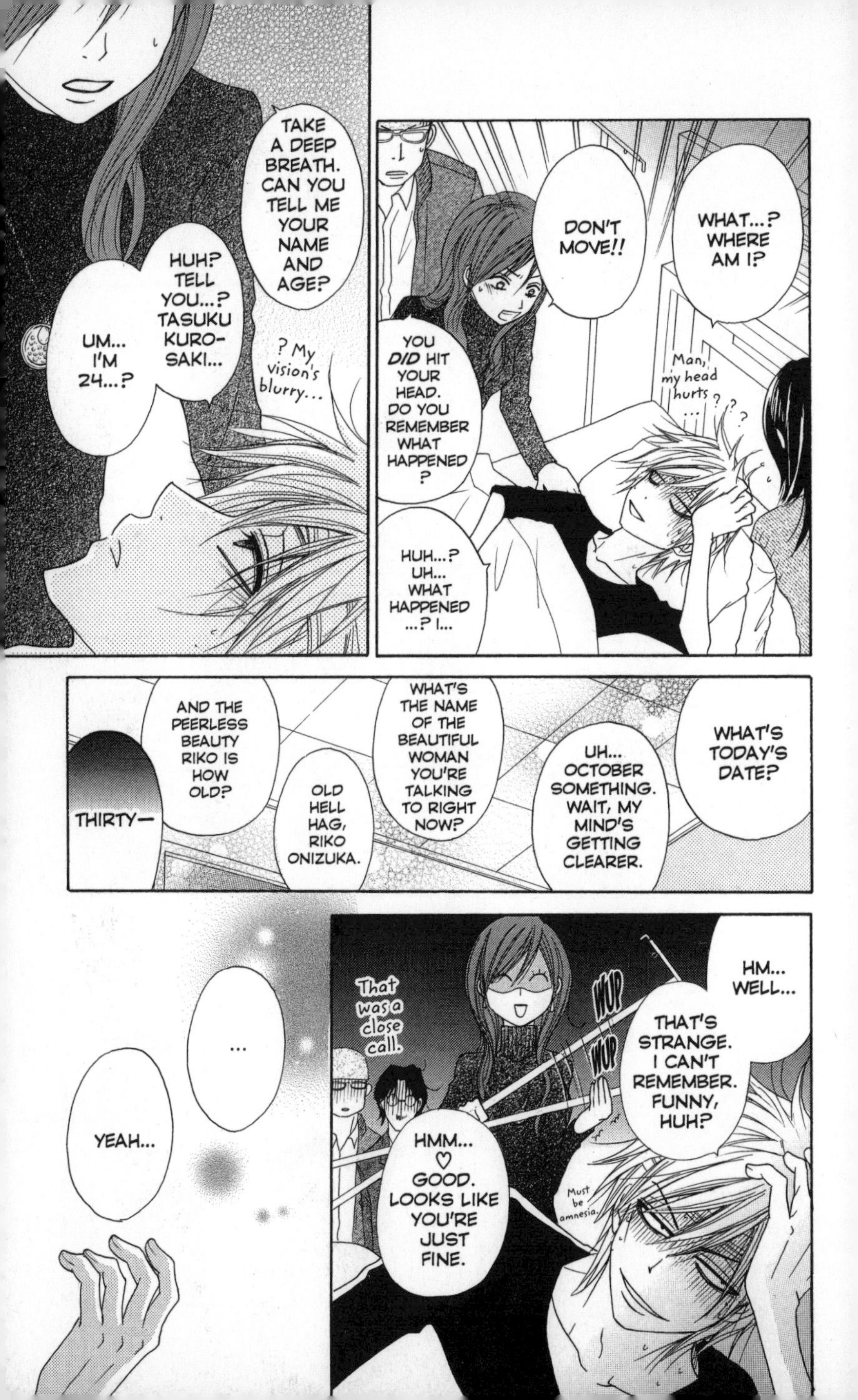
WHAT...? WHERE AM I?
DON'T MOVE!!
Man, my head hurts ...? ? ?
YOU DID HIT YOUR HEAD. DO YOU REMEMBER WHAT HAPPENED?
HUH...? UH... WHAT HAPPENED ...? I...
TAKE A DEEP BREATH. CAN YOU TELL ME YOUR NAME AND AGE?
HUH? TELL YOU...? TASUKU KURO-SAKI...
? My vision's blurry...
UM... I'M 24...?
WHAT'S TODAY'S DATE?
UH... OCTOBER SOMETHING. WAIT, MY MIND'S GETTING CLEARER.
WHAT'S THE NAME OF THE BEAUTIFUL WOMAN YOU'RE TALKING TO RIGHT NOW?
OLD HELL HAG, RIKO ONIZUKA.
AND THE PEERLESS BEAUTY RIKO IS HOW OLD?
THIRTY—
HM... WELL...
THAT'S STRANGE. I CAN'T REMEMBER. FUNNY, HUH?
Must be amnesia.
WUP
WUP
That was a close call.
HMM... ♡ GOOD. LOOKS LIKE YOU'RE JUST FINE.
...
YEAH...

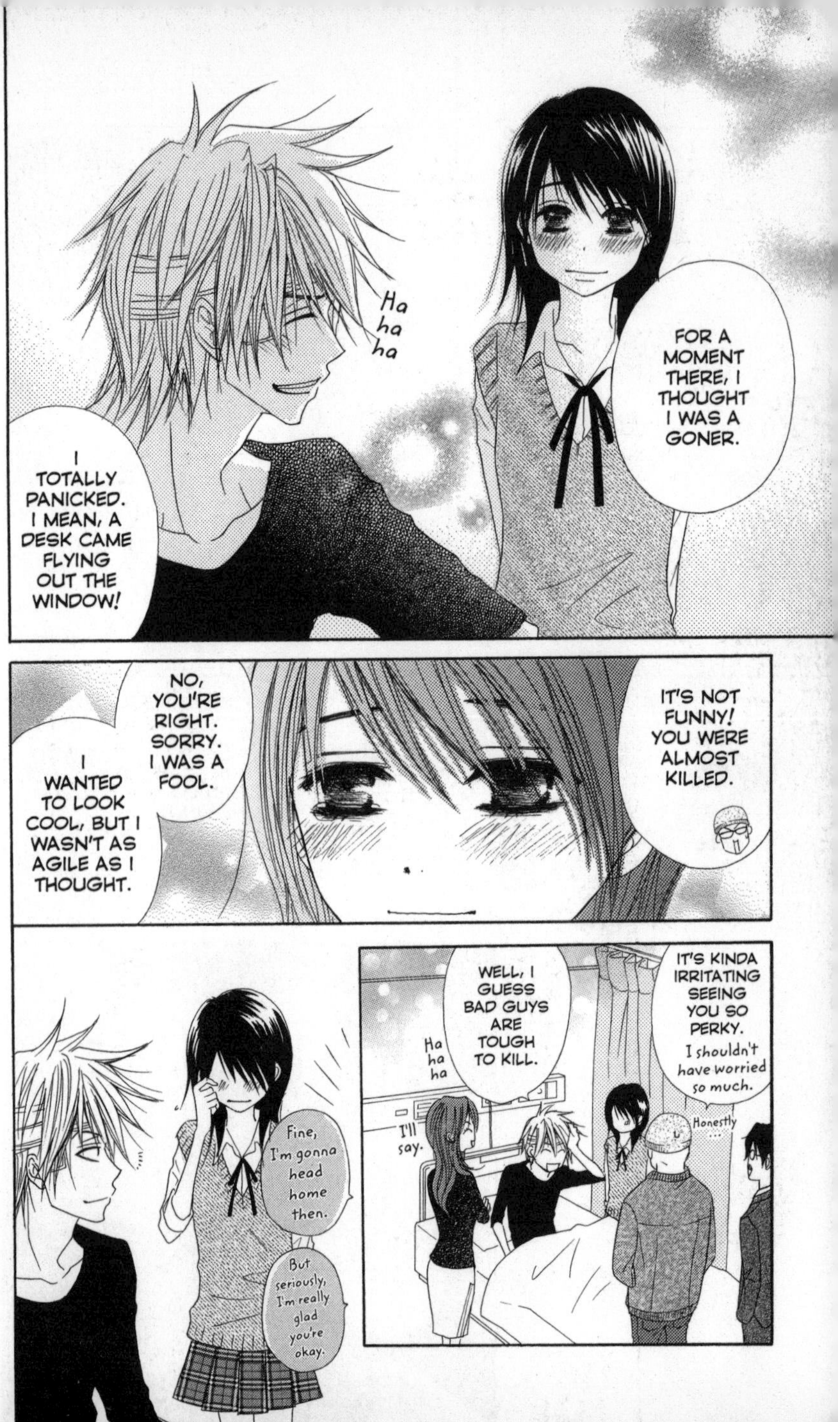
FOR A MOMENT THERE, I THOUGHT I WAS A GONER.
Ha ha ha
I TOTALLY PANICKED. I MEAN, A DESK CAME FLYING OUT THE WINDOW!
IT'S NOT FUNNY! YOU WERE ALMOST KILLED.
NO, YOU'RE RIGHT. SORRY. I WAS A FOOL.
I WANTED TO LOOK COOL, BUT I WASN'T AS AGILE AS I THOUGHT.
IT'S KINDA IRRITATING SEEING YOU SO PERKY.
I shouldn't have worried so much.
Honestly...
WELL, I GUESS BAD GUYS ARE TOUGH TO KILL.
Ha ha ha
I'll say.
Fine, I'm gonna head home then.
But seriously, I'm really glad you're okay.

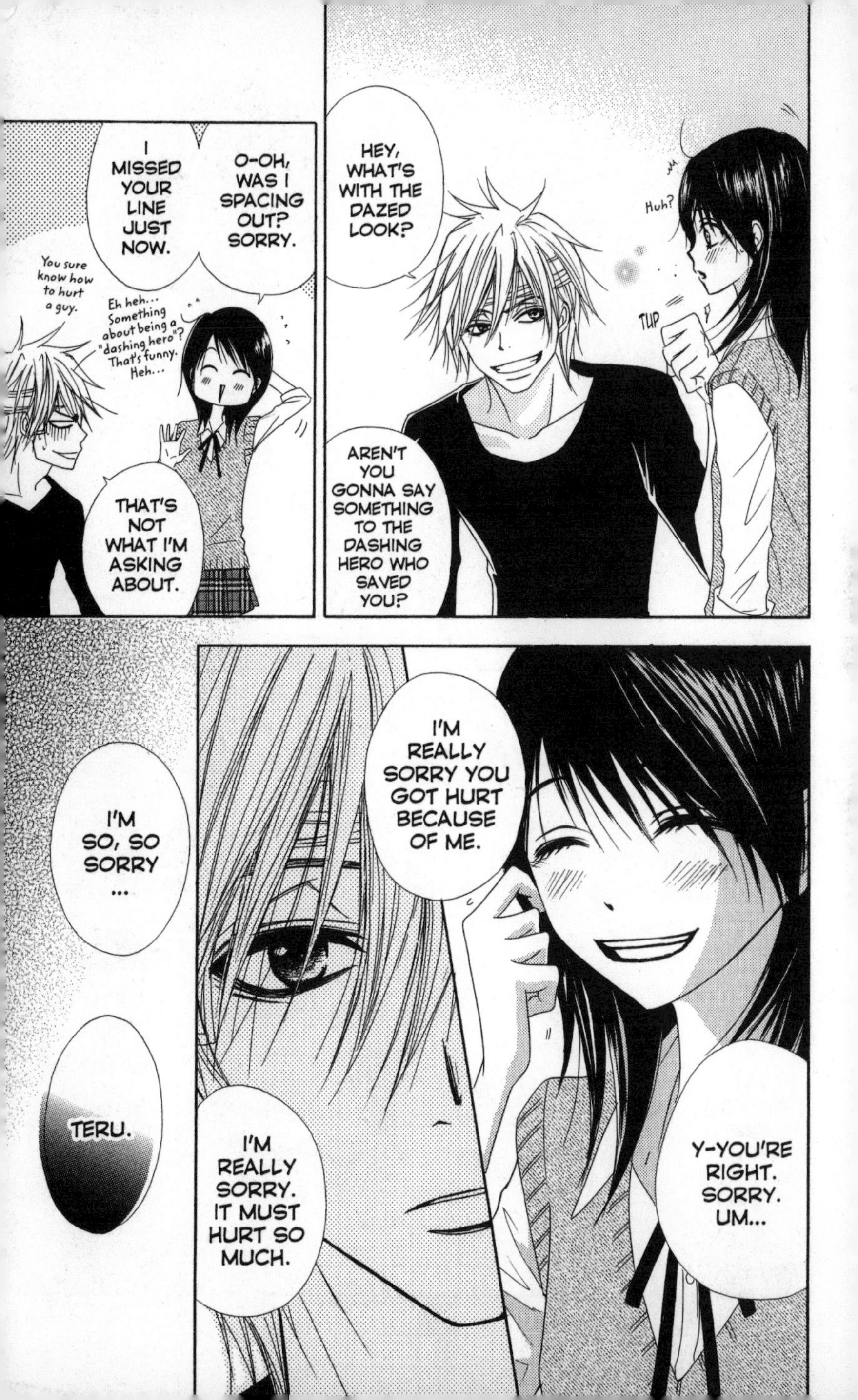
Huh?
HEY, WHAT'S WITH THE DAZED LOOK?
TUP
AREN'T YOU GONNA SAY SOMETHING TO THE DASHING HERO WHO SAVED YOU?
O-OH, WAS I SPACING OUT? SORRY.
I MISSED YOUR LINE JUST NOW.
Eh heh... Something about being a "dashing hero"? That's funny. Heh...
You sure know how to hurt a guy.
THAT'S NOT WHAT I'M ASKING ABOUT.
Y-YOU'RE RIGHT. SORRY. UM...
I'M REALLY SORRY YOU GOT HURT BECAUSE OF ME.
I'M REALLY SORRY. IT MUST HURT SO MUCH.
I'M SO, SO SORRY...
TERU.

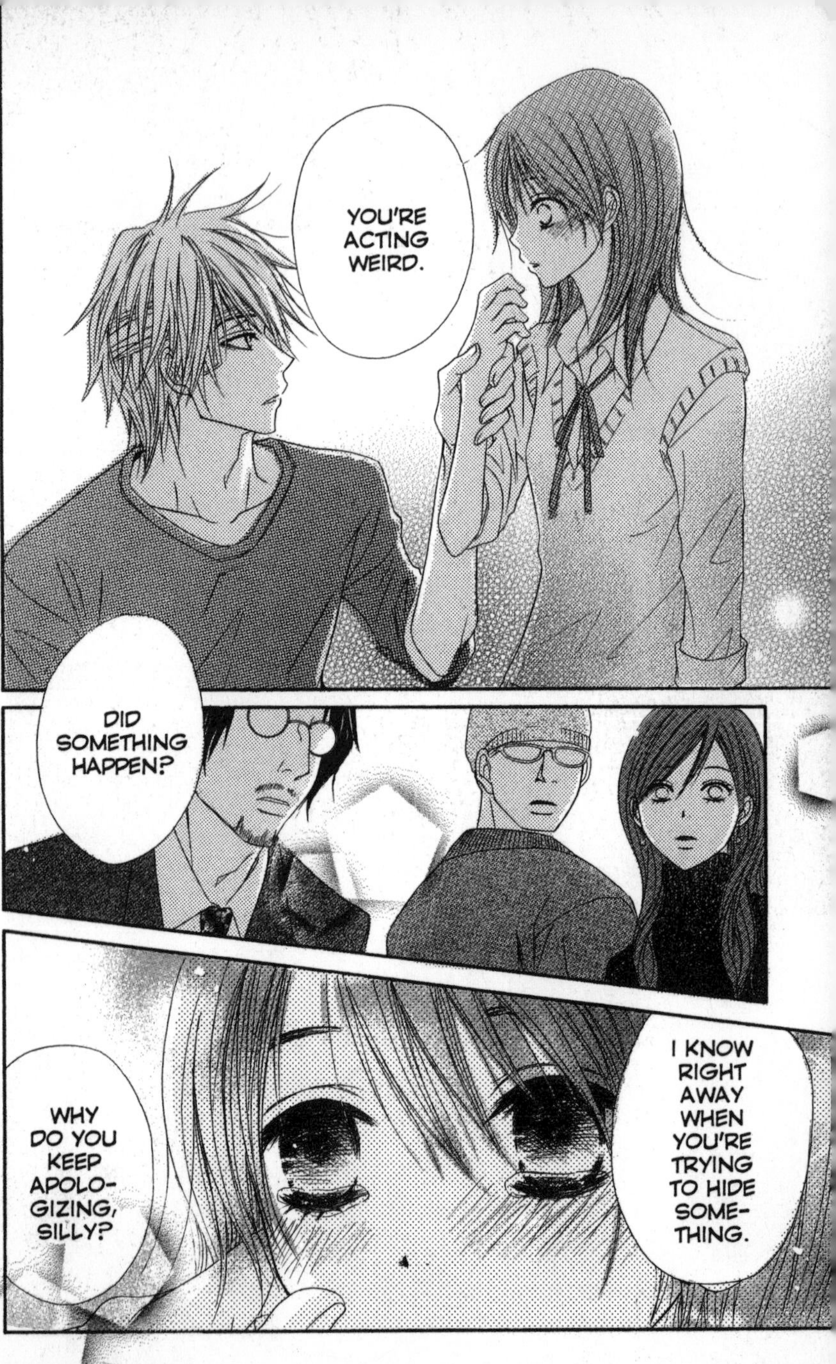
YOU'RE ACTING WEIRD.
DID SOMETHING HAPPEN?
I KNOW RIGHT AWAY WHEN YOU'RE TRYING TO HIDE SOME-THING.
WHY DO YOU KEEP APOLO-GIZING, SILLY?

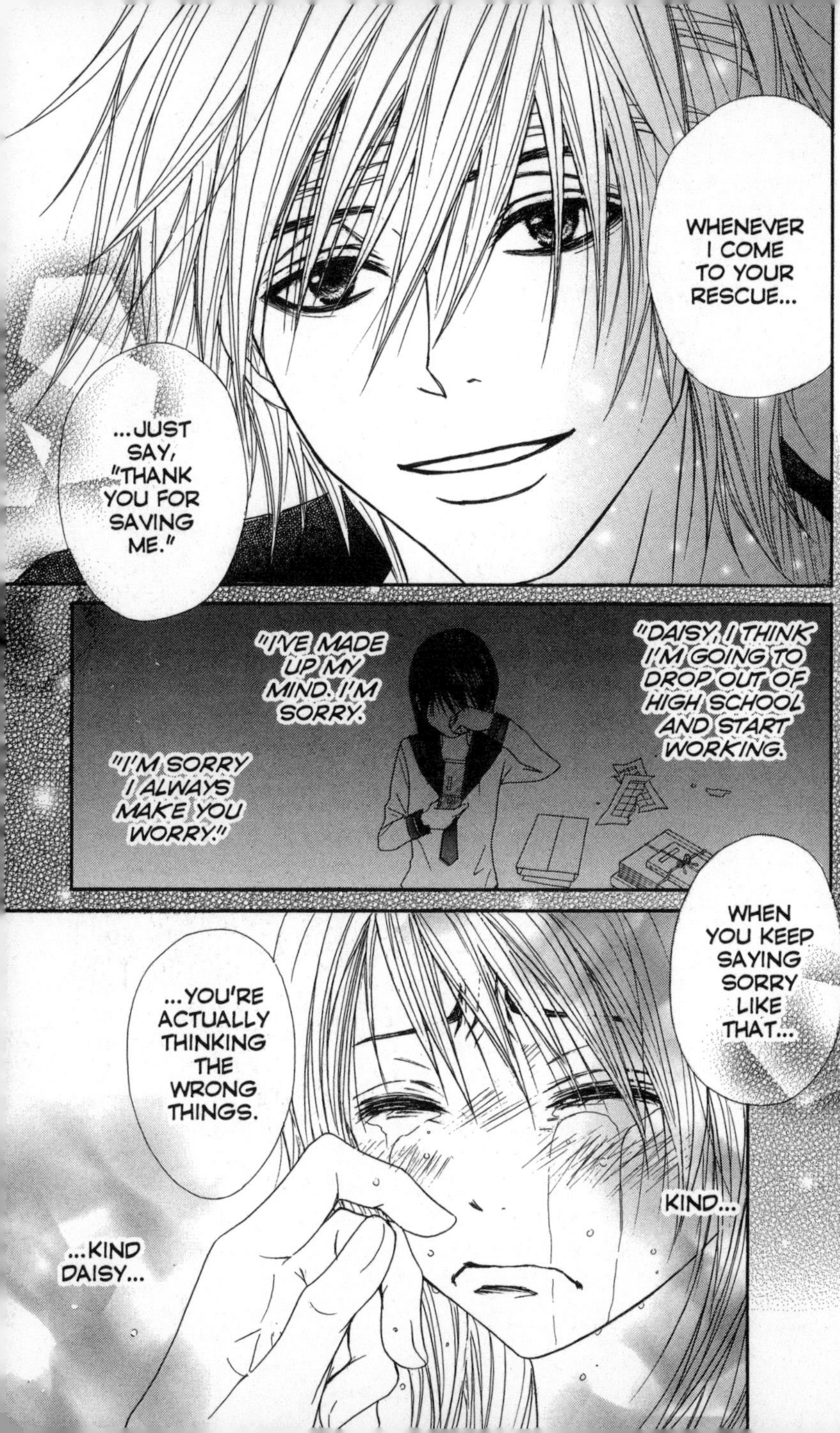
WHENEVER I COME TO YOUR RESCUE...
...JUST SAY, "THANK YOU FOR SAVING ME."
"DAISY, I THINK I'M GOING TO DROP OUT OF HIGH SCHOOL AND START WORKING.
"I'VE MADE UP MY MIND. I'M SORRY.
"I'M SORRY I ALWAYS MAKE YOU WORRY."
WHEN YOU KEEP SAYING SORRY LIKE THAT...
...YOU'RE ACTUALLY THINKING THE WRONG THINGS.
KIND...
...KIND DAISY...

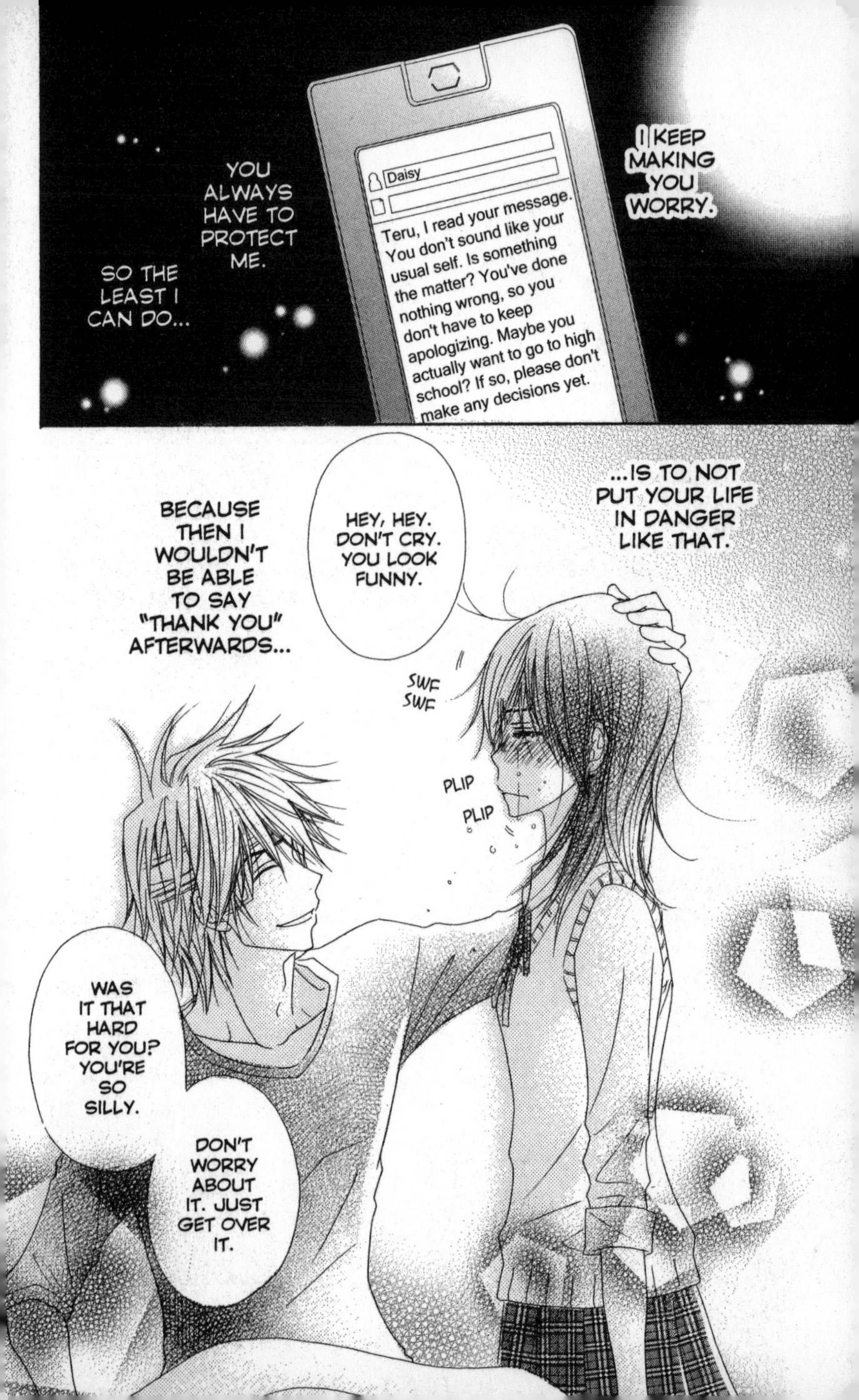
I KEEP MAKING YOU WORRY.
Daisy
Teru, I read your message. You don't sound like your usual self. Is something the matter? You've done nothing wrong, so you don't have to keep apologizing. Maybe you actually want to go to high school? If so, please don't make any decisions yet.
YOU ALWAYS HAVE TO PROTECT ME.
SO THE LEAST I CAN DO...
...IS TO NOT PUT YOUR LIFE IN DANGER LIKE THAT.
HEY, HEY. DON'T CRY. YOU LOOK FUNNY.
BECAUSE THEN I WOULDN'T BE ABLE TO SAY "THANK YOU" AFTERWARDS...
SWF SWF
PLIP
PLIP
WAS IT THAT HARD FOR YOU? YOU'RE SO SILLY.
DON'T WORRY ABOUT IT. JUST GET OVER IT.

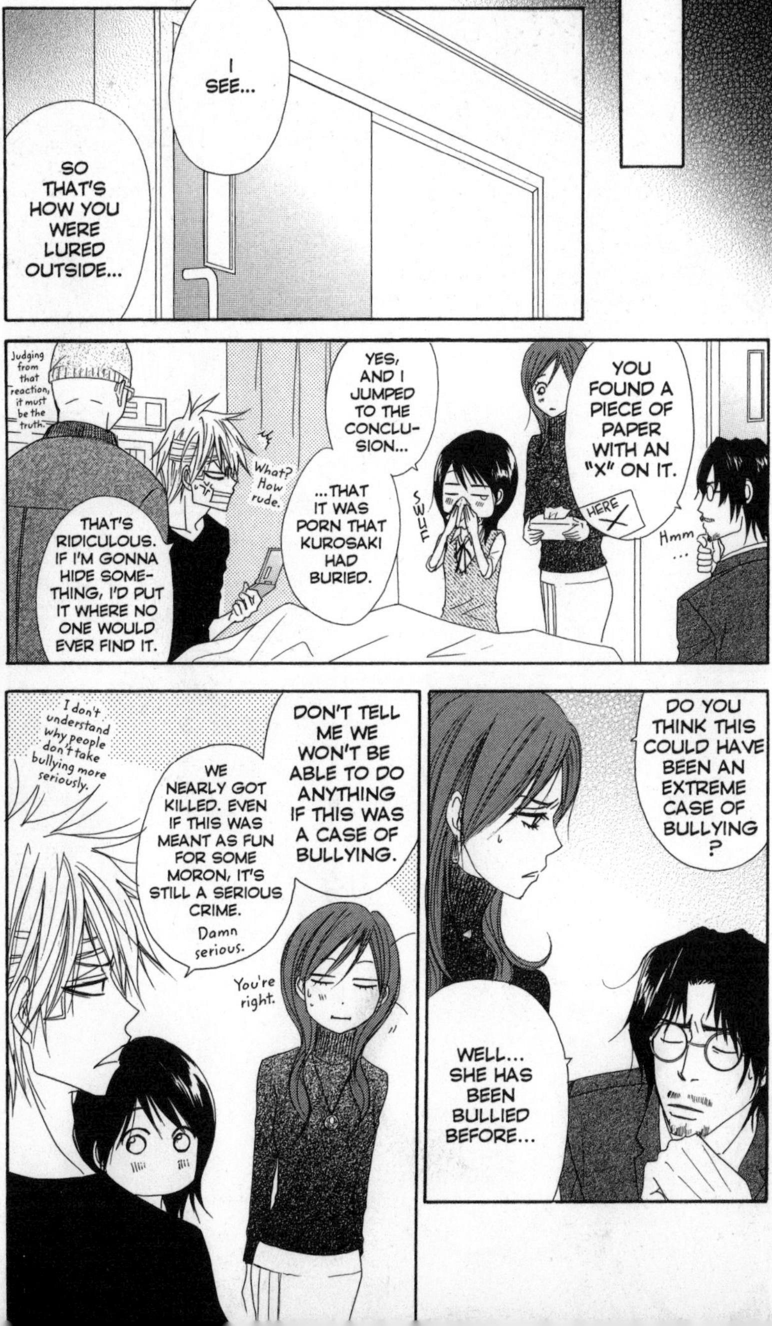
I SEE...
SO THAT'S HOW YOU WERE LURED OUTSIDE...
YOU FOUND A PIECE OF PAPER WITH AN "X" ON IT.
HERE
Hmm ...
SWUF
YES, AND I JUMPED TO THE CONCLUSION...
...THAT IT WAS PORN THAT KUROSAKI HAD BURIED.
What? How rude.
THAT'S RIDICULOUS. IF I'M GONNA HIDE SOMETHING, I'D PUT IT WHERE NO ONE WOULD EVER FIND IT.
Judging from that reaction, it must be the truth.
DO YOU THINK THIS COULD HAVE BEEN AN EXTREME CASE OF BULLYING?
WELL... SHE HAS BEEN BULLIED BEFORE...
DON'T TELL ME WE WON'T BE ABLE TO DO ANYTHING IF THIS WAS A CASE OF BULLYING.
WE NEARLY GOT KILLED. EVEN IF THIS WAS MEANT AS FUN FOR SOME MORON, IT'S STILL A SERIOUS CRIME.
Damn serious.
You're right.
I don't understand why people don't take bullying more seriously.

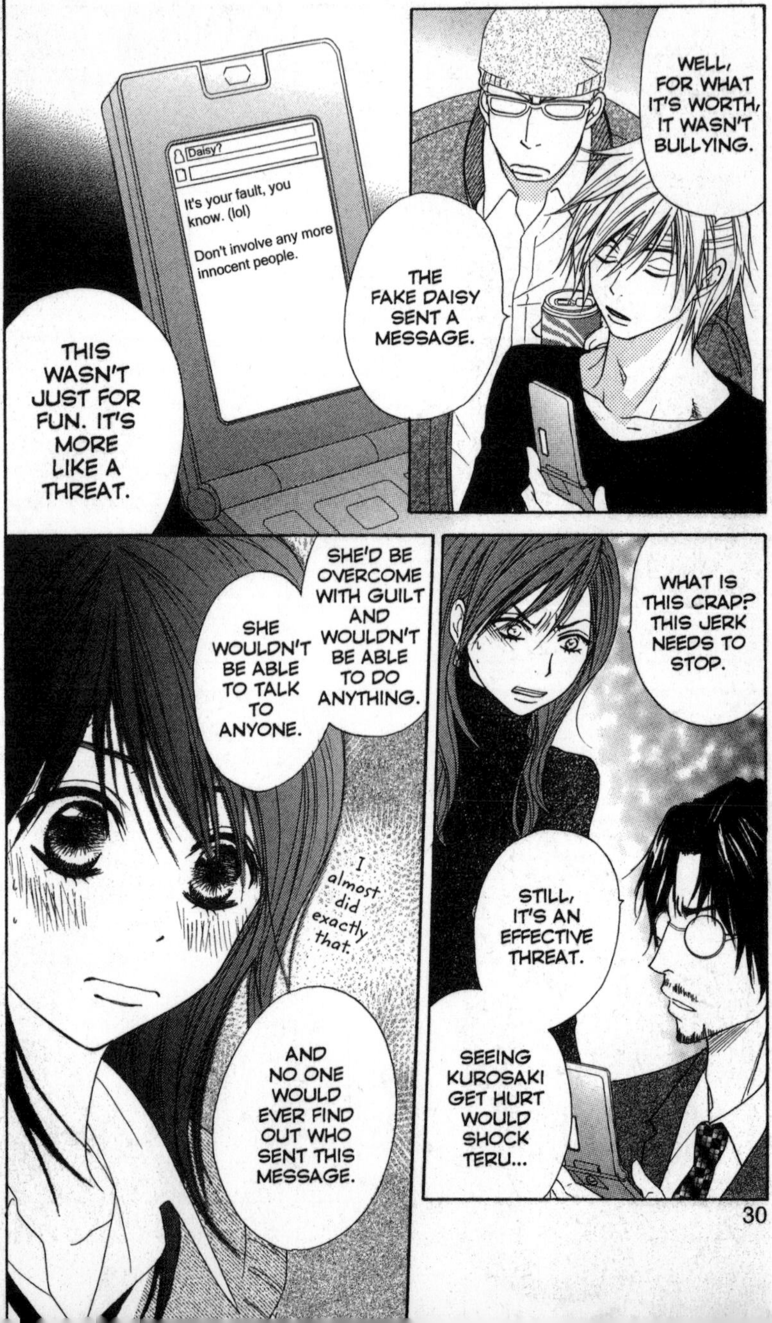
WELL, FOR WHAT IT'S WORTH, IT WASN'T BULLYING.
THE FAKE DAISY SENT A MESSAGE.
Daisy?
It's your fault, you know. (lol)
Don't involve any more innocent people.
THIS WASN'T JUST FOR FUN. IT'S MORE LIKE A THREAT.
WHAT IS THIS CRAP? THIS JERK NEEDS TO STOP.
STILL, IT'S AN EFFECTIVE THREAT.
SEEING KUROSAKI GET HURT WOULD SHOCK TERU...
SHE'D BE OVERCOME WITH GUILT AND WOULDN'T BE ABLE TO DO ANYTHING.
SHE WOULDN'T BE ABLE TO TALK TO ANYONE.
I almost did exactly that.
AND NO ONE WOULD EVER FIND OUT WHO SENT THIS MESSAGE.

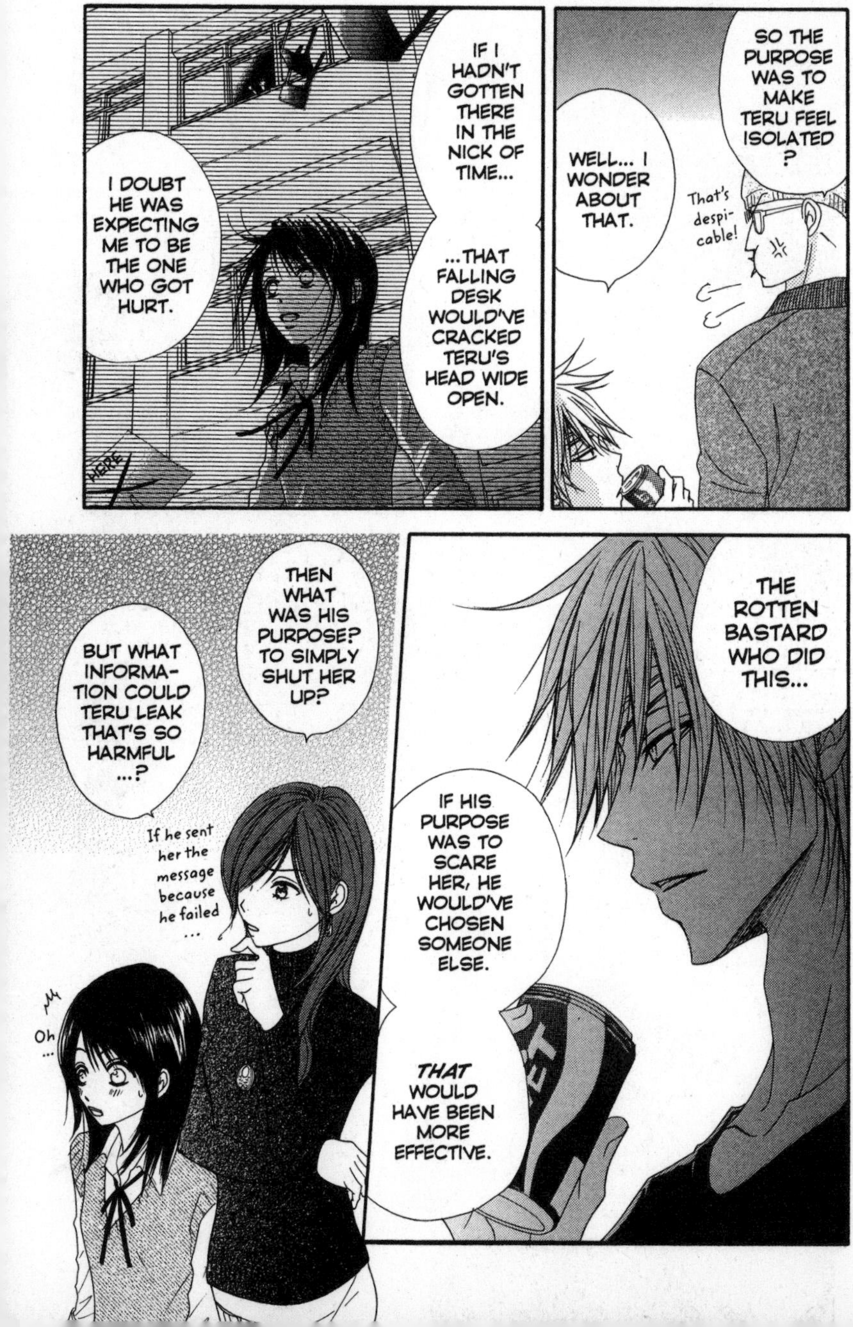
SO THE PURPOSE WAS TO MAKE TERU FEEL ISOLATED?
That's despicable!
WELL... I WONDER ABOUT THAT.
IF I HADN'T GOTTEN THERE IN THE NICK OF TIME...
...THAT FALLING DESK WOULD'VE CRACKED TERU'S HEAD WIDE OPEN.
I DOUBT HE WAS EXPECTING ME TO BE THE ONE WHO GOT HURT.
THE ROTTEN BASTARD WHO DID THIS...
IF HIS PURPOSE WAS TO SCARE HER, HE WOULD'VE CHOSEN SOMEONE ELSE.
THAT WOULD HAVE BEEN MORE EFFECTIVE.
THEN WHAT WAS HIS PURPOSE? TO SIMPLY SHUT HER UP?
BUT WHAT INFORMATION COULD TERU LEAK THAT'S SO HARMFUL...?
If he sent her the message because he failed...
Oh...

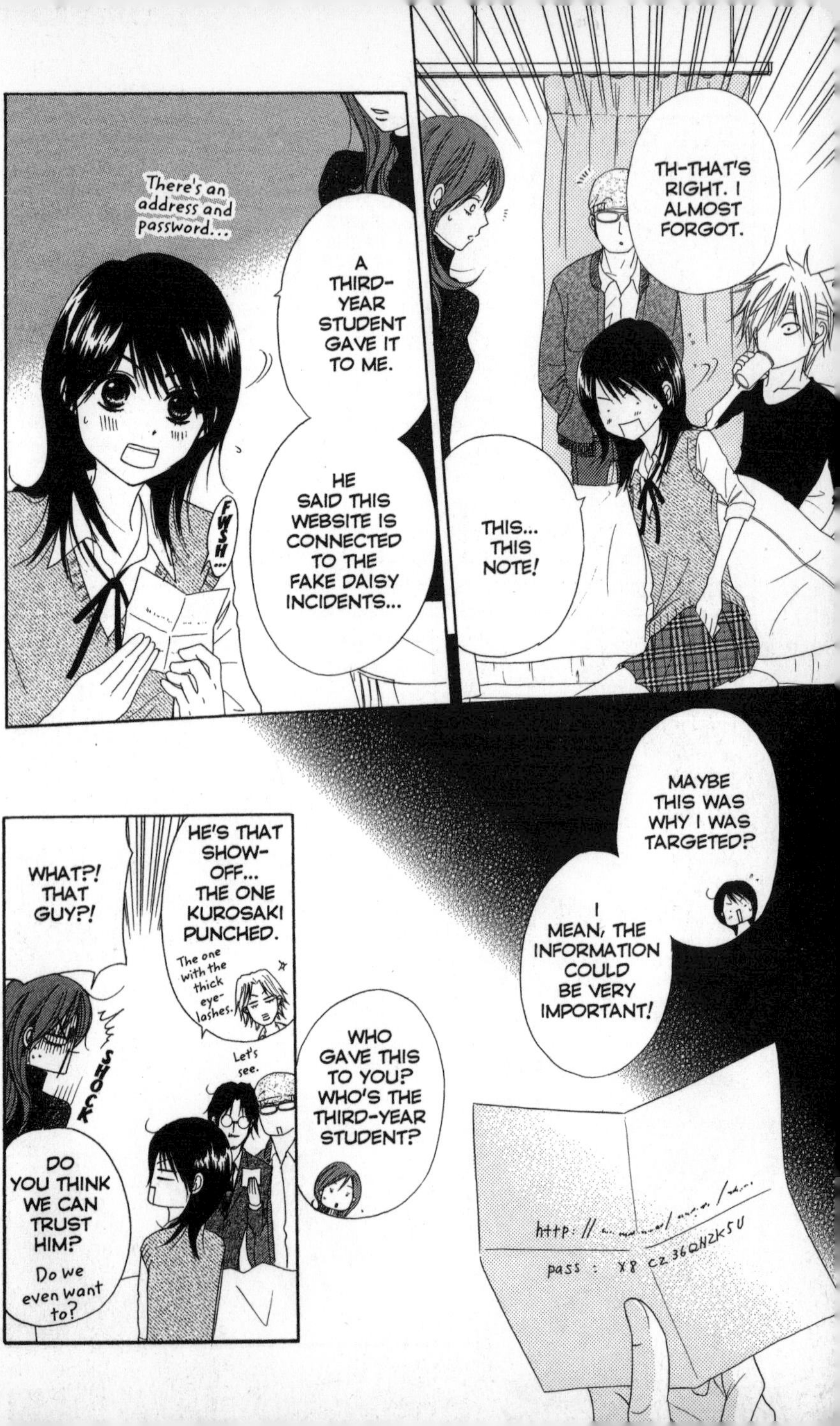

TH-THAT'S RIGHT. I ALMOST FORGOT.
THIS... THIS NOTE!
There's an address and password...
A THIRD-YEAR STUDENT GAVE IT TO ME.
FWSH...
HE SAID THIS WEBSITE IS CONNECTED TO THE FAKE DAISY INCIDENTS...
MAYBE THIS WAS WHY I WAS TARGETED?
I MEAN, THE INFORMATION COULD BE VERY IMPORTANT!
pass : X8 CZ36QNZK5U
WHO GAVE THIS TO YOU? WHO'S THE THIRD-YEAR STUDENT?
HE'S THAT SHOW-OFF... THE ONE KUROSAKI PUNCHED.
The one with the thick eye-lashes.
WHAT?! THAT GUY?!
SHOCK
Let's see.
DO YOU THINK WE CAN TRUST HIM?
Do we even want to?

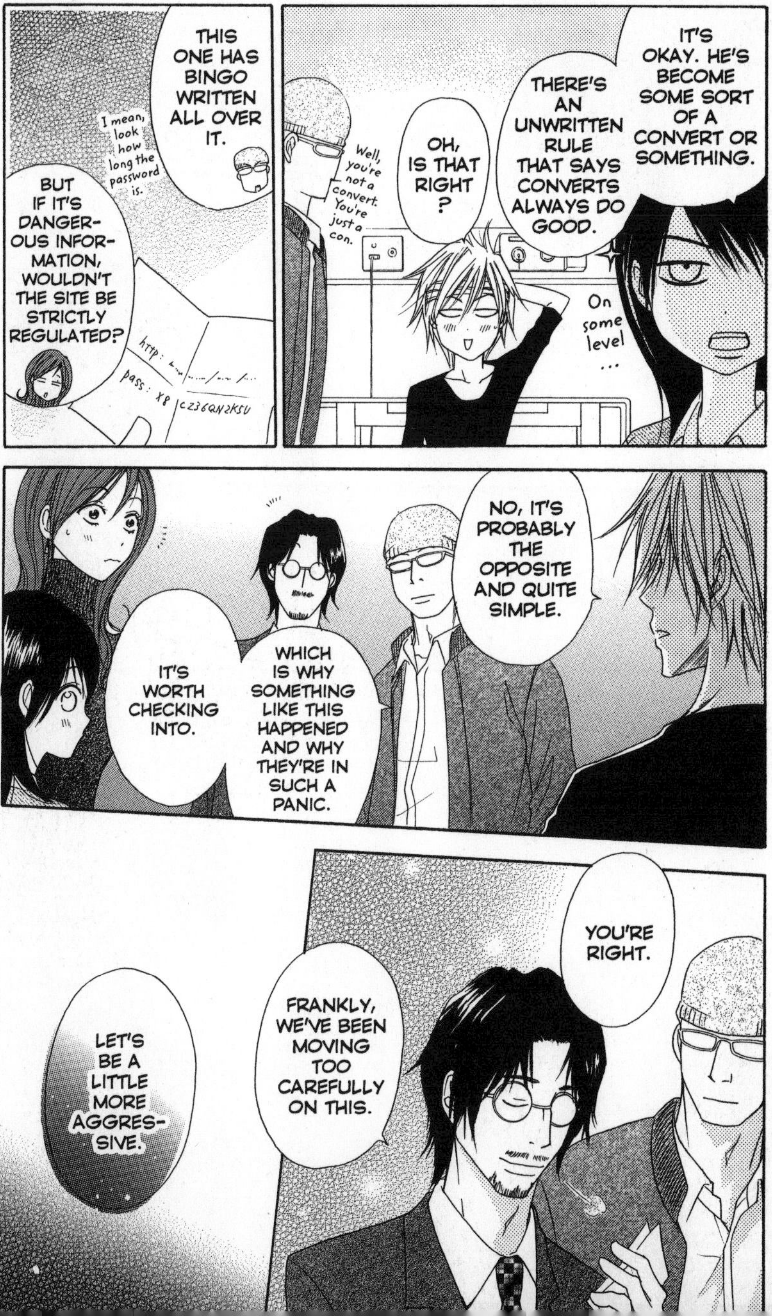
IT'S OKAY. HE'S BECOME SOME SORT OF A CONVERT OR SOMETHING.
THERE'S AN UNWRITTEN RULE THAT SAYS CONVERTS ALWAYS DO GOOD.
OH, IS THAT RIGHT?
Well, you're not a convert. You're just a con.
On some level...
THIS ONE HAS BINGO WRITTEN ALL OVER IT.
I mean, look how long the password is.
BUT IF IT'S DANGEROUS INFORMATION, WOULDN'T THE SITE BE STRICTLY REGULATED?
pass : X8 C236QN2K5U
NO, IT'S PROBABLY THE OPPOSITE AND QUITE SIMPLE.
WHICH IS WHY SOMETHING LIKE THIS HAPPENED AND WHY THEY'RE IN SUCH A PANIC.
IT'S WORTH CHECKING INTO.
YOU'RE RIGHT.
FRANKLY, WE'VE BEEN MOVING TOO CAREFULLY ON THIS.
LET'S BE A LITTLE MORE AGGRESSIVE.

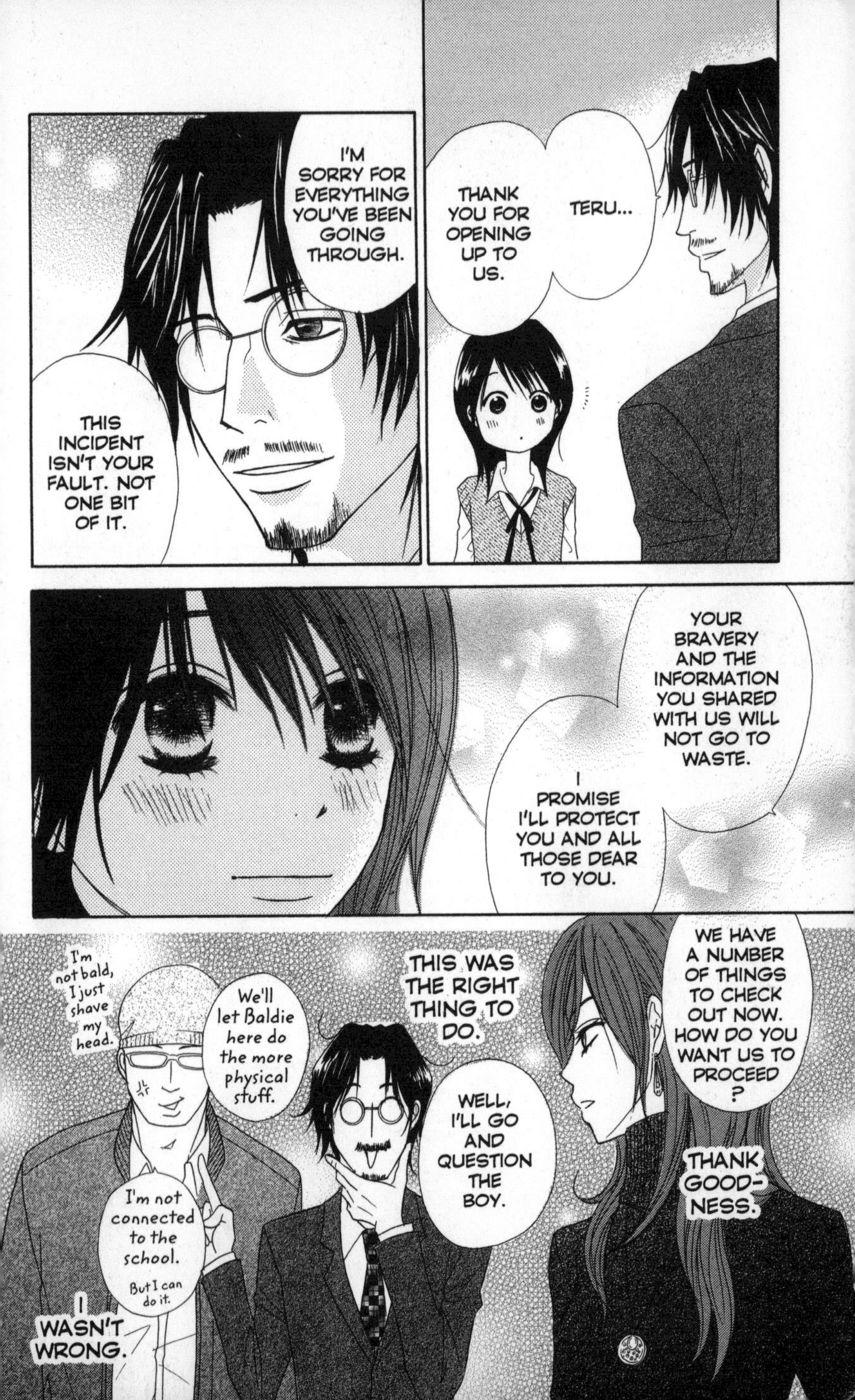
TERU...
THANK YOU FOR OPENING UP TO US.
I'M SORRY FOR EVERYTHING YOU'VE BEEN GOING THROUGH.
THIS INCIDENT ISN'T YOUR FAULT. NOT ONE BIT OF IT.
YOUR BRAVERY AND THE INFORMATION YOU SHARED WITH US WILL NOT GO TO WASTE.
I PROMISE I'LL PROTECT YOU AND ALL THOSE DEAR TO YOU.
WE HAVE A NUMBER OF THINGS TO CHECK OUT NOW. HOW DO YOU WANT US TO PROCEED?
THANK GOOD-NESS.
THIS WAS THE RIGHT THING TO DO.
WELL, I'LL GO AND QUESTION THE BOY.
We'll let Baldie here do the more physical stuff.
I'm not bald, I just shave my head.
I'm not connected to the school.
But I can do it.
I WASN'T WRONG.

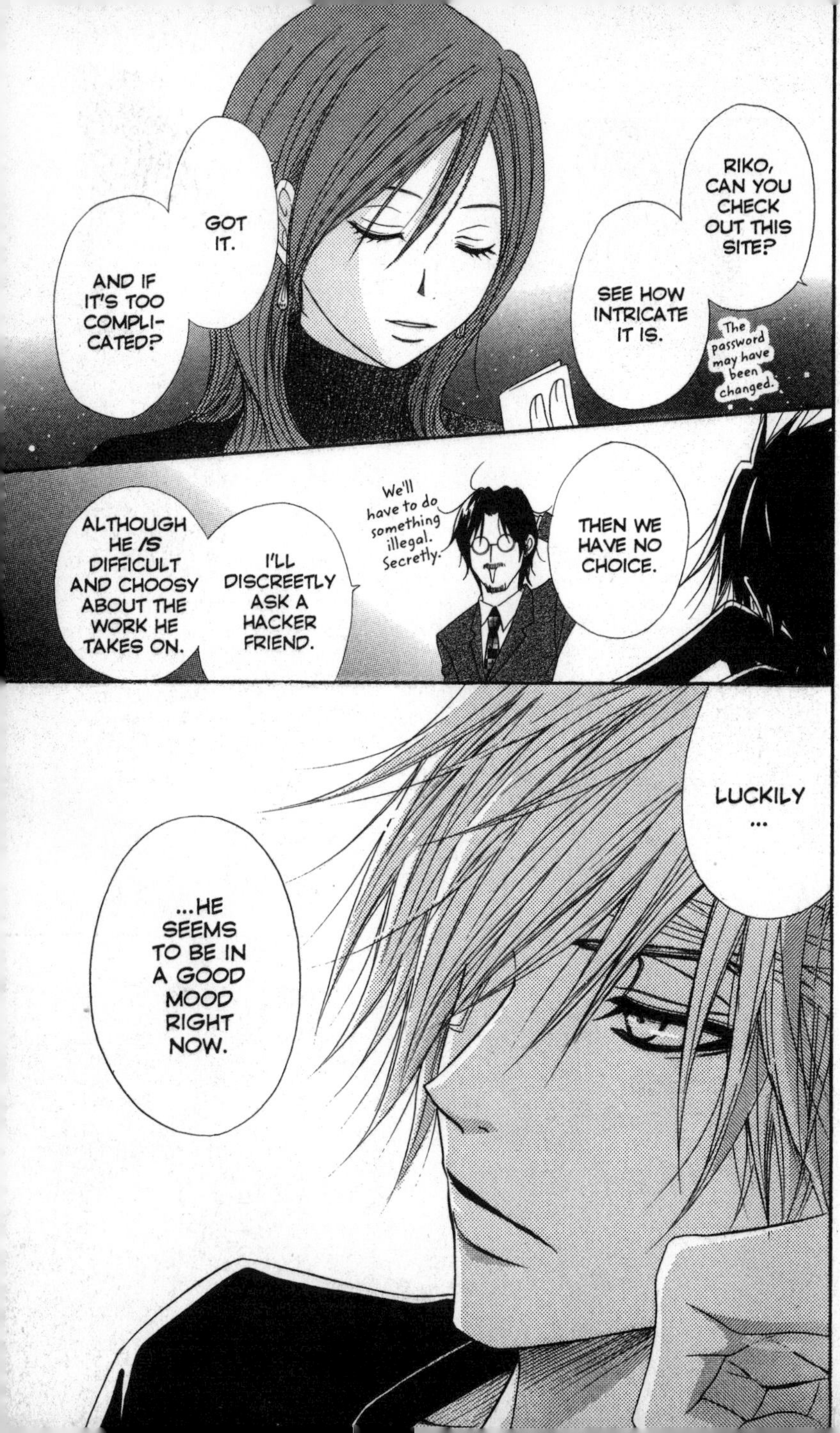
RIKO, CAN YOU CHECK OUT THIS SITE?
The password may have been changed.
SEE HOW INTRICATE IT IS.
GOT IT.
AND IF IT'S TOO COMPLICATED?
THEN WE HAVE NO CHOICE.
We'll have to do something illegal. Secretly.
I'LL DISCREETLY ASK A HACKER FRIEND.
ALTHOUGH HE *IS* DIFFICULT AND CHOOSY ABOUT THE WORK HE TAKES ON.
LUCKILY ...
...HE SEEMS TO BE IN A GOOD MOOD RIGHT NOW.

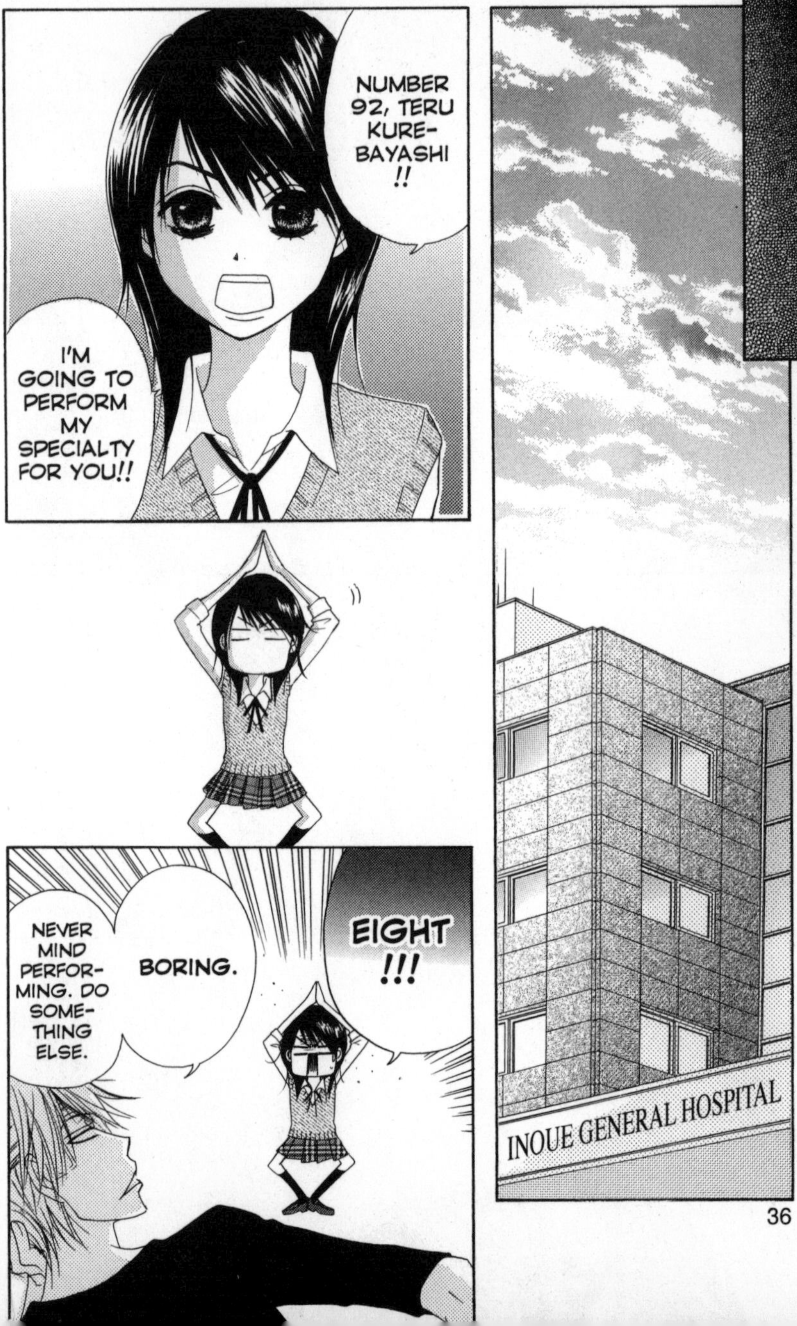
INOUE GENERAL HOSPITAL
NUMBER 92, TERU KURE-BAYASHI!!
I'M GOING TO PERFORM MY SPECIALTY FOR YOU!!
EIGHT!!!
BORING.
NEVER MIND PERFOR-MING. DO SOME-THING ELSE.

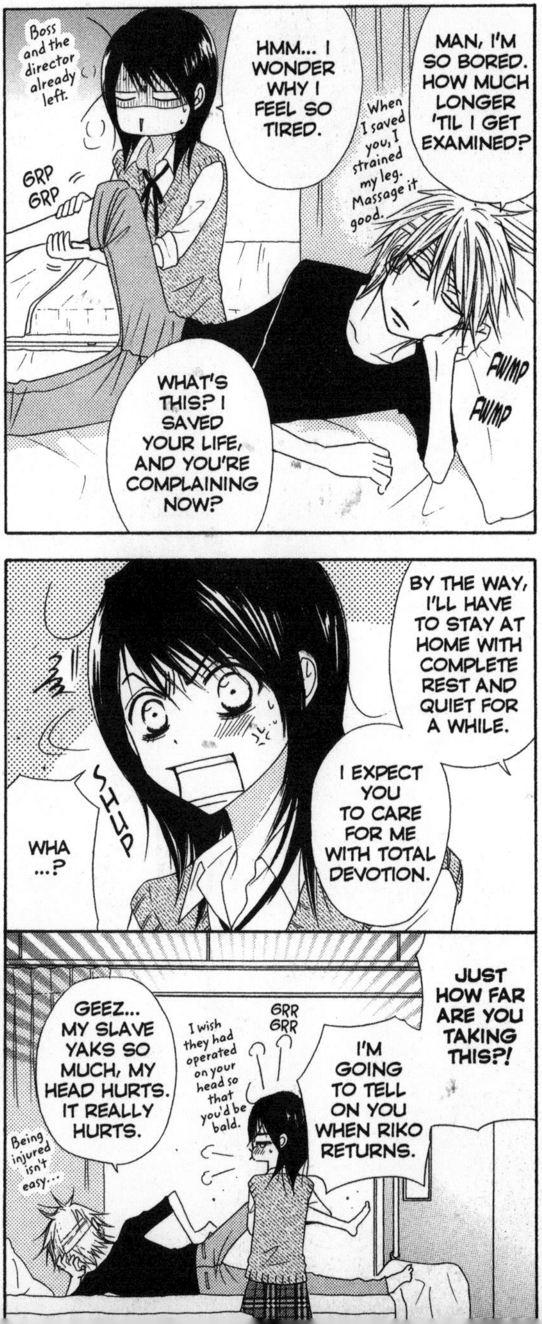
MAN, I'M SO BORED. HOW MUCH LONGER 'TIL I GET EXAMINED?
When I saved you, I strained my leg. Massage it good.
HMM... I WONDER WHY I FEEL SO TIRED.
Boss and the director already left.
GRP GRP
FWUMP
FWUMP
WHAT'S THIS? I SAVED YOUR LIFE, AND YOU'RE COMPLAINING NOW?
BY THE WAY, I'LL HAVE TO STAY AT HOME WITH COMPLETE REST AND QUIET FOR A WHILE.
I EXPECT YOU TO CARE FOR ME WITH TOTAL DEVOTION.
SHUP
WHA ...?
JUST HOW FAR ARE YOU TAKING THIS?!
I'M GOING TO TELL ON YOU WHEN RIKO RETURNS.
GRR GRR
I wish they had operated on your head so that you'd be bald.
GEEZ... MY SLAVE YAKS SO MUCH, MY HEAD HURTS. IT REALLY HURTS.
Being injured isn't easy...

DENGEKI DAISY QUESTION CORNER

BALDLY ASK!!

①

ERR, AS I EXPLAINED IN VOLUME 4, I'D LIKE TO DEDICATE THIS CORNER TO HONESTLY ANSWERING YOUR QUESTIONS.

THE CORNER'S NAME HAS BEEN CHANGED FROM "DAISY QUESTION CORNER (TEMPORARY)." I WANTED TO MAKE IT EASY TO REMEMBER AND WRITE BUT SLIGHTLY EMBARRASSING TO WRITE ON POSTCARDS AS WELL... I'M SORRY I DIDN'T PUT MORE THOUGHT INTO IT.

NOW THEN, THE FIRST MEMORABLE QUESTION.

Q.
I THOUGHT ZOGE (IVORY) WAS WRITTEN AS "象毛." IT'S ACTUALLY "象牙."

(M.O., HYOGO PREFECTURE)

A.
...YES.
OH, YES. I THINK SO.
M.O., THANK YOU!!!

...PLEASE KEEP SENDING THIS TYPE OF COMMENT TO THIS CORNER (AS WELL AS THINGS THAT CONCERN THE STORYLINE OF *DENGEKI DAISY*).

WHEN THE AUTHOR WAS A YOUNG, INNOCENT GIRL, SHE THOUGHT THAT A "HIGH WAVE ADVISORY" ACTUALLY MEANT A "HELLO ADVISORY."

GO TO I▶②

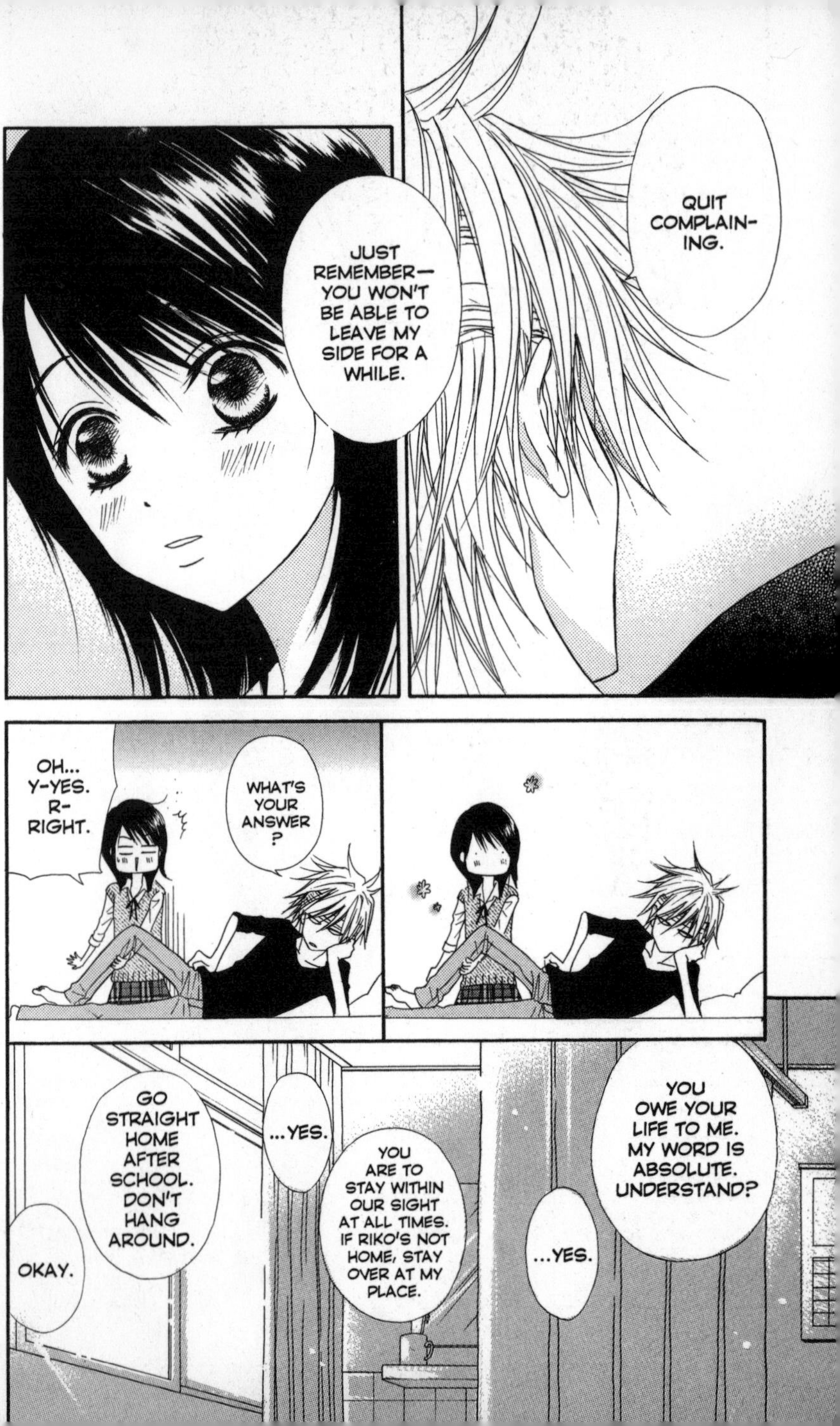
QUIT COMPLAINING.
JUST REMEMBER—YOU WON'T BE ABLE TO LEAVE MY SIDE FOR A WHILE.
WHAT'S YOUR ANSWER?
OH... Y-YES. R-RIGHT.
YOU OWE YOUR LIFE TO ME. MY WORD IS ABSOLUTE. UNDERSTAND?
...YES.
YOU ARE TO STAY WITHIN OUR SIGHT AT ALL TIMES. IF RIKO'S NOT HOME, STAY OVER AT MY PLACE.
...YES.
GO STRAIGHT HOME AFTER SCHOOL. DON'T HANG AROUND.
OKAY.

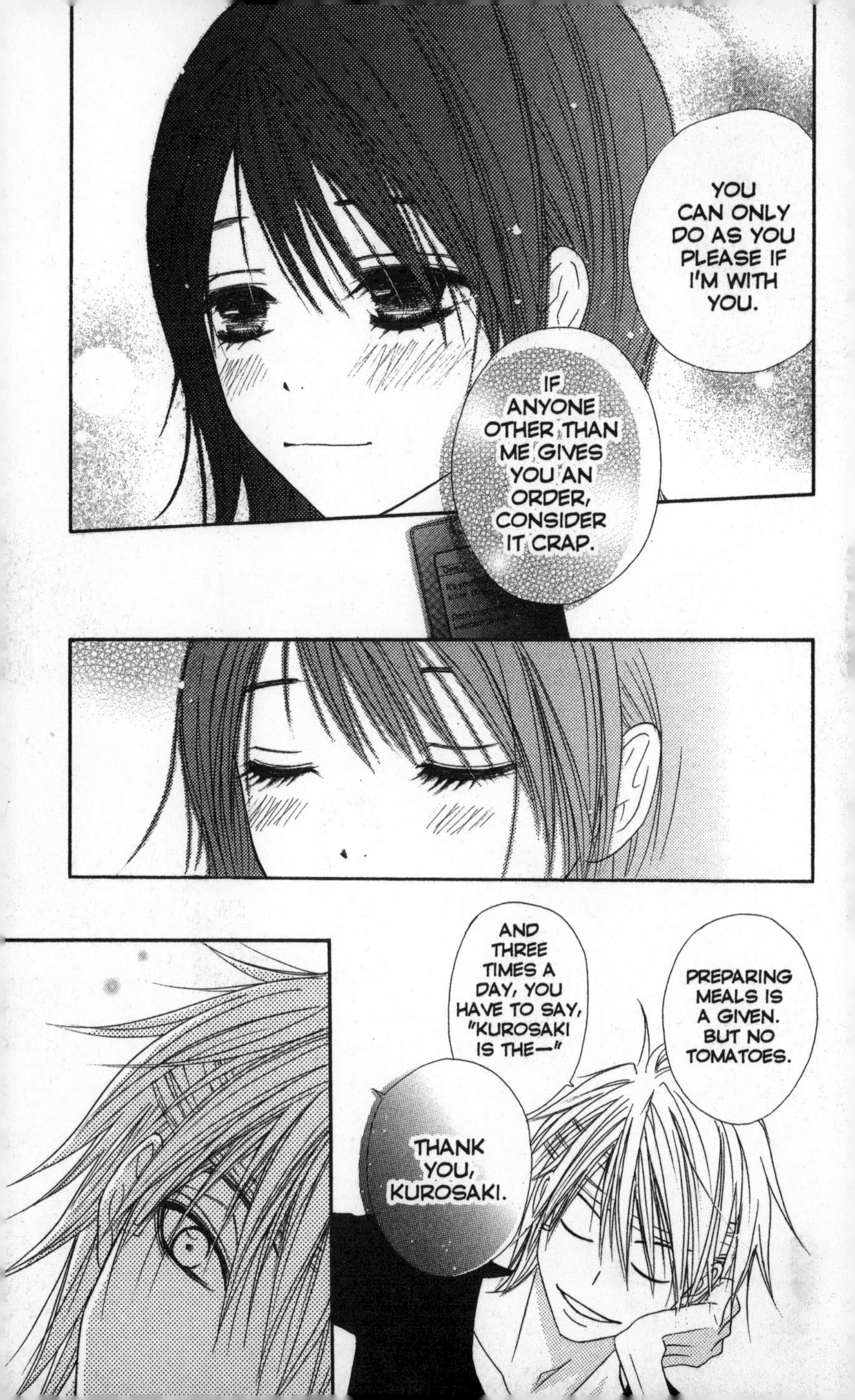
YOU CAN ONLY DO AS YOU PLEASE IF I'M WITH YOU.
IF ANYONE OTHER THAN ME GIVES YOU AN ORDER, CONSIDER IT CRAP.
PREPARING MEALS IS A GIVEN. BUT NO TOMATOES.
AND THREE TIMES A DAY, YOU HAVE TO SAY, "KUROSAKI IS THE—"
THANK YOU, KUROSAKI.

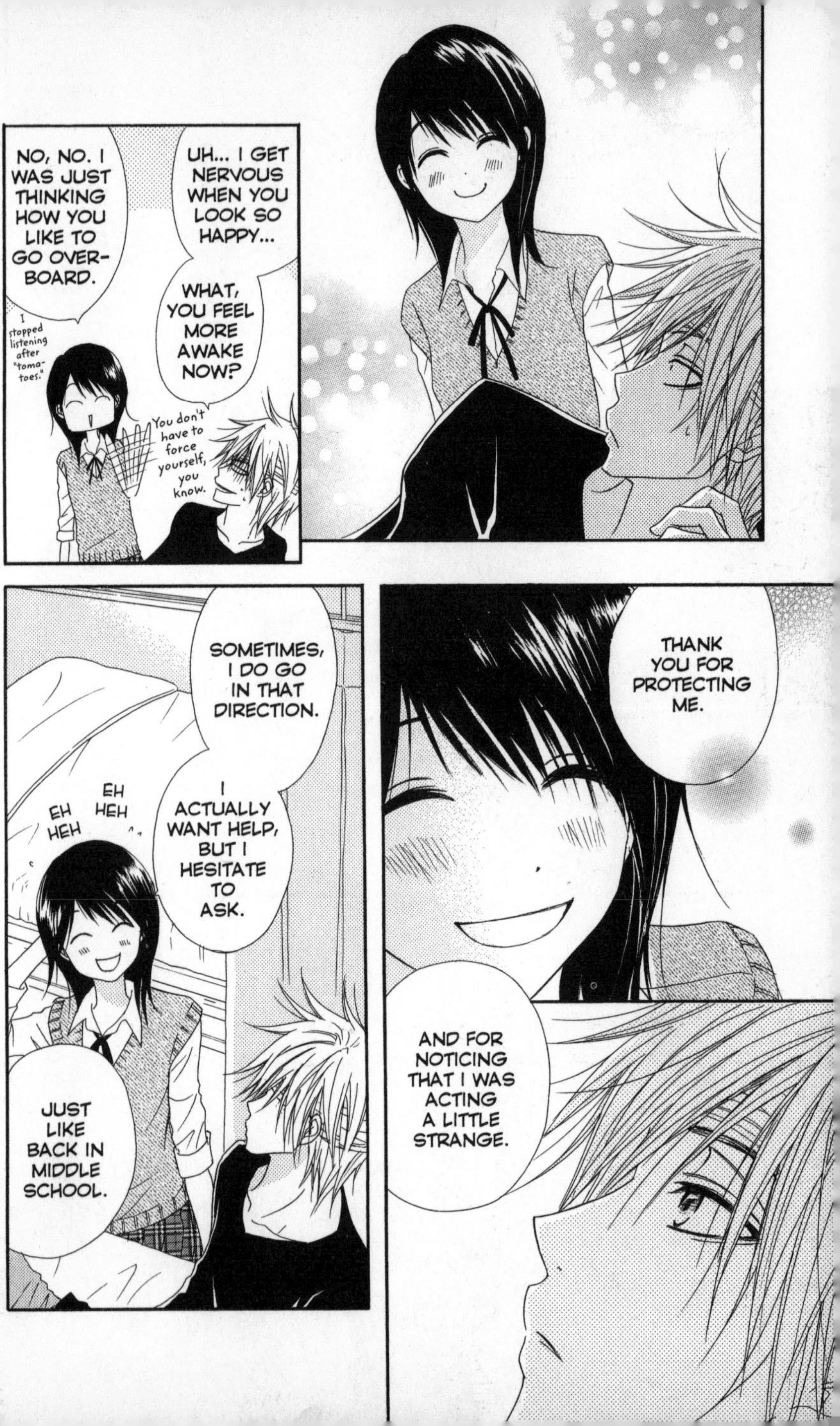
UH... I GET NERVOUS WHEN YOU LOOK SO HAPPY...
NO, NO. I WAS JUST THINKING HOW YOU LIKE TO GO OVER-BOARD.
WHAT, YOU FEEL MORE AWAKE NOW?
I stopped listening after "toma-toes."
You don't have to force yourself, you know.
THANK YOU FOR PROTECTING ME.
AND FOR NOTICING THAT I WAS ACTING A LITTLE STRANGE.
SOMETIMES, I DO GO IN THAT DIRECTION.
I ACTUALLY WANT HELP, BUT I HESITATE TO ASK.
EH HEH
EH HEH
JUST LIKE BACK IN MIDDLE SCHOOL.

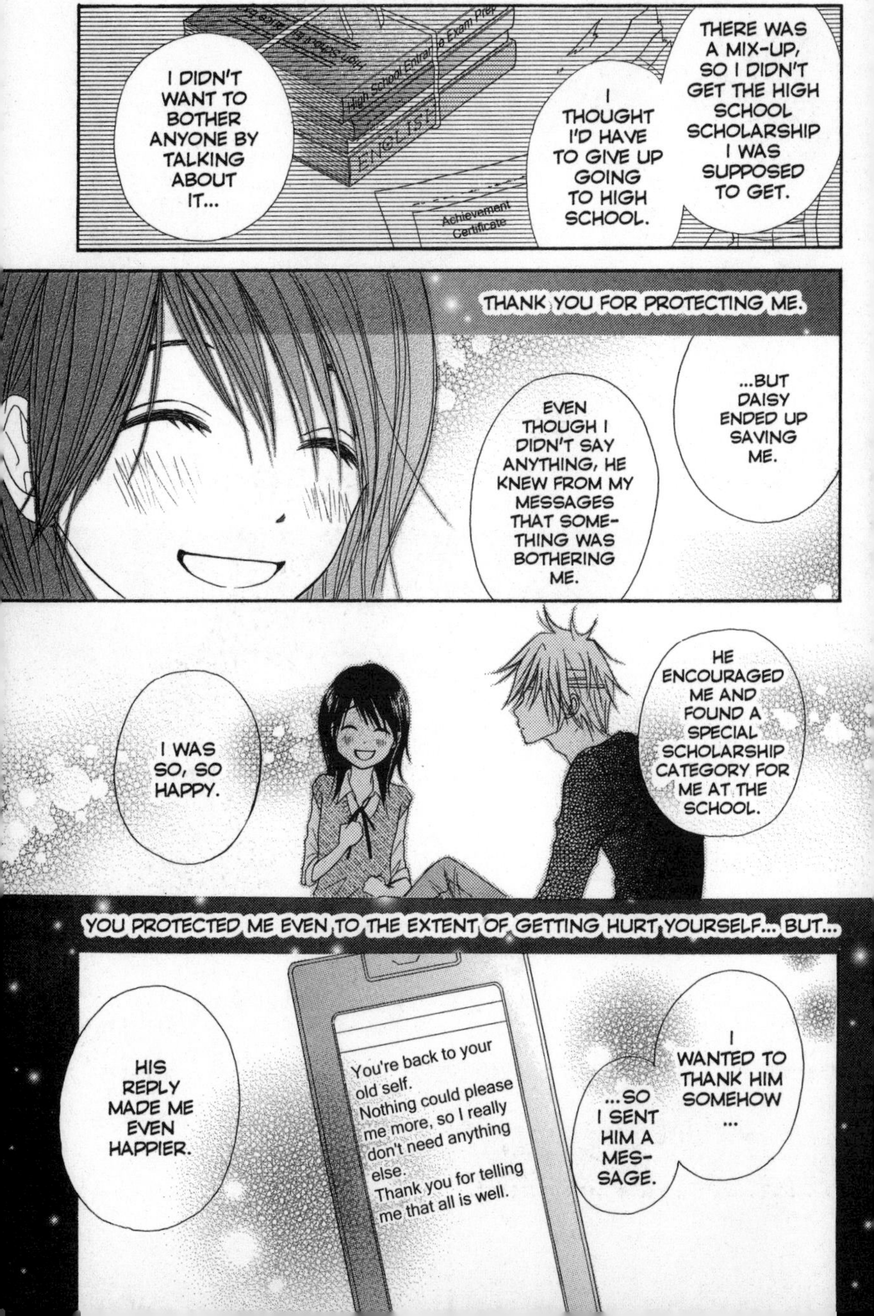
THERE WAS A MIX-UP, SO I DIDN'T GET THE HIGH SCHOOL SCHOLARSHIP I WAS SUPPOSED TO GET.
I THOUGHT I'D HAVE TO GIVE UP GOING TO HIGH SCHOOL.
Achievement Certificate
I DIDN'T WANT TO BOTHER ANYONE BY TALKING ABOUT IT...
THANK YOU FOR PROTECTING ME.
...BUT DAISY ENDED UP SAVING ME.
EVEN THOUGH I DIDN'T SAY ANYTHING, HE KNEW FROM MY MESSAGES THAT SOME-THING WAS BOTHERING ME.
HE ENCOURAGED ME AND FOUND A SPECIAL SCHOLARSHIP CATEGORY FOR ME AT THE SCHOOL.
I WAS SO, SO HAPPY.
YOU PROTECTED ME EVEN TO THE EXTENT OF GETTING HURT YOURSELF... BUT...
I WANTED TO THANK HIM SOMEHOW...
...SO I SENT HIM A MES-SAGE.
You're back to your old self. Nothing could please me more, so I really don't need anything else. Thank you for telling me that all is well.
HIS REPLY MADE ME EVEN HAPPIER.

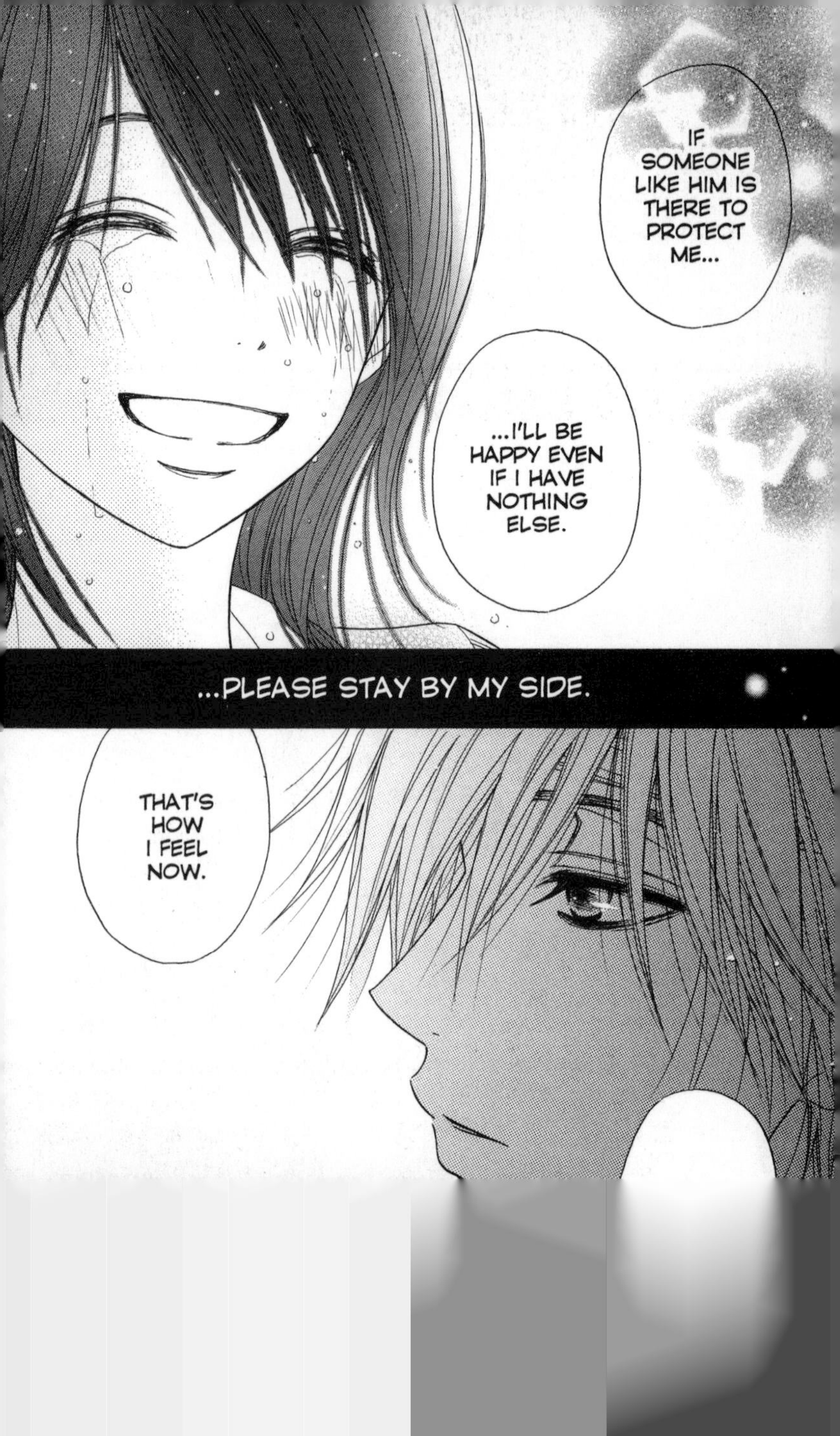
IF SOMEONE LIKE HIM IS THERE TO PROTECT ME...
...I'LL BE HAPPY EVEN IF I HAVE NOTHING ELSE.
...PLEASE STAY BY MY SIDE.
THAT'S HOW I FEEL NOW.

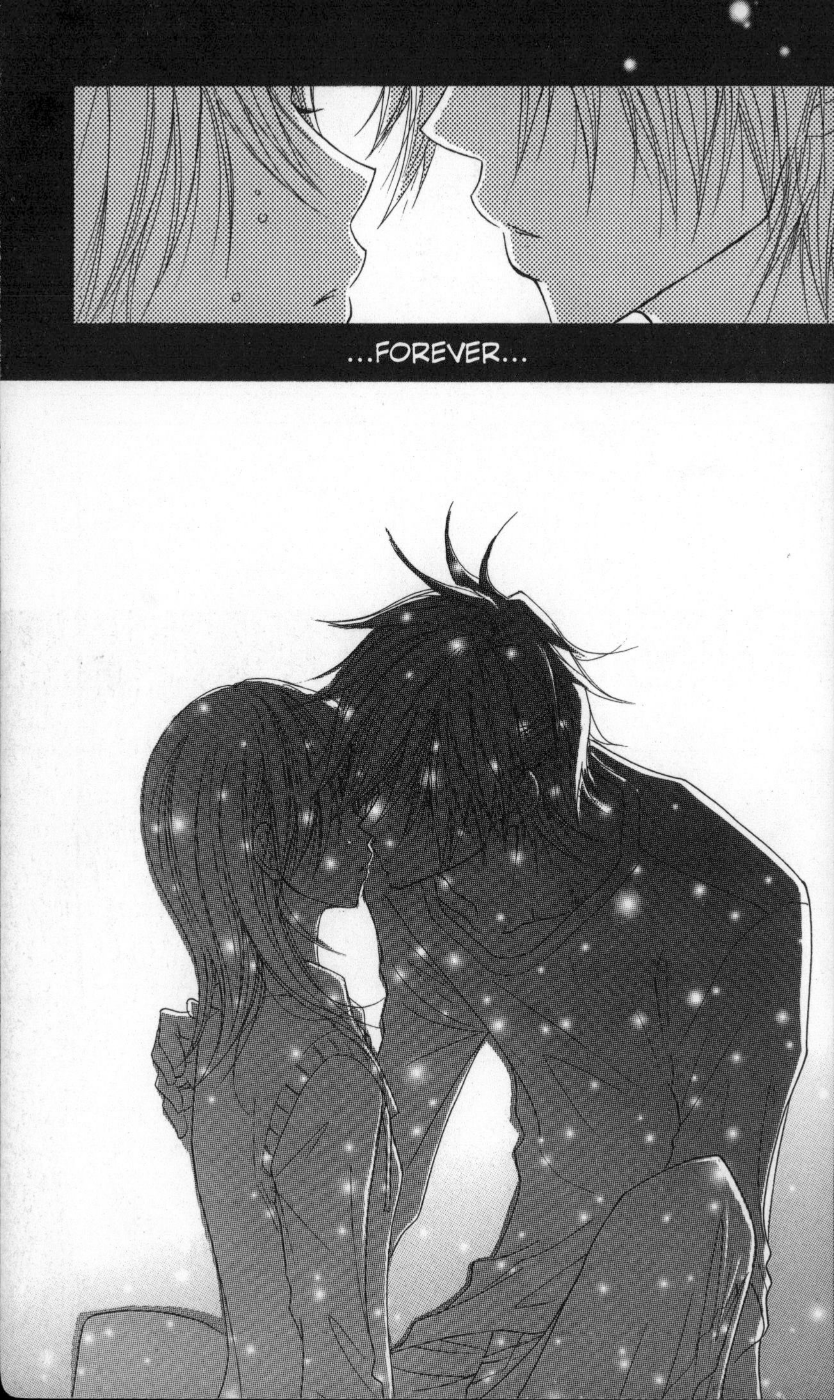
...FOREVER...

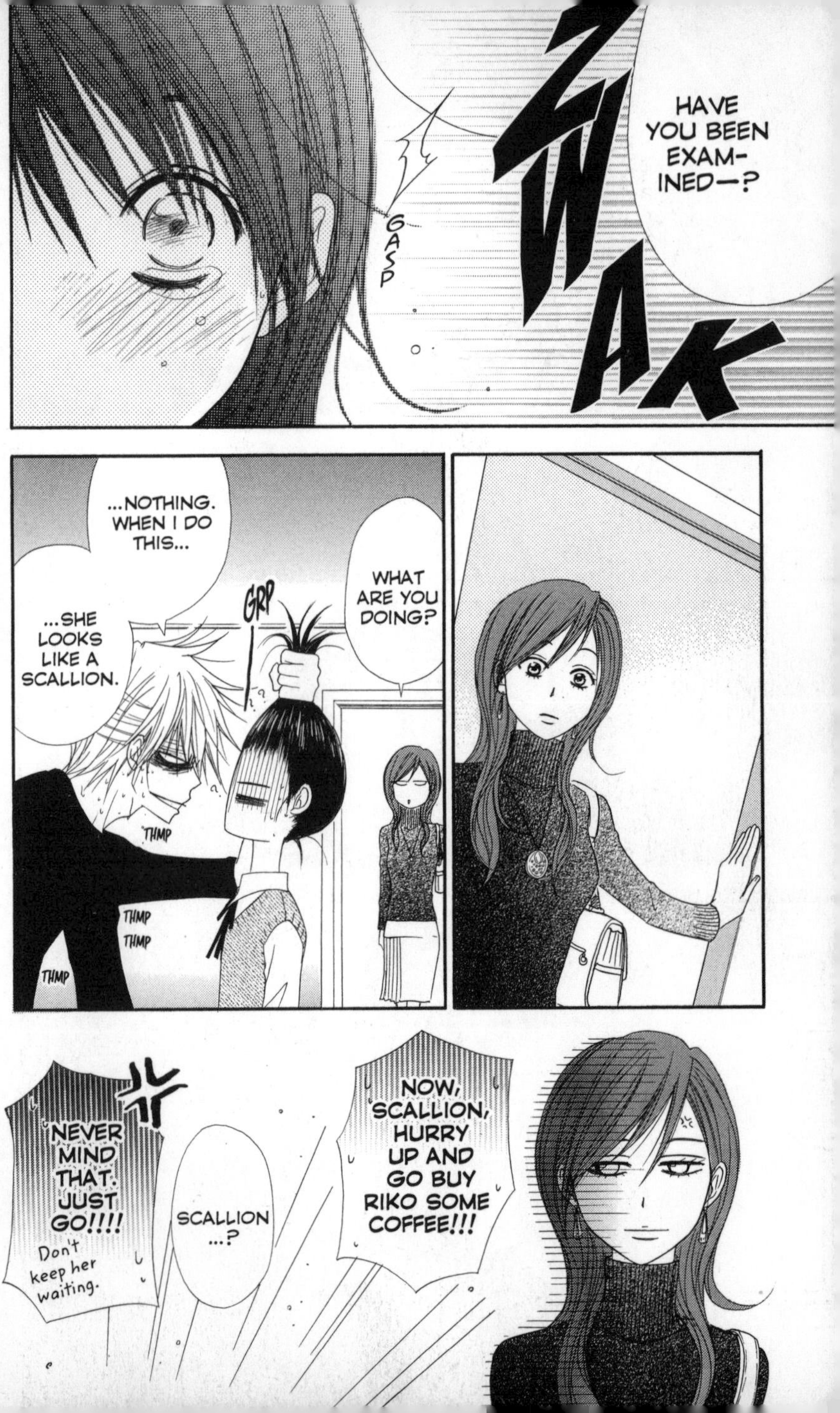

HAVE YOU BEEN EXAM-INED—?
ZWAK
GASP
WHAT ARE YOU DOING?
...NOTHING. WHEN I DO THIS...
...SHE LOOKS LIKE A SCALLION.
GRP
THMP
THMP
THMP
THMP
NOW, SCALLION, HURRY UP AND GO BUY RIKO SOME COFFEE!!!
SCALLION ...?
NEVER MIND THAT. JUST GO!!!!
Don't keep her waiting.

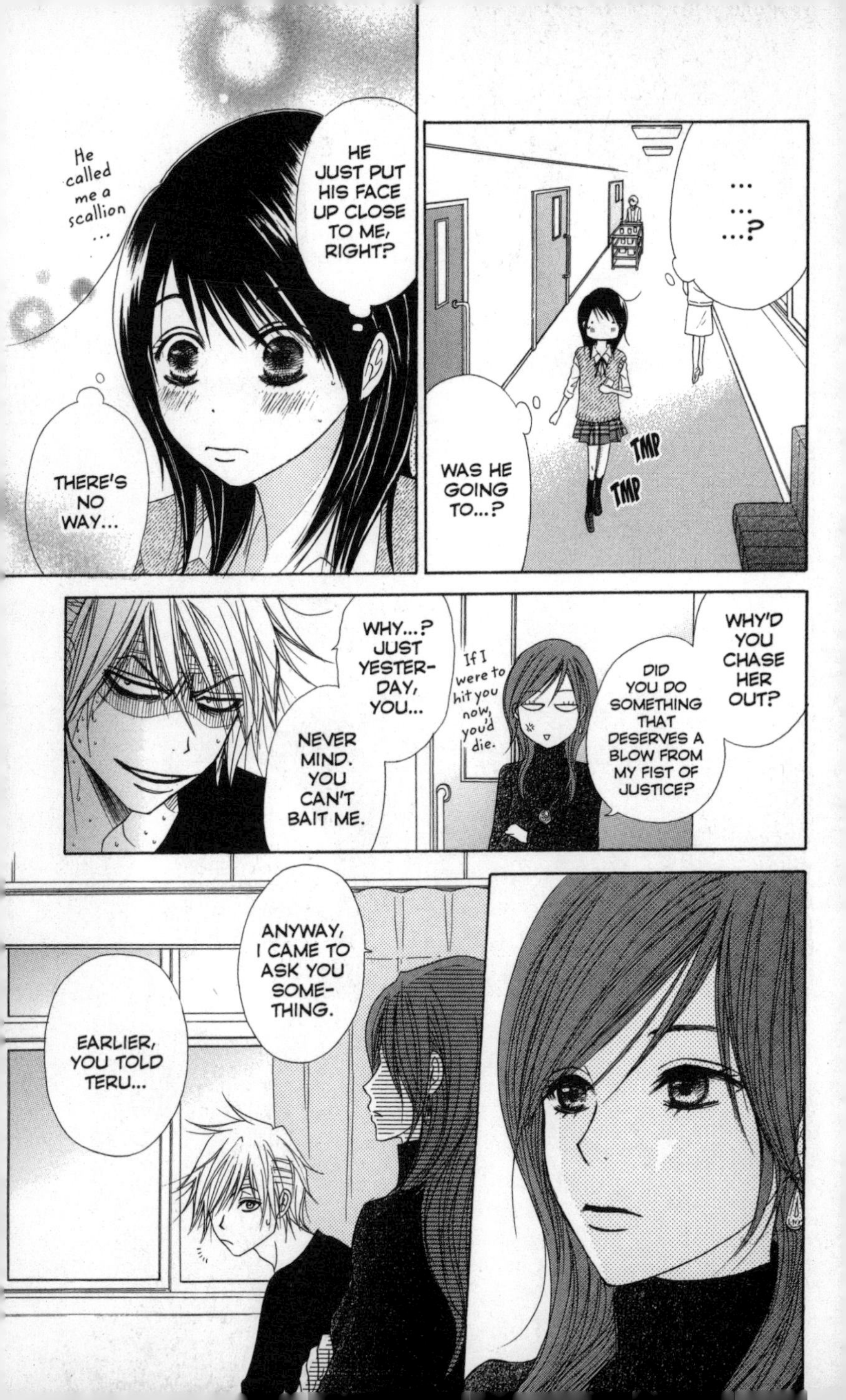
......?
WAS HE GOING TO...?
HE JUST PUT HIS FACE UP CLOSE TO ME, RIGHT?
He called me a scallion...
THERE'S NO WAY...
WHY'D YOU CHASE HER OUT?
DID YOU DO SOMETHING THAT DESERVES A BLOW FROM MY FIST OF JUSTICE?
If I were to hit you now, you'd die.
WHY...? JUST YESTER-DAY, YOU...
NEVER MIND. YOU CAN'T BAIT ME.
ANYWAY, I CAME TO ASK YOU SOME-THING.
EARLIER, YOU TOLD TERU...

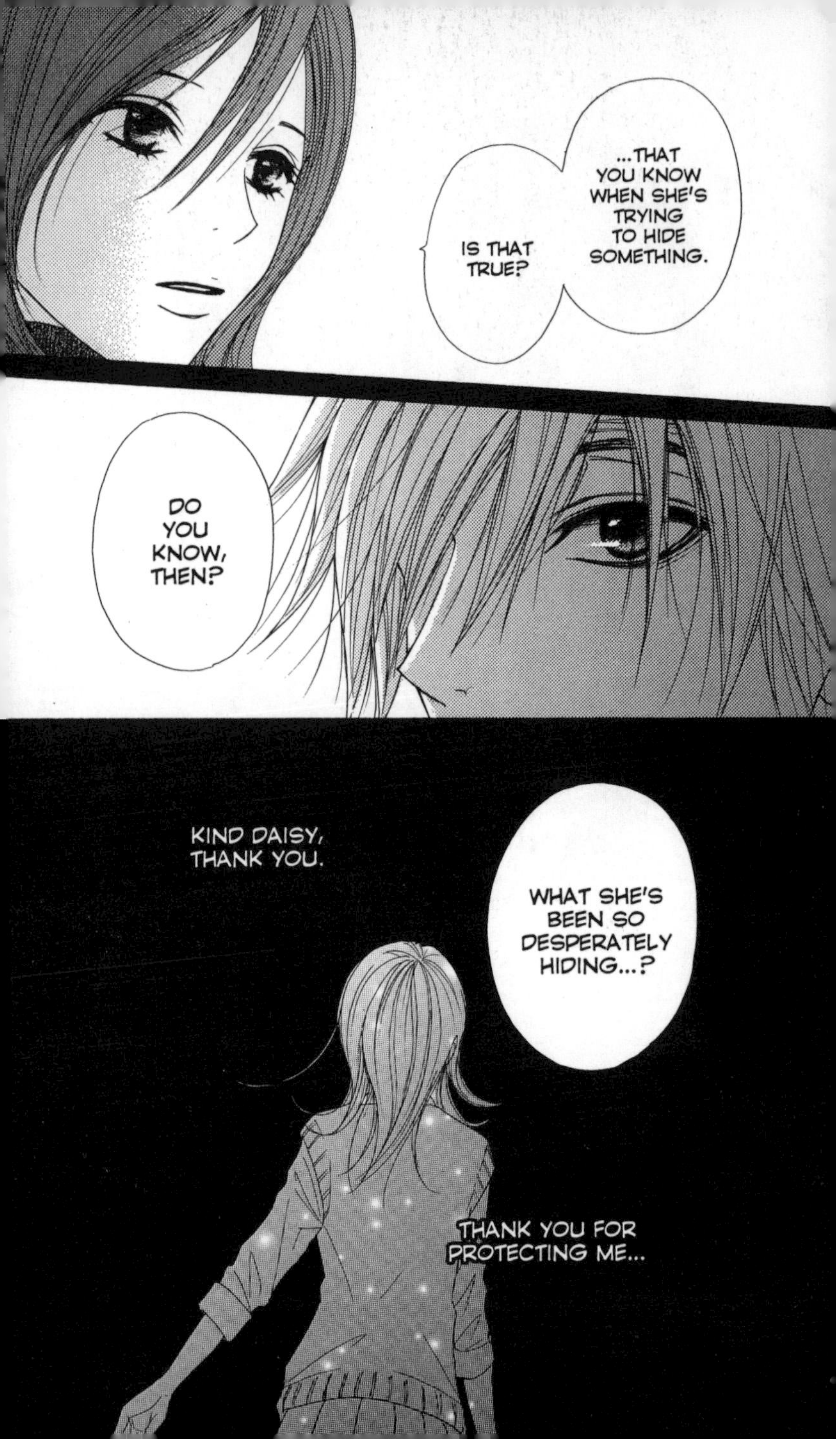
...THAT YOU KNOW WHEN SHE'S TRYING TO HIDE SOMETHING.
IS THAT TRUE?
DO YOU KNOW, THEN?
WHAT SHE'S BEEN SO DESPERATELY HIDING...?
KIND DAISY, THANK YOU.
THANK YOU FOR PROTECTING ME...

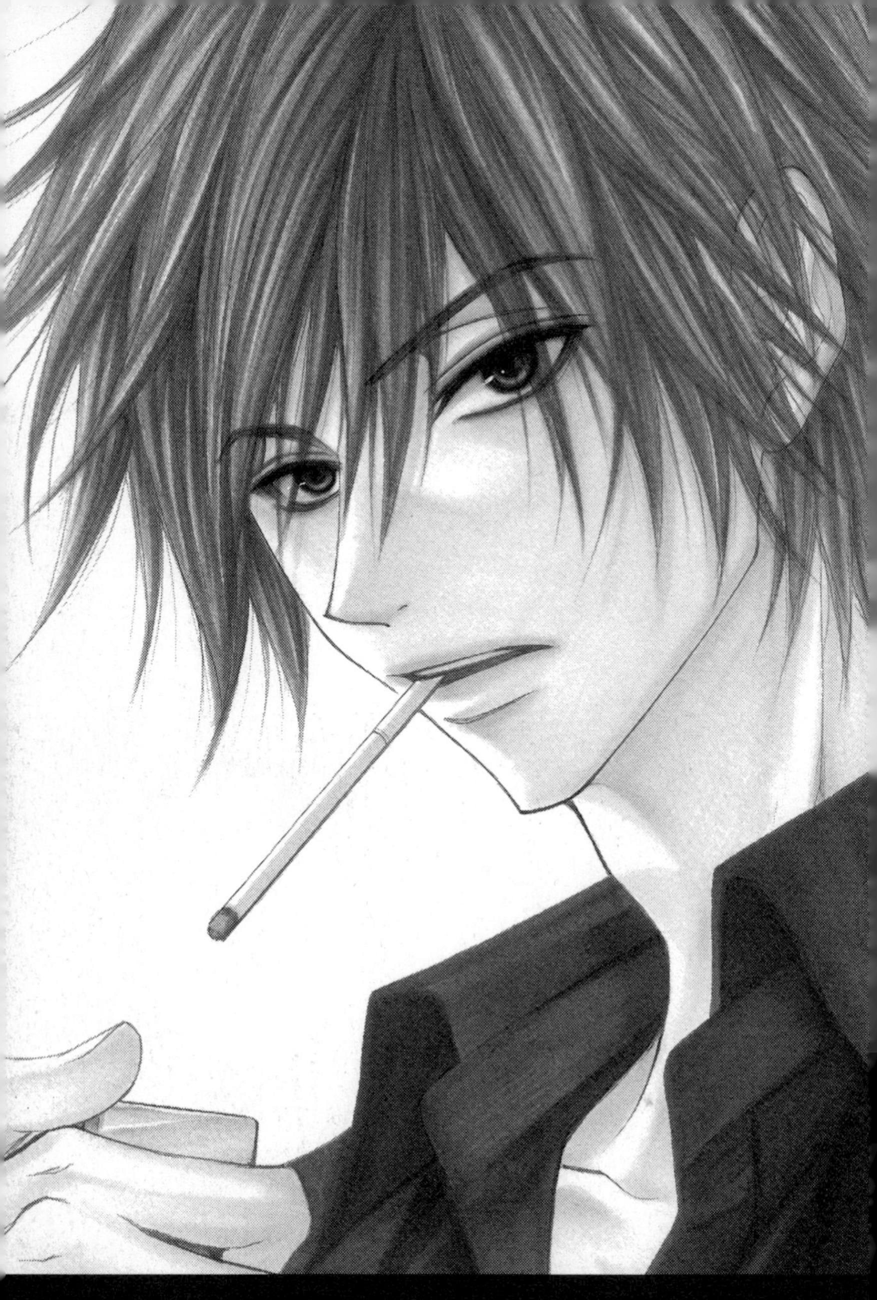

CHAPTER 21: THE FIRST...

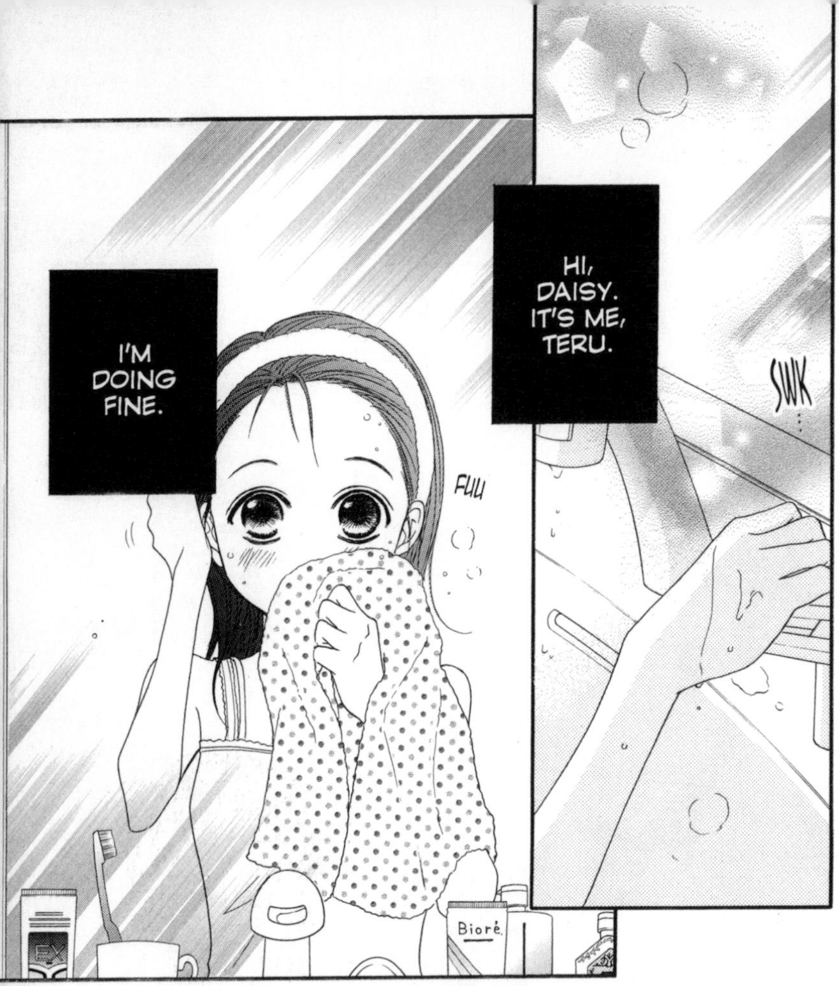
HI, DAISY. IT'S ME, TERU.
SWK
I'M DOING FINE.
FUU
Bioré

LATELY, HE'S STAYED IN THE SHADOWS AND TAKEN ON A MEANER ROLE IN THE STORY, BUT AS I MENTIONED A COUPLE OF TIMES BEFORE, I REALLY LIKE BOSS.

MY EDITOR AND I HAD A DISCUSSION RECENTLY ABOUT HOW HE LOOKS GOOD NO MATTER WHAT HE'S MADE TO DO OR WEAR. WHETHER HE'S IN A SUIT, IN MILITARY GARB, IN SWIM SHORTS, OR IN ANY TYPE OF SPORTS UNIFORM, HE ALWAYS TURNS OUT LOOKING COOL.

(IT'S PAINFUL TO SEE KUROSAKI IN EVEN A BASKETBALL UNIFORM THOUGH.)

ESPECIALLY THIS DIFFICULT-TO-WEAR SPEED SKATING OUFIT... SEE HOW GOOD HE LOOKS IN IT?

BY THE WAY, TERU LOOKS GOOD IN IT TOO.

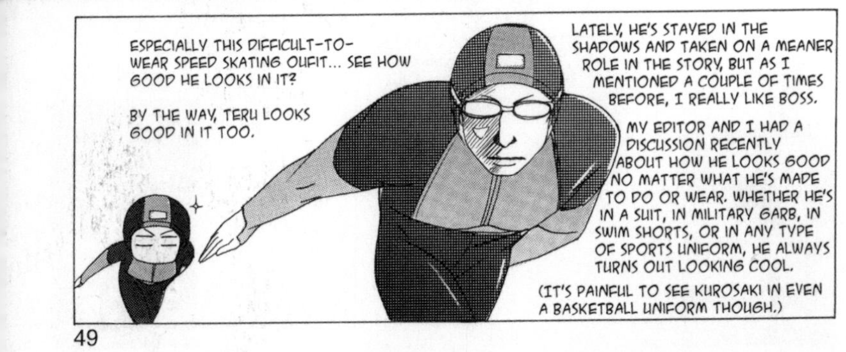

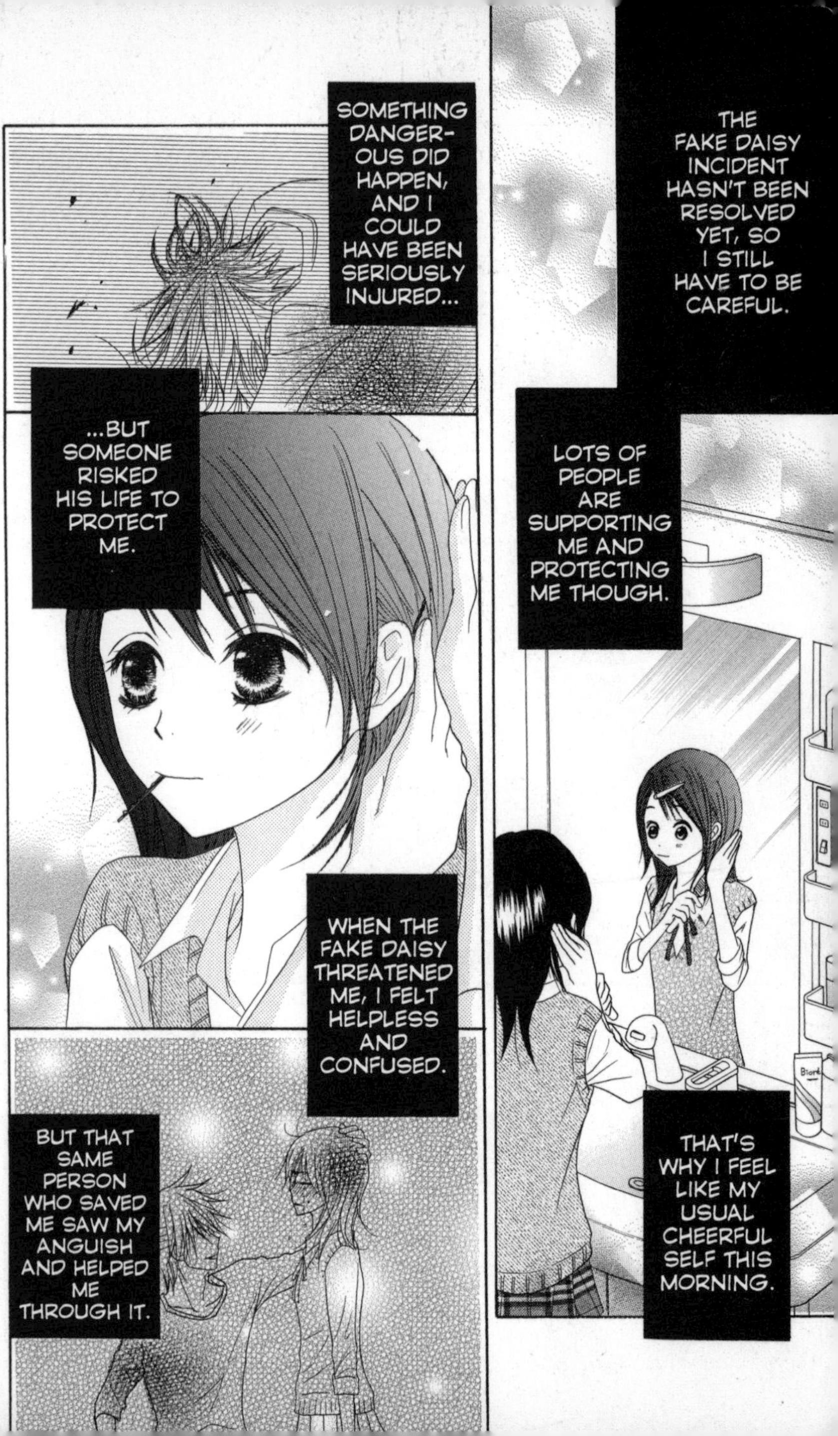
THE FAKE DAISY INCIDENT HASN'T BEEN RESOLVED YET, SO I STILL HAVE TO BE CAREFUL.
LOTS OF PEOPLE ARE SUPPORTING ME AND PROTECTING ME THOUGH.
THAT'S WHY I FEEL LIKE MY USUAL CHEERFUL SELF THIS MORNING.
SOMETHING DANGER-OUS DID HAPPEN, AND I COULD HAVE BEEN SERIOUSLY INJURED...
...BUT SOMEONE RISKED HIS LIFE TO PROTECT ME.
WHEN THE FAKE DAISY THREATENED ME, I FELT HELPLESS AND CONFUSED.
BUT THAT SAME PERSON WHO SAVED ME SAW MY ANGUISH AND HELPED ME THROUGH IT.

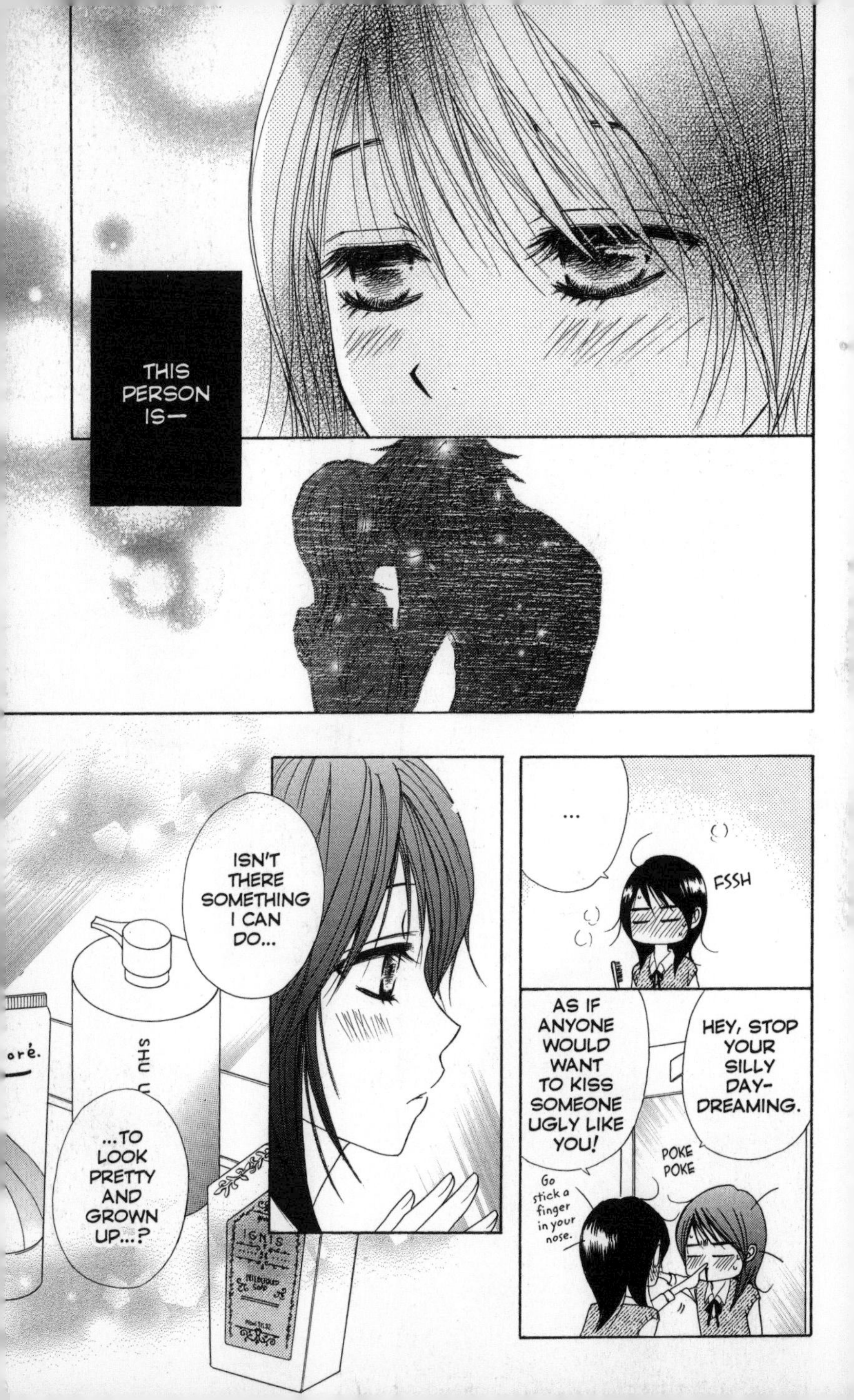
THIS PERSON IS—
...
FSSH
HEY, STOP YOUR SILLY DAY-DREAMING.
AS IF ANYONE WOULD WANT TO KISS SOMEONE UGLY LIKE YOU!
POKE POKE
Go stick a finger in your nose.
ISN'T THERE SOMETHING I CAN DO...
...TO LOOK PRETTY AND GROWN UP...?
SHU U
IGNIS

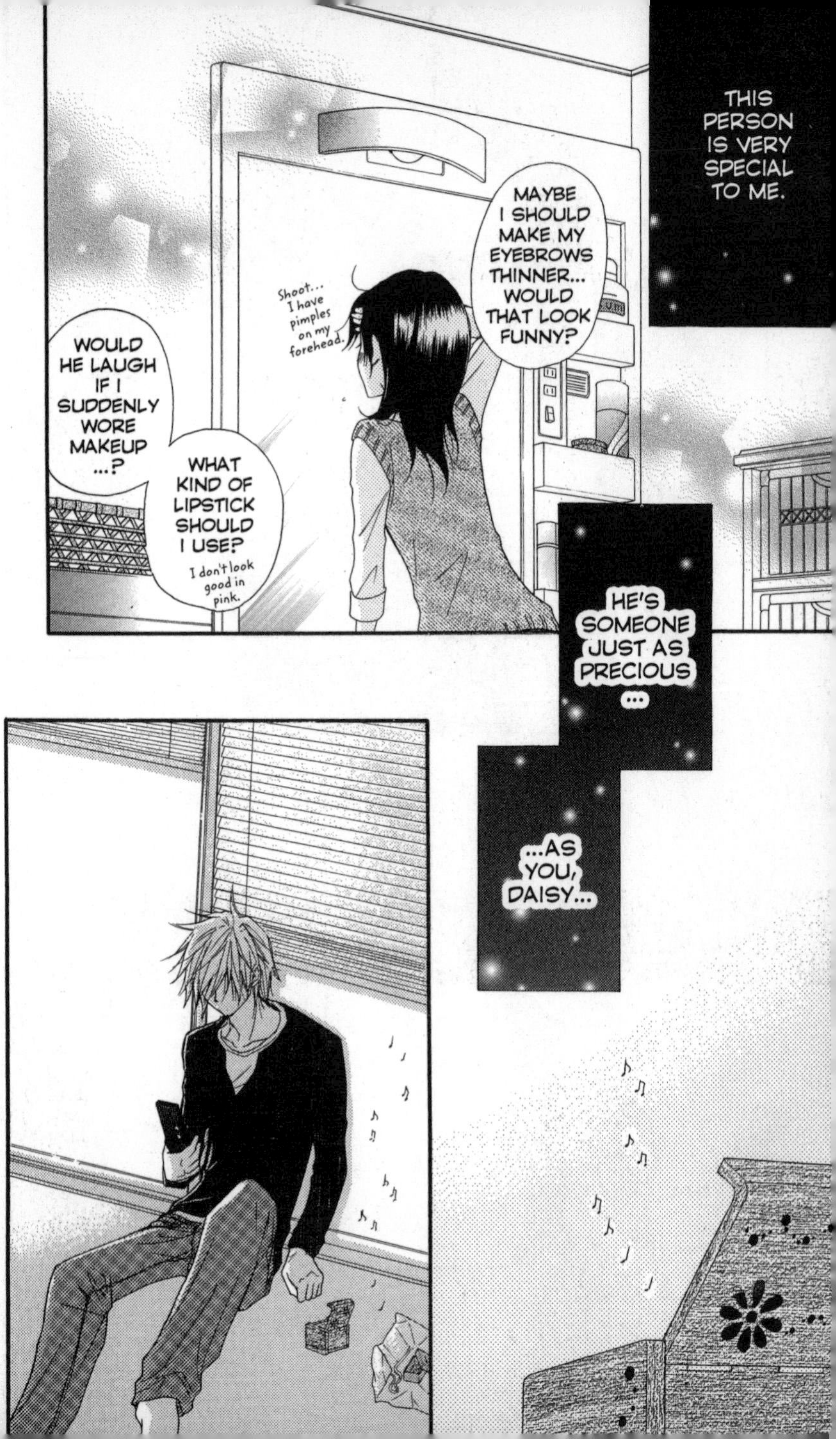
THIS PERSON IS VERY SPECIAL TO ME.
MAYBE I SHOULD MAKE MY EYEBROWS THINNER... WOULD THAT LOOK FUNNY?
Shoot... I have pimples on my forehead.
WOULD HE LAUGH IF I SUDDENLY WORE MAKEUP ...?
WHAT KIND OF LIPSTICK SHOULD I USE?
I don't look good in pink.
HE'S SOMEONE JUST AS PRECIOUS ...
...AS YOU, DAISY...

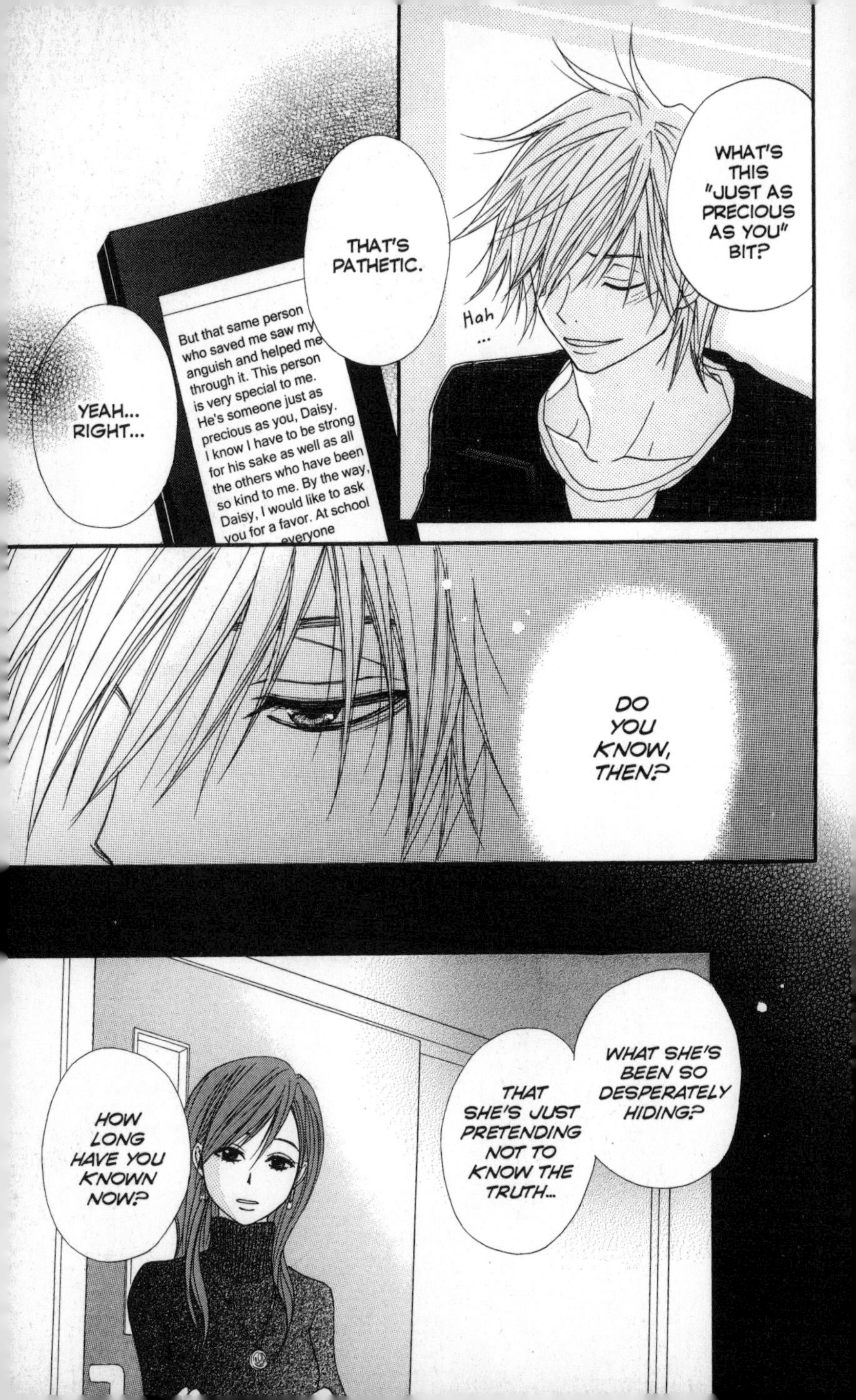
WHAT'S THIS "JUST AS PRECIOUS AS YOU" BIT?
Hah...
THAT'S PATHETIC.
But that same person who saved me saw my anguish and helped me through it. This person is very special to me. He's someone just as precious as you, Daisy. I know I have to be strong for his sake as well as all the others who have been so kind to me. By the way, Daisy, I would like to ask you for a favor. At school everyone
YEAH... RIGHT...
DO YOU KNOW, THEN?
WHAT SHE'S BEEN SO DESPERATELY HIDING?
THAT SHE'S JUST PRETENDING NOT TO KNOW THE TRUTH...
HOW LONG HAVE YOU KNOWN NOW?

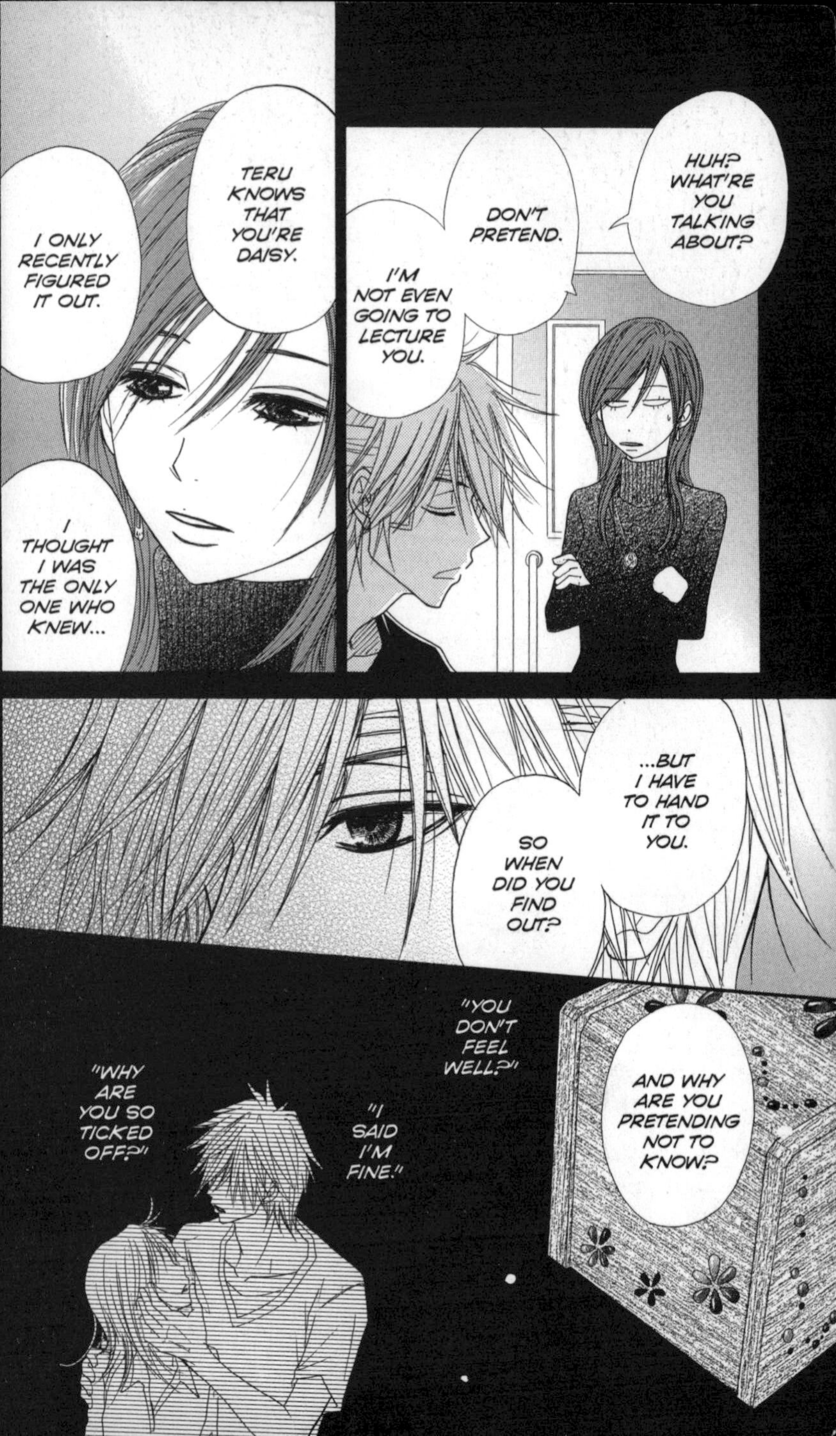
HUH? WHAT'RE YOU TALKING ABOUT?
DON'T PRETEND.
I'M NOT EVEN GOING TO LECTURE YOU.
TERU KNOWS THAT YOU'RE DAISY.
I ONLY RECENTLY FIGURED IT OUT.
I THOUGHT I WAS THE ONLY ONE WHO KNEW...
...BUT I HAVE TO HAND IT TO YOU.
SO WHEN DID YOU FIND OUT?
AND WHY ARE YOU PRETENDING NOT TO KNOW?
"YOU DON'T FEEL WELL?"
"I SAID I'M FINE."
"WHY ARE YOU SO TICKED OFF?"

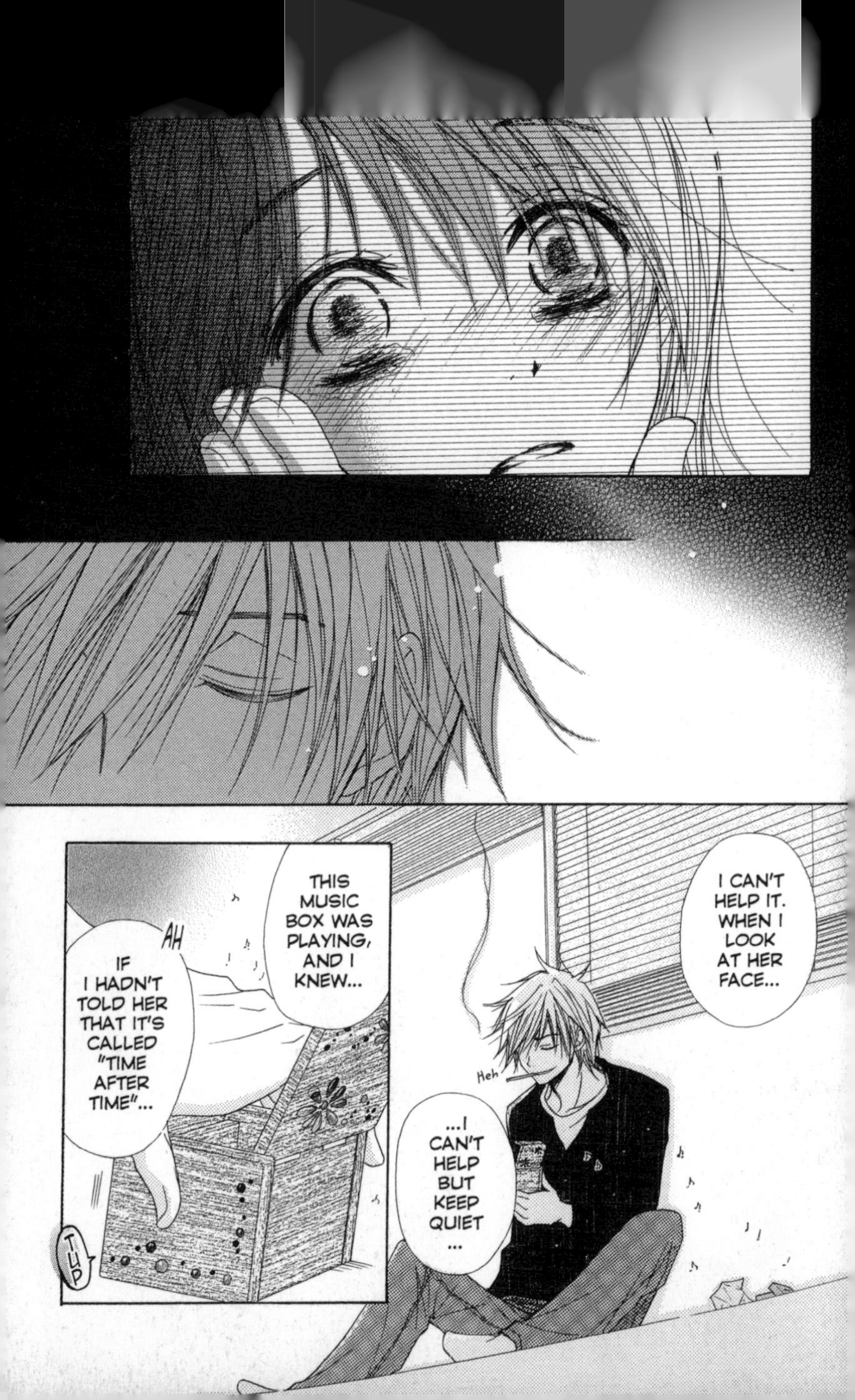
I CAN'T HELP IT. WHEN I LOOK AT HER FACE...
Heh
...I CAN'T HELP BUT KEEP QUIET ...
THIS MUSIC BOX WAS PLAYING, AND I KNEW...
AH
IF I HADN'T TOLD HER THAT IT'S CALLED "TIME AFTER TIME"...
TUP

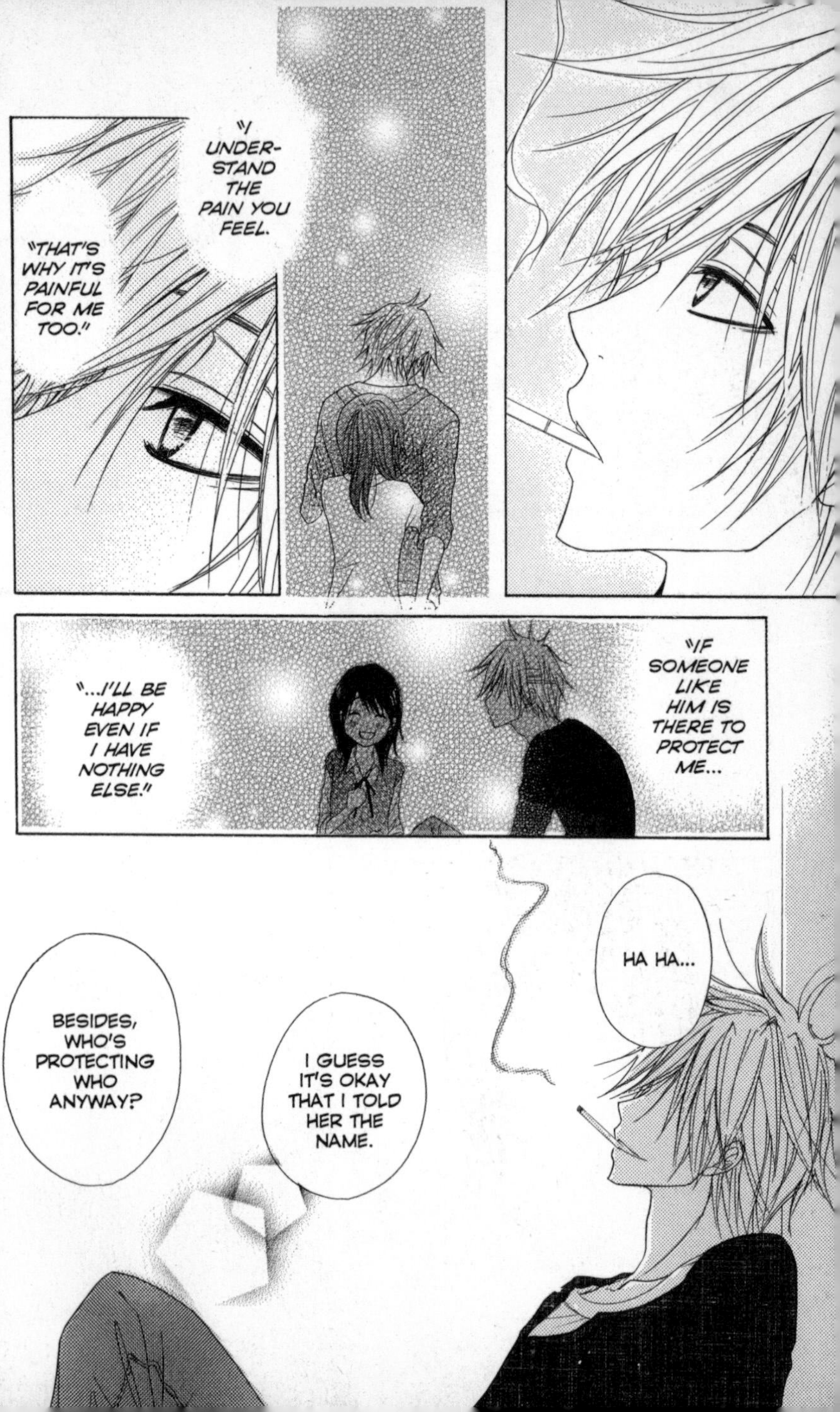
"I UNDERSTAND THE PAIN YOU FEEL.
"THAT'S WHY IT'S PAINFUL FOR ME TOO."
"IF SOMEONE LIKE HIM IS THERE TO PROTECT ME...
"...I'LL BE HAPPY EVEN IF I HAVE NOTHING ELSE."
HA HA...
I GUESS IT'S OKAY THAT I TOLD HER THE NAME.
BESIDES, WHO'S PROTECTING WHO ANYWAY?

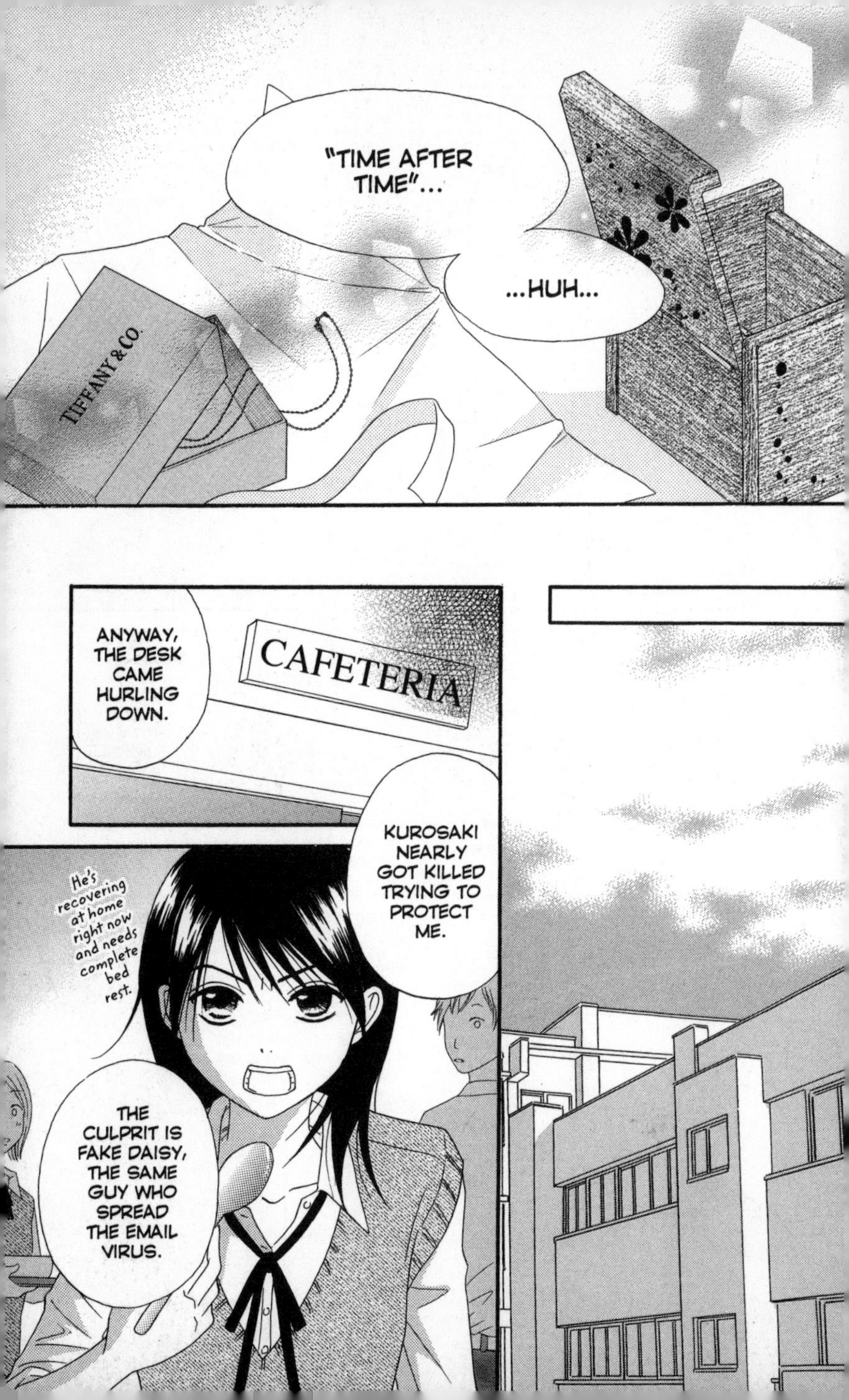
"TIME AFTER TIME"...
...HUH...
TIFFANY & CO.
CAFETERIA
ANYWAY, THE DESK CAME HURLING DOWN.
KUROSAKI NEARLY GOT KILLED TRYING TO PROTECT ME.
He's recovering at home right now and needs complete bed rest.
THE CULPRIT IS FAKE DAISY, THE SAME GUY WHO SPREAD THE EMAIL VIRUS.

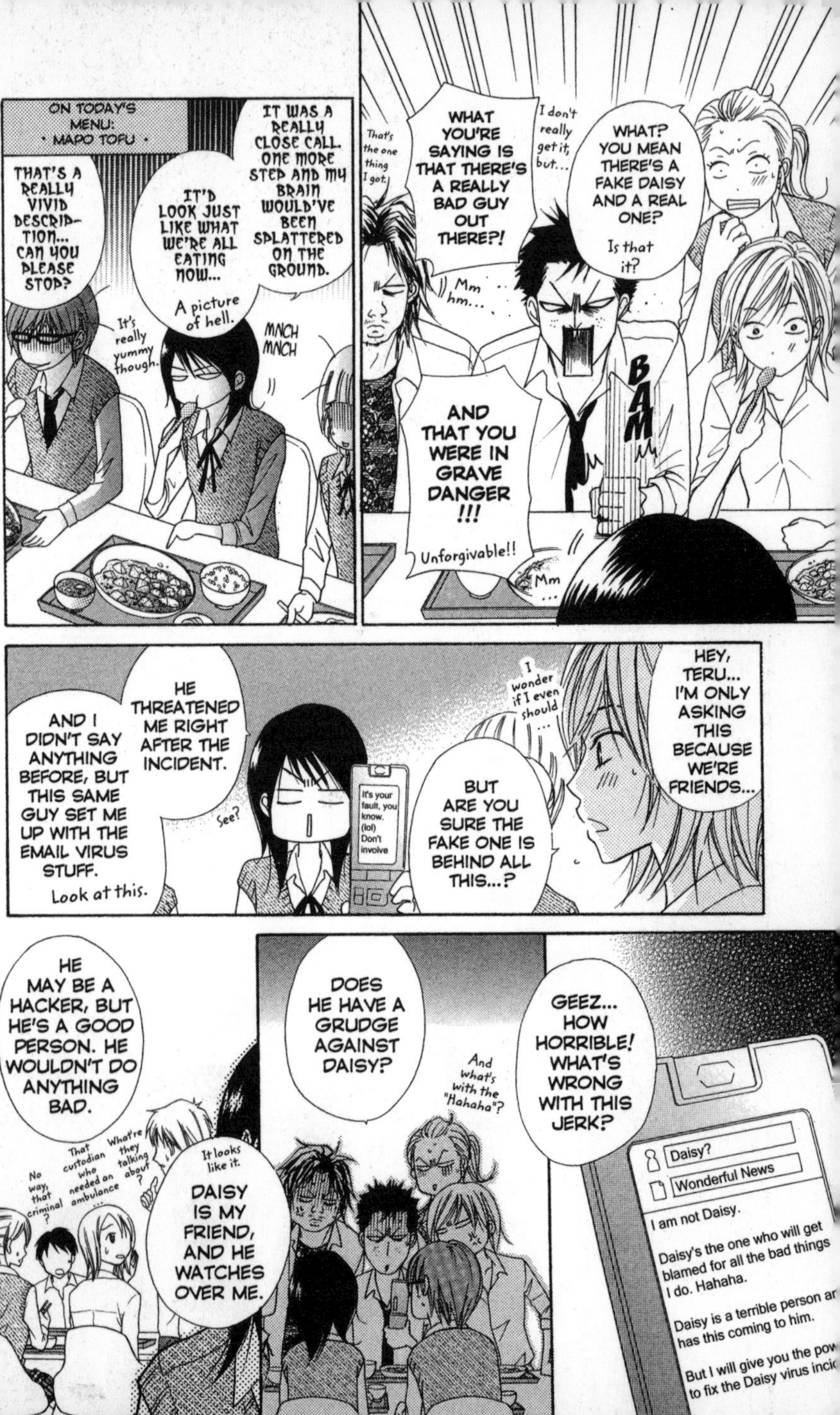
WHAT? YOU MEAN THERE'S A FAKE DAISY AND A REAL ONE?
Is that it?
I don't really get it, but...
WHAT YOU'RE SAYING IS THAT THERE'S A REALLY BAD GUY OUT THERE?!
That's the one thing I got.
Mm hm...
BAM
AND THAT YOU WERE IN GRAVE DANGER !!!
Unforgivable!!
Mm...
IT WAS A REALLY CLOSE CALL. ONE MORE STEP AND MY BRAIN WOULD'VE BEEN SPLATTERED ON THE GROUND.
ON TODAY'S MENU: • MAPO TOFU •
IT'D LOOK JUST LIKE WHAT WE'RE ALL EATING NOW...
A picture of hell.
MNCH MNCH
THAT'S A REALLY VIVID DESCRIPTION... CAN YOU PLEASE STOP?
It's really yummy though.
HEY, TERU... I'M ONLY ASKING THIS BECAUSE WE'RE FRIENDS...
I wonder if I even should...
BUT ARE YOU SURE THE FAKE ONE IS BEHIND ALL THIS...?
HE THREATENED ME RIGHT AFTER THE INCIDENT.
It's your fault, you know. (lol) Don't involve
See?
AND I DIDN'T SAY ANYTHING BEFORE, BUT THIS SAME GUY SET ME UP WITH THE EMAIL VIRUS STUFF.
Look at this.
Daisy?
Wonderful News
I am not Daisy.
Daisy's the one who will get blamed for all the bad things I do. Hahaha.
Daisy is a terrible person ar has this coming to him.
But I will give you the pow to fix the Daisy virus inci
GEEZ... HOW HORRIBLE! WHAT'S WRONG WITH THIS JERK?
And what's with the "Hahaha"?
DOES HE HAVE A GRUDGE AGAINST DAISY?
It looks like it.
DAISY IS MY FRIEND, AND HE WATCHES OVER ME.
What're they talking about?
That custodian who needed an ambulance...
No way, that criminal?
HE MAY BE A HACKER, BUT HE'S A GOOD PERSON. HE WOULDN'T DO ANYTHING BAD.

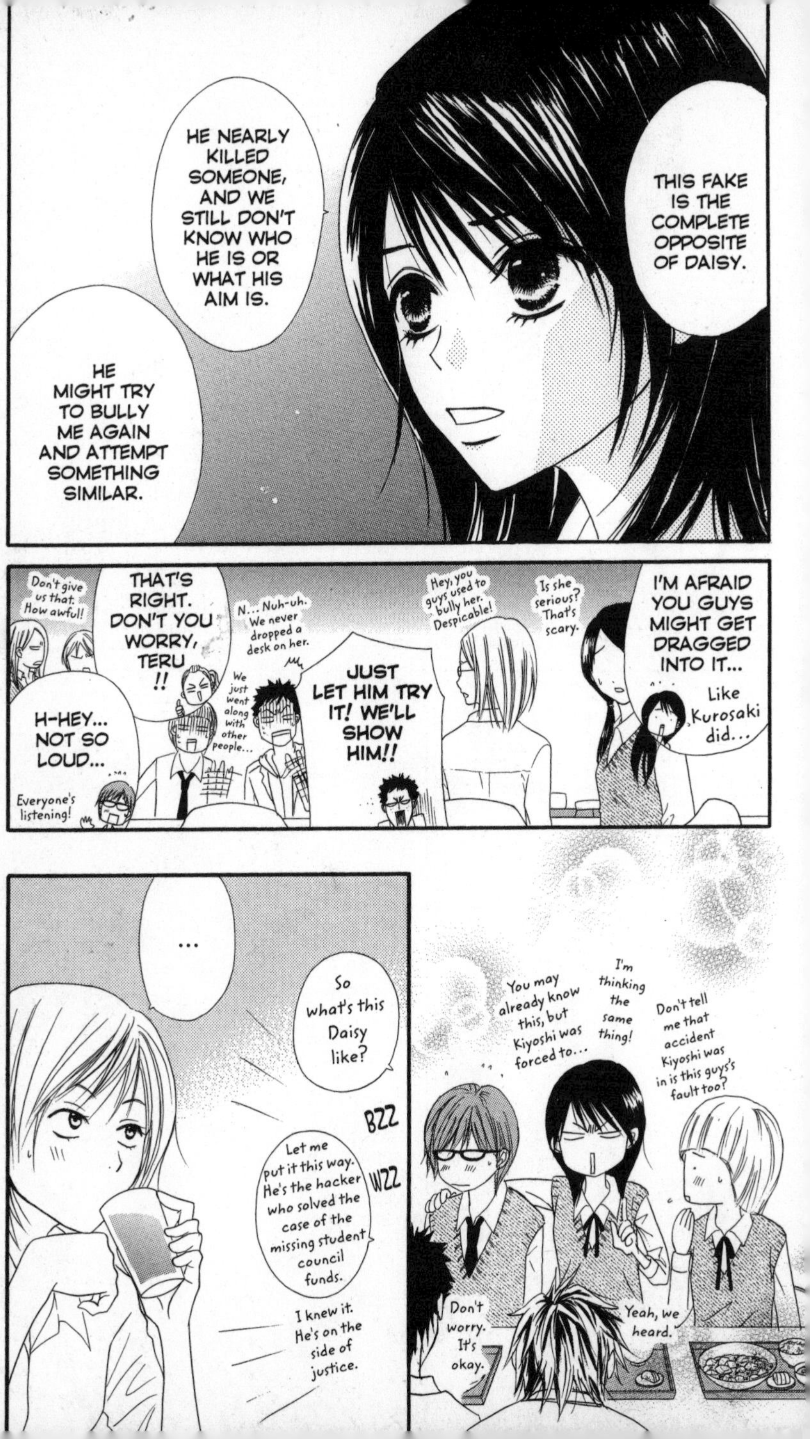
THIS FAKE IS THE COMPLETE OPPOSITE OF DAISY.
HE NEARLY KILLED SOMEONE, AND WE STILL DON'T KNOW WHO HE IS OR WHAT HIS AIM IS.
HE MIGHT TRY TO BULLY ME AGAIN AND ATTEMPT SOMETHING SIMILAR.
I'M AFRAID YOU GUYS MIGHT GET DRAGGED INTO IT...
Like Kurosaki did...
Is she serious? That's scary.
Hey, you guys used to bully her. Despicable!
JUST LET HIM TRY IT! WE'LL SHOW HIM!!
N... Nuh-uh. We never dropped a desk on her.
We just went along with other people...
THAT'S RIGHT. DON'T YOU WORRY, TERU!!
Don't give us that. How awful!
H-HEY... NOT SO LOUD...
Everyone's listening!
Don't tell me that accident Kiyoshi was in is this guys's fault too?
I'm thinking the same thing!
You may already know this, but Kiyoshi was forced to...
Yeah, we heard.
Don't worry. It's okay.
...
So what's this Daisy like?
BZZ
WZZ
Let me put it this way. He's the hacker who solved the case of the missing student council funds.
I knew it. He's on the side of justice.

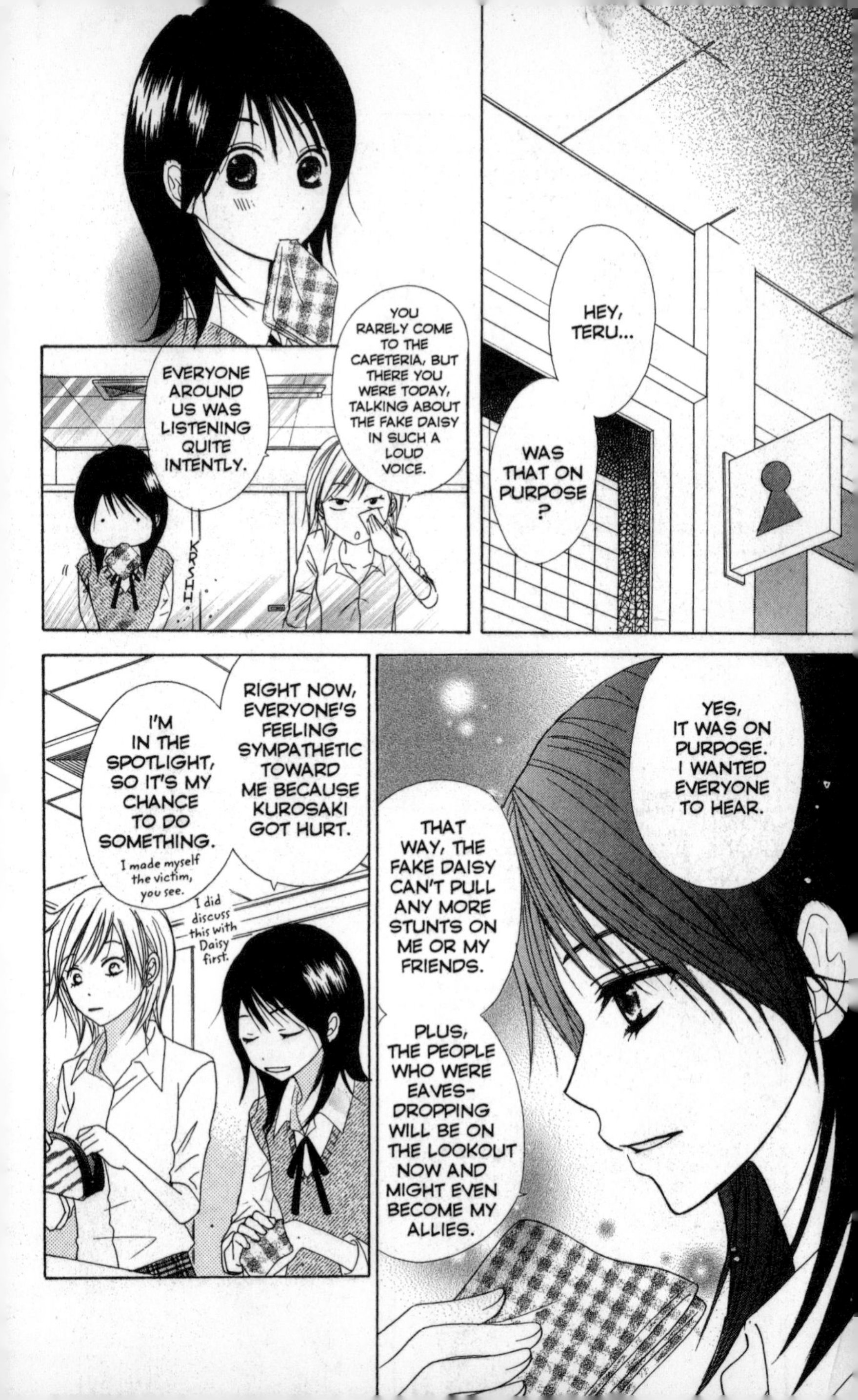
HEY, TERU...
WAS THAT ON PURPOSE?
YOU RARELY COME TO THE CAFETERIA, BUT THERE YOU WERE TODAY, TALKING ABOUT THE FAKE DAISY IN SUCH A LOUD VOICE.
EVERYONE AROUND US WAS LISTENING QUITE INTENTLY.
KRSHH
YES, IT WAS ON PURPOSE. I WANTED EVERYONE TO HEAR.
THAT WAY, THE FAKE DAISY CAN'T PULL ANY MORE STUNTS ON ME OR MY FRIENDS.
PLUS, THE PEOPLE WHO WERE EAVES-DROPPING WILL BE ON THE LOOKOUT NOW AND MIGHT EVEN BECOME MY ALLIES.
RIGHT NOW, EVERYONE'S FEELING SYMPATHETIC TOWARD ME BECAUSE KUROSAKI GOT HURT.
I'M IN THE SPOTLIGHT, SO IT'S MY CHANCE TO DO SOMETHING.
I made myself the victim, you see.
I did discuss this with Daisy first.

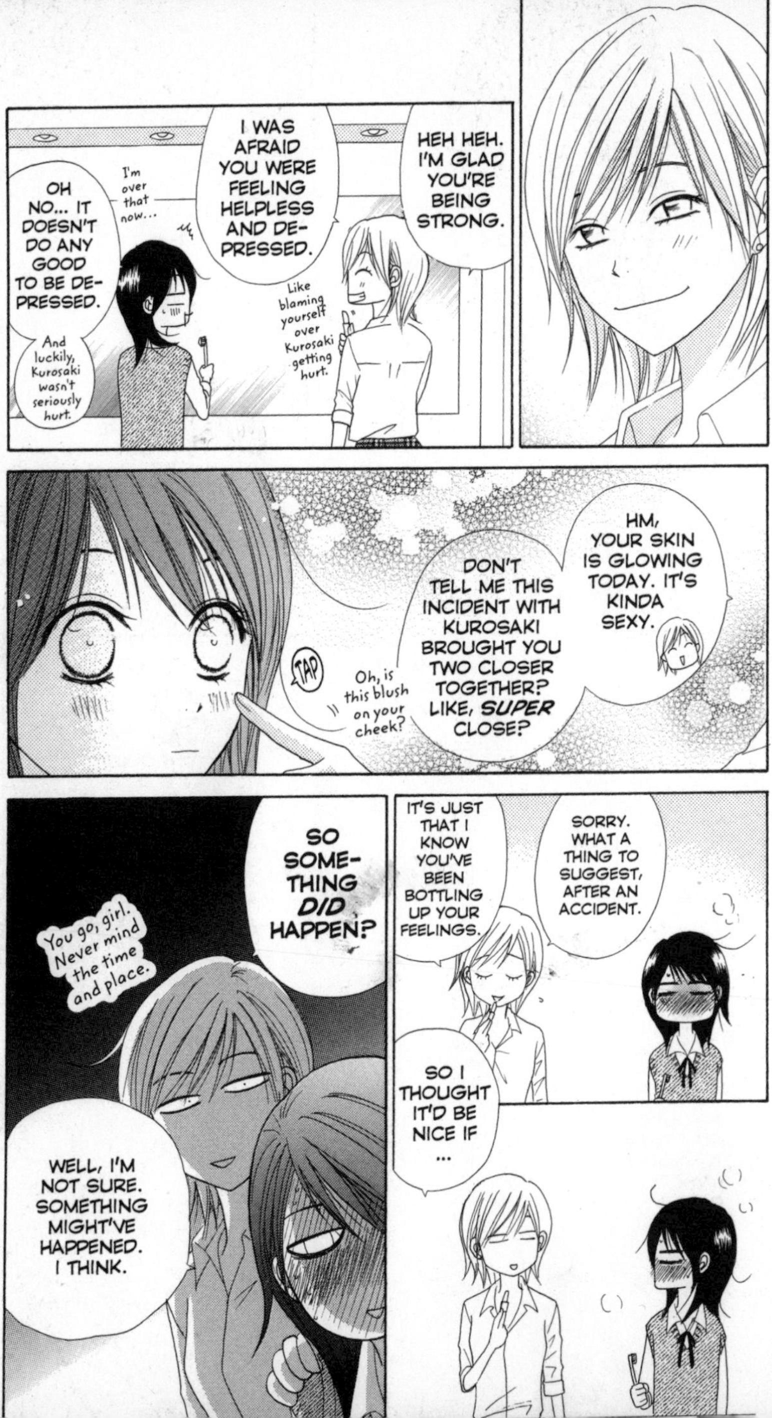
HEH HEH. I'M GLAD YOU'RE BEING STRONG.
I WAS AFRAID YOU WERE FEELING HELPLESS AND DE-PRESSED.
Like blaming yourself over Kurosaki getting hurt.
I'm over that now...
OH NO... IT DOESN'T DO ANY GOOD TO BE DE-PRESSED.
And luckily, Kurosaki wasn't seriously hurt.
HM, YOUR SKIN IS GLOWING TODAY. IT'S KINDA SEXY.
DON'T TELL ME THIS INCIDENT WITH KUROSAKI BROUGHT YOU TWO CLOSER TOGETHER? LIKE, *SUPER* CLOSE?
Oh, is this blush on your cheek?
TAP
SORRY. WHAT A THING TO SUGGEST, AFTER AN ACCIDENT.
IT'S JUST THAT I KNOW YOU'VE BEEN BOTTLING UP YOUR FEELINGS.
SO I THOUGHT IT'D BE NICE IF ...
SO SOMETHING *DID* HAPPEN?
You go, girl. Never mind the time and place.
WELL, I'M NOT SURE. SOMETHING MIGHT'VE HAPPENED. I THINK.

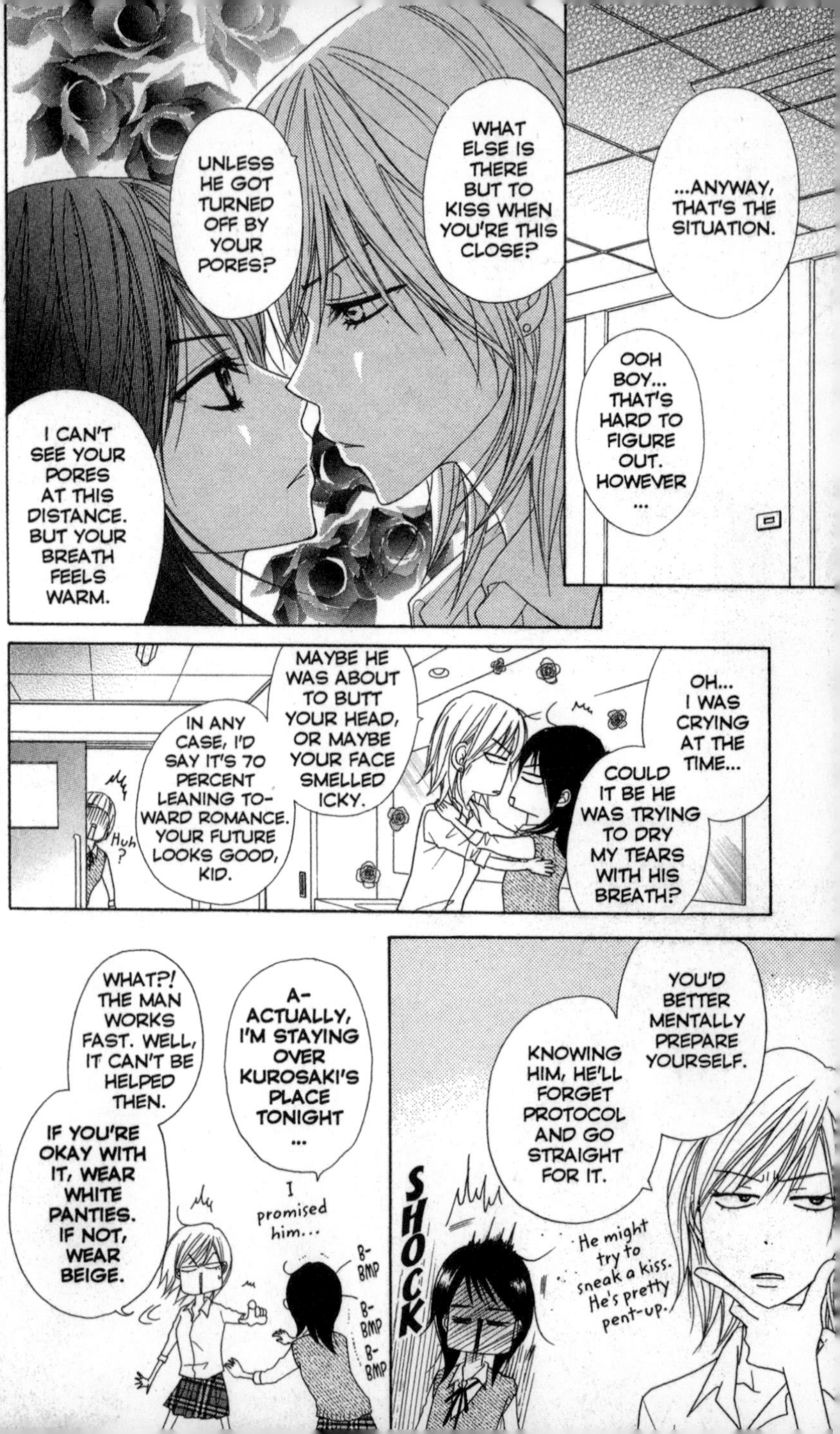
...ANYWAY, THAT'S THE SITUATION.
OOH BOY... THAT'S HARD TO FIGURE OUT. HOWEVER...
WHAT ELSE IS THERE BUT TO KISS WHEN YOU'RE THIS CLOSE?
UNLESS HE GOT TURNED OFF BY YOUR PORES?
I CAN'T SEE YOUR PORES AT THIS DISTANCE. BUT YOUR BREATH FEELS WARM.
OH... I WAS CRYING AT THE TIME...
COULD IT BE HE WAS TRYING TO DRY MY TEARS WITH HIS BREATH?
MAYBE HE WAS ABOUT TO BUTT YOUR HEAD, OR MAYBE YOUR FACE SMELLED ICKY.
IN ANY CASE, I'D SAY IT'S 70 PERCENT LEANING TO-WARD ROMANCE. YOUR FUTURE LOOKS GOOD, KID.
Huh?
YOU'D BETTER MENTALLY PREPARE YOURSELF.
KNOWING HIM, HE'LL FORGET PROTOCOL AND GO STRAIGHT FOR IT.
SHOCK
He might try to sneak a kiss. He's pretty pent-up.
A-ACTUALLY, I'M STAYING OVER KUROSAKI'S PLACE TONIGHT...
I promised him...
B-BMP
B-BMP
B-BMP
WHAT?! THE MAN WORKS FAST. WELL, IT CAN'T BE HELPED THEN.
IF YOU'RE OKAY WITH IT, WEAR WHITE PANTIES. IF NOT, WEAR BEIGE.

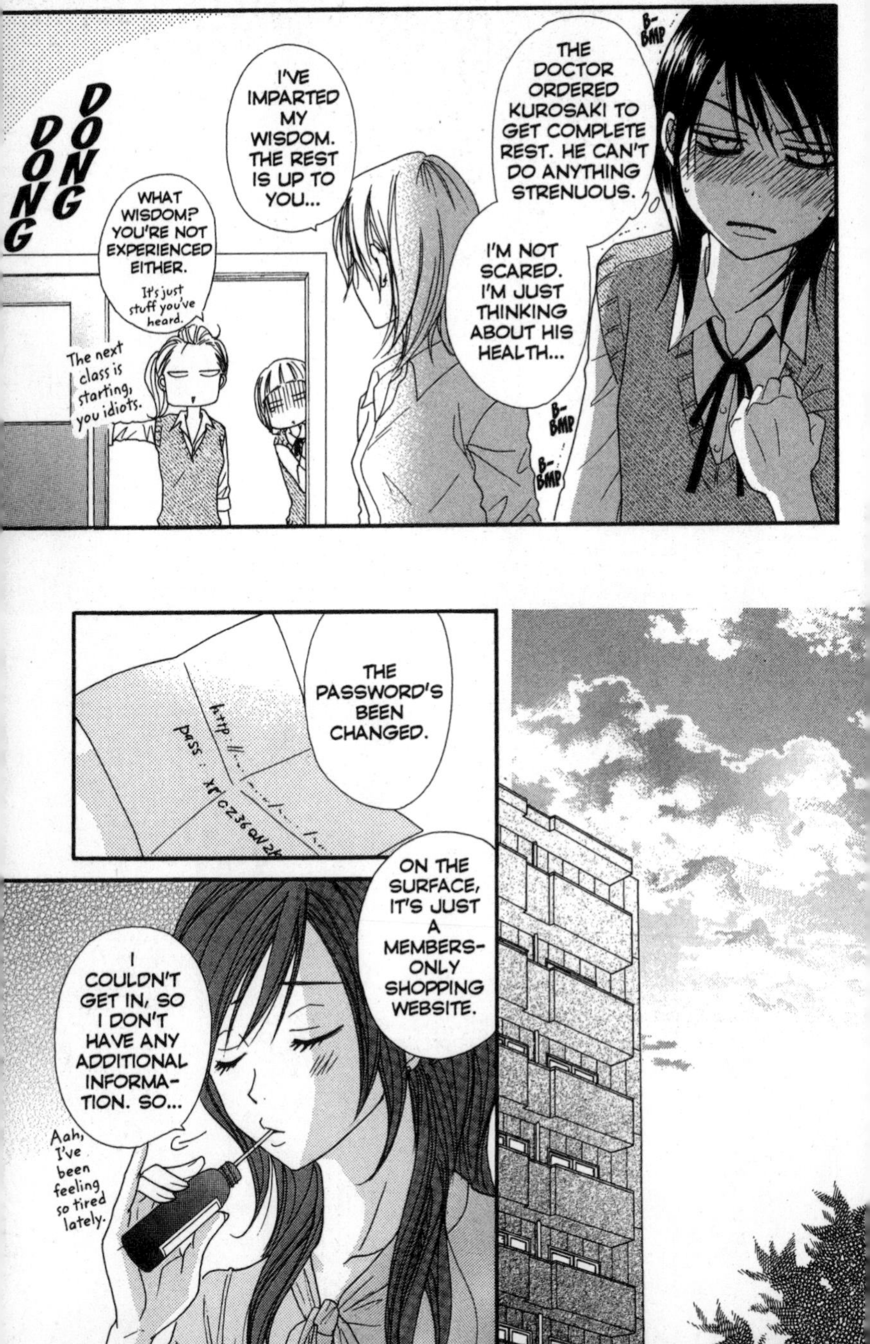
B-BMP
THE DOCTOR ORDERED KUROSAKI TO GET COMPLETE REST. HE CAN'T DO ANYTHING STRENUOUS.
I'M NOT SCARED. I'M JUST THINKING ABOUT HIS HEALTH...
B-BMP
B-BMP
I'VE IMPARTED MY WISDOM. THE REST IS UP TO YOU...
DONG DONG
WHAT WISDOM? YOU'RE NOT EXPERIENCED EITHER.
It's just stuff you've heard.
The next class is starting, you idiots.
THE PASSWORD'S BEEN CHANGED.
http://
pass:
ON THE SURFACE, IT'S JUST A MEMBERS-ONLY SHOPPING WEBSITE.
I COULDN'T GET IN, SO I DON'T HAVE ANY ADDITIONAL INFORMATION. SO...
Aah, I've been feeling so tired lately.

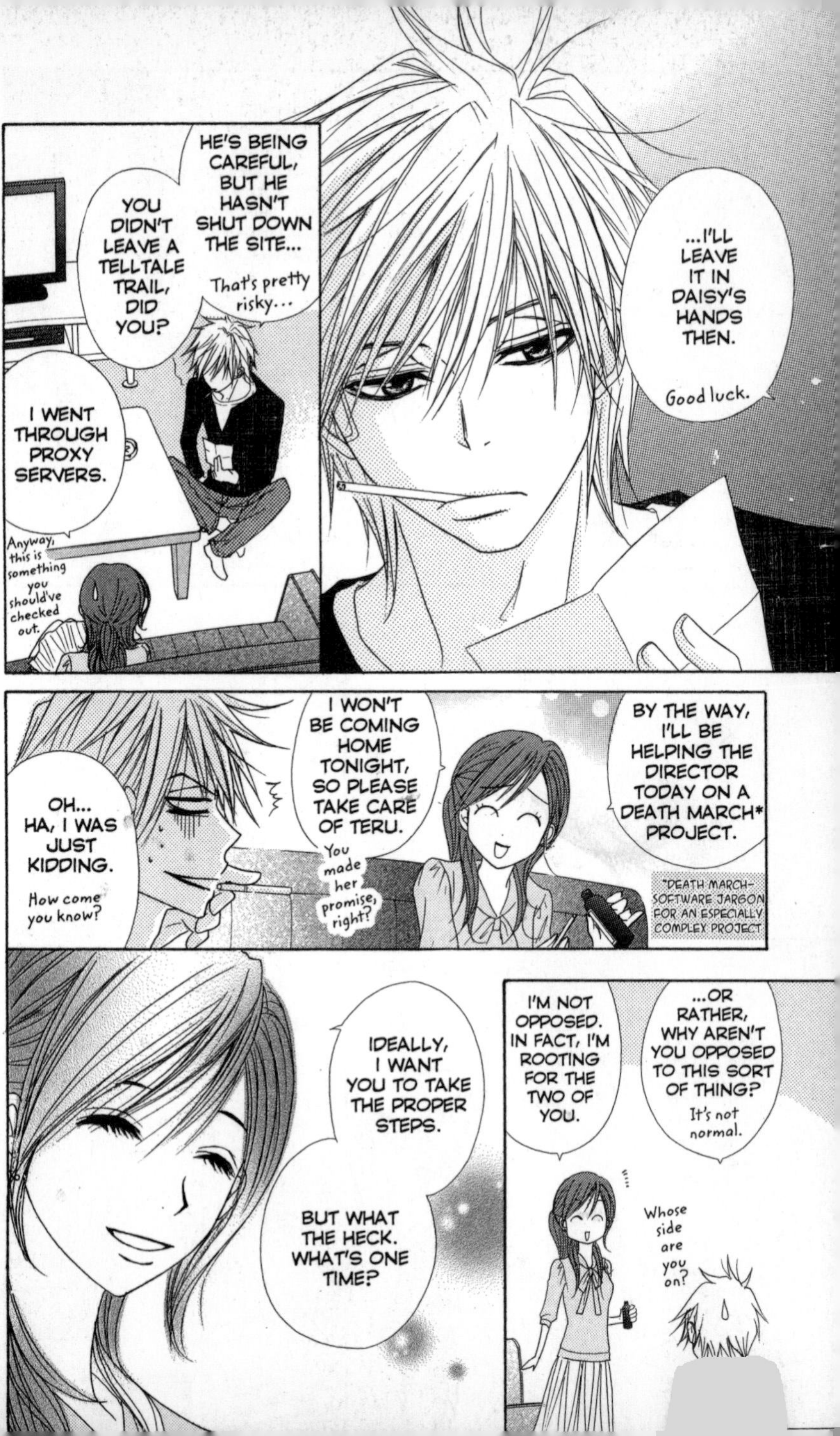
...I'LL LEAVE IT IN DAISY'S HANDS THEN.
Good luck.
HE'S BEING CAREFUL, BUT HE HASN'T SHUT DOWN THE SITE...
That's pretty risky...
YOU DIDN'T LEAVE A TELLTALE TRAIL, DID YOU?
I WENT THROUGH PROXY SERVERS.
Anyway, this is something you should've checked out.
BY THE WAY, I'LL BE HELPING THE DIRECTOR TODAY ON A DEATH MARCH* PROJECT.
*DEATH MARCH- SOFTWARE JARGON FOR AN ESPECIALLY COMPLEX PROJECT
I WON'T BE COMING HOME TONIGHT, SO PLEASE TAKE CARE OF TERU.
You made her promise, right?
OH... HA, I WAS JUST KIDDING.
How come you know?
...OR RATHER, WHY AREN'T YOU OPPOSED TO THIS SORT OF THING?
It's not normal.
I'M NOT OPPOSED. IN FACT, I'M ROOTING FOR THE TWO OF YOU.
Whose side are you on?
IDEALLY, I WANT YOU TO TAKE THE PROPER STEPS.
BUT WHAT THE HECK. WHAT'S ONE TIME?

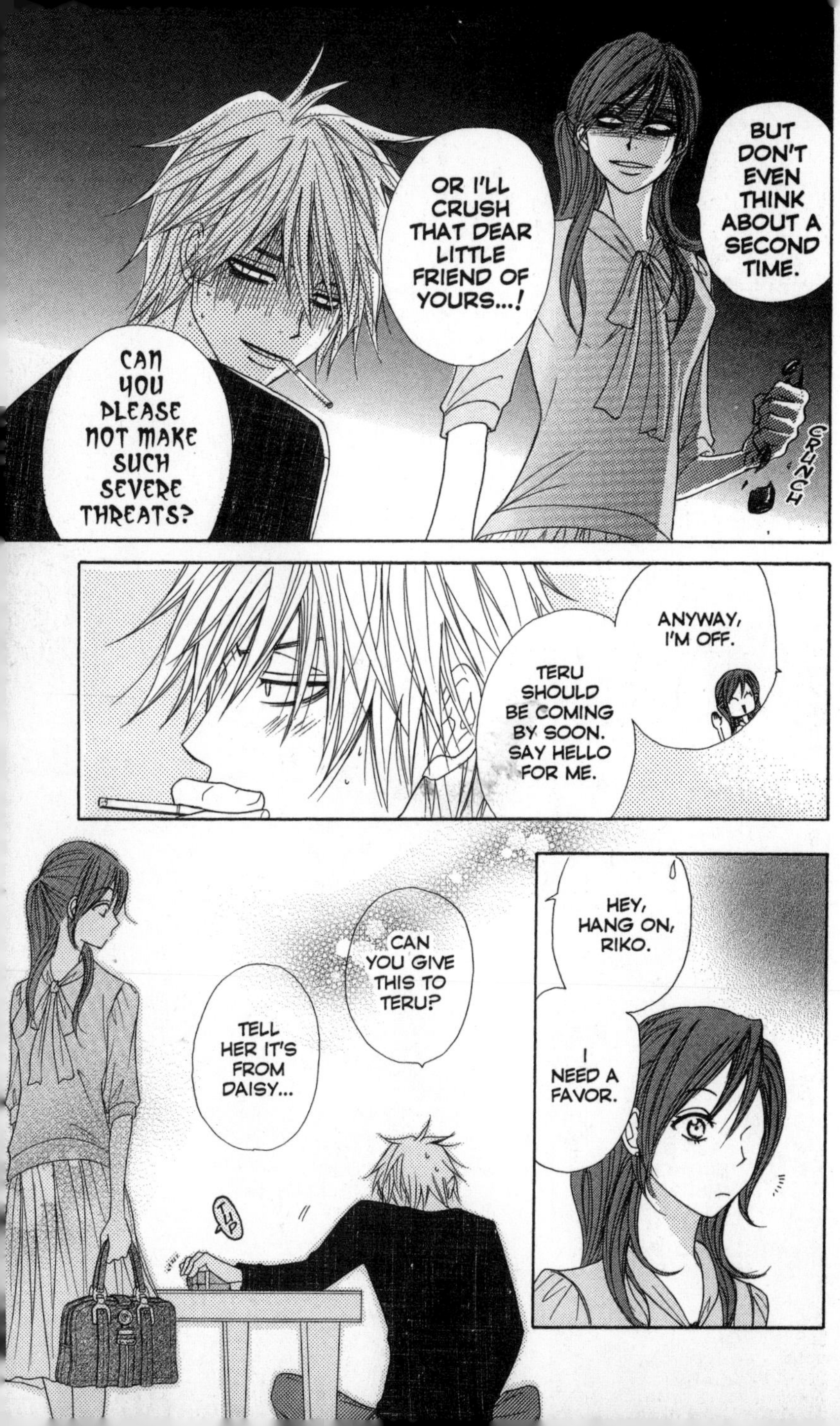
BUT DON'T EVEN THINK ABOUT A SECOND TIME.
OR I'LL CRUSH THAT DEAR LITTLE FRIEND OF YOURS...!
CRUNCH
CAN YOU PLEASE NOT MAKE SUCH SEVERE THREATS?
ANYWAY, I'M OFF.
TERU SHOULD BE COMING BY SOON. SAY HELLO FOR ME.
HEY, HANG ON, RIKO.
I NEED A FAVOR.
CAN YOU GIVE THIS TO TERU?
TELL HER IT'S FROM DAISY...
TUP

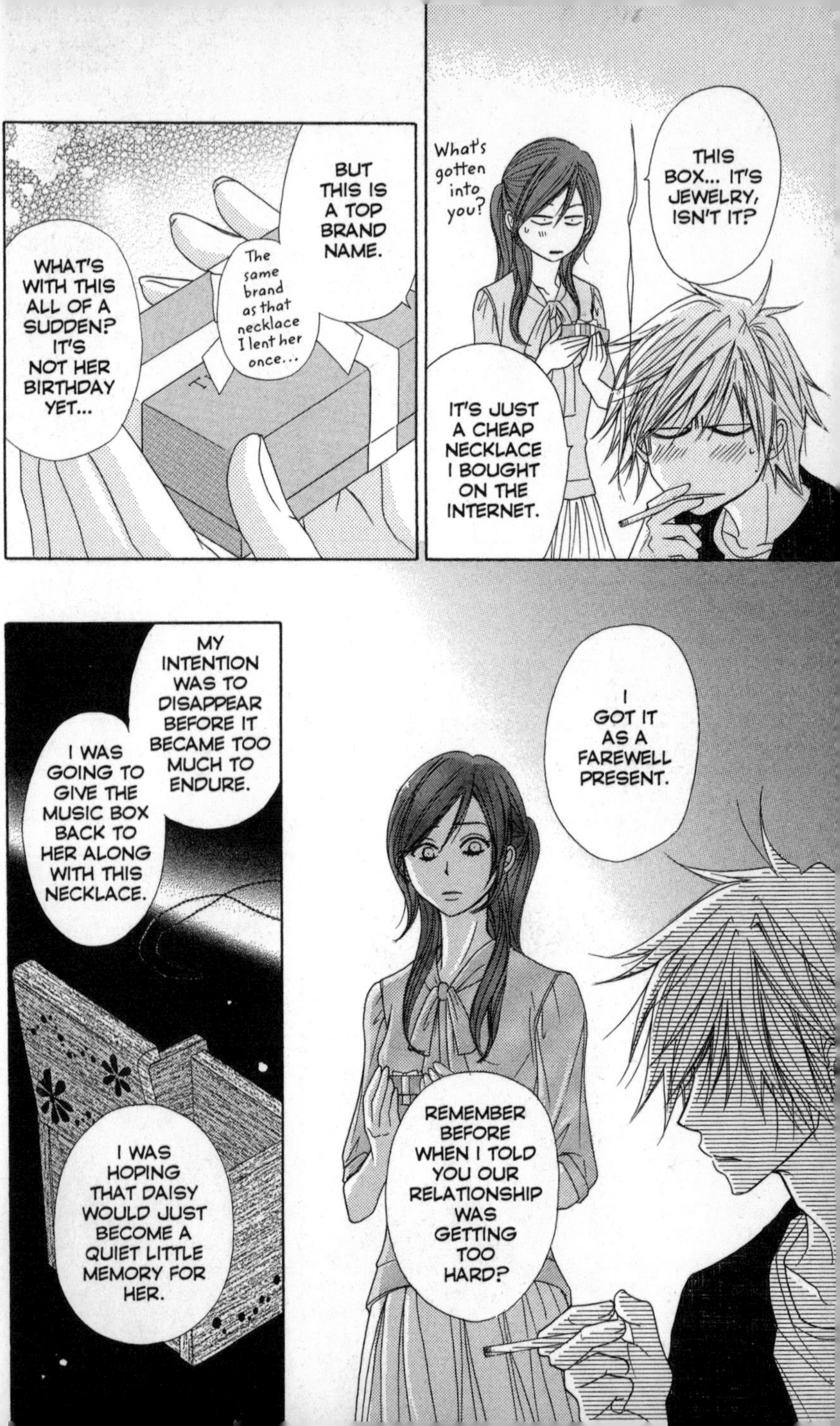
THIS BOX... IT'S JEWELRY, ISN'T IT?
What's gotten into you?
IT'S JUST A CHEAP NECKLACE I BOUGHT ON THE INTERNET.
BUT THIS IS A TOP BRAND NAME.
The same brand as that necklace I lent her once...
WHAT'S WITH THIS ALL OF A SUDDEN? IT'S NOT HER BIRTHDAY YET...
I GOT IT AS A FAREWELL PRESENT.
REMEMBER BEFORE WHEN I TOLD YOU OUR RELATIONSHIP WAS GETTING TOO HARD?
MY INTENTION WAS TO DISAPPEAR BEFORE IT BECAME TOO MUCH TO ENDURE.
I WAS GOING TO GIVE THE MUSIC BOX BACK TO HER ALONG WITH THIS NECKLACE.
I WAS HOPING THAT DAISY WOULD JUST BECOME A QUIET LITTLE MEMORY FOR HER.

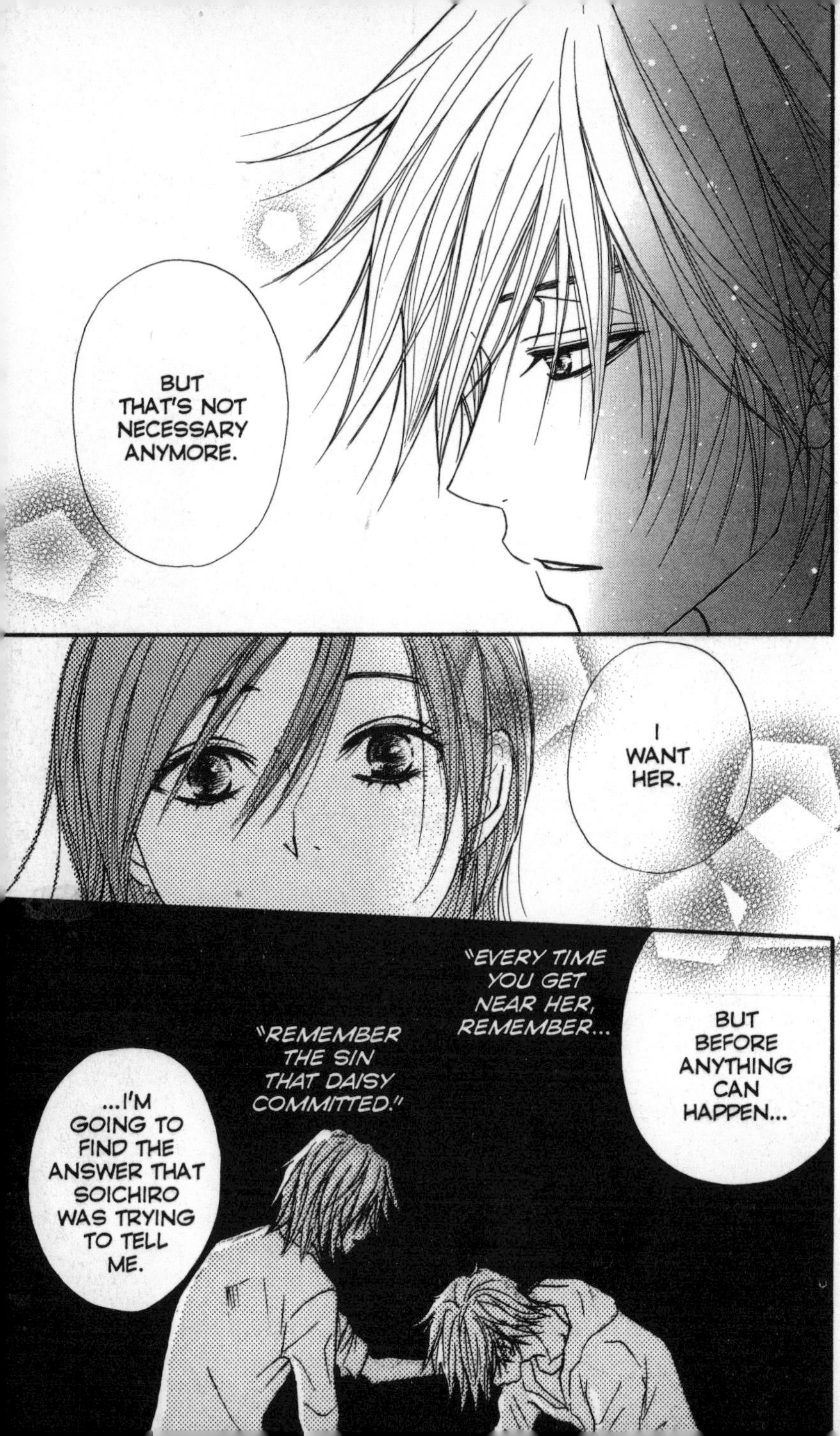
BUT THAT'S NOT NECESSARY ANYMORE.
I WANT HER.
BUT BEFORE ANYTHING CAN HAPPEN...
"EVERY TIME YOU GET NEAR HER, REMEMBER...
"REMEMBER THE SIN THAT DAISY COMMITTED."
...I'M GOING TO FIND THE ANSWER THAT SOICHIRO WAS TRYING TO TELL ME.

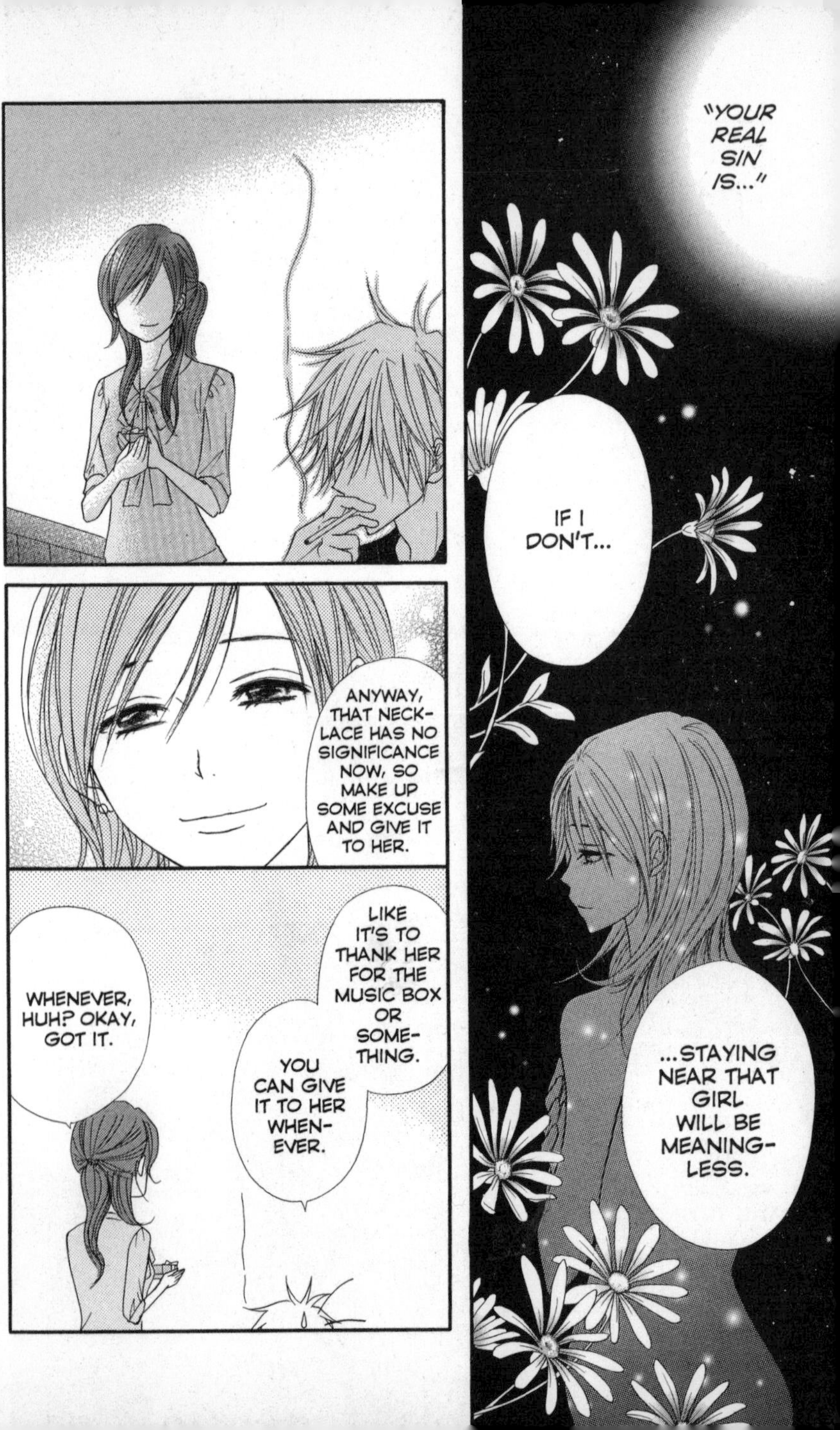
"YOUR REAL SIN IS..."
IF I DON'T...
...STAYING NEAR THAT GIRL WILL BE MEANING-LESS.
ANYWAY, THAT NECK-LACE HAS NO SIGNIFICANCE NOW, SO MAKE UP SOME EXCUSE AND GIVE IT TO HER.
LIKE IT'S TO THANK HER FOR THE MUSIC BOX OR SOME-THING.
YOU CAN GIVE IT TO HER WHEN-EVER.
WHENEVER, HUH? OKAY, GOT IT.

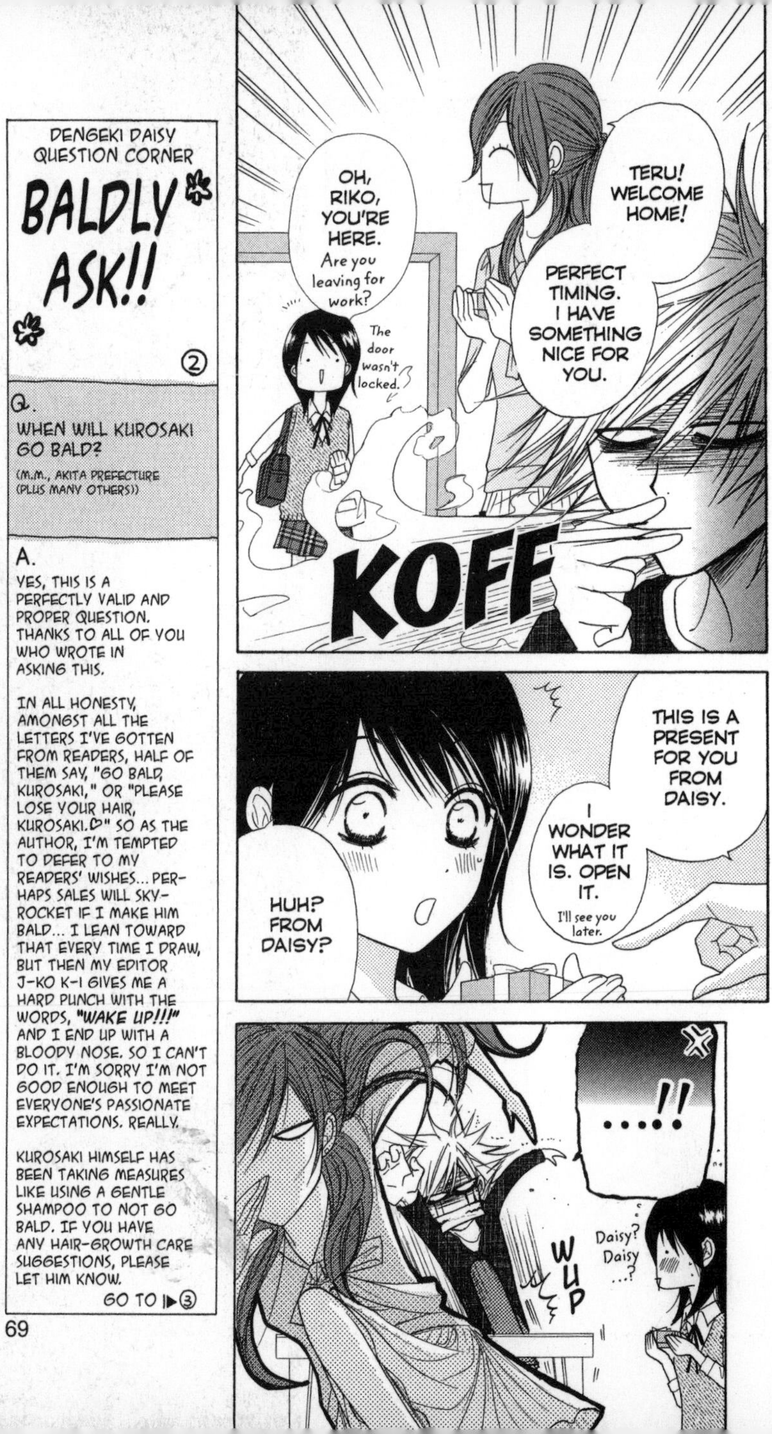
TERU! WELCOME HOME!
PERFECT TIMING. I HAVE SOMETHING NICE FOR YOU.
OH, RIKO, YOU'RE HERE. Are you leaving for work?
The door wasn't locked.
KOFF
THIS IS A PRESENT FOR YOU FROM DAISY.
I WONDER WHAT IT IS. OPEN IT.
I'll see you later.
HUH? FROM DAISY?
....!!
Daisy? Daisy ...?
WUP

DENGEKI DAISY QUESTION CORNER

BALDLY ASK!!

②

Q.

WHEN WILL KUROSAKI GO BALD?

(M.M., AKITA PREFECTURE (PLUS MANY OTHERS))

A.

YES, THIS IS A PERFECTLY VALID AND PROPER QUESTION. THANKS TO ALL OF YOU WHO WROTE IN ASKING THIS.

IN ALL HONESTY, AMONGST ALL THE LETTERS I'VE GOTTEN FROM READERS, HALF OF THEM SAY, "GO BALD, KUROSAKI," OR "PLEASE LOSE YOUR HAIR, KUROSAKI.♡" SO AS THE AUTHOR, I'M TEMPTED TO DEFER TO MY READERS' WISHES... PERHAPS SALES WILL SKYROCKET IF I MAKE HIM BALD... I LEAN TOWARD THAT EVERY TIME I DRAW, BUT THEN MY EDITOR J-KO K-I GIVES ME A HARD PUNCH WITH THE WORDS, ***"WAKE UP!!!"*** AND I END UP WITH A BLOODY NOSE. SO I CAN'T DO IT. I'M SORRY I'M NOT GOOD ENOUGH TO MEET EVERYONE'S PASSIONATE EXPECTATIONS. REALLY.

KUROSAKI HIMSELF HAS BEEN TAKING MEASURES LIKE USING A GENTLE SHAMPOO TO NOT GO BALD. IF YOU HAVE ANY HAIR-GROWTH CARE SUGGESTIONS, PLEASE LET HIM KNOW.

GO TO ▶③

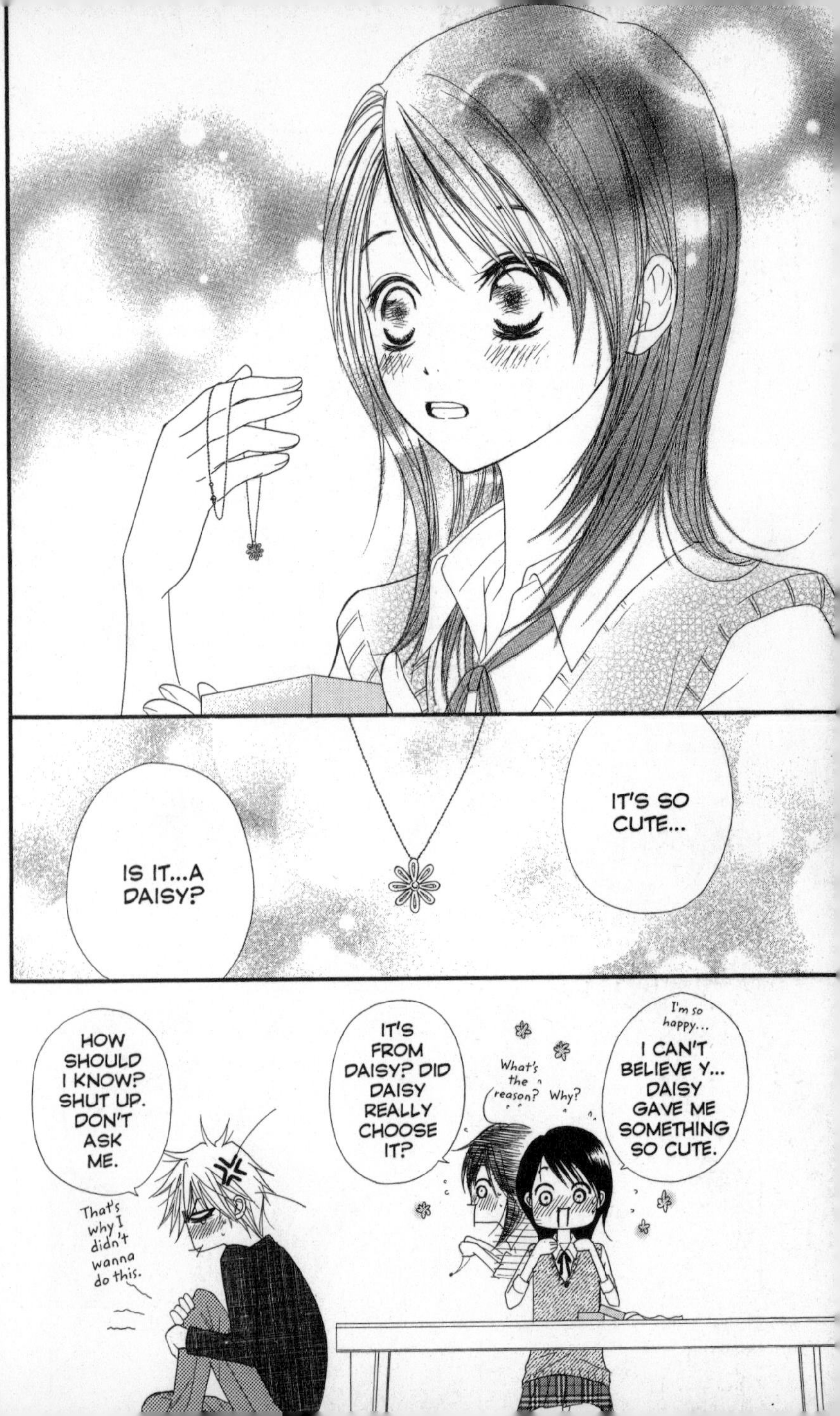
IT'S SO CUTE...
IS IT...A DAISY?
I'm so happy...
I CAN'T BELIEVE Y... DAISY GAVE ME SOMETHING SO CUTE.
What's the reason? Why?
IT'S FROM DAISY? DID DAISY REALLY CHOOSE IT?
HOW SHOULD I KNOW? SHUT UP. DON'T ASK ME.
That's why I didn't wanna do this.

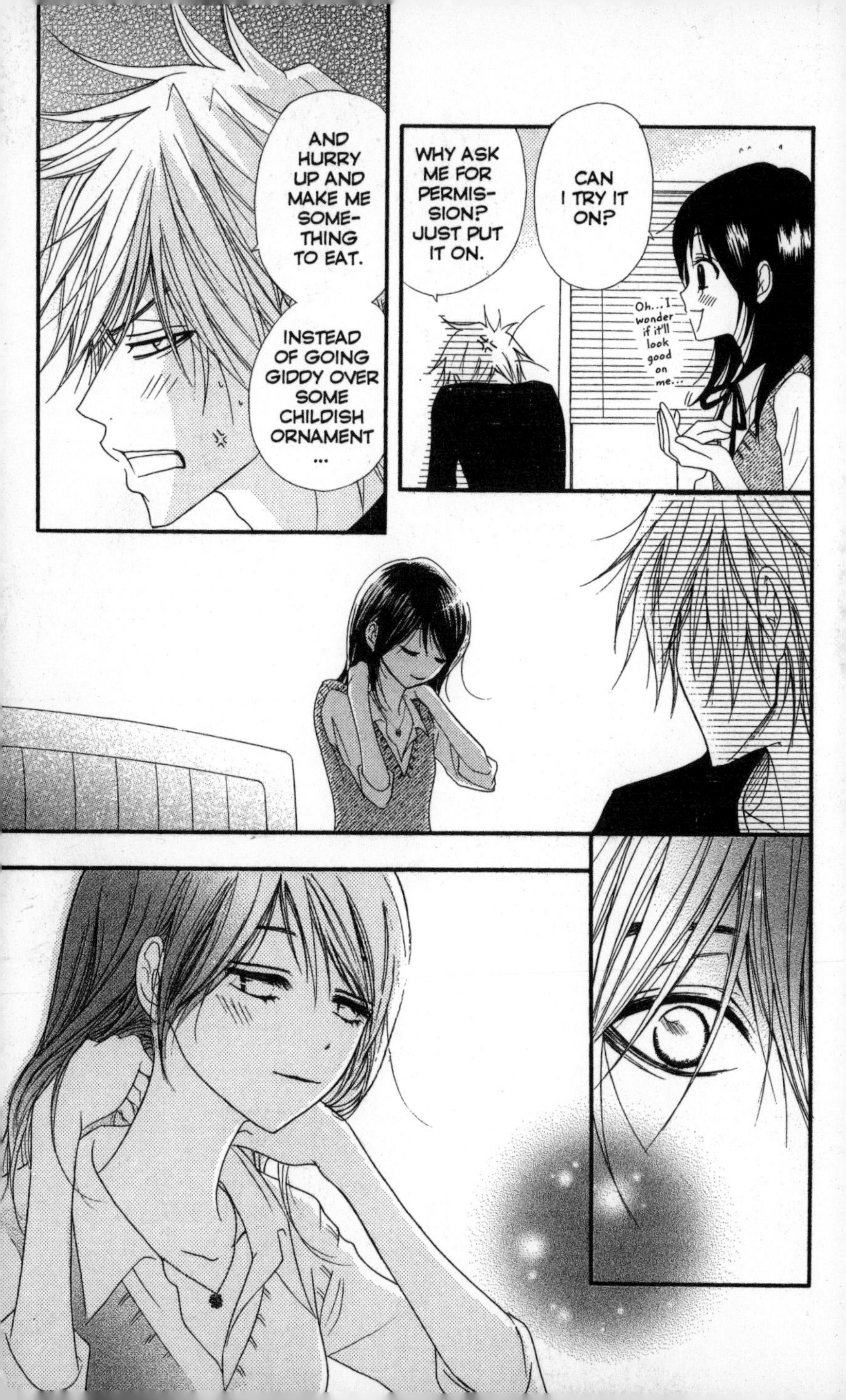
CAN I TRY IT ON?
Oh... I wonder if it'll look good on me...
WHY ASK ME FOR PERMISSION? JUST PUT IT ON.
AND HURRY UP AND MAKE ME SOMETHING TO EAT.
INSTEAD OF GOING GIDDY OVER SOME CHILDISH ORNAMENT ...

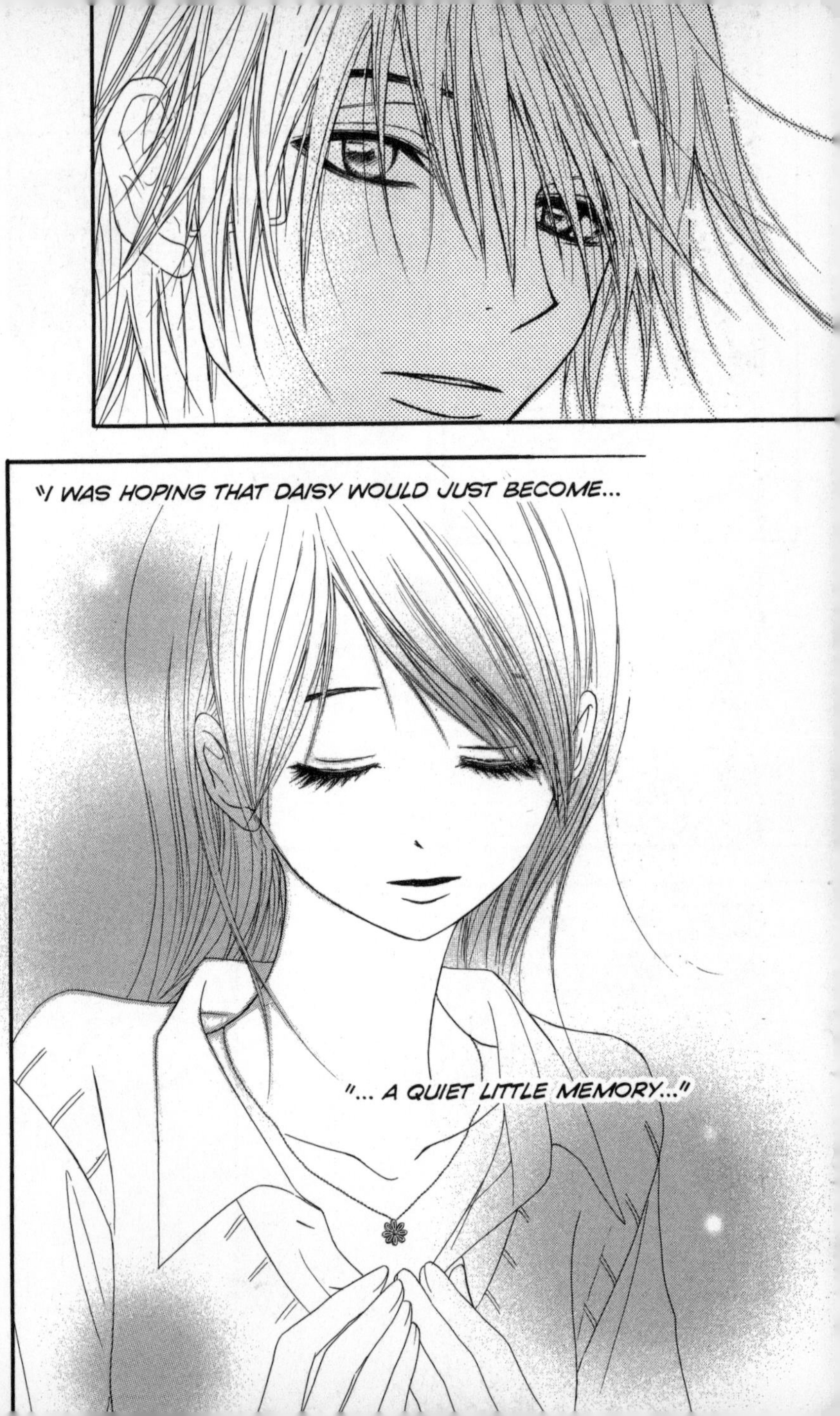
"I WAS HOPING THAT DAISY WOULD JUST BECOME...
"... A QUIET LITTLE MEMORY..."

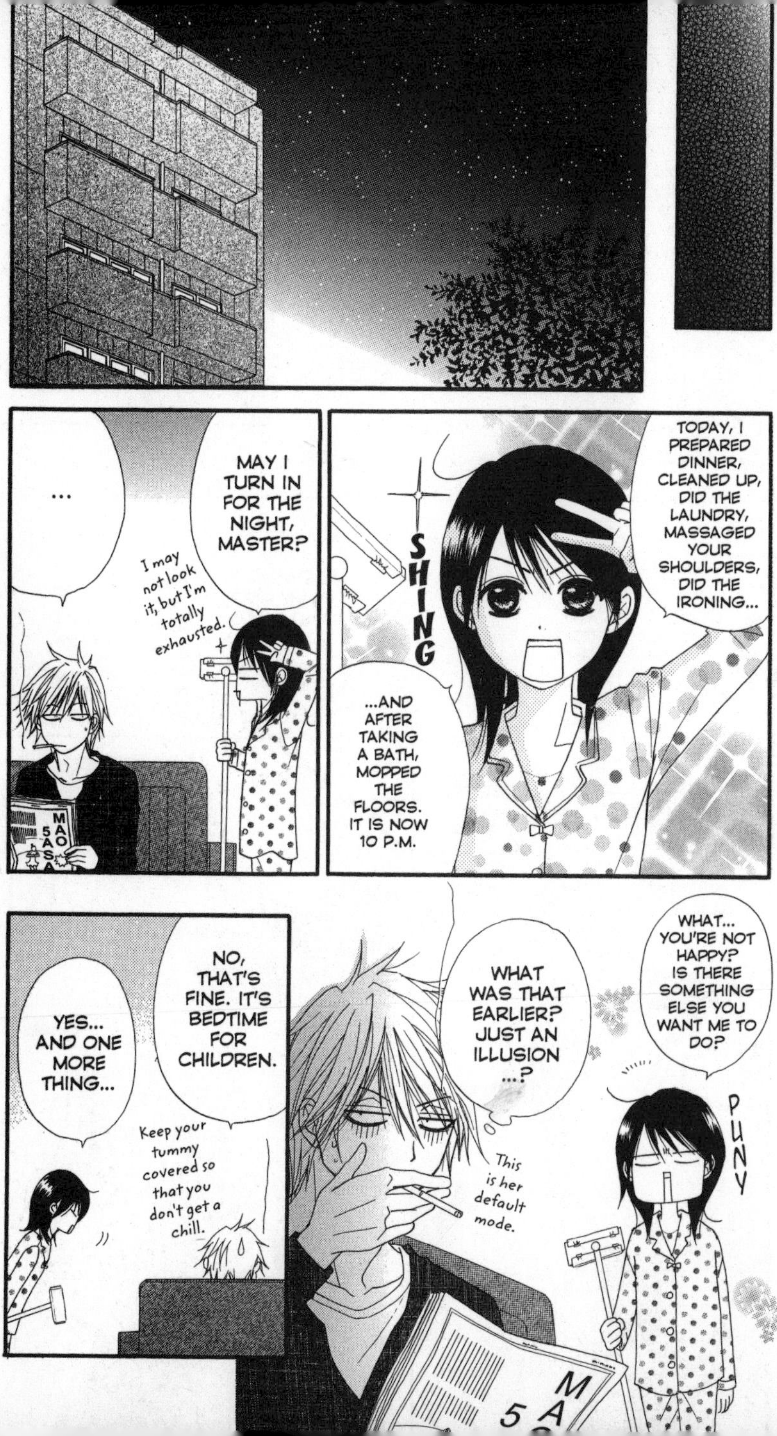
TODAY, I PREPARED DINNER, CLEANED UP, DID THE LAUNDRY, MASSAGED YOUR SHOULDERS, DID THE IRONING...
SHING
...AND AFTER TAKING A BATH, MOPPED THE FLOORS. IT IS NOW 10 P.M.
MAY I TURN IN FOR THE NIGHT, MASTER?
I may not look it, but I'm totally exhausted.
...
WHAT... YOU'RE NOT HAPPY? IS THERE SOMETHING ELSE YOU WANT ME TO DO?
PUNY
WHAT WAS THAT EARLIER? JUST AN ILLUSION ...?
This is her default mode.
NO, THAT'S FINE. IT'S BEDTIME FOR CHILDREN.
YES... AND ONE MORE THING...
Keep your tummy covered so that you don't get a chill.

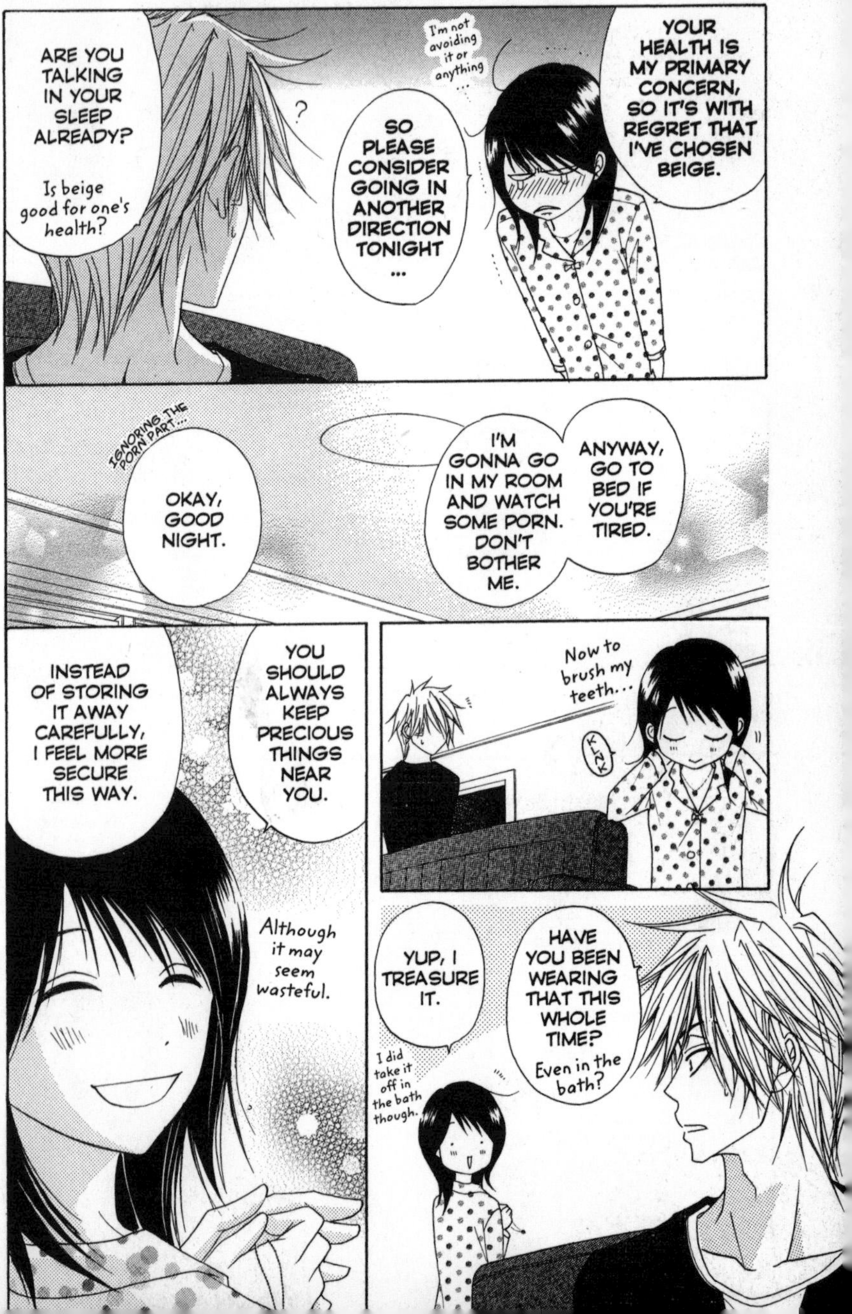
YOUR HEALTH IS MY PRIMARY CONCERN, SO IT'S WITH REGRET THAT I'VE CHOSEN BEIGE.
I'm not avoiding it or anything...
SO PLEASE CONSIDER GOING IN ANOTHER DIRECTION TONIGHT...
?
ARE YOU TALKING IN YOUR SLEEP ALREADY?
Is beige good for one's health?
ANYWAY, GO TO BED IF YOU'RE TIRED.
I'M GONNA GO IN MY ROOM AND WATCH SOME PORN. DON'T BOTHER ME.
IGNORING THE PORN PART...
OKAY, GOOD NIGHT.
Now to brush my teeth...
KLNK
HAVE YOU BEEN WEARING THAT THIS WHOLE TIME?
Even in the bath?
YUP, I TREASURE IT.
I did take it off in the bath though.
YOU SHOULD ALWAYS KEEP PRECIOUS THINGS NEAR YOU.
INSTEAD OF STORING IT AWAY CAREFULLY, I FEEL MORE SECURE THIS WAY.
Although it may seem wasteful.

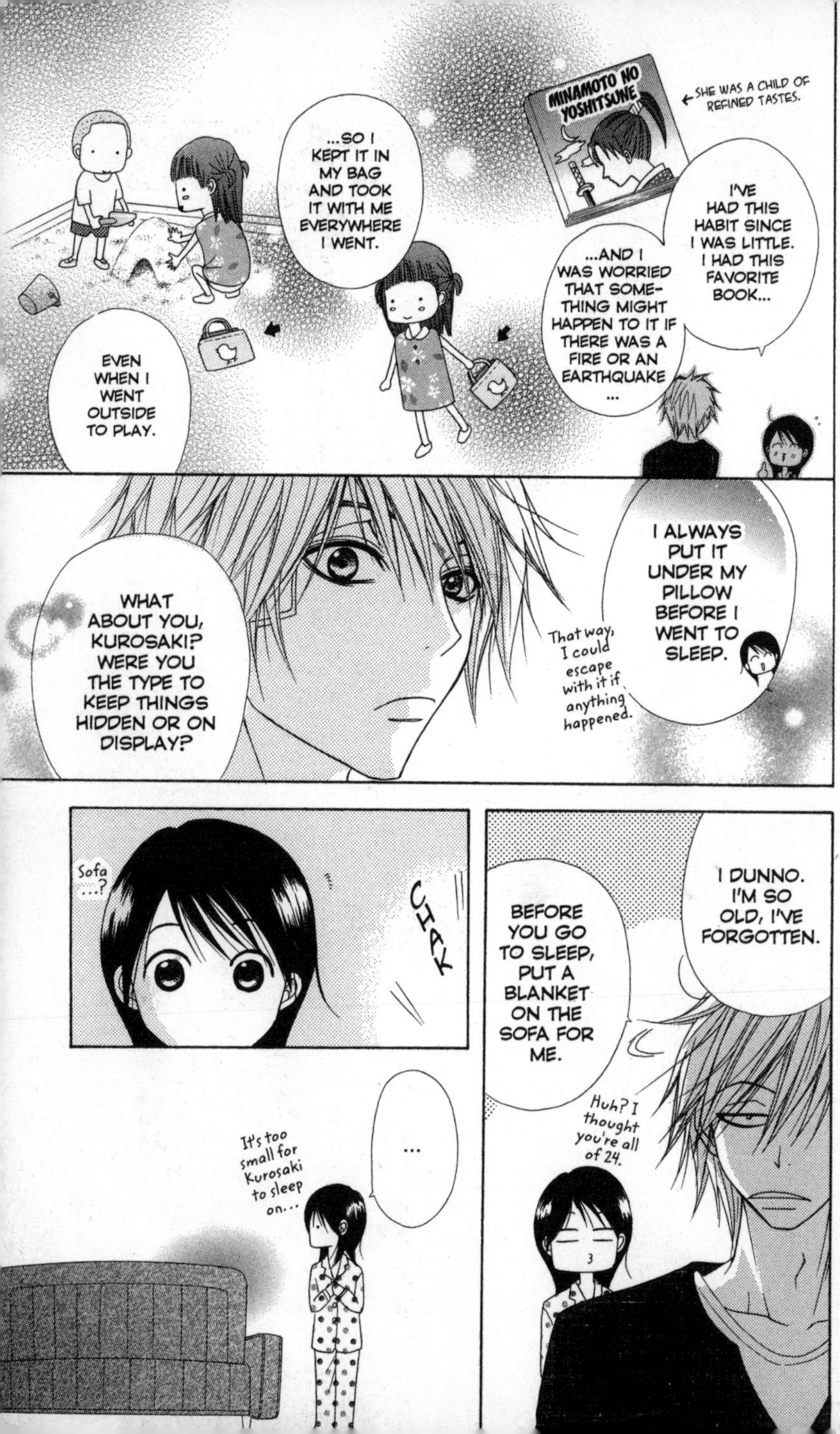
MINAMOTO NO YOSHITSUNE
← SHE WAS A CHILD OF REFINED TASTES.
I'VE HAD THIS HABIT SINCE I WAS LITTLE. I HAD THIS FAVORITE BOOK...
...AND I WAS WORRIED THAT SOME-THING MIGHT HAPPEN TO IT IF THERE WAS A FIRE OR AN EARTHQUAKE...
...SO I KEPT IT IN MY BAG AND TOOK IT WITH ME EVERYWHERE I WENT.
EVEN WHEN I WENT OUTSIDE TO PLAY.
I ALWAYS PUT IT UNDER MY PILLOW BEFORE I WENT TO SLEEP.
That way, I could escape with it if anything happened.
WHAT ABOUT YOU, KUROSAKI? WERE YOU THE TYPE TO KEEP THINGS HIDDEN OR ON DISPLAY?
I DUNNO. I'M SO OLD, I'VE FORGOTTEN.
BEFORE YOU GO TO SLEEP, PUT A BLANKET ON THE SOFA FOR ME.
Huh? I thought you're all of 24.
CHAK
Sofa ...?
...
It's too small for Kurosaki to sleep on...

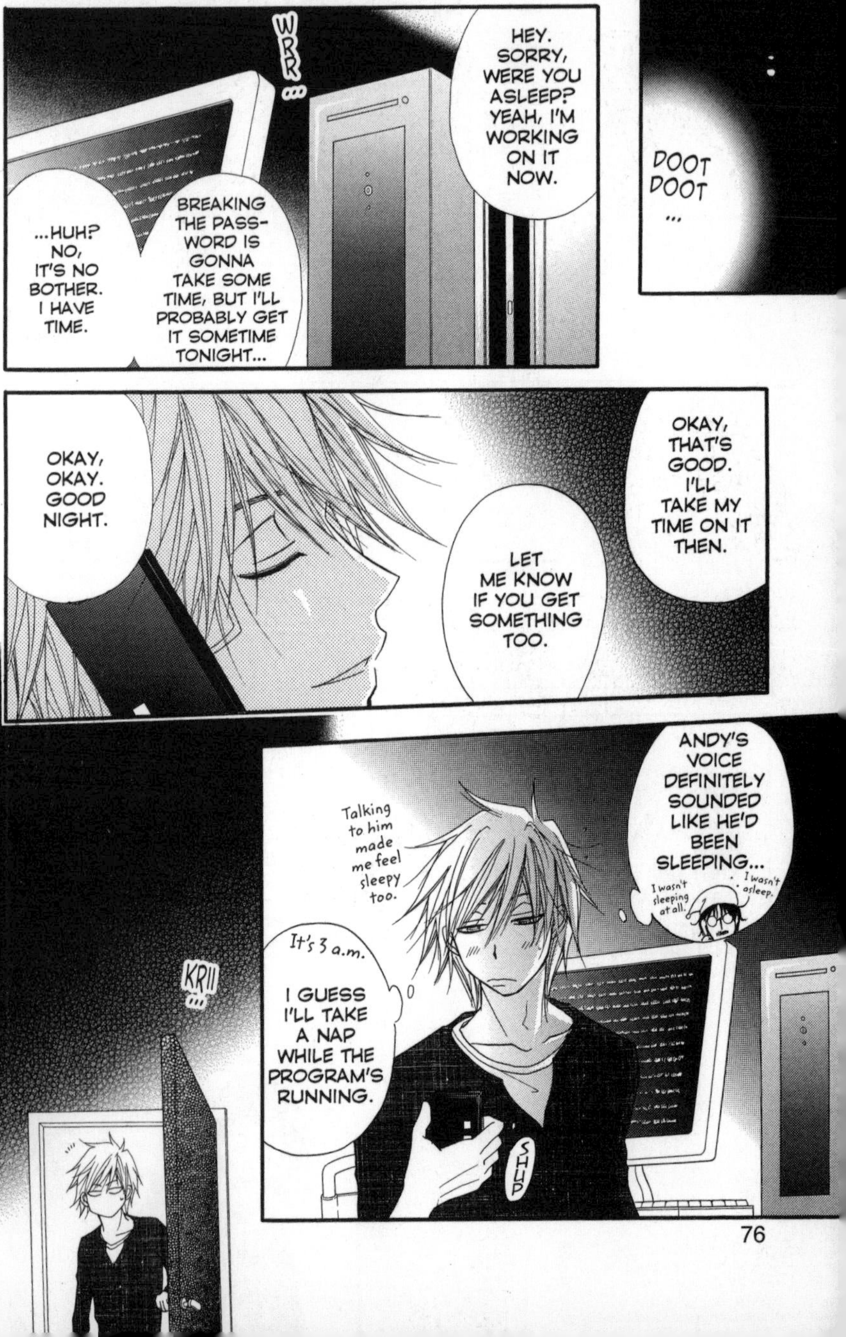
DOOT DOOT ...
HEY. SORRY, WERE YOU ASLEEP? YEAH, I'M WORKING ON IT NOW.
WRR...
BREAKING THE PASS-WORD IS GONNA TAKE SOME TIME, BUT I'LL PROBABLY GET IT SOMETIME TONIGHT...
...HUH? NO, IT'S NO BOTHER. I HAVE TIME.
OKAY, THAT'S GOOD. I'LL TAKE MY TIME ON IT THEN.
LET ME KNOW IF YOU GET SOMETHING TOO.
OKAY, OKAY. GOOD NIGHT.
ANDY'S VOICE DEFINITELY SOUNDED LIKE HE'D BEEN SLEEPING...
I wasn't asleep.
I wasn't sleeping at all.
Talking to him made me feel sleepy too.
It's 3 a.m.
I GUESS I'LL TAKE A NAP WHILE THE PROGRAM'S RUNNING.
SHUP
KRII...

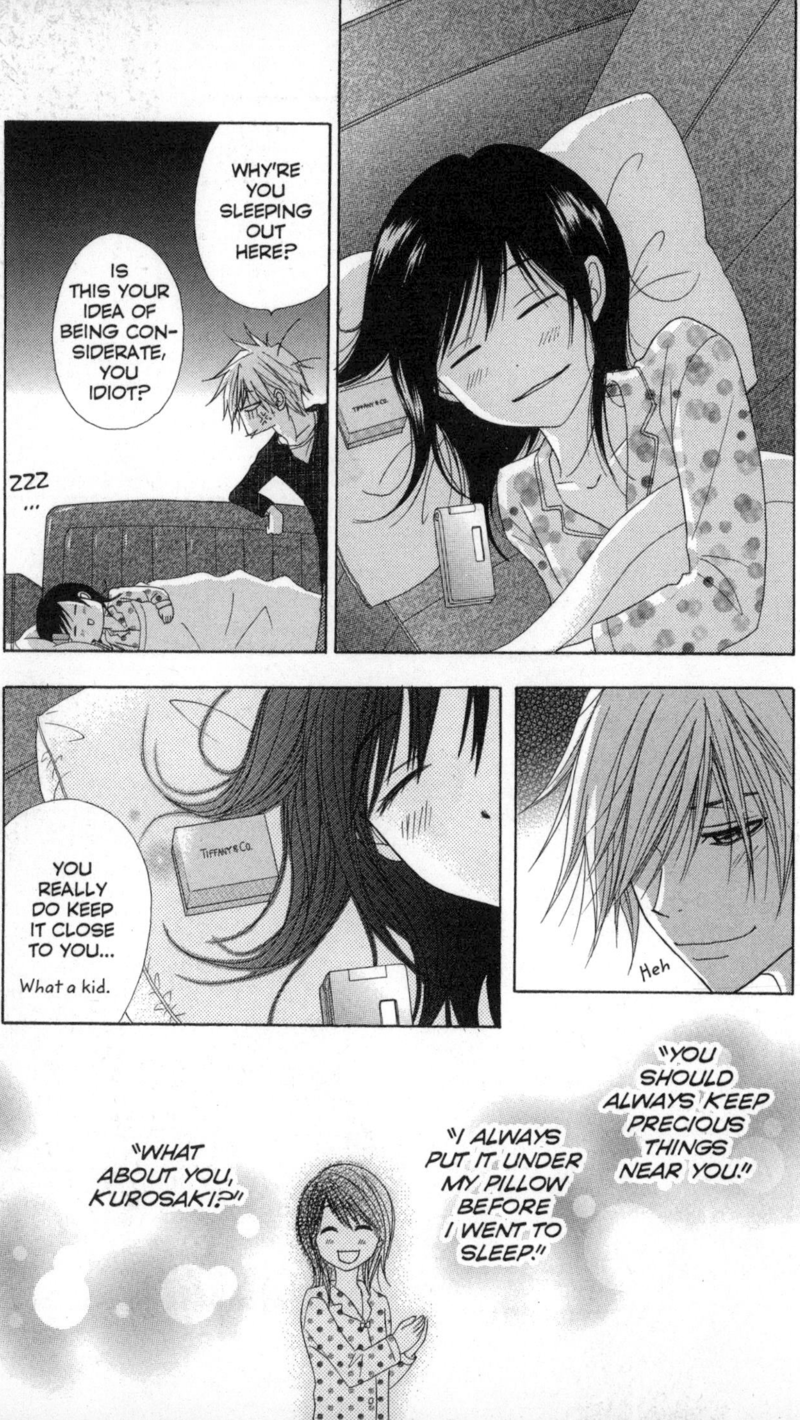
WHY'RE YOU SLEEPING OUT HERE?
IS THIS YOUR IDEA OF BEING CONSIDERATE, YOU IDIOT?
ZZZ ...
Heh
YOU REALLY DO KEEP IT CLOSE TO YOU...
What a kid.
"YOU SHOULD ALWAYS KEEP PRECIOUS THINGS NEAR YOU."
"I ALWAYS PUT IT UNDER MY PILLOW BEFORE I WENT TO SLEEP."
"WHAT ABOUT YOU, KUROSAKI?"

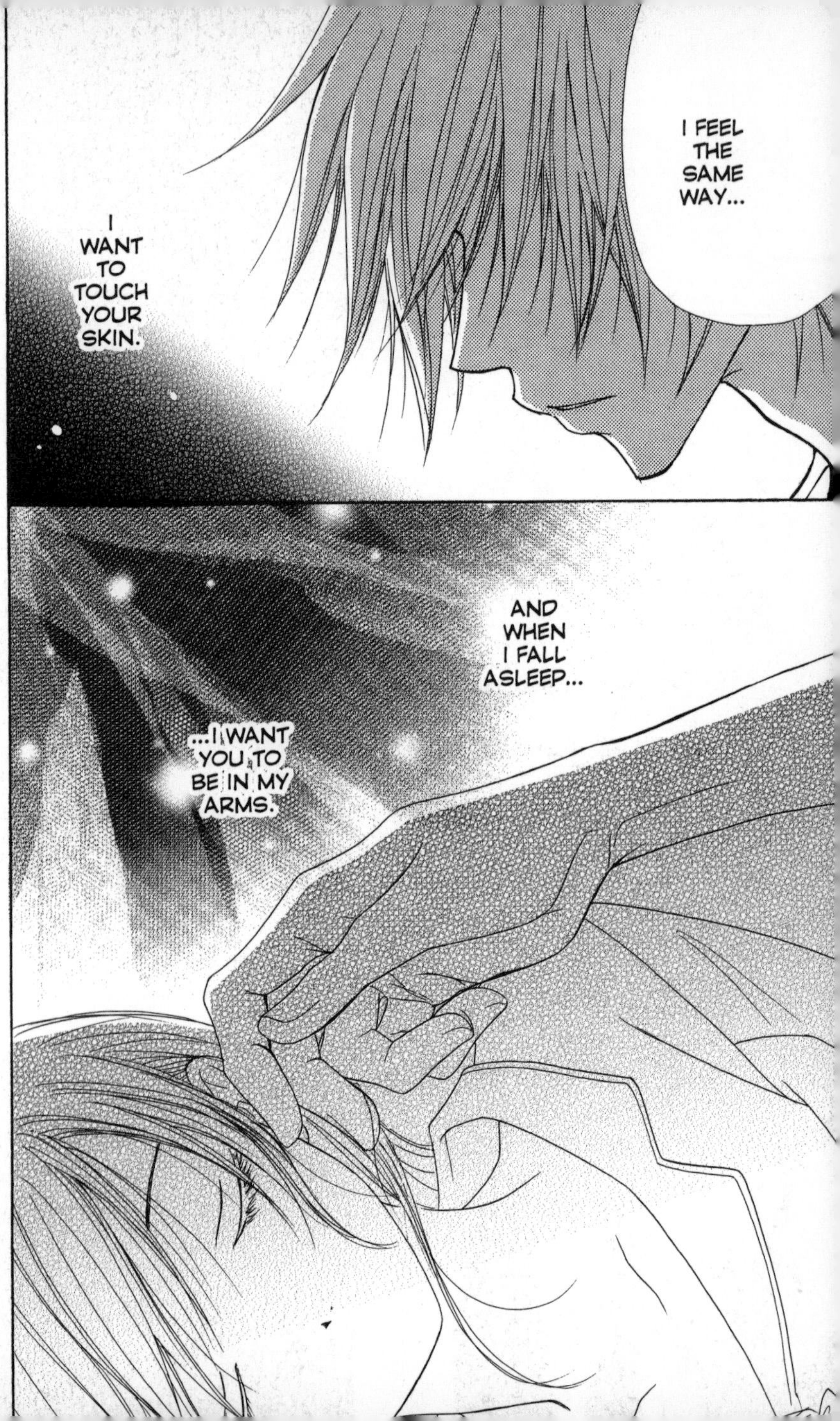
I FEEL THE SAME WAY...
I WANT TO TOUCH YOUR SKIN.
AND WHEN I FALL ASLEEP...
...I WANT YOU TO BE IN MY ARMS.

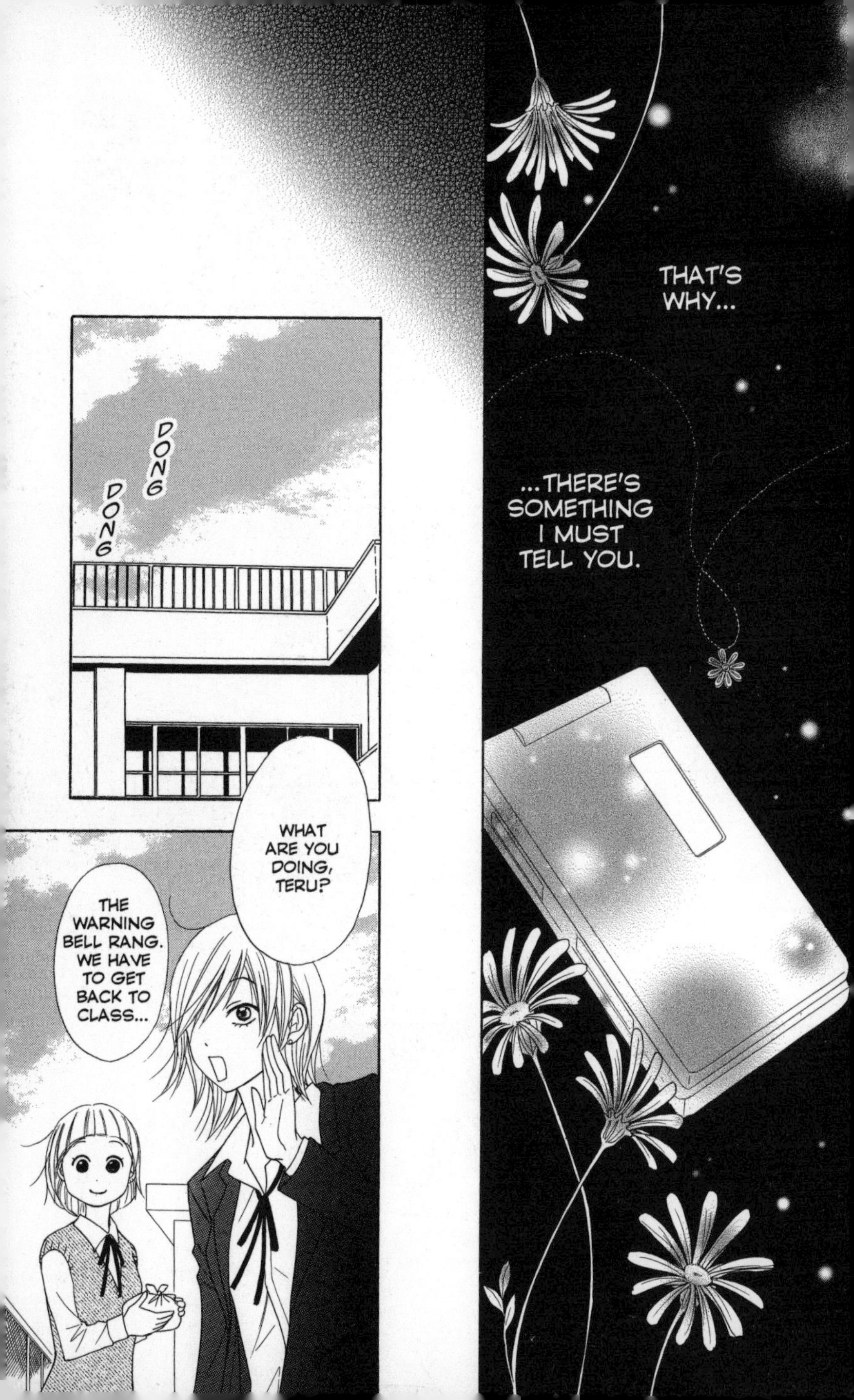
THAT'S WHY...
...THERE'S SOMETHING I MUST TELL YOU.
DONG DONG
WHAT ARE YOU DOING, TERU?
THE WARNING BELL RANG. WE HAVE TO GET BACK TO CLASS...

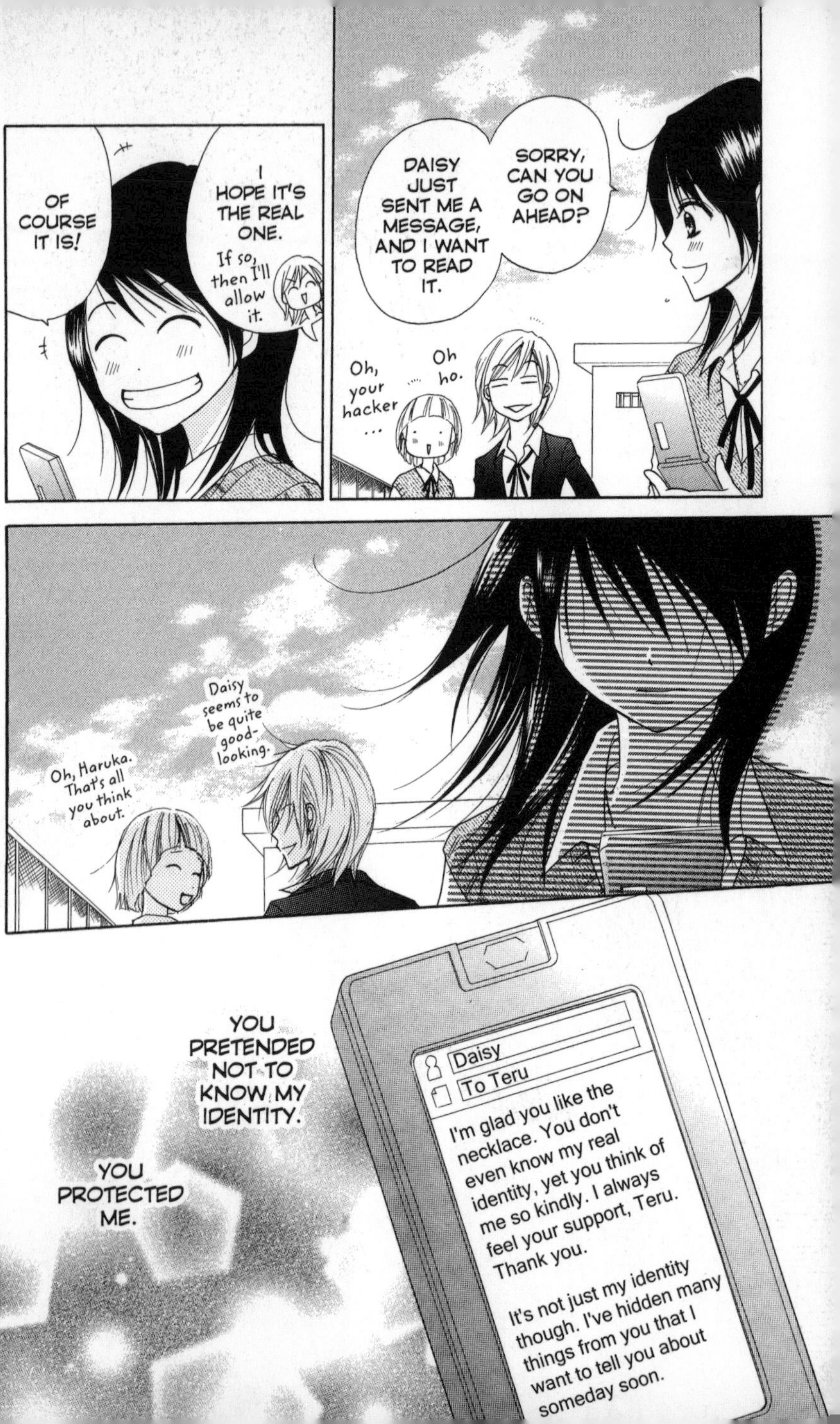
SORRY, CAN YOU GO ON AHEAD?
DAISY JUST SENT ME A MESSAGE, AND I WANT TO READ IT.
Oh ho.
Oh, your hacker...
I HOPE IT'S THE REAL ONE.
If so, then I'll allow it.
OF COURSE IT IS!
Daisy seems to be quite good-looking.
Oh, Haruka. That's all you think about.
Daisy
To Teru
I'm glad you like the necklace. You don't even know my real identity, yet you think of me so kindly. I always feel your support, Teru. Thank you.
It's not just my identity though. I've hidden many things from you that I want to tell you about someday soon.
YOU PRETENDED NOT TO KNOW MY IDENTITY.
YOU PROTECTED ME.

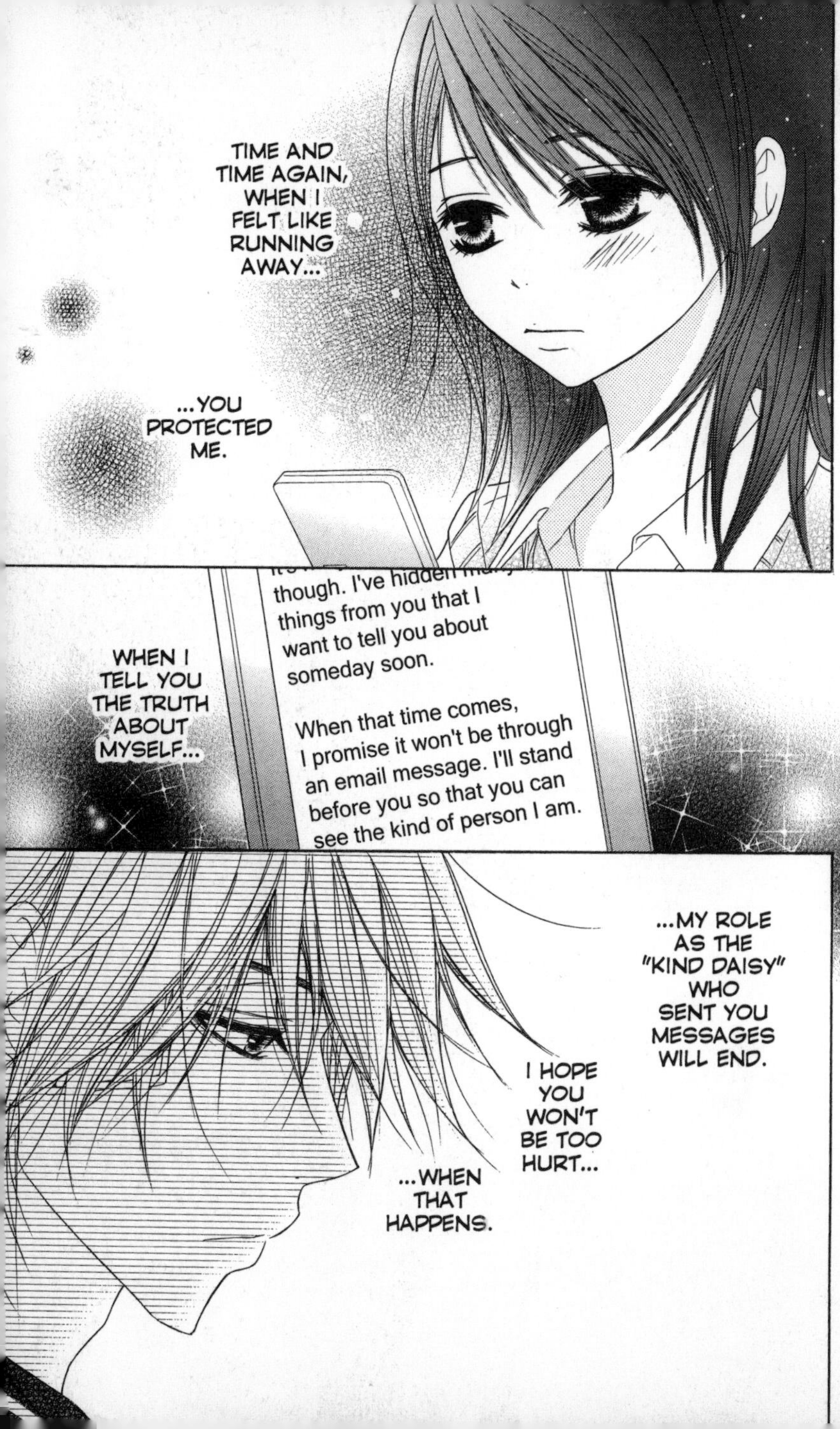
TIME AND TIME AGAIN, WHEN I FELT LIKE RUNNING AWAY...
...YOU PROTECTED ME.
though. I've hidden
things from you that I want to tell you about someday soon.
When that time comes, I promise it won't be through an email message. I'll stand before you so that you can see the kind of person I am.
WHEN I TELL YOU THE TRUTH ABOUT MYSELF...
...MY ROLE AS THE "KIND DAISY" WHO SENT YOU MESSAGES WILL END.
I HOPE YOU WON'T BE TOO HURT...
...WHEN THAT HAPPENS.

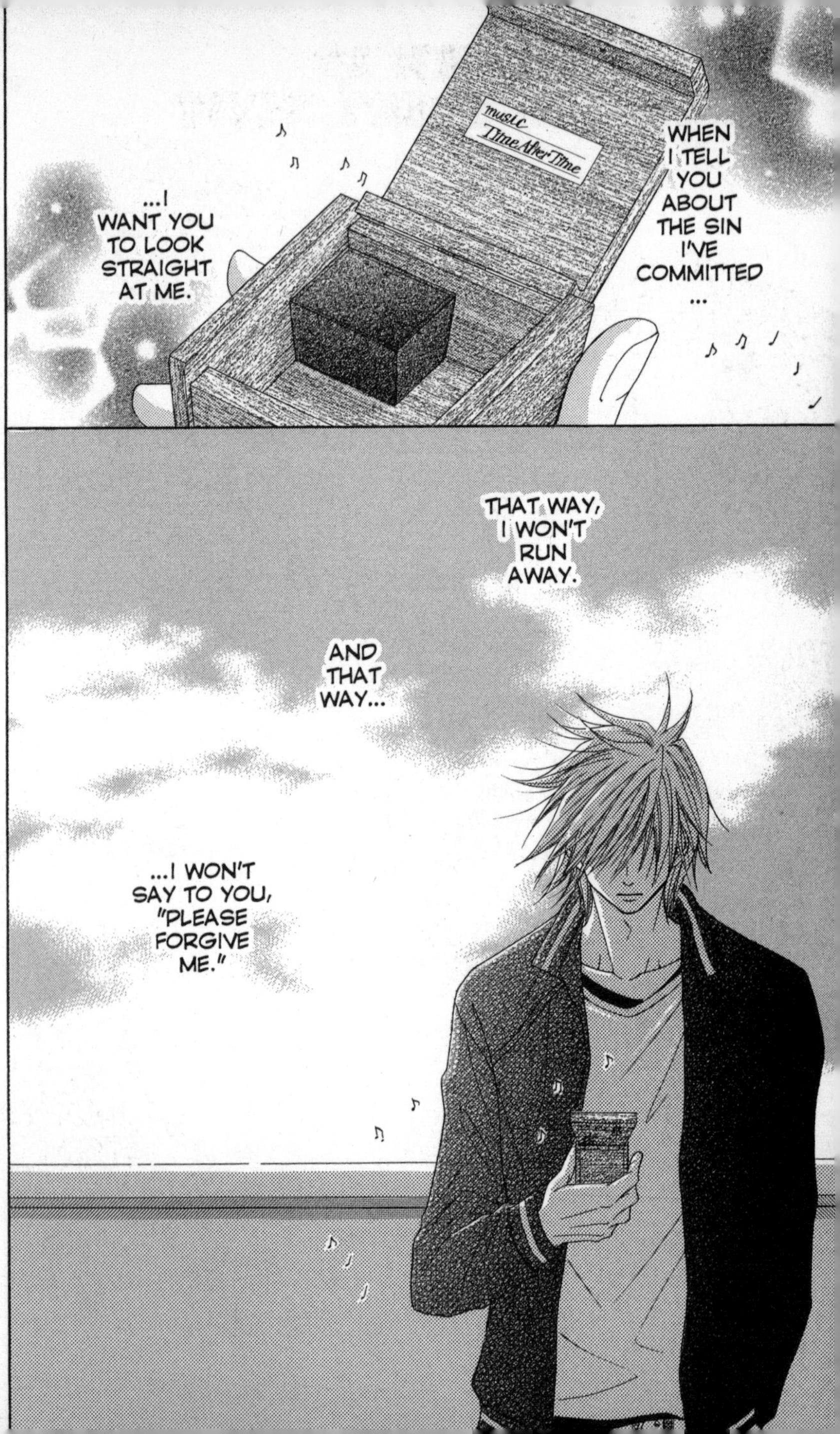
music
Time After Time
WHEN I TELL YOU ABOUT THE SIN I'VE COMMITTED ...
...I WANT YOU TO LOOK STRAIGHT AT ME.
THAT WAY, I WON'T RUN AWAY.
AND THAT WAY...
...I WON'T SAY TO YOU, "PLEASE FORGIVE ME."

CHAPTER 22:
EACH AND EVERY HURT

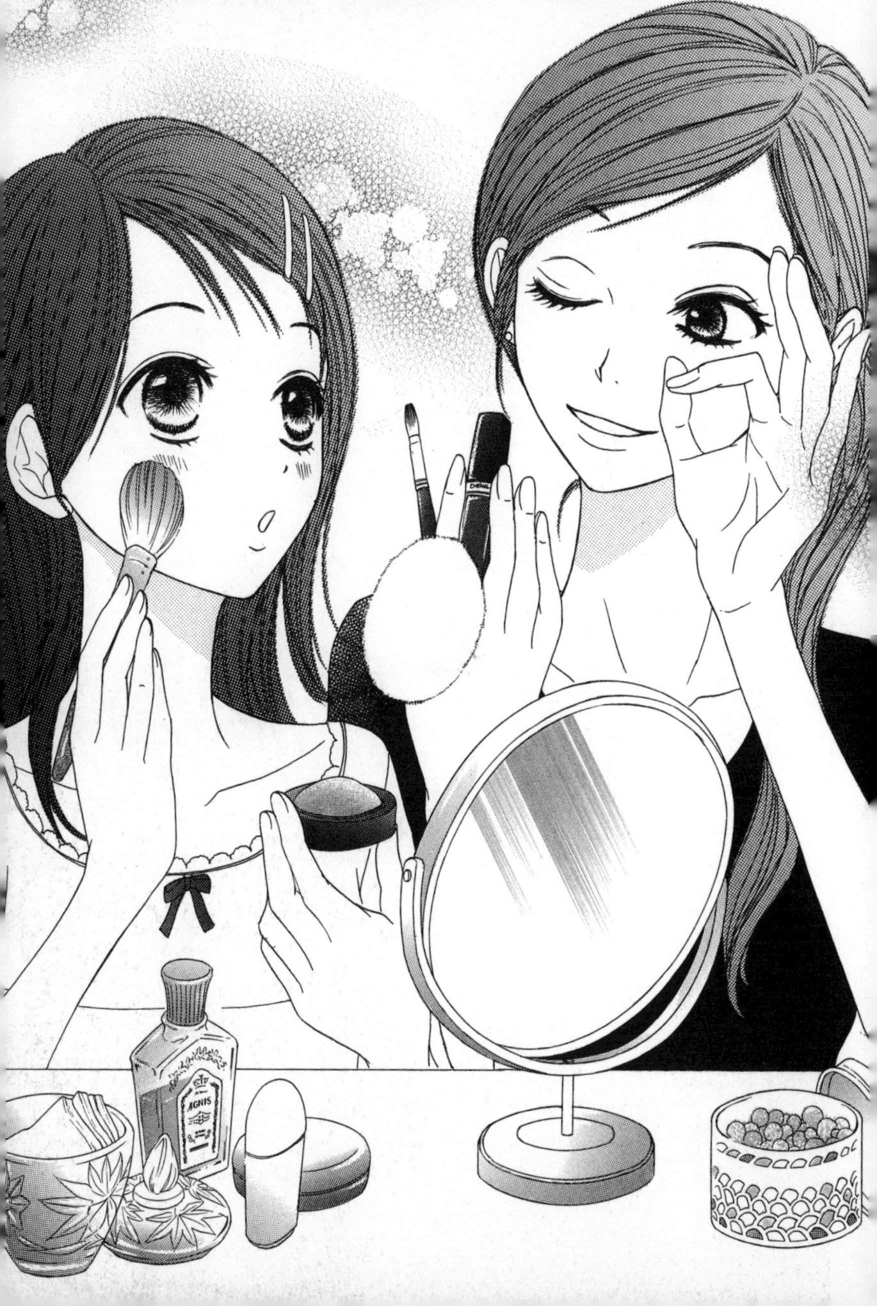
AGNIS

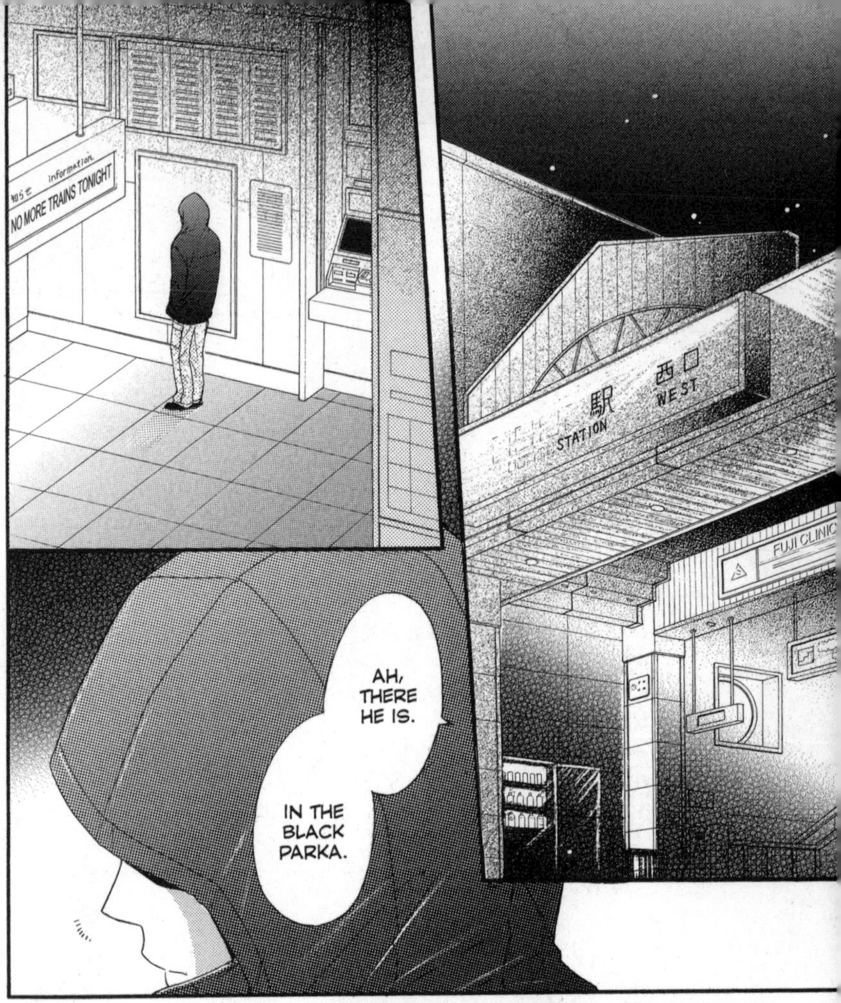
STATION
WEST
FUJI CLINIC
information
NO MORE TRAINS TONIGHT
AH, THERE HE IS.
IN THE BLACK PARKA.

NOT THAT ANYONE CARES, BUT IF KUROSAKI WAS CAST IN A HISTORICAL DRAMA, I THINK HE'D BE "BANDIT 2," SOMEONE WHO PICKS A FIGHT WITH THE HANDSOME MAIN SAMURAI CHARACTER DURING THE FIRST TEN MINUTES OF THE STORY OR SO AND GETS KILLED OFF.

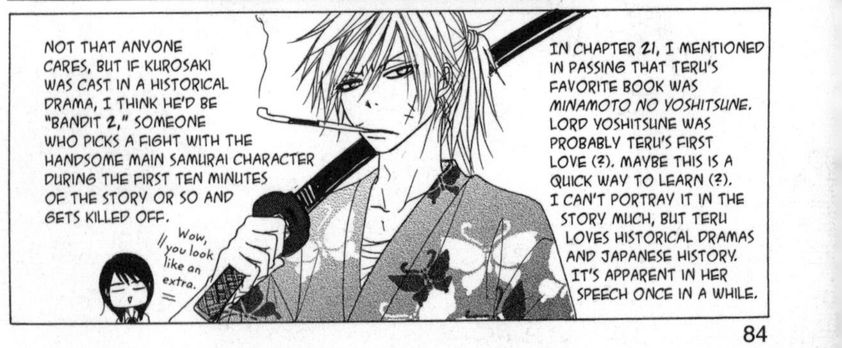
Wow, you look like an extra.

IN CHAPTER 21, I MENTIONED IN PASSING THAT TERU'S FAVORITE BOOK WAS *MINAMOTO NO YOSHITSUNE*. LORD YOSHITSUNE WAS PROBABLY TERU'S FIRST LOVE (?). MAYBE THIS IS A QUICK WAY TO LEARN (?). I CAN'T PORTRAY IT IN THE STORY MUCH, BUT TERU LOVES HISTORICAL DRAMAS AND JAPANESE HISTORY. IT'S APPARENT IN HER SPEECH ONCE IN A WHILE.

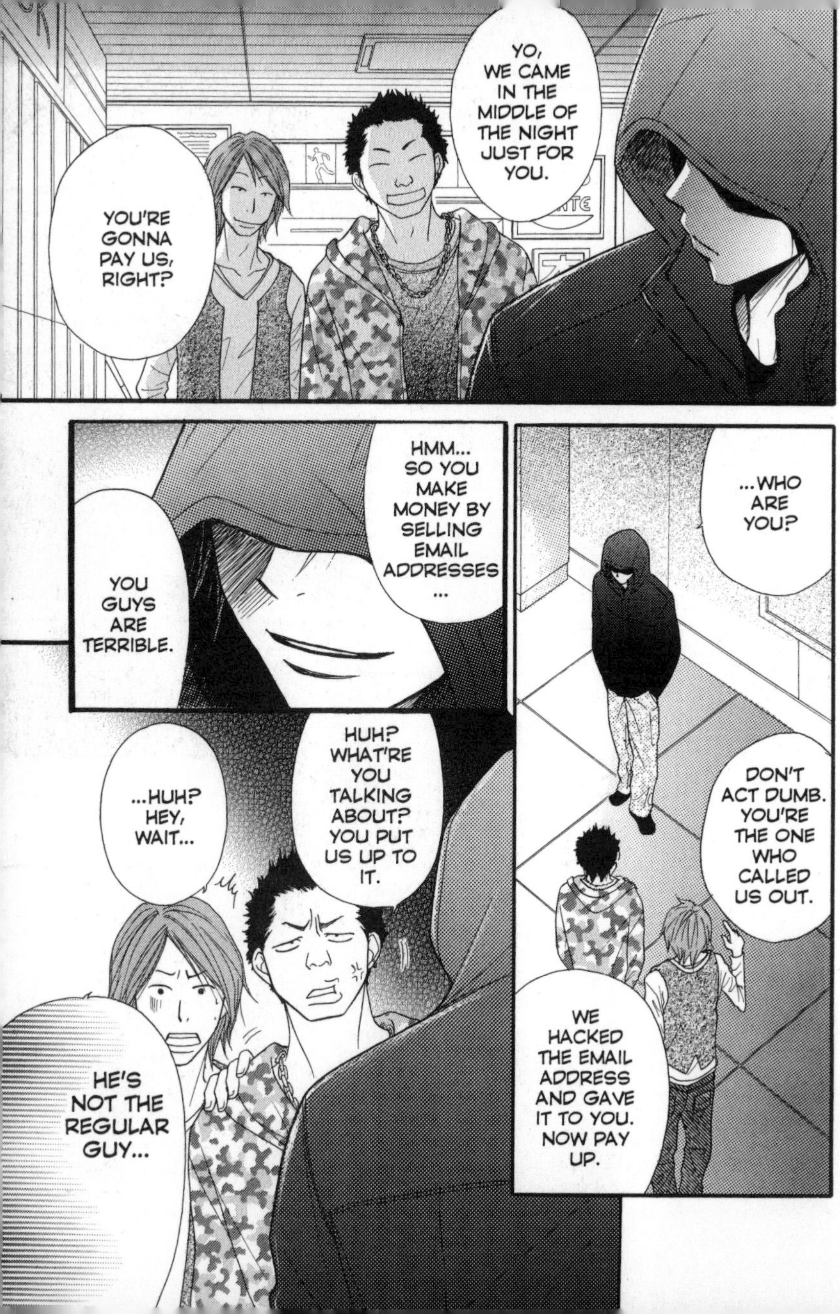
YO, WE CAME IN THE MIDDLE OF THE NIGHT JUST FOR YOU.
YOU'RE GONNA PAY US, RIGHT?
...WHO ARE YOU?
DON'T ACT DUMB. YOU'RE THE ONE WHO CALLED US OUT.
WE HACKED THE EMAIL ADDRESS AND GAVE IT TO YOU. NOW PAY UP.
HMM... SO YOU MAKE MONEY BY SELLING EMAIL ADDRESSES...
YOU GUYS ARE TERRIBLE.
HUH? WHAT'RE YOU TALKING ABOUT? YOU PUT US UP TO IT.
...HUH? HEY, WAIT...
HE'S NOT THE REGULAR GUY...

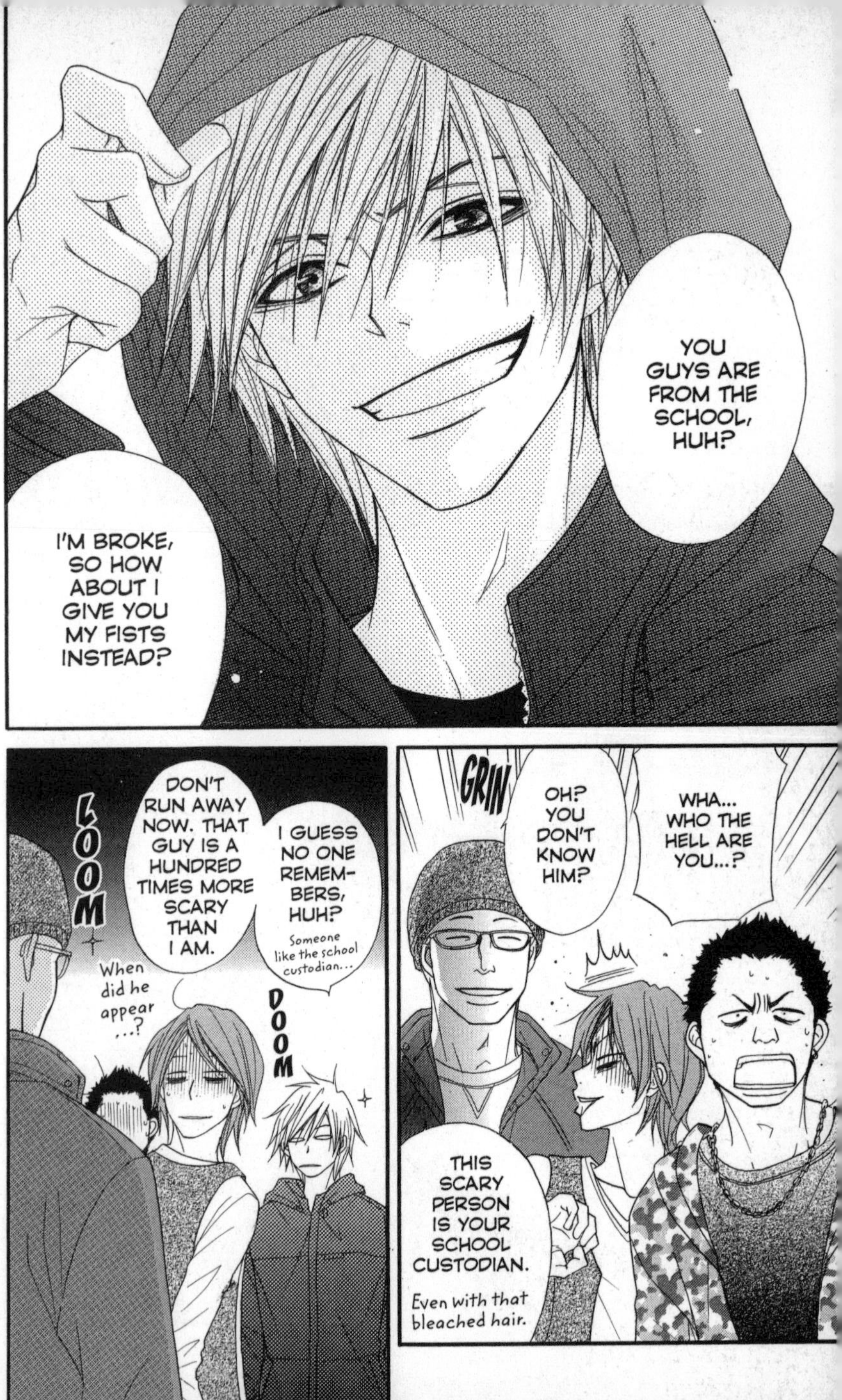
YOU GUYS ARE FROM THE SCHOOL, HUH?
I'M BROKE, SO HOW ABOUT I GIVE YOU MY FISTS INSTEAD?
GRIN
WHA... WHO THE HELL ARE YOU...?
OH? YOU DON'T KNOW HIM?
THIS SCARY PERSON IS YOUR SCHOOL CUSTODIAN.
Even with that bleached hair.
I GUESS NO ONE REMEM-BERS, HUH?
Someone like the school custodian...
DON'T RUN AWAY NOW. THAT GUY IS A HUNDRED TIMES MORE SCARY THAN I AM.
LOOM
DOOM
When did he appear...?

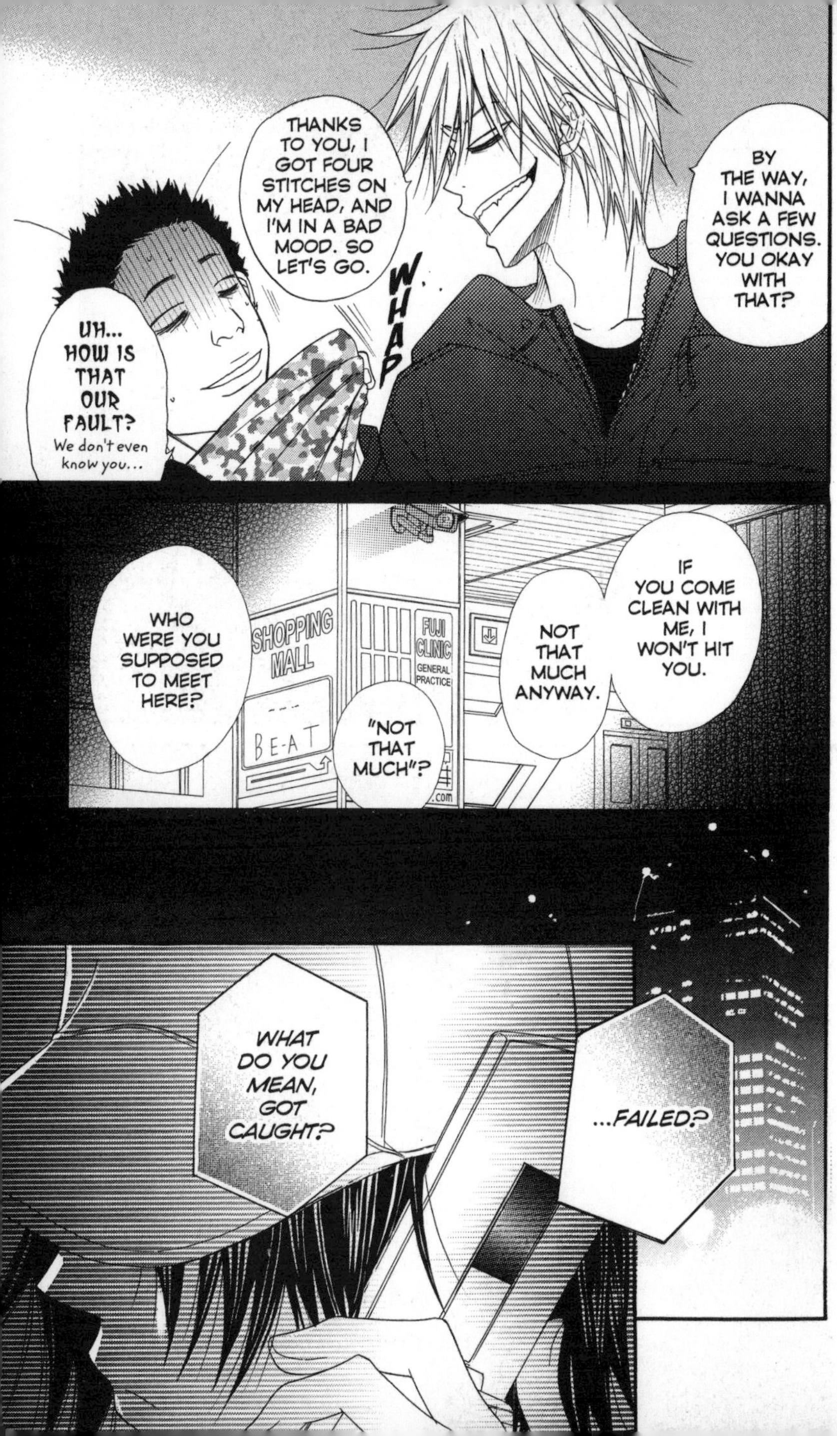
BY THE WAY, I WANNA ASK A FEW QUESTIONS. YOU OKAY WITH THAT?
THANKS TO YOU, I GOT FOUR STITCHES ON MY HEAD, AND I'M IN A BAD MOOD. SO LET'S GO.
WHAP
UH... HOW IS THAT OUR FAULT?
We don't even know you...
IF YOU COME CLEAN WITH ME, I WON'T HIT YOU.
NOT THAT MUCH ANYWAY.
FUJI CLINIC
GENERAL PRACTICE
SHOPPING MALL
BE-AT
.com
"NOT THAT MUCH"?
WHO WERE YOU SUPPOSED TO MEET HERE?
...FAILED?
WHAT DO YOU MEAN, GOT CAUGHT?

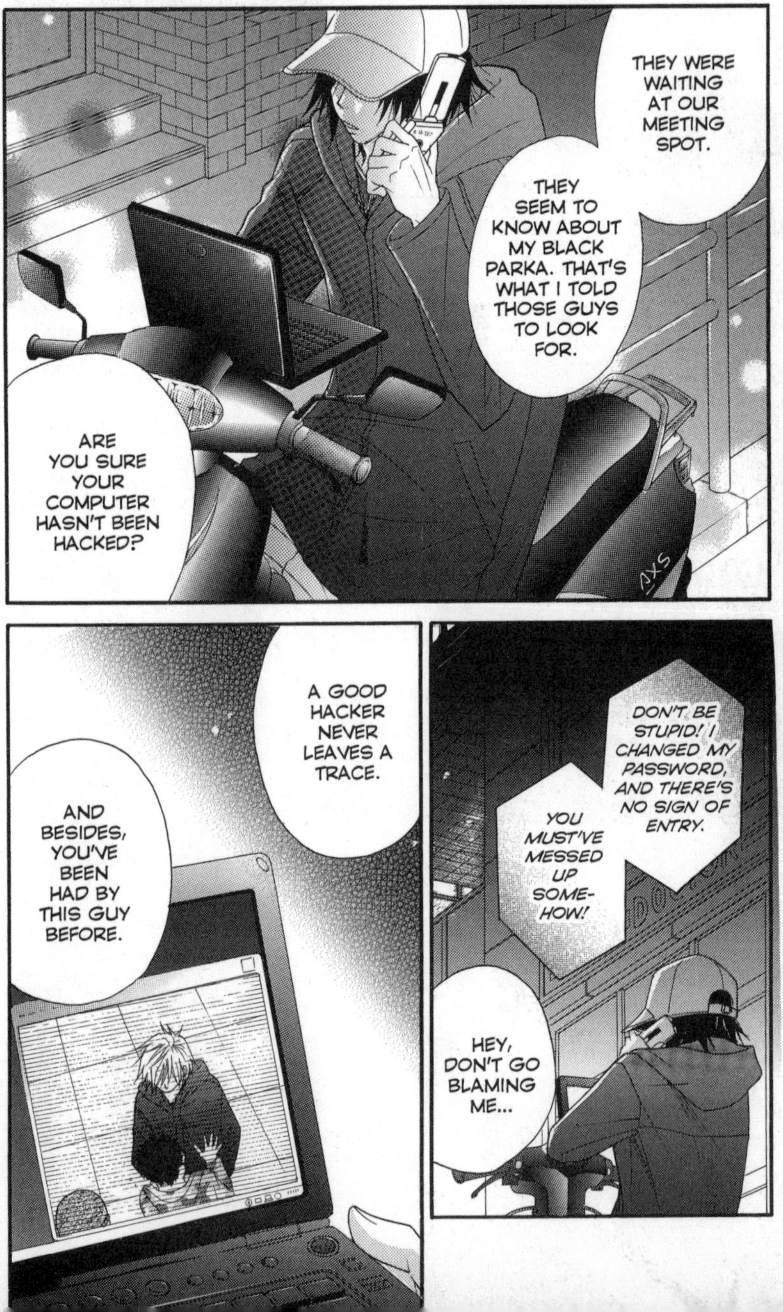
THEY WERE WAITING AT OUR MEETING SPOT.
THEY SEEM TO KNOW ABOUT MY BLACK PARKA. THAT'S WHAT I TOLD THOSE GUYS TO LOOK FOR.
ARE YOU SURE YOUR COMPUTER HASN'T BEEN HACKED?
DON'T BE STUPID! I CHANGED MY PASSWORD, AND THERE'S NO SIGN OF ENTRY.
YOU MUST'VE MESSED UP SOME-HOW!
HEY, DON'T GO BLAMING ME...
A GOOD HACKER NEVER LEAVES A TRACE.
AND BESIDES, YOU'VE BEEN HAD BY THIS GUY BEFORE.

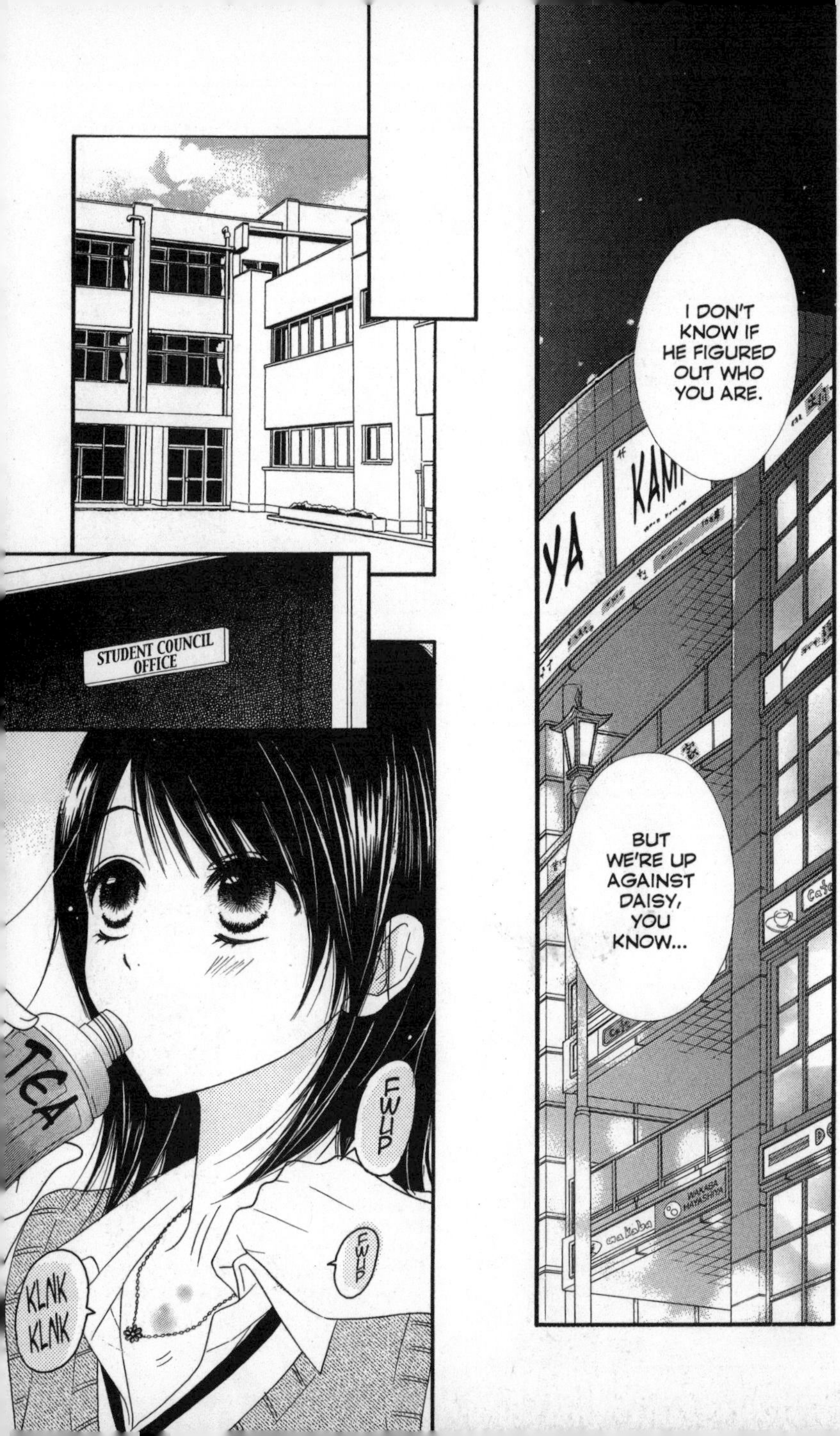
I DON'T KNOW IF HE FIGURED OUT WHO YOU ARE.
BUT WE'RE UP AGAINST DAISY, YOU KNOW...
STUDENT COUNCIL OFFICE
TEA
FWLP
FWLP
KLNK KLNK

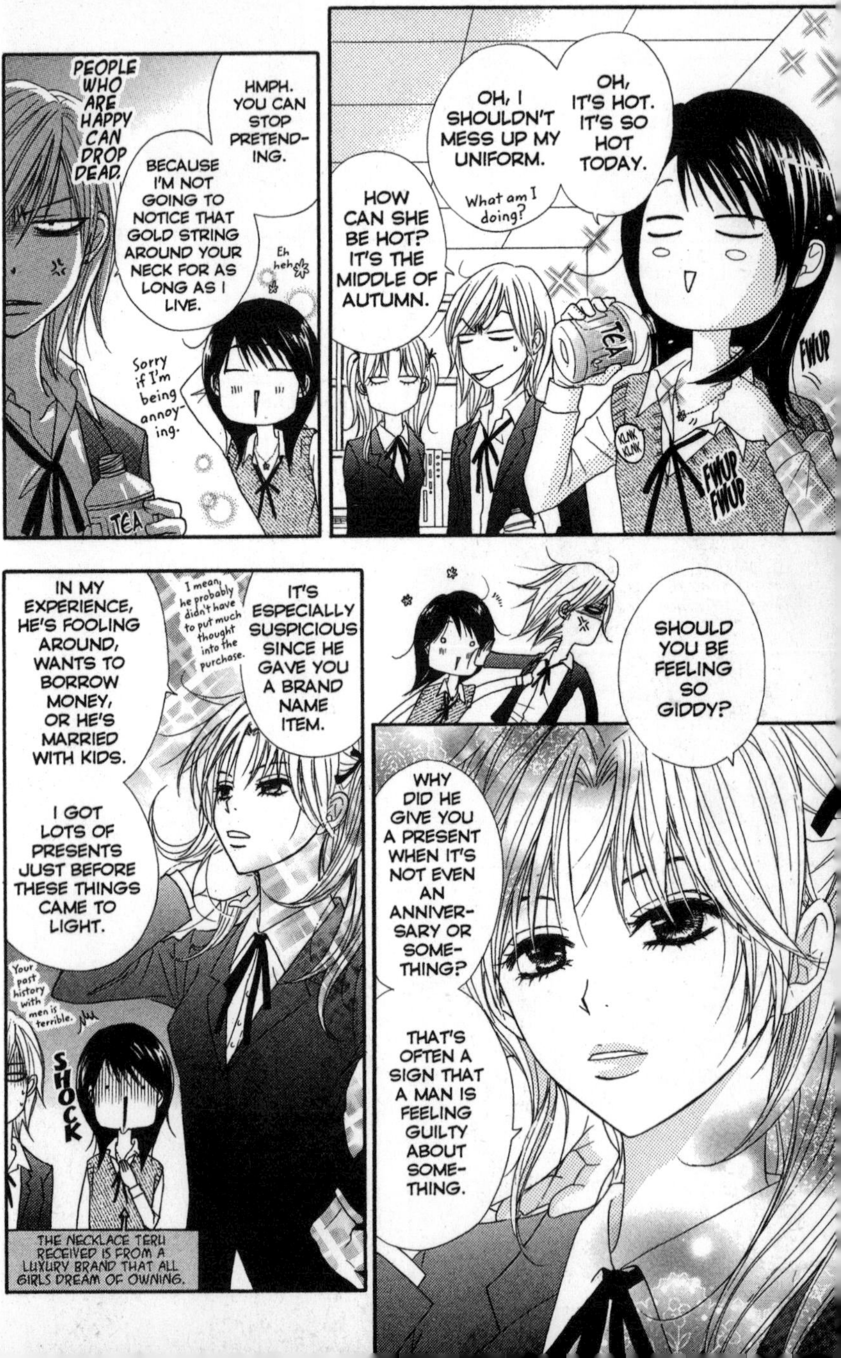
OH, IT'S HOT. IT'S SO HOT TODAY.
OH, I SHOULDN'T MESS UP MY UNIFORM.
What am I doing?
HOW CAN SHE BE HOT? IT'S THE MIDDLE OF AUTUMN.
FWUP
TEA
KLNK KLNK
FWUP FWUP
HMPH. YOU CAN STOP PRETENDING.
BECAUSE I'M NOT GOING TO NOTICE THAT GOLD STRING AROUND YOUR NECK FOR AS LONG AS I LIVE.
PEOPLE WHO ARE HAPPY CAN DROP DEAD.
Eh heh
Sorry if I'm being annoying.
TEA
SHOULD YOU BE FEELING SO GIDDY?
WHY DID HE GIVE YOU A PRESENT WHEN IT'S NOT EVEN AN ANNIVERSARY OR SOMETHING?
THAT'S OFTEN A SIGN THAT A MAN IS FEELING GUILTY ABOUT SOMETHING.
IT'S ESPECIALLY SUSPICIOUS SINCE HE GAVE YOU A BRAND NAME ITEM.
I mean, he probably didn't have to put much thought into the purchase.
IN MY EXPERIENCE, HE'S FOOLING AROUND, WANTS TO BORROW MONEY, OR HE'S MARRIED WITH KIDS.
I GOT LOTS OF PRESENTS JUST BEFORE THESE THINGS CAME TO LIGHT.
Your past history with men is terrible.
SHOCK
THE NECKLACE TERU RECEIVED IS FROM A LUXURY BRAND THAT ALL GIRLS DREAM OF OWNING.

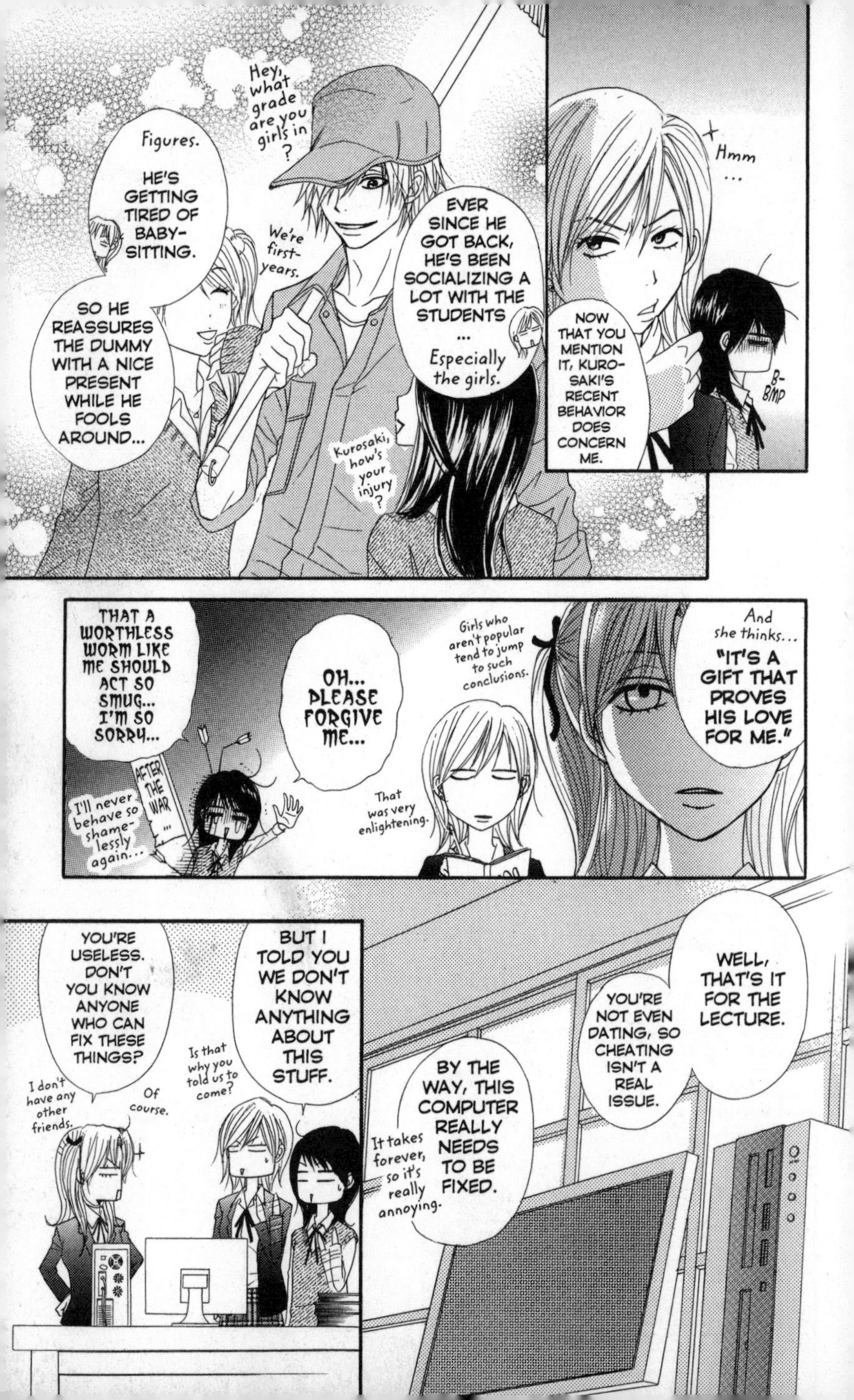
Hmm...
NOW THAT YOU MENTION IT, KURO-SAKI'S RECENT BEHAVIOR DOES CONCERN ME.
B-BMP
Hey, what grade are you girls in?
EVER SINCE HE GOT BACK, HE'S BEEN SOCIALIZING A LOT WITH THE STUDENTS... Especially the girls.
Figures. HE'S GETTING TIRED OF BABY-SITTING.
We're first-years.
Kurosaki, how's your injury?
SO HE REASSURES THE DUMMY WITH A NICE PRESENT WHILE HE FOOLS AROUND...
And she thinks... "IT'S A GIFT THAT PROVES HIS LOVE FOR ME."
Girls who aren't popular tend to jump to such conclusions.
That was very enlightening.
OH... PLEASE FORGIVE ME...
THAT A WORTHLESS WORM LIKE ME SHOULD ACT SO SMUG... I'M SO SORRY...
AFTER THE WAR ...
I'll never behave so shame-lessly again...
WELL, THAT'S IT FOR THE LECTURE.
YOU'RE NOT EVEN DATING, SO CHEATING ISN'T A REAL ISSUE.
BY THE WAY, THIS COMPUTER REALLY NEEDS TO BE FIXED.
It takes forever, so it's really annoying.
BUT I TOLD YOU WE DON'T KNOW ANYTHING ABOUT THIS STUFF.
Is that why you told us to come?
YOU'RE USELESS. DON'T YOU KNOW ANYONE WHO CAN FIX THESE THINGS?
Of course.
I don't have any other friends.

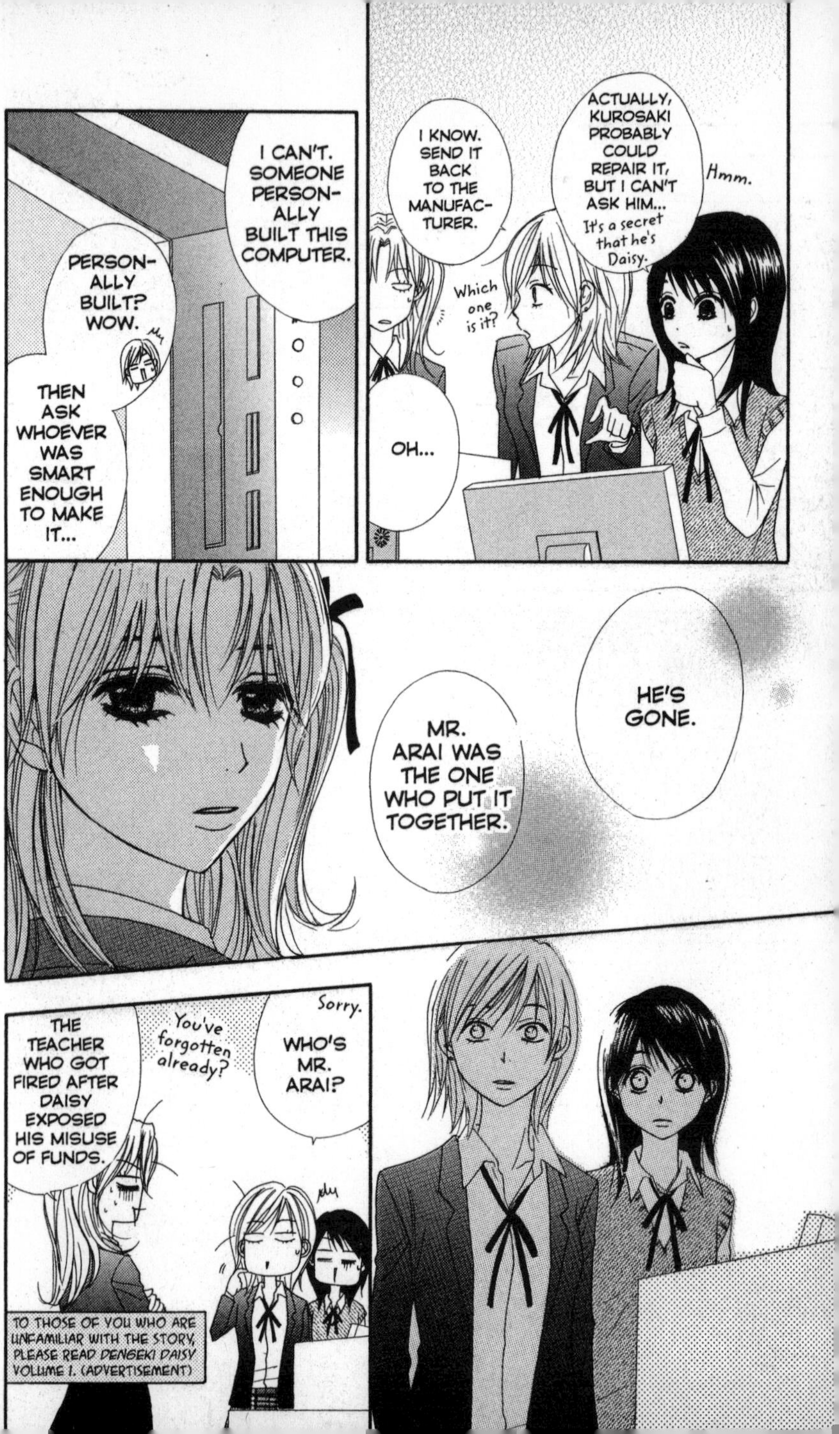
Hmm.
ACTUALLY, KUROSAKI PROBABLY COULD REPAIR IT, BUT I CAN'T ASK HIM...
It's a secret that he's Daisy.
I KNOW. SEND IT BACK TO THE MANUFACTURER.
Which one is it?
OH...
I CAN'T. SOMEONE PERSONALLY BUILT THIS COMPUTER.
PERSONALLY BUILT? WOW.
THEN ASK WHOEVER WAS SMART ENOUGH TO MAKE IT...
HE'S GONE.
MR. ARAI WAS THE ONE WHO PUT IT TOGETHER.
Sorry.
WHO'S MR. ARAI?
You've forgotten already?
THE TEACHER WHO GOT FIRED AFTER DAISY EXPOSED HIS MISUSE OF FUNDS.
TO THOSE OF YOU WHO ARE UNFAMILIAR WITH THE STORY, PLEASE READ DENGEKI DAISY VOLUME 1. (ADVERTISEMENT)

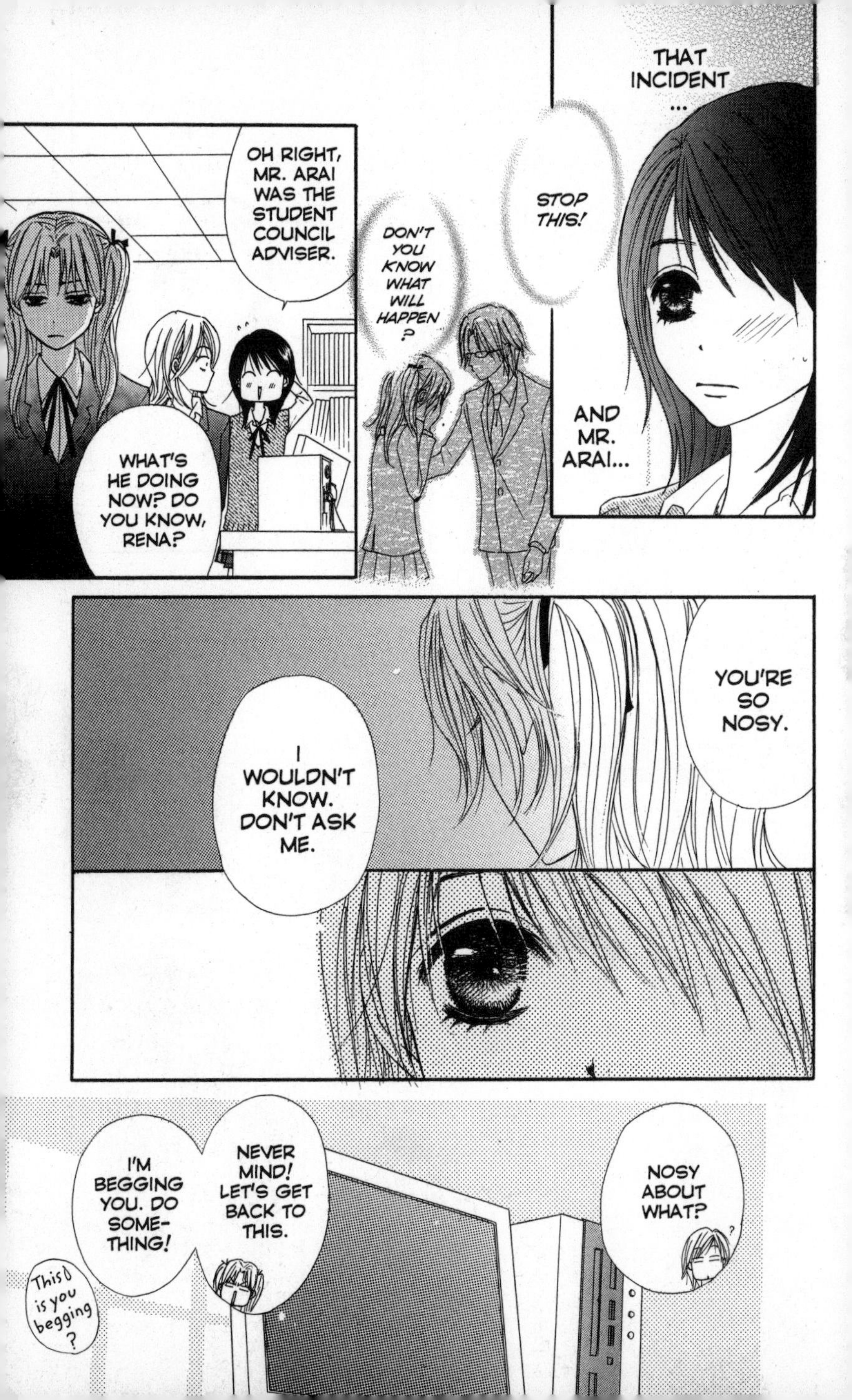
THAT INCIDENT ...
STOP THIS!
DON'T YOU KNOW WHAT WILL HAPPEN?
AND MR. ARAI...
OH RIGHT, MR. ARAI WAS THE STUDENT COUNCIL ADVISER.
WHAT'S HE DOING NOW? DO YOU KNOW, RENA?
YOU'RE SO NOSY.
I WOULDN'T KNOW. DON'T ASK ME.
NOSY ABOUT WHAT?
NEVER MIND! LET'S GET BACK TO THIS.
I'M BEGGING YOU. DO SOME-THING!
This is you begging?

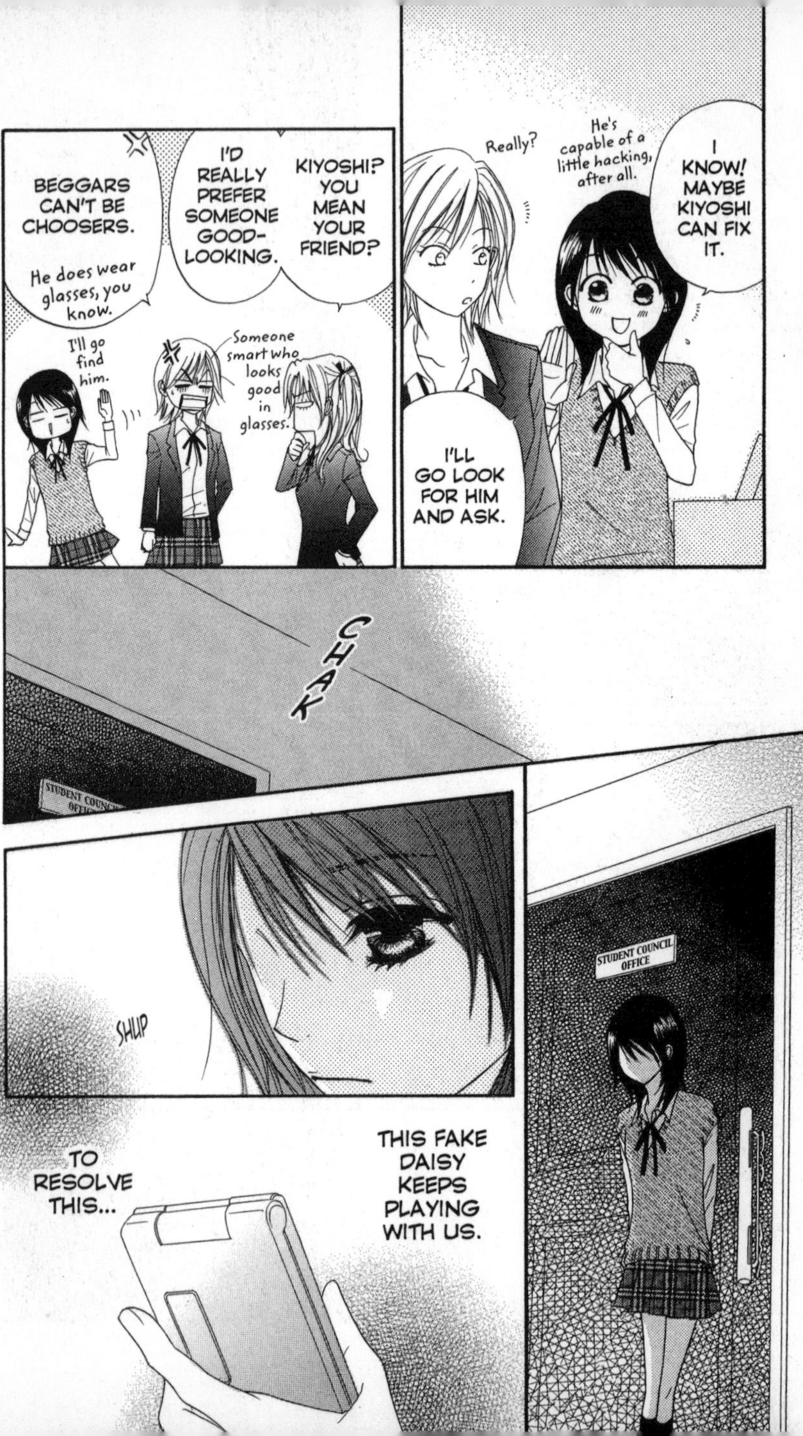
I KNOW! MAYBE KIYOSHI CAN FIX IT.
He's capable of a little hacking, after all.
Really?
I'LL GO LOOK FOR HIM AND ASK.
KIYOSHI? YOU MEAN YOUR FRIEND?
I'D REALLY PREFER SOMEONE GOOD-LOOKING.
BEGGARS CAN'T BE CHOOSERS.
He does wear glasses, you know.
Someone smart who looks good in glasses.
I'll go find him.
CHAK
STUDENT COUNCIL OFFICE
THIS FAKE DAISY KEEPS PLAYING WITH US.
SHUP
TO RESOLVE THIS...

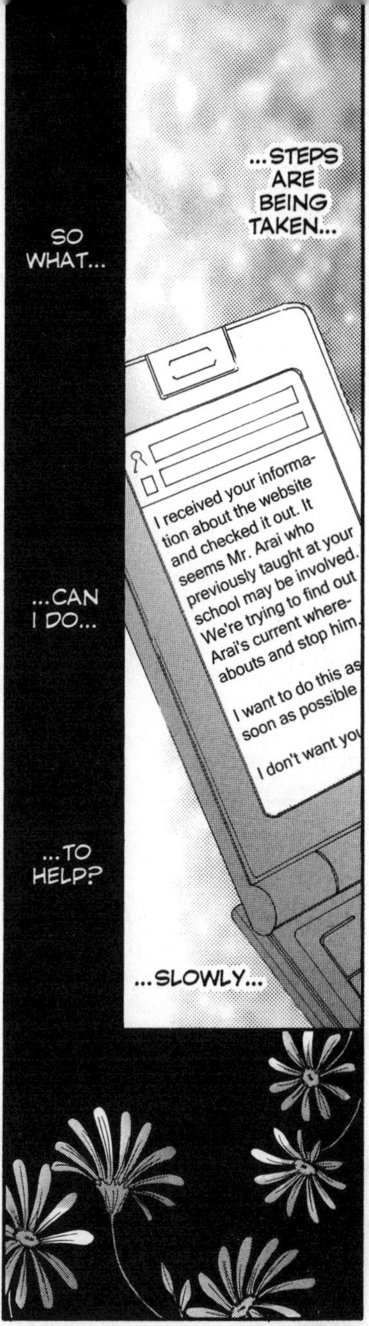
...STEPS ARE BEING TAKEN...
SO WHAT...
I received your information about the website and checked it out. It seems Mr. Arai who previously taught at your school may be involved. We're trying to find out Arai's current whereabouts and stop him.
I want to do this as soon as possible
I don't want you
...CAN I DO...
...TO HELP?
...SLOWLY...
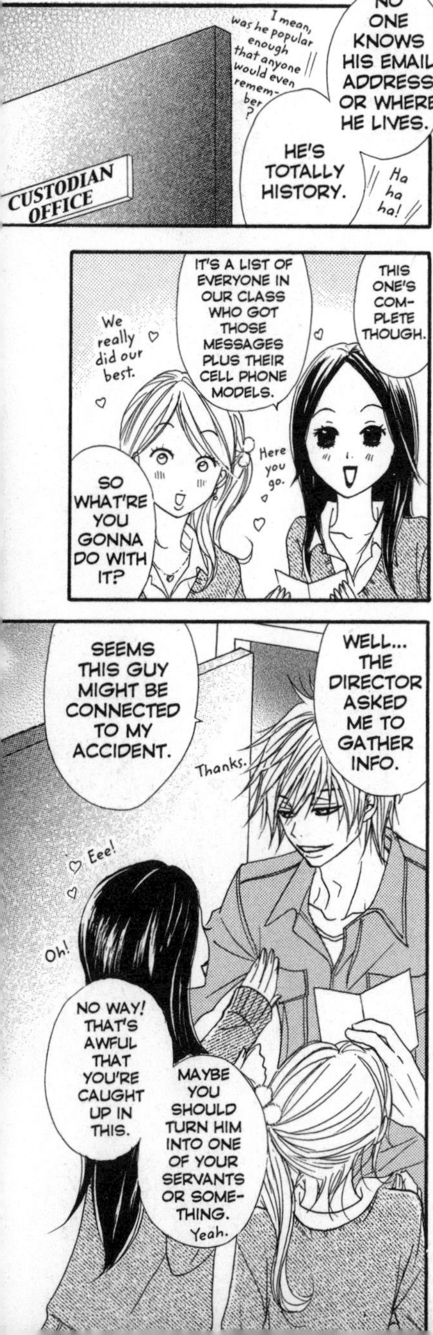
NO ONE KNOWS HIS EMAIL ADDRESS OR WHERE HE LIVES.
I mean, was he popular enough that anyone would even remember?
CUSTODIAN OFFICE
HE'S TOTALLY HISTORY.
Ha ha ha!
THIS ONE'S COMPLETE THOUGH.
IT'S A LIST OF EVERYONE IN OUR CLASS WHO GOT THOSE MESSAGES PLUS THEIR CELL PHONE MODELS.
We really did our best.
Here you go.
SO WHAT'RE YOU GONNA DO WITH IT?
WELL... THE DIRECTOR ASKED ME TO GATHER INFO.
SEEMS THIS GUY MIGHT BE CONNECTED TO MY ACCIDENT.
Thanks.
Eee!
Oh!
NO WAY! THAT'S AWFUL THAT YOU'RE CAUGHT UP IN THIS.
MAYBE YOU SHOULD TURN HIM INTO ONE OF YOUR SERVANTS OR SOMETHING.
Yeah.

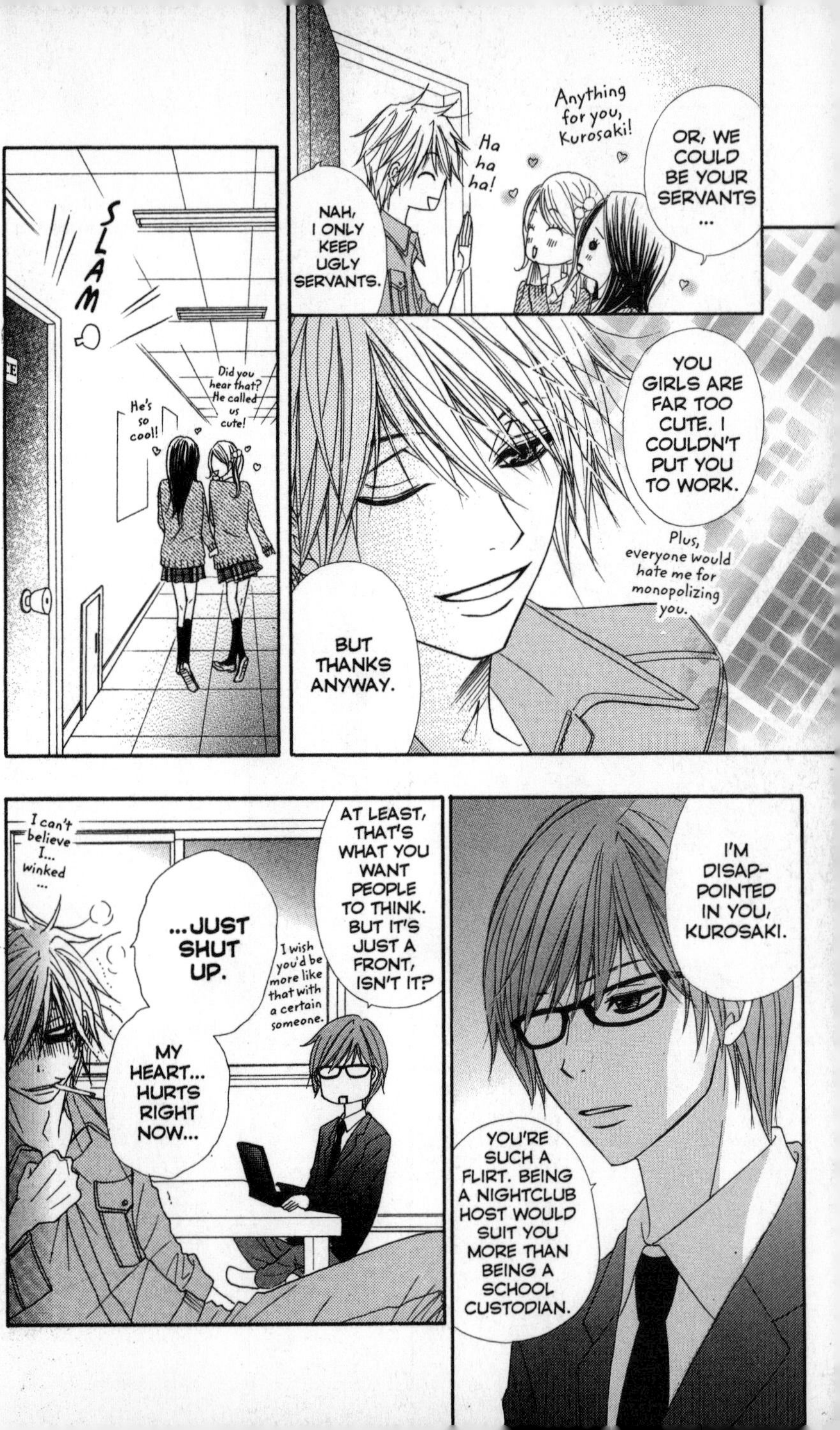
OR, WE COULD BE YOUR SERVANTS ...
Anything for you, Kurosaki!
Ha ha ha!
NAH, I ONLY KEEP UGLY SERVANTS.
YOU GIRLS ARE FAR TOO CUTE. I COULDN'T PUT YOU TO WORK.
Plus, everyone would hate me for monopolizing you.
BUT THANKS ANYWAY.
SLAM
Did you hear that? He called us cute!
He's so cool!
I'M DISAP-POINTED IN YOU, KUROSAKI.
YOU'RE SUCH A FLIRT. BEING A NIGHTCLUB HOST WOULD SUIT YOU MORE THAN BEING A SCHOOL CUSTODIAN.
AT LEAST, THAT'S WHAT YOU WANT PEOPLE TO THINK. BUT IT'S JUST A FRONT, ISN'T IT?
I wish you'd be more like that with a certain someone.
...JUST SHUT UP.
I can't believe I... winked ...
MY HEART... HURTS RIGHT NOW...

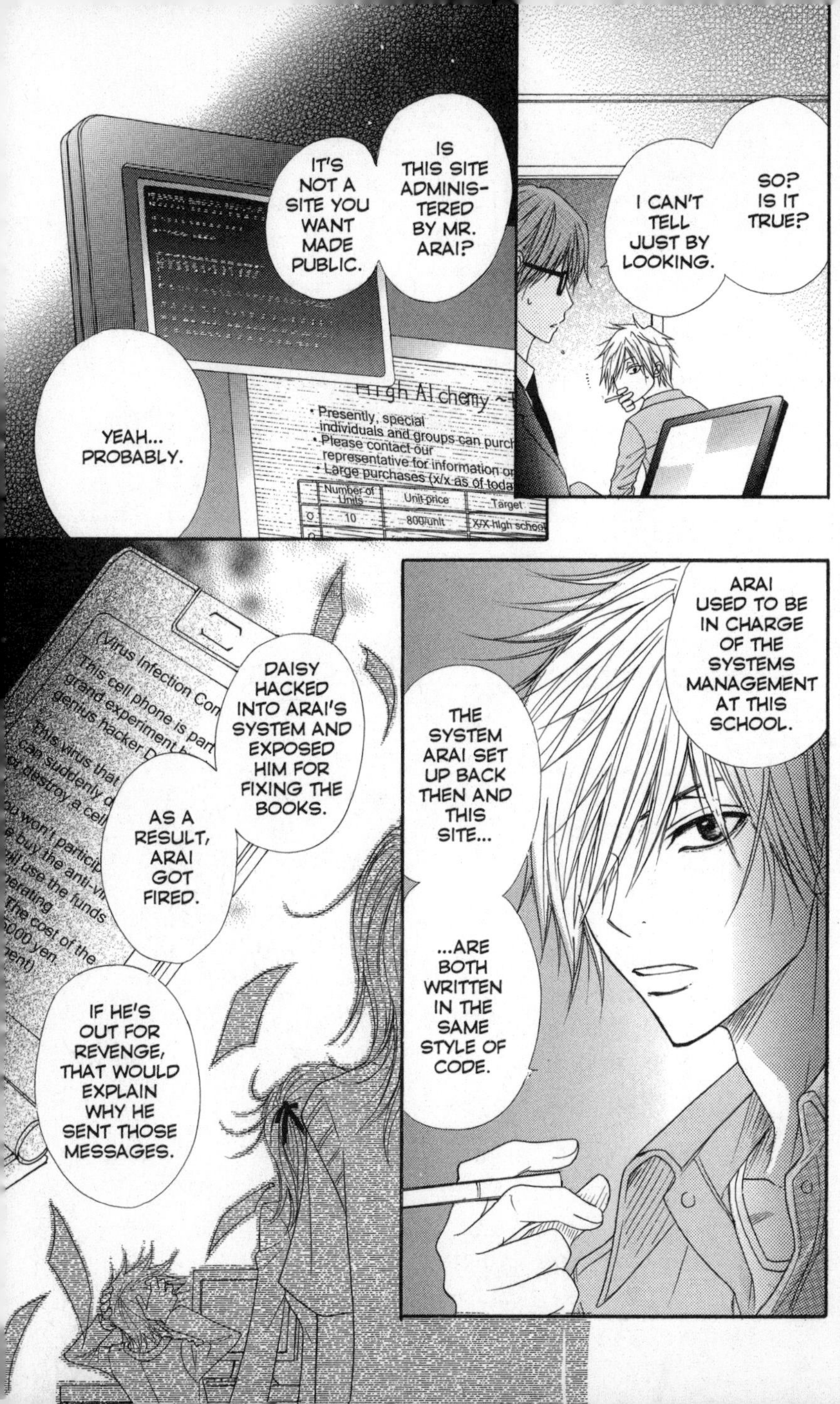
SO? IS IT TRUE?
I CAN'T TELL JUST BY LOOKING.
IS THIS SITE ADMINIS-TERED BY MR. ARAI?
IT'S NOT A SITE YOU WANT MADE PUBLIC.
YEAH... PROBABLY.
• Presently, special
Number of Units
Unit-price
Target
10
800/unit
ARAI USED TO BE IN CHARGE OF THE SYSTEMS MANAGEMENT AT THIS SCHOOL.
THE SYSTEM ARAI SET UP BACK THEN AND THIS SITE...
...ARE BOTH WRITTEN IN THE SAME STYLE OF CODE.
DAISY HACKED INTO ARAI'S SYSTEM AND EXPOSED HIM FOR FIXING THE BOOKS.
AS A RESULT, ARAI GOT FIRED.
IF HE'S OUT FOR REVENGE, THAT WOULD EXPLAIN WHY HE SENT THOSE MESSAGES.

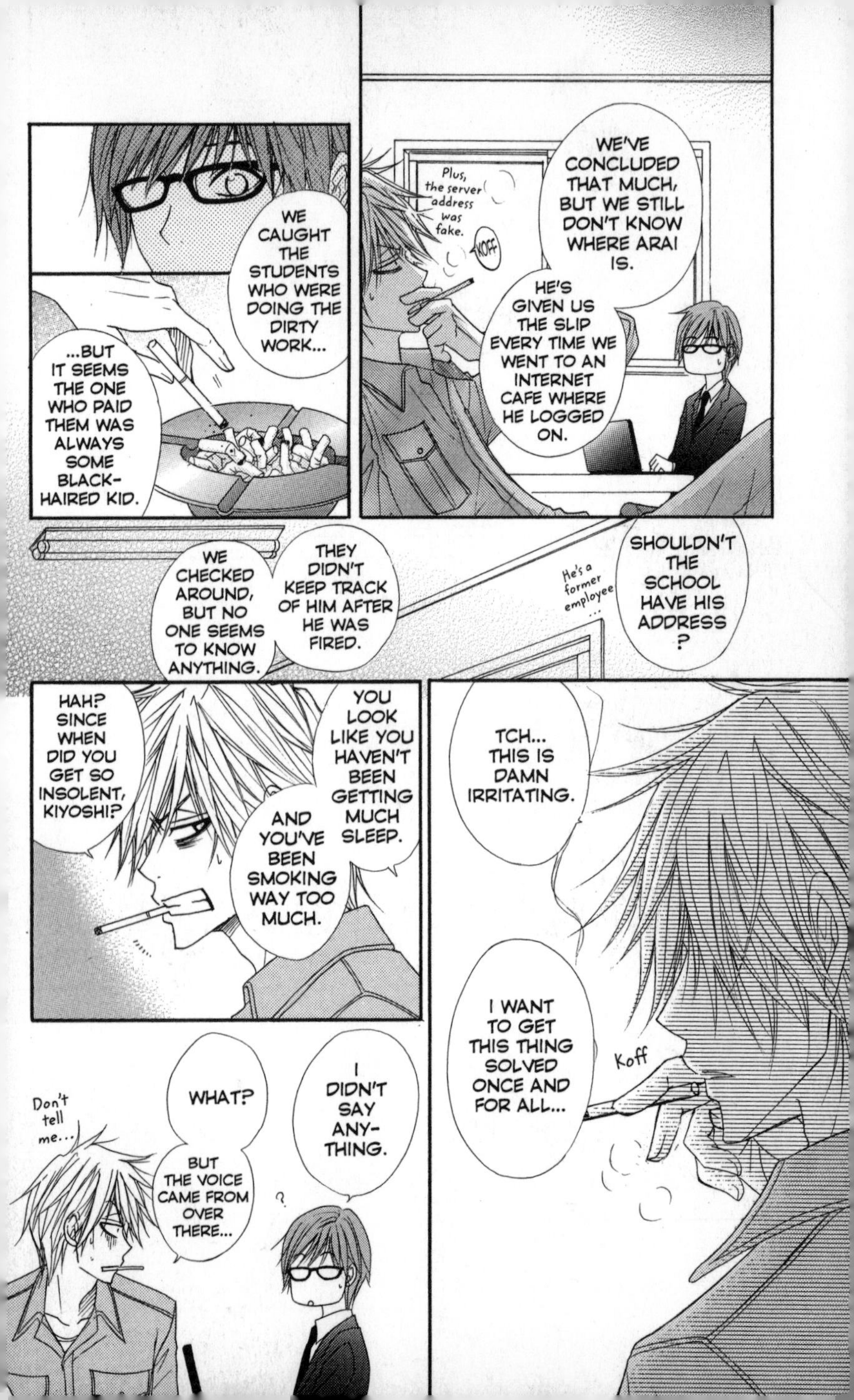
WE'VE CONCLUDED THAT MUCH, BUT WE STILL DON'T KNOW WHERE ARAI IS.
Plus, the server address was fake.
KOFF
HE'S GIVEN US THE SLIP EVERY TIME WE WENT TO AN INTERNET CAFE WHERE HE LOGGED ON.
WE CAUGHT THE STUDENTS WHO WERE DOING THE DIRTY WORK...
...BUT IT SEEMS THE ONE WHO PAID THEM WAS ALWAYS SOME BLACK-HAIRED KID.
SHOULDN'T THE SCHOOL HAVE HIS ADDRESS?
He's a former employee...
THEY DIDN'T KEEP TRACK OF HIM AFTER HE WAS FIRED.
WE CHECKED AROUND, BUT NO ONE SEEMS TO KNOW ANYTHING.
TCH... THIS IS DAMN IRRITATING.
I WANT TO GET THIS THING SOLVED ONCE AND FOR ALL...
Koff
YOU LOOK LIKE YOU HAVEN'T BEEN GETTING MUCH SLEEP.
AND YOU'VE BEEN SMOKING WAY TOO MUCH.
HAH? SINCE WHEN DID YOU GET SO INSOLENT, KIYOSHI?
I DIDN'T SAY ANY-THING.
WHAT?
BUT THE VOICE CAME FROM OVER THERE...
?
Don't tell me...

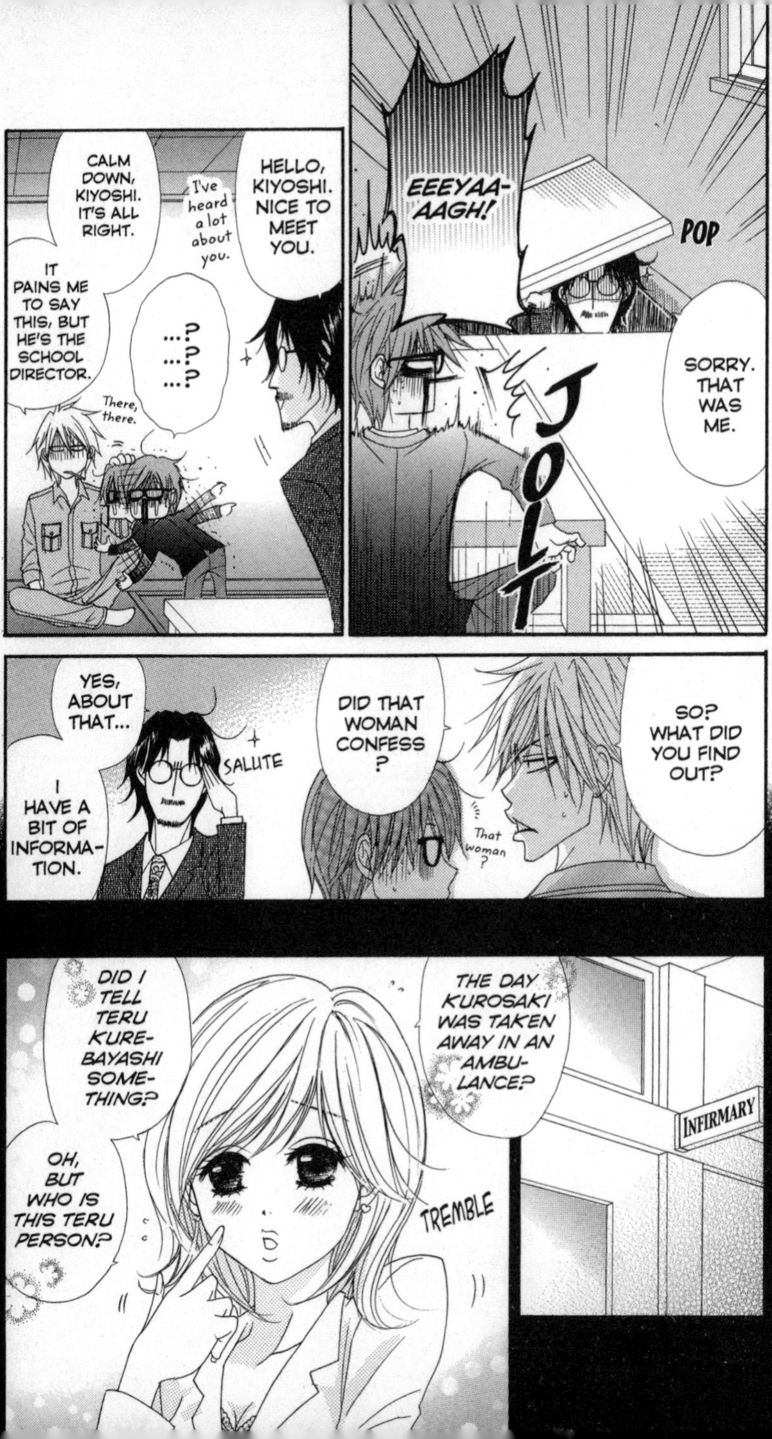
EEEYAA-AAGH!
POP
SORRY. THAT WAS ME.
JOLT
HELLO, KIYOSHI. NICE TO MEET YOU.
I've heard a lot about you.
CALM DOWN, KIYOSHI. IT'S ALL RIGHT.
IT PAINS ME TO SAY THIS, BUT HE'S THE SCHOOL DIRECTOR.
...? ...? ...?
There, there.
SO? WHAT DID YOU FIND OUT?
That woman?
DID THAT WOMAN CONFESS?
YES, ABOUT THAT...
SALUTE
I HAVE A BIT OF INFORMATION.
INFIRMARY
THE DAY KUROSAKI WAS TAKEN AWAY IN AN AMBULANCE?
DID I TELL TERU KUREBAYASHI SOMETHING?
TREMBLE
OH, BUT WHO IS THIS TERU PERSON?

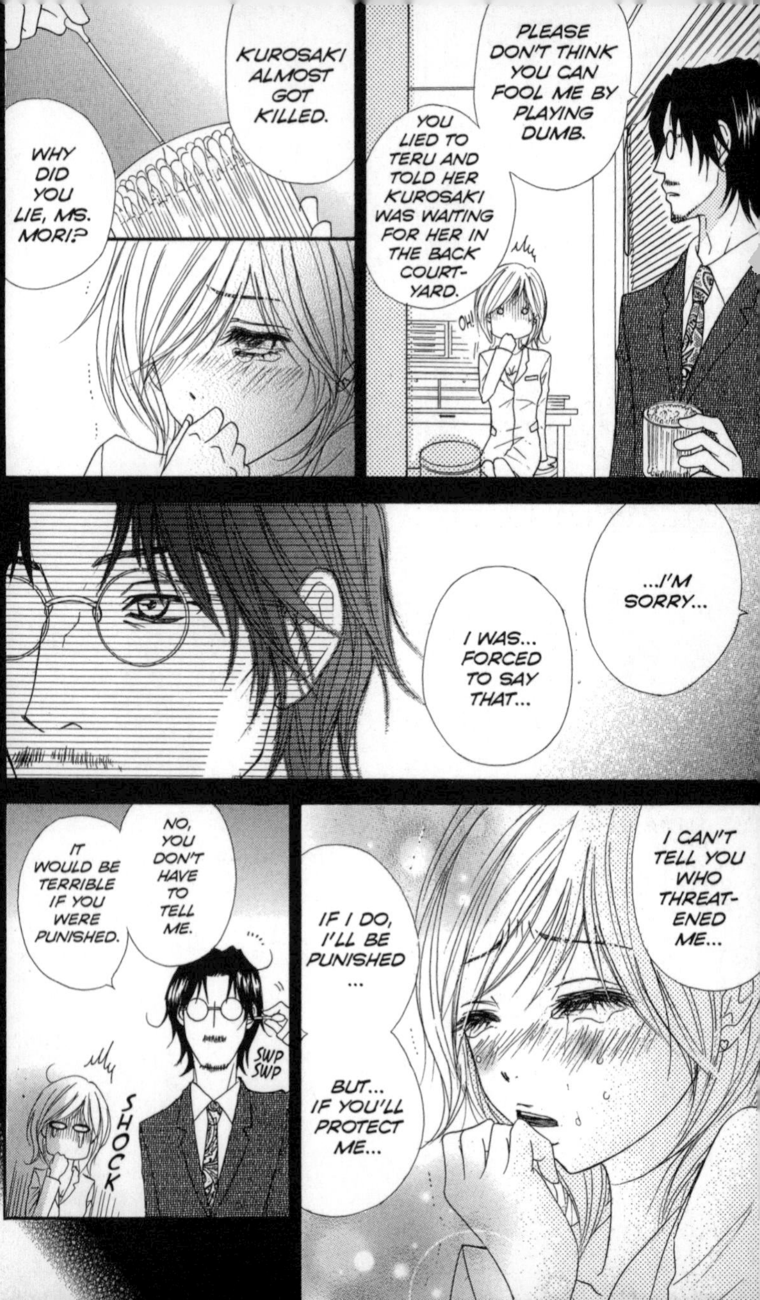
PLEASE DON'T THINK YOU CAN FOOL ME BY PLAYING DUMB.
YOU LIED TO TERU AND TOLD HER KUROSAKI WAS WAITING FOR HER IN THE BACK COURT-YARD.
OH!
KUROSAKI ALMOST GOT KILLED.
WHY DID YOU LIE, MS. MORI?
...I'M SORRY...
I WAS... FORCED TO SAY THAT...
I CAN'T TELL YOU WHO THREAT-ENED ME...
IF I DO, I'LL BE PUNISHED ...
BUT... IF YOU'LL PROTECT ME...
NO, YOU DON'T HAVE TO TELL ME.
IT WOULD BE TERRIBLE IF YOU WERE PUNISHED.
SWP SWP
SHOCK

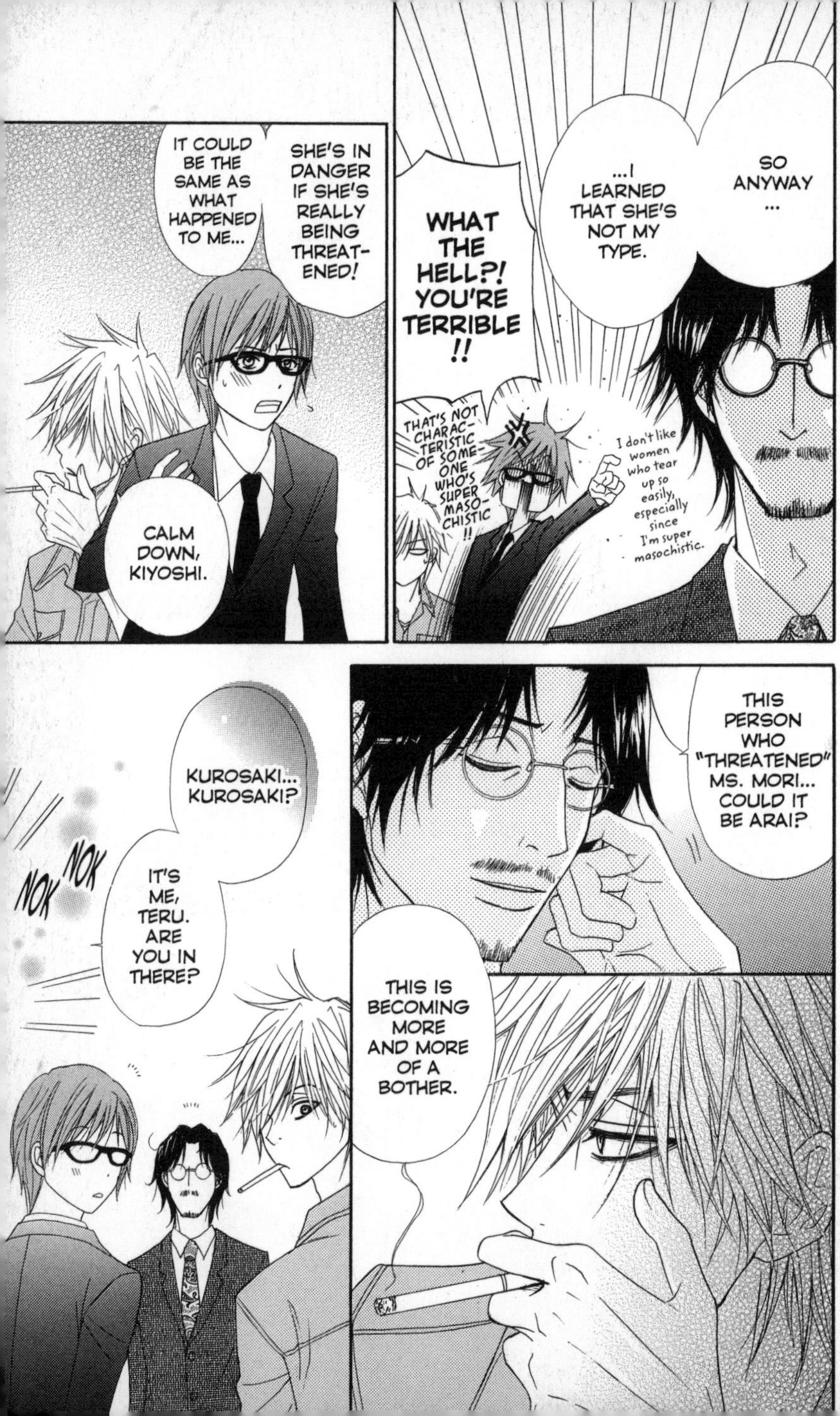
SO ANYWAY ...
...I LEARNED THAT SHE'S NOT MY TYPE.
I don't like women who tear up so easily, especially since I'm super masochistic.
WHAT THE HELL?! YOU'RE TERRIBLE!!
THAT'S NOT CHARAC-TERISTIC OF SOME-ONE WHO'S SUPER MASO-CHISTIC!!
SHE'S IN DANGER IF SHE'S REALLY BEING THREAT-ENED!
IT COULD BE THE SAME AS WHAT HAPPENED TO ME...
CALM DOWN, KIYOSHI.
THIS PERSON WHO "THREATENED" MS. MORI... COULD IT BE ARAI?
THIS IS BECOMING MORE AND MORE OF A BOTHER.
KUROSAKI... KUROSAKI?
NOK NOK
IT'S ME, TERU. ARE YOU IN THERE?

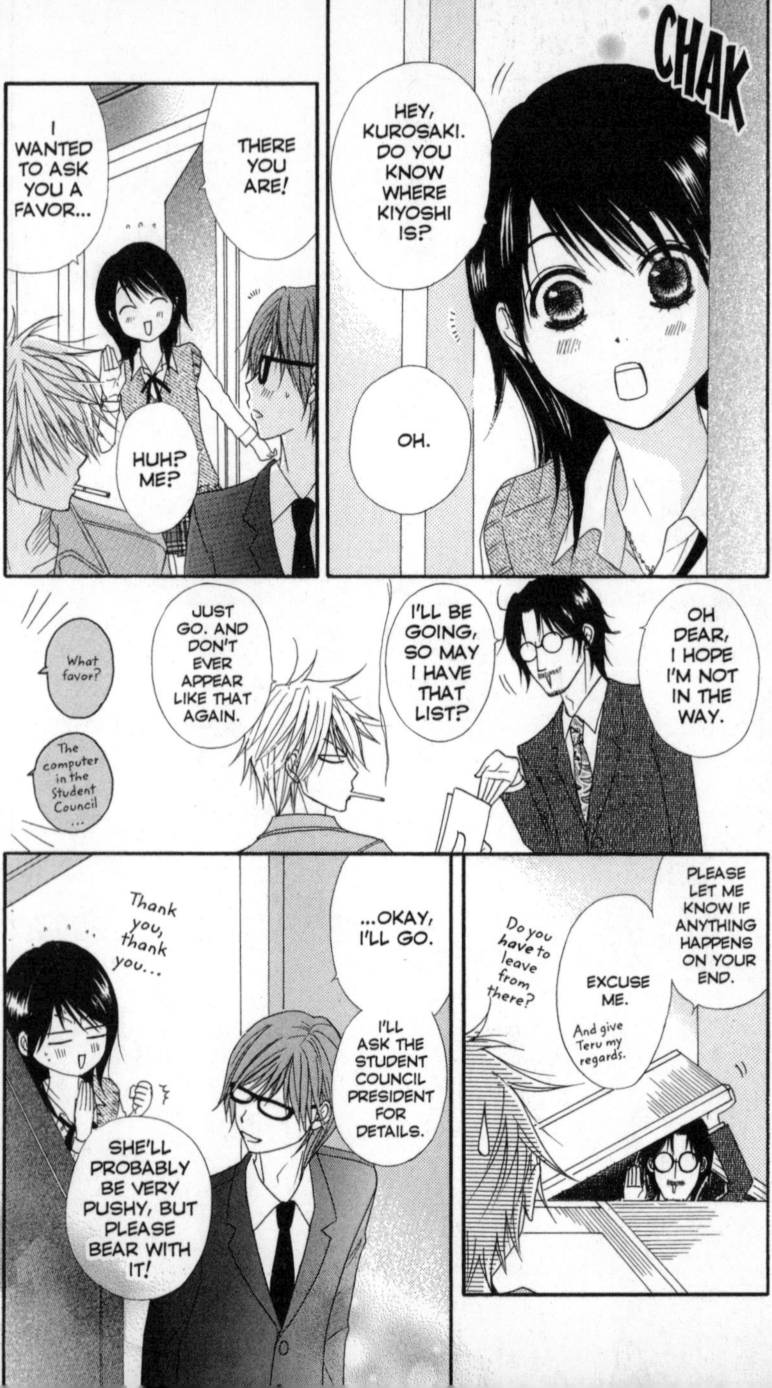
CHAK
HEY, KUROSAKI. DO YOU KNOW WHERE KIYOSHI IS?
OH.
THERE YOU ARE!
I WANTED TO ASK YOU A FAVOR...
HUH? ME?
OH DEAR, I HOPE I'M NOT IN THE WAY.
I'LL BE GOING, SO MAY I HAVE THAT LIST?
JUST GO. AND DON'T EVER APPEAR LIKE THAT AGAIN.
What favor?
The computer in the Student Council...
PLEASE LET ME KNOW IF ANYTHING HAPPENS ON YOUR END.
EXCUSE ME.
And give Teru my regards.
Do you have to leave from there?
...OKAY, I'LL GO.
I'LL ASK THE STUDENT COUNCIL PRESIDENT FOR DETAILS.
Thank you, thank you...
SHE'LL PROBABLY BE VERY PUSHY, BUT PLEASE BEAR WITH IT!

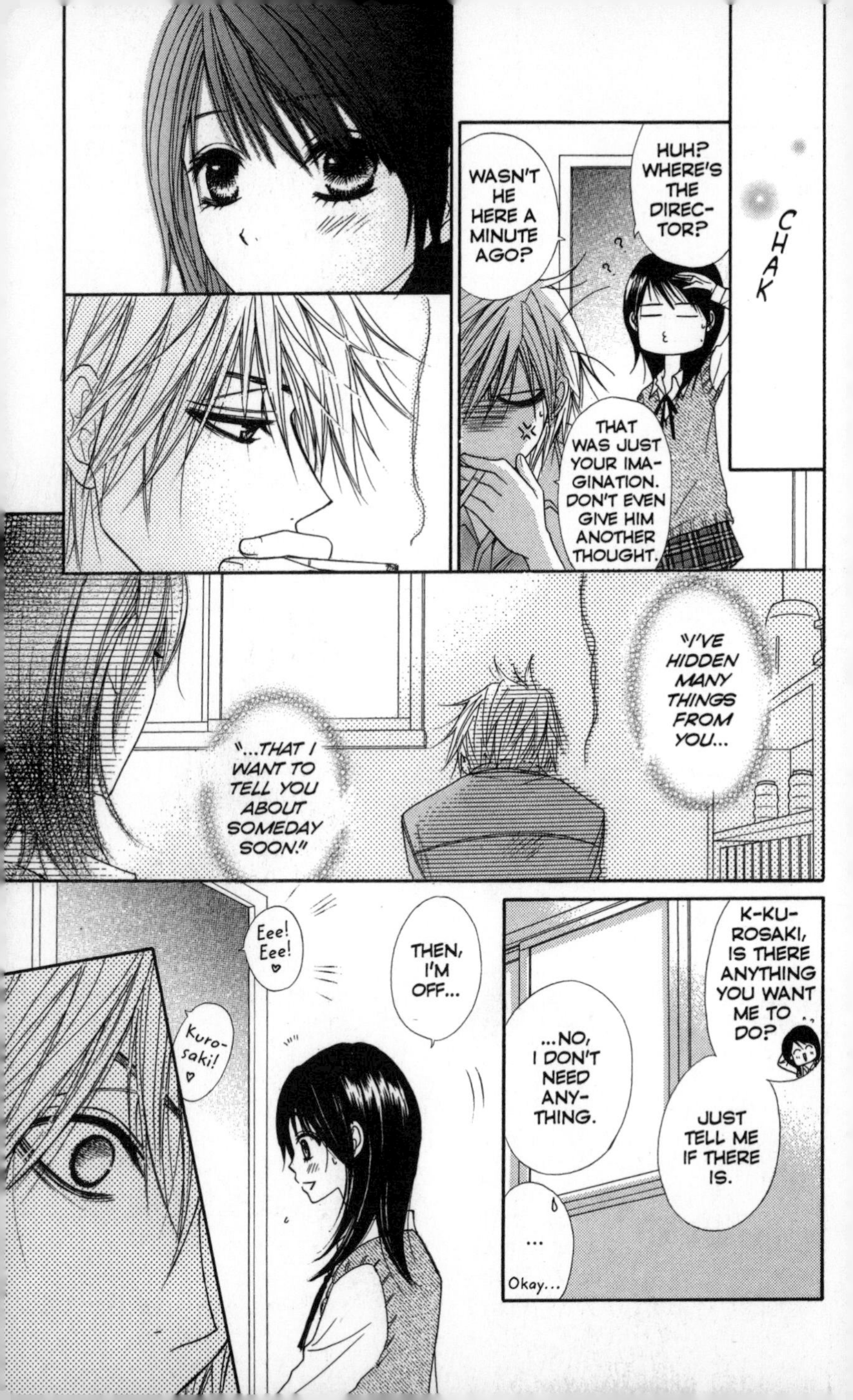
CHAK
HUH? WHERE'S THE DIRECTOR?
WASN'T HE HERE A MINUTE AGO?
THAT WAS JUST YOUR IMAGINATION. DON'T EVEN GIVE HIM ANOTHER THOUGHT.
"I'VE HIDDEN MANY THINGS FROM YOU...
"...THAT I WANT TO TELL YOU ABOUT SOMEDAY SOON."
K-KUROSAKI, IS THERE ANYTHING YOU WANT ME TO DO?
JUST TELL ME IF THERE IS.
...NO, I DON'T NEED ANYTHING.
...
Okay...
THEN, I'M OFF...
Eee! Eee!
Kurosaki!

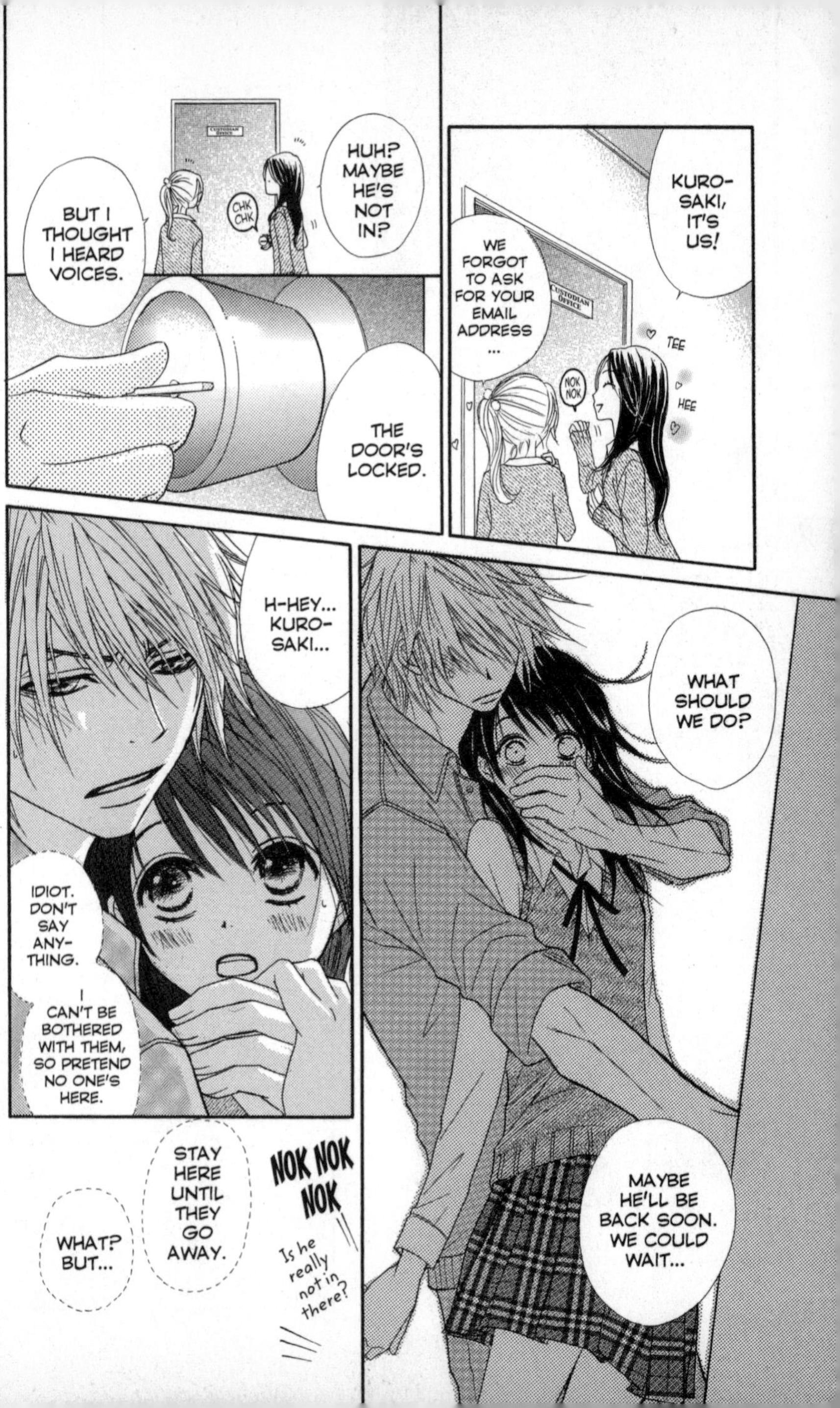
CUSTODIAN OFFICE
HUH? MAYBE HE'S NOT IN?
CHK CHK
BUT I THOUGHT I HEARD VOICES.
THE DOOR'S LOCKED.
KURO-SAKI, IT'S US!
WE FORGOT TO ASK FOR YOUR EMAIL ADDRESS ...
TEE HEE
NOK NOK
WHAT SHOULD WE DO?
MAYBE HE'LL BE BACK SOON. WE COULD WAIT...
H-HEY... KURO-SAKI...
IDIOT. DON'T SAY ANY-THING.
I CAN'T BE BOTHERED WITH THEM, SO PRETEND NO ONE'S HERE.
NOK NOK NOK
Is he really not in there?
STAY HERE UNTIL THEY GO AWAY.
WHAT? BUT...

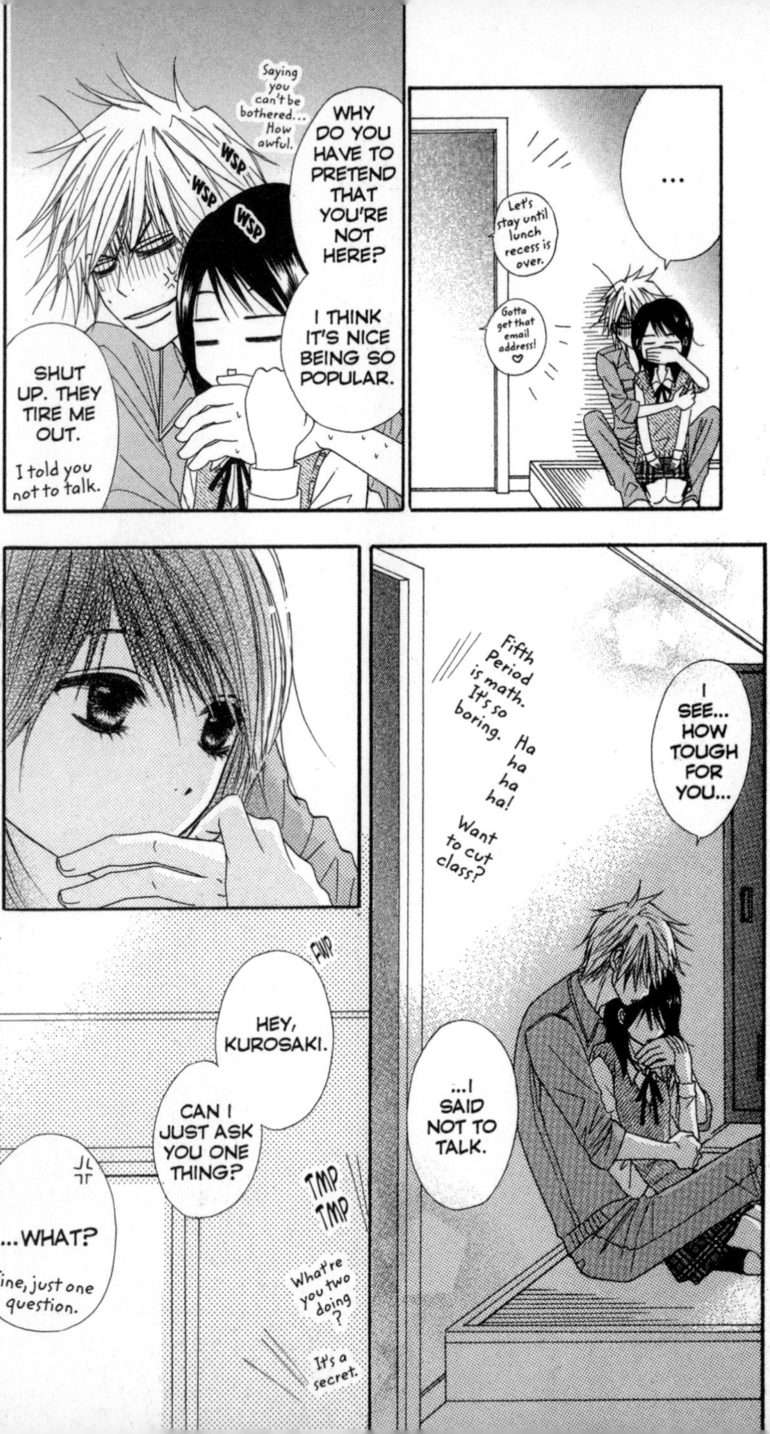
...
Let's stay until lunch recess is over.
Gotta get that email address! ♡
Saying you can't be bothered... How awful.
WHY DO YOU HAVE TO PRETEND THAT YOU'RE NOT HERE?
WSP
WSP
WSP
I THINK IT'S NICE BEING SO POPULAR.
SHUT UP. THEY TIRE ME OUT.
I told you not to talk.
Fifth Period is math. It's so boring.
Ha ha ha ha!
Want to cut class?
I SEE... HOW TOUGH FOR YOU...
...I SAID NOT TO TALK.
FWIP
HEY, KUROSAKI.
CAN I JUST ASK YOU ONE THING?
TMP TMP
What're you two doing?
It's a secret.
...WHAT?
Fine, just one question.

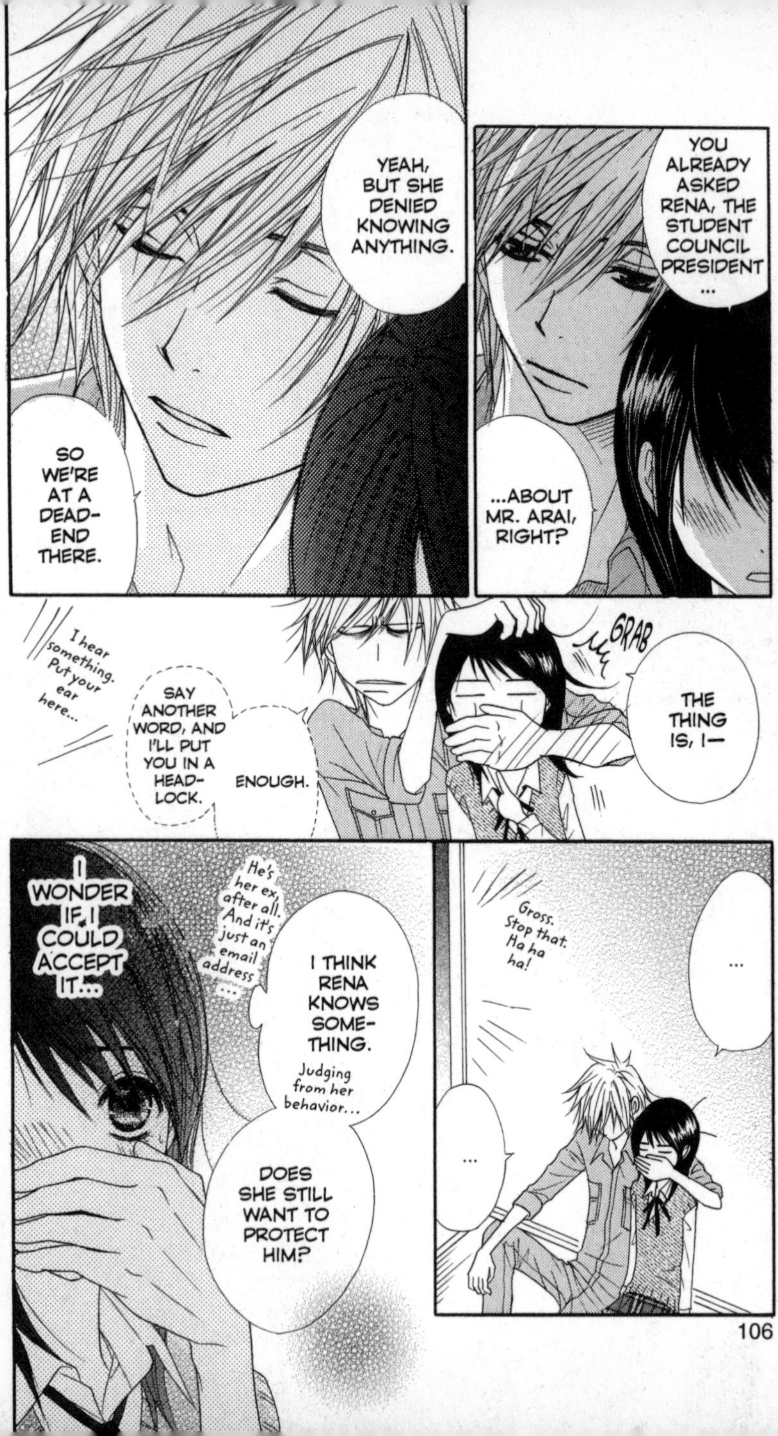
YOU ALREADY ASKED RENA, THE STUDENT COUNCIL PRESIDENT...
...ABOUT MR. ARAI, RIGHT?
YEAH, BUT SHE DENIED KNOWING ANYTHING.
SO WE'RE AT A DEAD-END THERE.
GRAB
THE THING IS, I—
ENOUGH.
SAY ANOTHER WORD, AND I'LL PUT YOU IN A HEADLOCK.
I hear something. Put your ear here...
...
Gross. Stop that. Ha ha ha!
...
I THINK RENA KNOWS SOME-THING.
Judging from her behavior...
He's her ex, after all. And it's just an email address...
DOES SHE STILL WANT TO PROTECT HIM?
I WONDER IF I COULD ACCEPT IT...

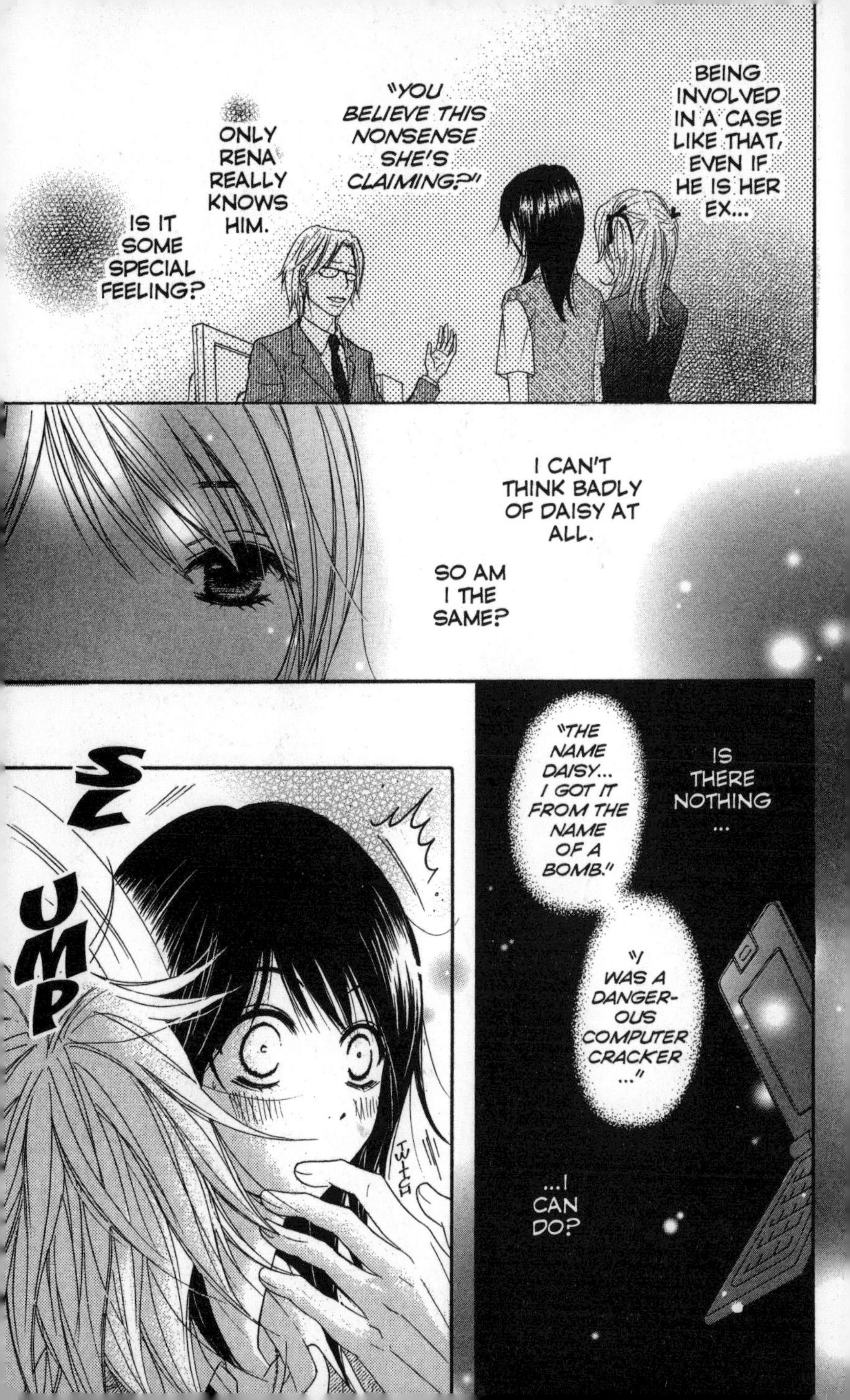
BEING INVOLVED IN A CASE LIKE THAT, EVEN IF HE IS HER EX...
"YOU BELIEVE THIS NONSENSE SHE'S CLAIMING?"
ONLY RENA REALLY KNOWS HIM.
IS IT SOME SPECIAL FEELING?
I CAN'T THINK BADLY OF DAISY AT ALL.
SO AM I THE SAME?
IS THERE NOTHING ...
"THE NAME DAISY... I GOT IT FROM THE NAME OF A BOMB."
"I WAS A DANGER-OUS COMPUTER CRACKER ..."
...I CAN DO?
SLUMP
TWITCH

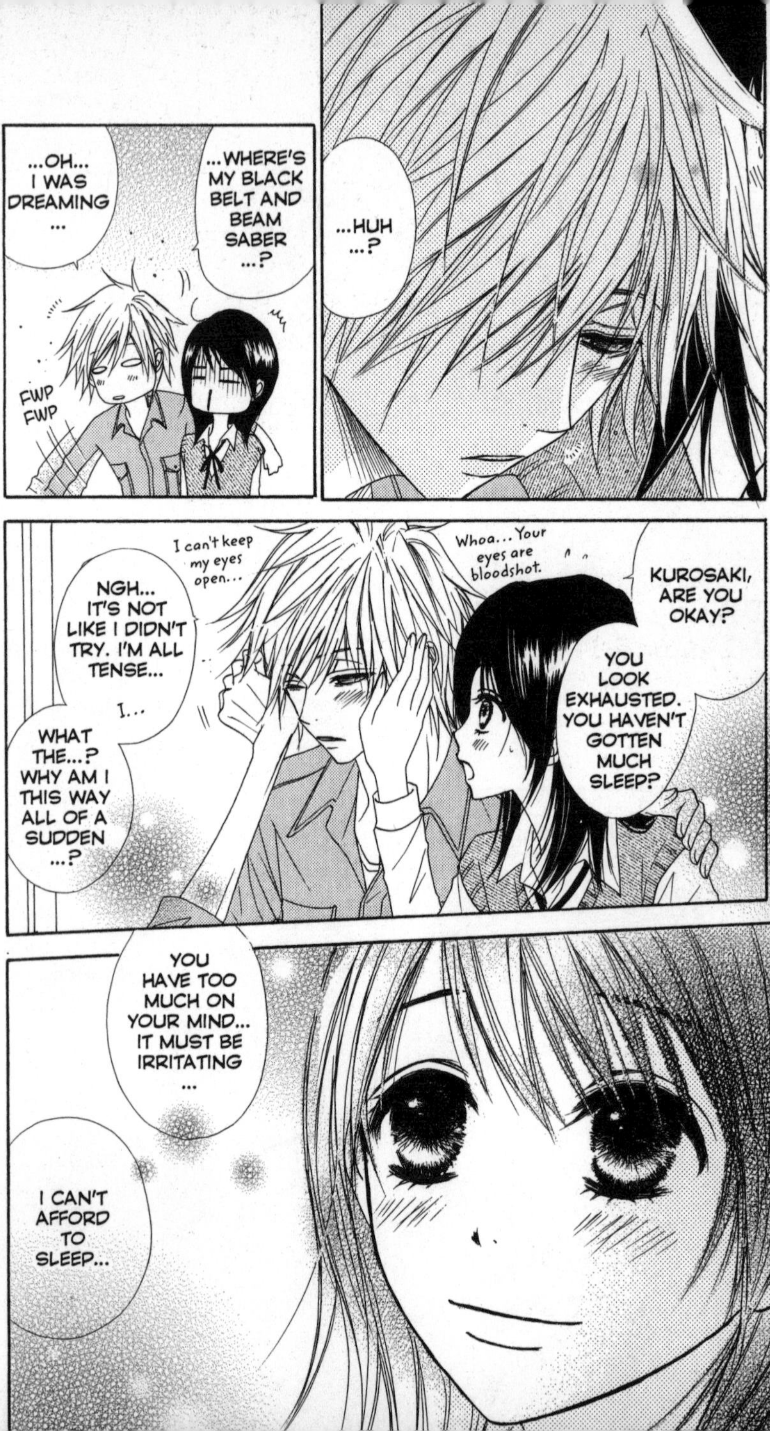
...HUH ...?
...WHERE'S MY BLACK BELT AND BEAM SABER ...?
...OH... I WAS DREAMING ...
FWP FWP
KUROSAKI, ARE YOU OKAY?
YOU LOOK EXHAUSTED. YOU HAVEN'T GOTTEN MUCH SLEEP?
Whoa... Your eyes are bloodshot.
I can't keep my eyes open...
NGH... IT'S NOT LIKE I DIDN'T TRY. I'M ALL TENSE...
I...
WHAT THE...? WHY AM I THIS WAY ALL OF A SUDDEN ...?
YOU HAVE TOO MUCH ON YOUR MIND... IT MUST BE IRRITATING ...
I CAN'T AFFORD TO SLEEP...

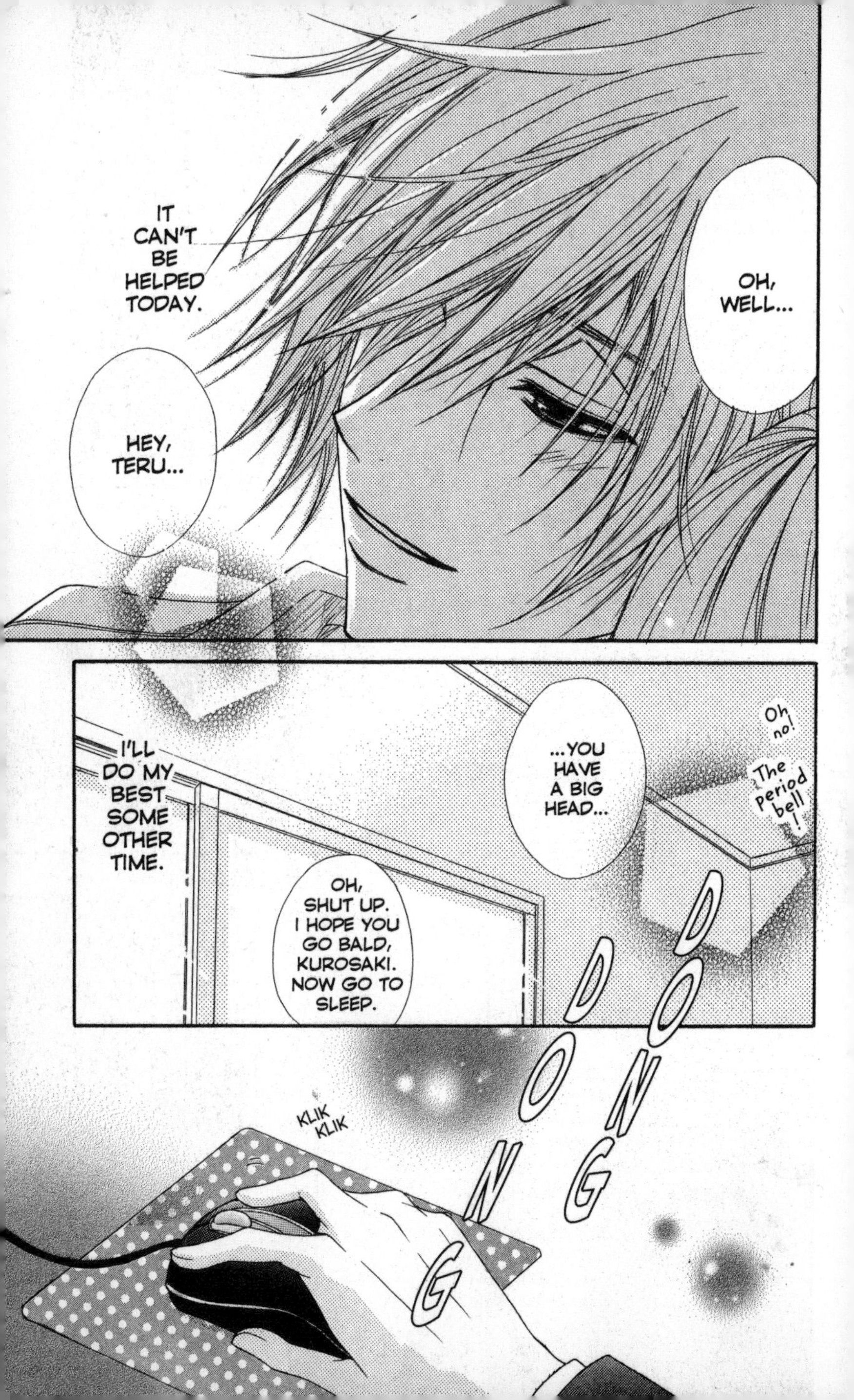
OH, WELL...
IT CAN'T BE HELPED TODAY.
HEY, TERU...
Oh no! The period bell!
...YOU HAVE A BIG HEAD...
OH, SHUT UP. I HOPE YOU GO BALD, KUROSAKI. NOW GO TO SLEEP.
I'LL DO MY BEST SOME OTHER TIME.
DONG
DONG
KLIK KLIK

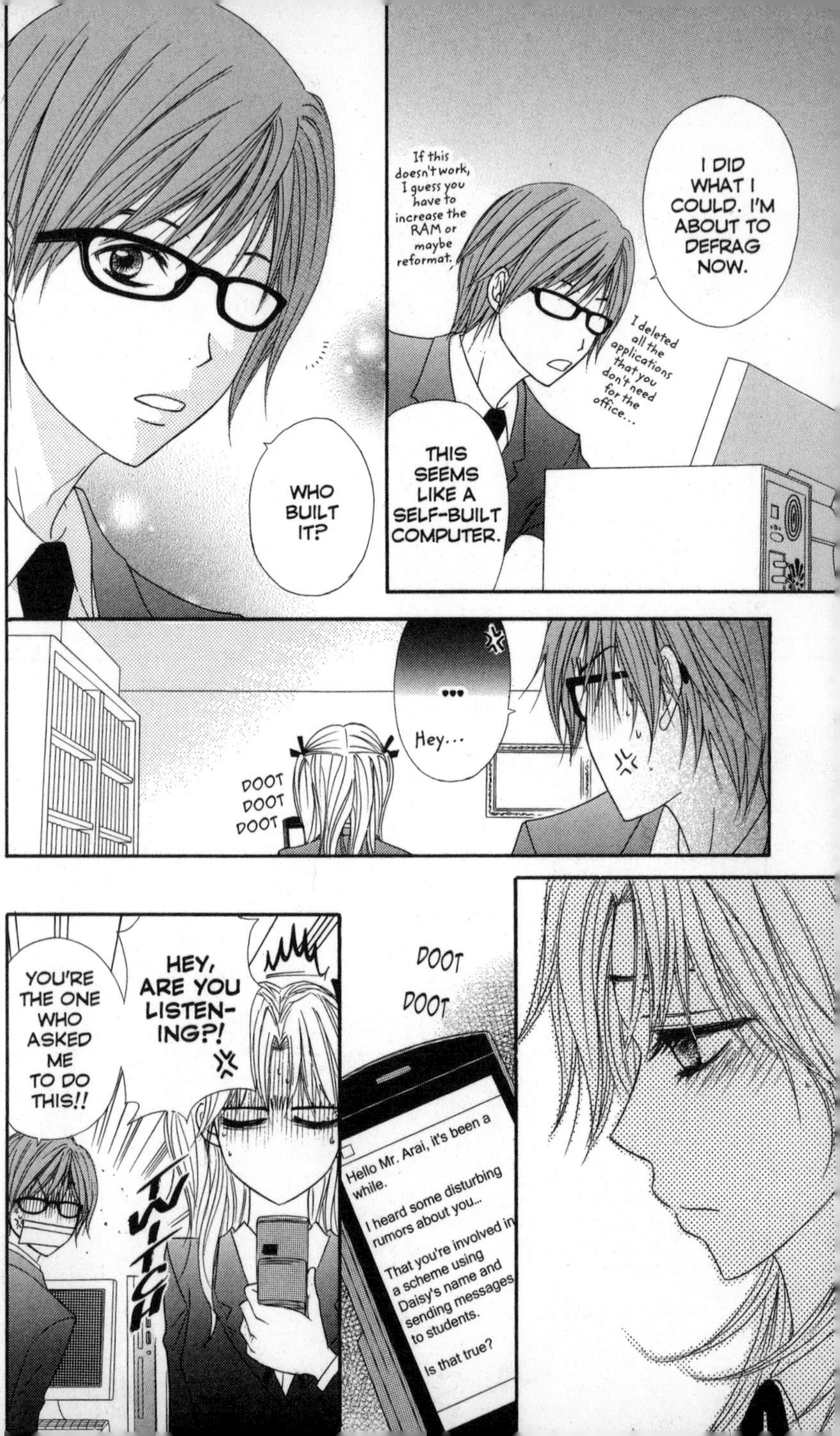
I DID WHAT I COULD. I'M ABOUT TO DEFRAG NOW.
If this doesn't work, I guess you have to increase the RAM or maybe reformat.
I deleted all the applications that you don't need for the office...
THIS SEEMS LIKE A SELF-BUILT COMPUTER.
WHO BUILT IT?
...
Hey...
DOOT DOOT DOOT
DOOT DOOT
Hello Mr. Arai, it's been a while.
I heard some disturbing rumors about you...
That you're involved in a scheme using Daisy's name and sending messages to students.
Is that true?
HEY, ARE YOU LISTENING?!
YOU'RE THE ONE WHO ASKED ME TO DO THIS!!
TWITCH

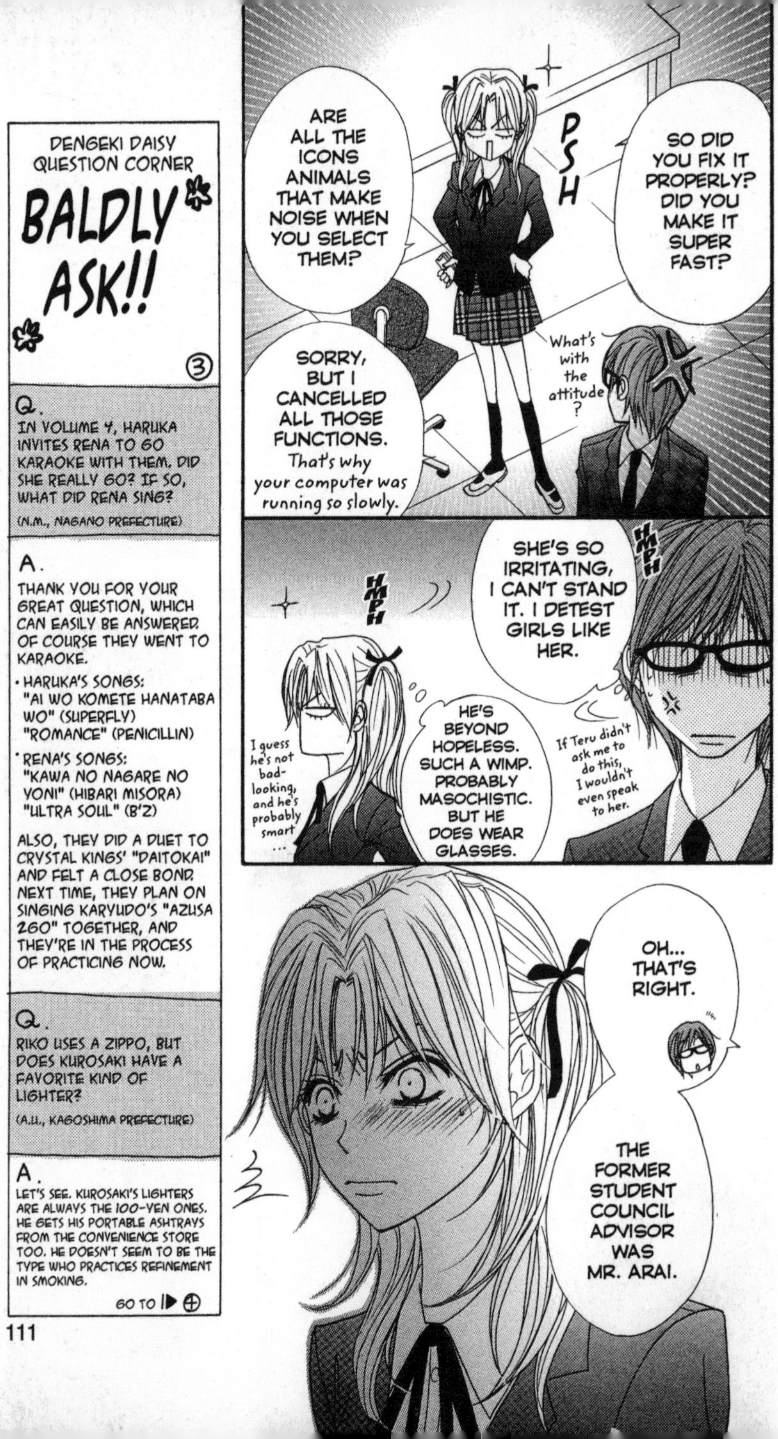
SO DID YOU FIX IT PROPERLY? DID YOU MAKE IT SUPER FAST?
PSH
ARE ALL THE ICONS ANIMALS THAT MAKE NOISE WHEN YOU SELECT THEM?
What's with the attitude?
SORRY, BUT I CANCELLED ALL THOSE FUNCTIONS. That's why your computer was running so slowly.
HMPH
SHE'S SO IRRITATING, I CAN'T STAND IT. I DETEST GIRLS LIKE HER.
If Teru didn't ask me to do this, I wouldn't even speak to her.
HMPH
HE'S BEYOND HOPELESS. SUCH A WIMP. PROBABLY MASOCHISTIC. BUT HE DOES WEAR GLASSES.
I guess he's not bad-looking, and he's probably smart...
OH... THAT'S RIGHT.
THE FORMER STUDENT COUNCIL ADVISOR WAS MR. ARAI.

DENGEKI DAISY QUESTION CORNER

BALDLY ASK!!

③

Q.

IN VOLUME 4, HARUKA INVITES RENA TO GO KARAOKE WITH THEM. DID SHE REALLY GO? IF SO, WHAT DID RENA SING?

(N.M., NAGANO PREFECTURE)

A.

THANK YOU FOR YOUR GREAT QUESTION, WHICH CAN EASILY BE ANSWERED. OF COURSE THEY WENT TO KARAOKE.

- HARUKA'S SONGS: "AI WO KOMETE HANATABA WO" (SUPERFLY) "ROMANCE" (PENICILLIN)
- RENA'S SONGS: "KAWA NO NAGARE NO YONI" (HIBARI MISORA) "ULTRA SOUL" (B'Z)

ALSO, THEY DID A DUET TO CRYSTAL KINGS' "DAITOKAI" AND FELT A CLOSE BOND. NEXT TIME, THEY PLAN ON SINGING KARYUDO'S "AZUSA 2GO" TOGETHER, AND THEY'RE IN THE PROCESS OF PRACTICING NOW.

Q.

RIKO USES A ZIPPO, BUT DOES KUROSAKI HAVE A FAVORITE KIND OF LIGHTER?

(A.U., KAGOSHIMA PREFECTURE)

A.

LET'S SEE. KUROSAKI'S LIGHTERS ARE ALWAYS THE 100-YEN ONES. HE GETS HIS PORTABLE ASHTRAYS FROM THE CONVENIENCE STORE TOO. HE DOESN'T SEEM TO BE THE TYPE WHO PRACTICES REFINEMENT IN SMOKING.

GO TO ▶ ④

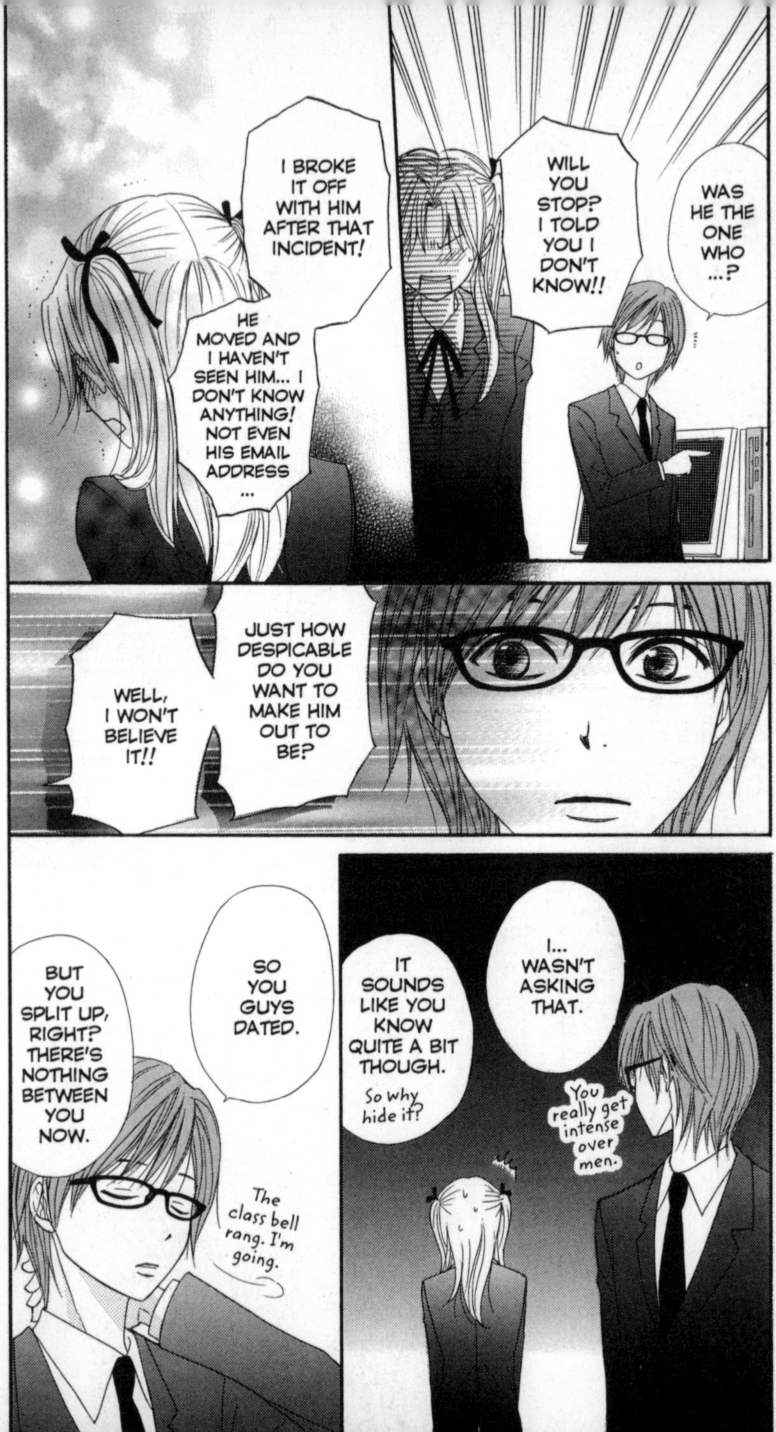
WAS HE THE ONE WHO ...?
WILL YOU STOP? I TOLD YOU I DON'T KNOW!!
I BROKE IT OFF WITH HIM AFTER THAT INCIDENT!
HE MOVED AND I HAVEN'T SEEN HIM... I DON'T KNOW ANYTHING! NOT EVEN HIS EMAIL ADDRESS ...
JUST HOW DESPICABLE DO YOU WANT TO MAKE HIM OUT TO BE?
WELL, I WON'T BELIEVE IT!!
I... WASN'T ASKING THAT.
You really get intense over men.
IT SOUNDS LIKE YOU KNOW QUITE A BIT THOUGH.
So why hide it?
SO YOU GUYS DATED.
BUT YOU SPLIT UP, RIGHT? THERE'S NOTHING BETWEEN YOU NOW.
The class bell rang. I'm going.

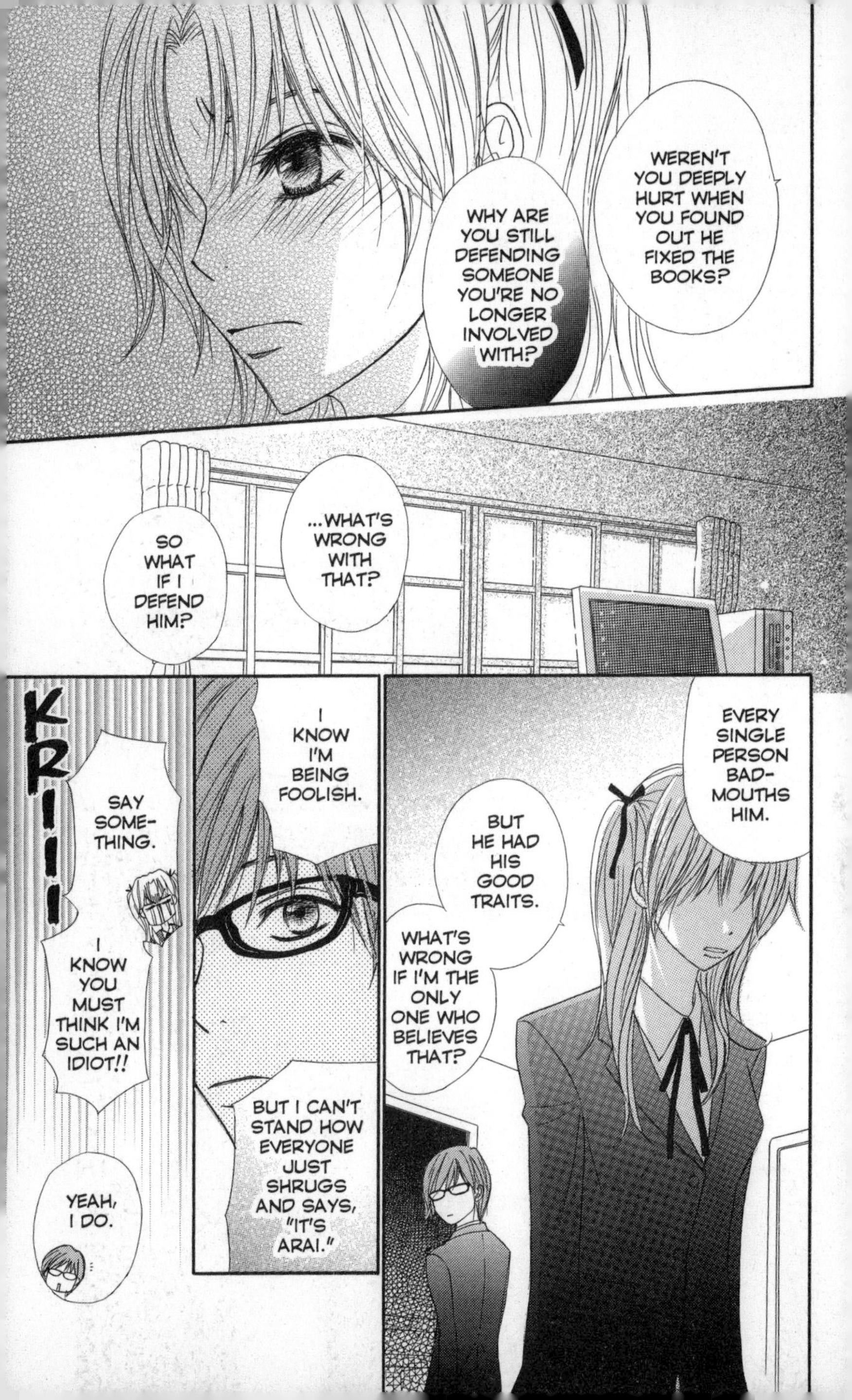
WEREN'T YOU DEEPLY HURT WHEN YOU FOUND OUT HE FIXED THE BOOKS?
WHY ARE YOU STILL DEFENDING SOMEONE YOU'RE NO LONGER INVOLVED WITH?
...WHAT'S WRONG WITH THAT?
SO WHAT IF I DEFEND HIM?
EVERY SINGLE PERSON BAD-MOUTHS HIM.
BUT HE HAD HIS GOOD TRAITS.
WHAT'S WRONG IF I'M THE ONLY ONE WHO BELIEVES THAT?
I KNOW I'M BEING FOOLISH.
BUT I CAN'T STAND HOW EVERYONE JUST SHRUGS AND SAYS, "IT'S ARAI."
KRIII
SAY SOME-THING.
I KNOW YOU MUST THINK I'M SUCH AN IDIOT!!
YEAH, I DO.

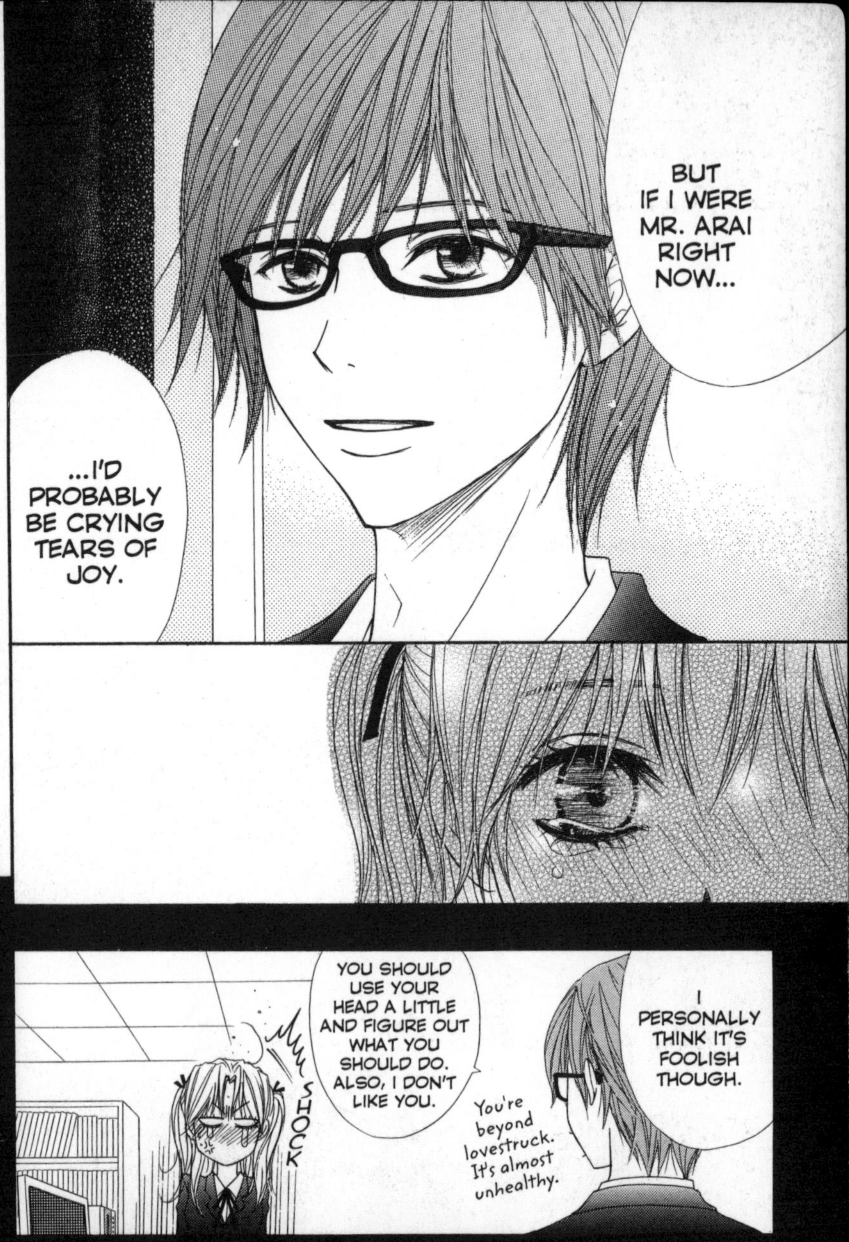
BUT IF I WERE MR. ARAI RIGHT NOW...
...I'D PROBABLY BE CRYING TEARS OF JOY.
I PERSONALLY THINK IT'S FOOLISH THOUGH.
You're beyond lovestruck. It's almost unhealthy.
YOU SHOULD USE YOUR HEAD A LITTLE AND FIGURE OUT WHAT YOU SHOULD DO. ALSO, I DON'T LIKE YOU.
SHOCK

THINGS ARE STARTING TO MOVE...

I GUESS I SHOULD CALL HIM.

Since I'm his servant.

Kurosaki
090-XXXXXXX

IT'S SOMEWHAT RELATED TO THE CASE.

...?

He's not answering...

PLEASE LET ME BE OF SOME HELP.

Tetsuya Arai
It's Rena

Hello Mr. Arai, it's been a while.

I heard some disturbing rumors about you...

That you're involved in scheme using ...sy's name and ...ing messa...

Tetsuya Arai
It's Rena

Delete mail?

Yes
No
Save

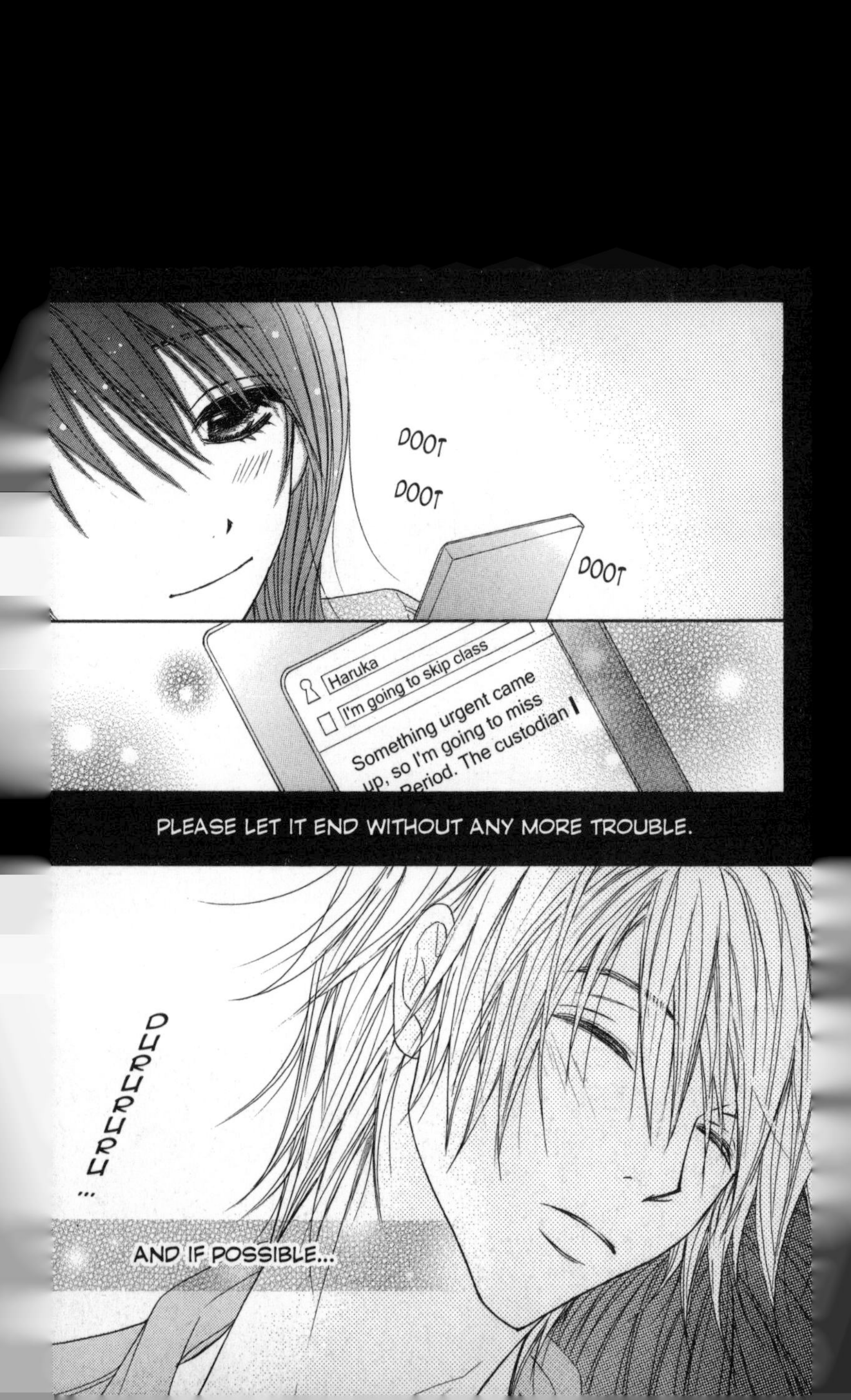
DOOT
DOOT
DOOT
Haruka
I'm going to skip class
Something urgent came up, so I'm going to miss
Period. The custodian
PLEASE LET IT END WITHOUT ANY MORE TROUBLE.
DURURURU...
AND IF POSSIBLE...

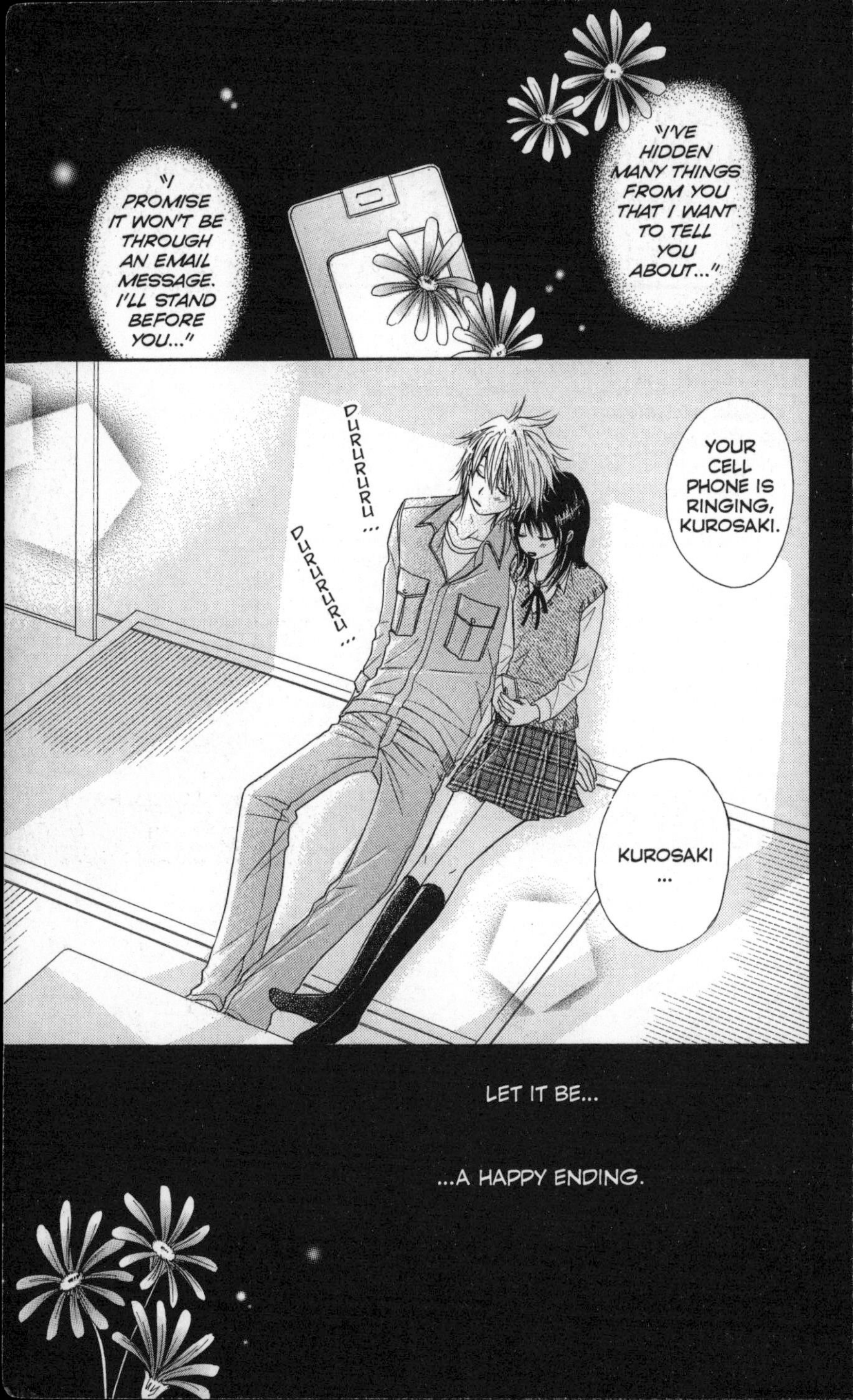
"I'VE HIDDEN MANY THINGS FROM YOU THAT I WANT TO TELL YOU ABOUT..."
"I PROMISE IT WON'T BE THROUGH AN EMAIL MESSAGE. I'LL STAND BEFORE YOU..."
YOUR CELL PHONE IS RINGING, KUROSAKI.
DURURURU...
DURURURU...
KUROSAKI...
LET IT BE...
...A HAPPY ENDING.

PROBABLY A SUPER POPULAR SECTION

DENGEKI DAISY
COMMENTS FROM THE LAST PAGE THAT CANNOT BE MISSED

~ THANK YOU, GENIUS K-TANI ~

ON THE LAST PAGE OF THE CHAPTER SERIALIZATIONS IN *BETSUCOMI*, THERE ARE CAPTIONS NEXT TO THE "TO BE CONTINUED IN..." LINE THAT WRAP UP THE CHAPTER AND GIVE HINTS TO THE UPCOMING CHAPTER. THE SHARP EDITOR WHO OVERSAW THIS PAGE, K-TANI, ALSO KNOWN AS THE GENIUS OF BA◯◯BON, IS SADLY, AND UNBELIEVABLY, BEING TRANSFERRED TO ANOTHER DEPARTMENT.
AND SO, IN THIS VOLUME, WE PRESENT K-TANI'S LAST BRILLIANT WORK ~~THAT WAS REJECTED.~~ SO LONG, K-TANI...!!!

CH. 20	THE UNFINISHED KISS WITH THE "SCALLION"... DON'T LOSE HEART, KUROSAKI. YOU'LL BE ON THE COVER IN THE NEXT ISSUE. STAY STRONG!		"STAY STRONG!" YOU SAY...? (IF YOU ROUND UP HIS AGE, K-TANI IS A 30-YEAR-OLD MALE. HE'S A SUPER FOOL WHO THINKS HE LOOKS LIKE KEN SATO.)
CH. 21	WE'LL CLEAN KUROSAKI'S TARNISHED IMAGE AS "MR. COWARD." WHAT WILL BE HIS NEXT MOVE?! NEXT TIME : CONFESSION TIME?!		SO WHAT DOES "CONFESSION TIME" MEAN? DID YOU THINK THIS WOULD TITILLATE THE READERS OF *BETSUCOMI*? ALTHOUGH IT DID FOR ME.
CH. 22	I MAY ACT LIKE A NIGHTCLUB HOST, BUT MY HEART BELONGS TO ONLY ONE PERSON. ♡		THIS IS A CUTE AND PITHY CAPTION FOR K-TANI, BUT THERE'S NOT EVEN A HINT OF WHAT'S TO COME IN THE NEXT CHAPTER.
CH. 23	IF TERU WAS ASLEEP, RIGHT NOW...?! NEXT TIME : DON'T TAKE YOUR EYES OFF KUROSAKI!	REJECTED	THINKING BACK, THE FACT THAT KUROSAKI APPEARS MORE LIKE A PERVERT THAN I MAKE HIM OUT TO BE IS THANKS TO THE GOOD JOB K-TANI DOES.
CH. 24	TO PROTECT TERU'S SMILE. GO! KUROPANMAN!!	REJECTED	...TO THINK THIS WAS HIS LAST PIECE OF WORK... ...AND TO THINK THAT IT WAS REJECTED...

K-TANI'S ODD JOBS WILL NOW BE IN THE CAPABLE HANDS OF HIS SUPERIOR WHO MENTORED HIM, ITO-U (THE WIZ WHO SUDDENLY STOOD UP IN THE MIDDLE OF AN ALL-NIGHTER AT THE OFFICE AND BEGAN PLAYING IMAGINARY CATCH WITH AN IMAGINARY AYA UETO). PLEASE REST ASSURED THAT HIS BA◯◯BON SKILL LEVEL WILL BE HIGHER AND THAT IT WON'T BE LOWER. PLEASE CHECK OUT "THE SECRET SCHOOL CUSTODIAN OFFICE" FAN PAGE IN *BETSUCOMI*. YOU WON'T BELIEVE THE DEGREE OF DIFFERENCE FROM THE OTHER FAN PAGES.

CHAPTER 23: LOSING SOMETHING IN ORDER TO PROTECT IT

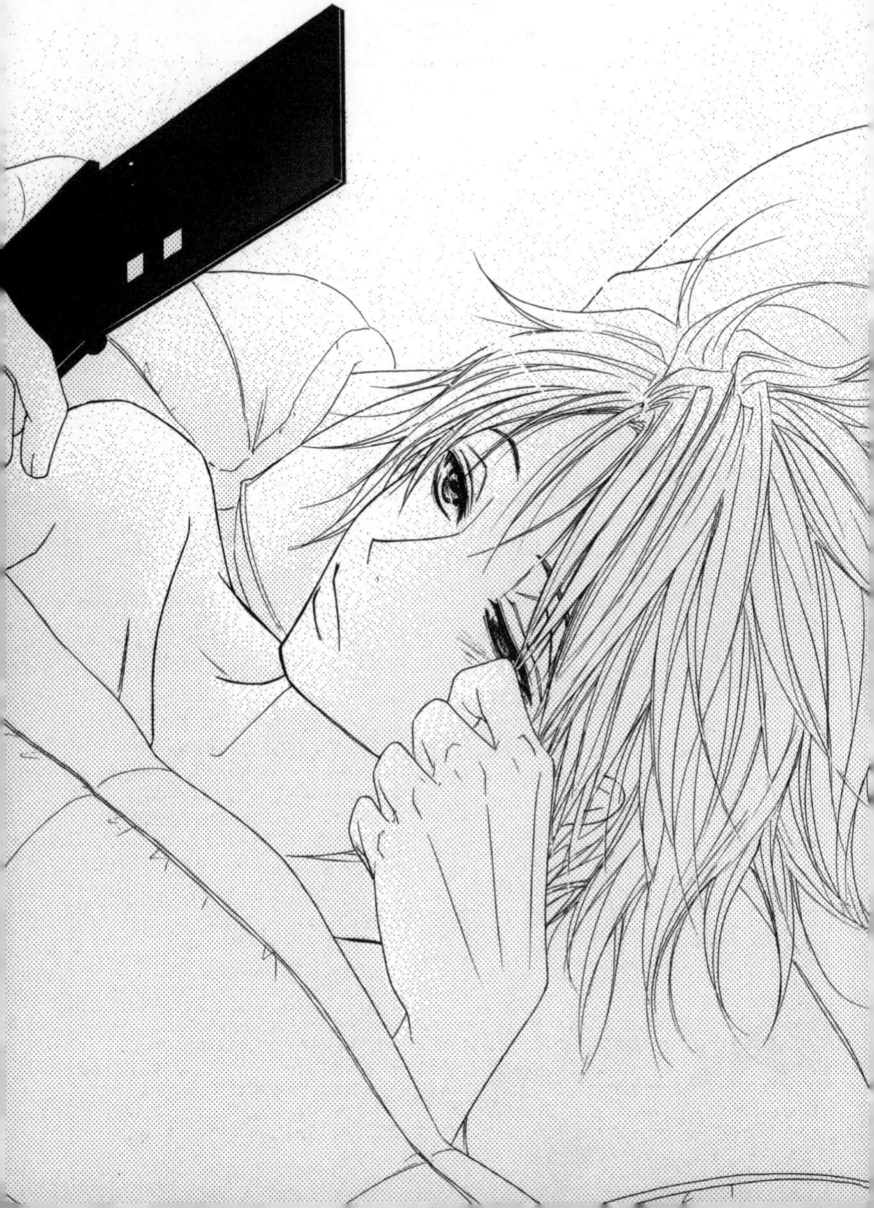

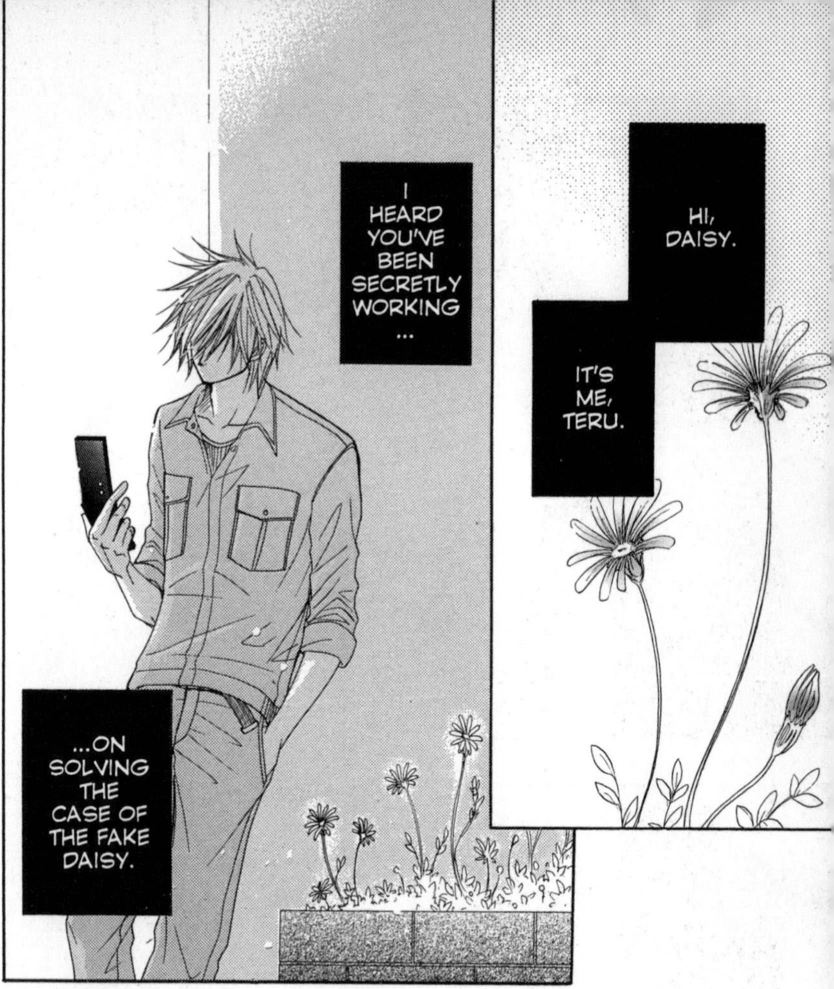
HI, DAISY.
IT'S ME, TERU.
I HEARD YOU'VE BEEN SECRETLY WORKING...
...ON SOLVING THE CASE OF THE FAKE DAISY.

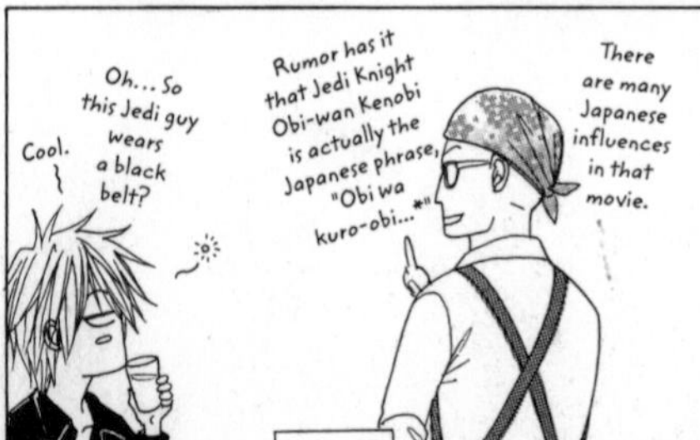
There are many Japanese influences in that movie.
Rumor has it that Jedi Knight Obi-wan Kenobi is actually the Japanese phrase, "Obi wa kuro-obi...*"
Oh... So this Jedi guy wears a black belt?
Cool.

IN CHAPTER 22, KUROSAKI TALKS WHILE HE'S STILL HALF-ASLEEP. (HE SAYS, "WHERE'S MY BLACK BELT AND BEAM SABER...?") KUROSAKI ISN'T FAMILIAR WITH STAR WAR● AND WAS DREAMING ABOUT SOMETHING AKIN TO IT... I REALIZED THAT I TOTALLY MESSED UP THE WORDS AND THAT READERS MAY HAVE GOTTEN CONFUSED.

"BEAM SABER" SHOULD HAVE BEEN "LIGHT SABER." "BEAM SABER" IS FROM GUN●M. IT SEEMS THAT THIS AUTHOR IS JUST AS IGNORANT AS KUROSAKI (ABOUT SW AND GUNDAM). MY APOLOGIES.

*Translates to "My belt is a black belt."

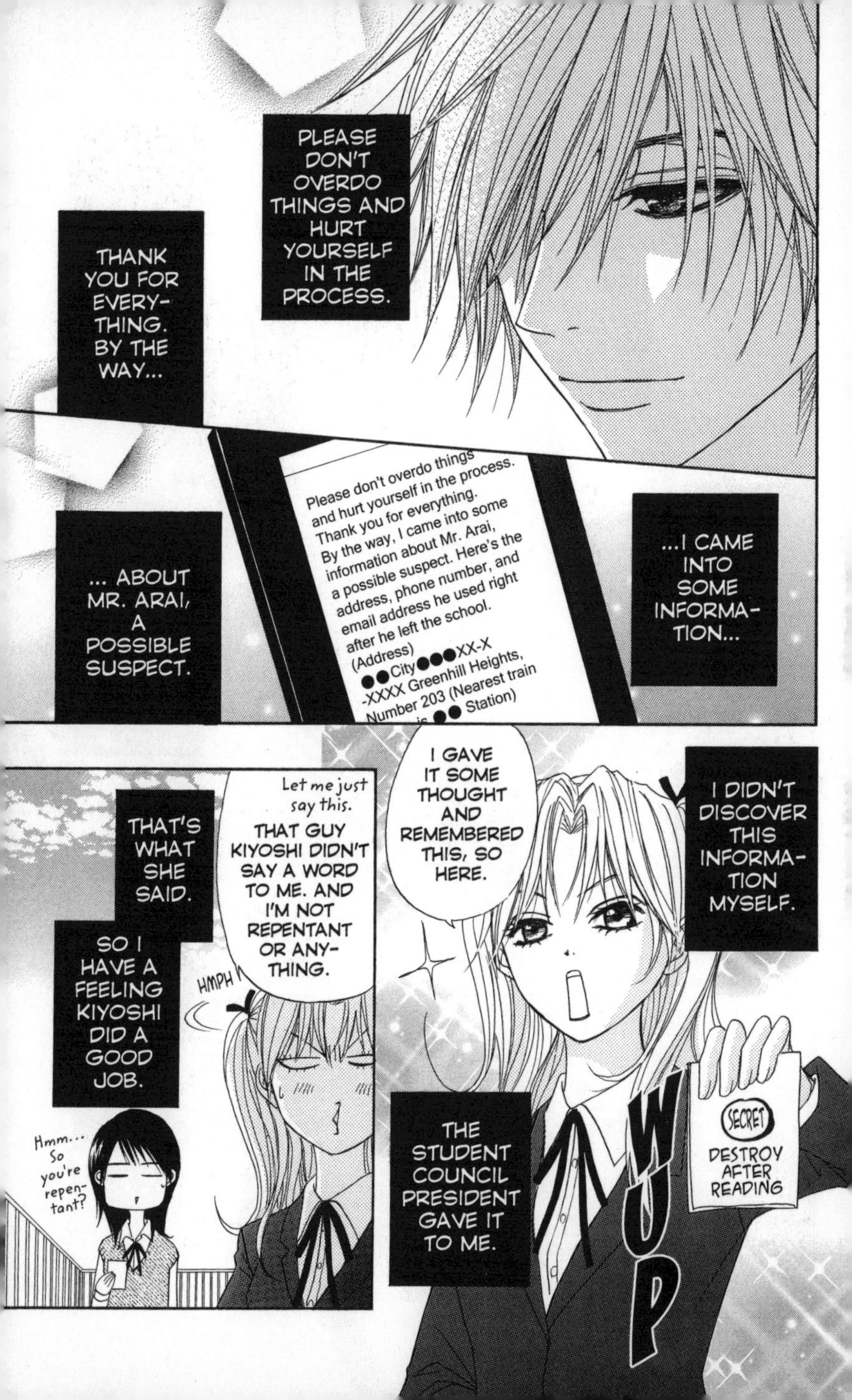

PLEASE DON'T OVERDO THINGS AND HURT YOURSELF IN THE PROCESS.
THANK YOU FOR EVERY-THING. BY THE WAY...
...I CAME INTO SOME INFORMA-TION...
Please don't overdo things and hurt yourself in the process. Thank you for everything. By the way, I came into some information about Mr. Arai, a possible suspect. Here's the address, phone number, and email address he used right after he left the school.
(Address)
●●City●●●XX-X
-XXXX Greenhill Heights,
Number 203 (Nearest train
●● Station)
... ABOUT MR. ARAI, A POSSIBLE SUSPECT.
I DIDN'T DISCOVER THIS INFORMA-TION MYSELF.
I GAVE IT SOME THOUGHT AND REMEMBERED THIS, SO HERE.
THE STUDENT COUNCIL PRESIDENT GAVE IT TO ME.
WUP
SECRET
DESTROY AFTER READING
Let me just say this.
THAT GUY KIYOSHI DIDN'T SAY A WORD TO ME. AND I'M NOT REPENTANT OR ANY-THING.
HMPH
THAT'S WHAT SHE SAID.
SO I HAVE A FEELING KIYOSHI DID A GOOD JOB.
Hmm... So you're repen-tant?

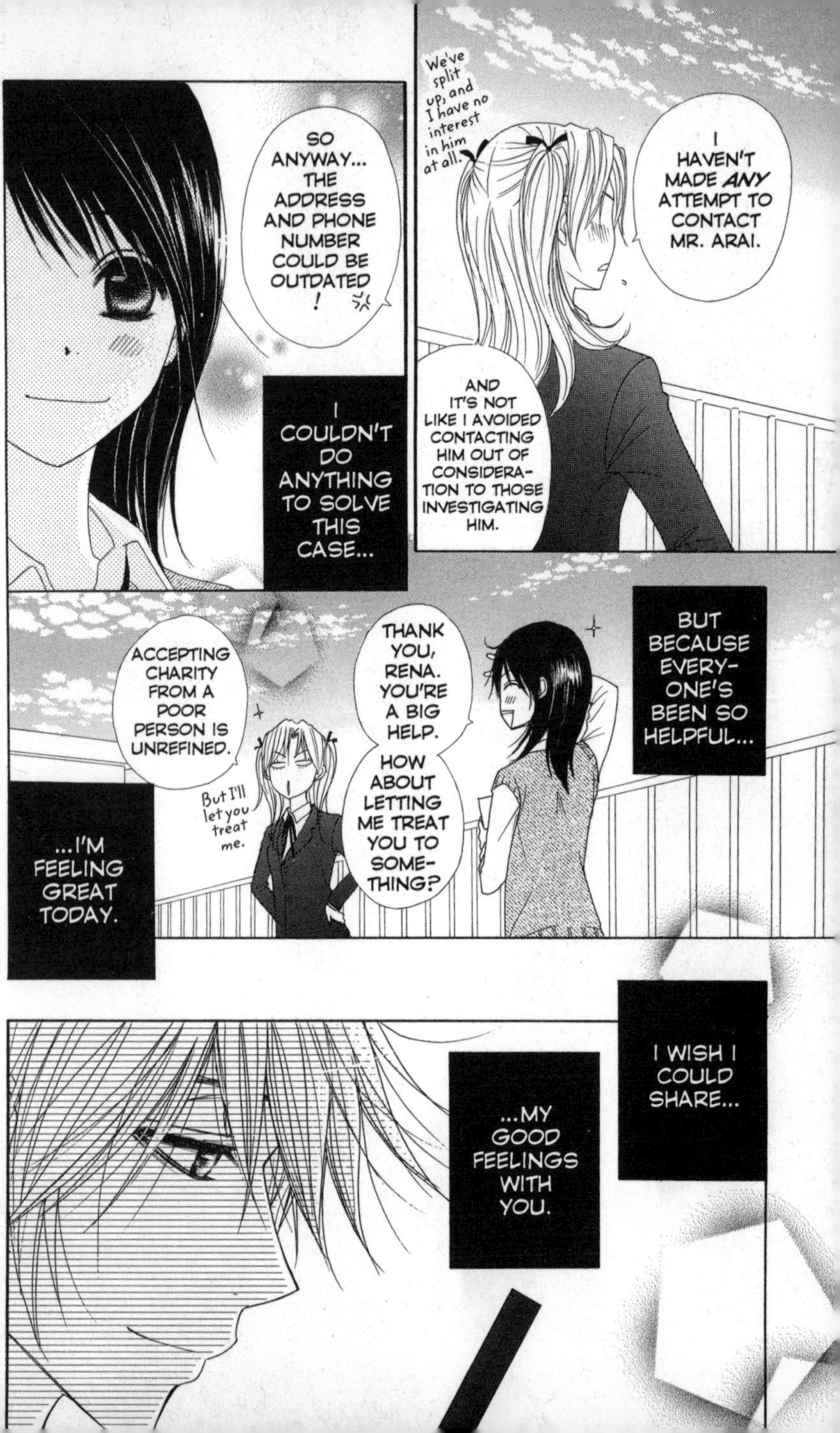
I HAVEN'T MADE ANY ATTEMPT TO CONTACT MR. ARAI.
We've split up, and I have no interest in him at all.
AND IT'S NOT LIKE I AVOIDED CONTACTING HIM OUT OF CONSIDERATION TO THOSE INVESTIGATING HIM.
SO ANYWAY... THE ADDRESS AND PHONE NUMBER COULD BE OUTDATED!
I COULDN'T DO ANYTHING TO SOLVE THIS CASE...
BUT BECAUSE EVERYONE'S BEEN SO HELPFUL...
THANK YOU, RENA. YOU'RE A BIG HELP.
HOW ABOUT LETTING ME TREAT YOU TO SOMETHING?
ACCEPTING CHARITY FROM A POOR PERSON IS UNREFINED.
But I'll let you treat me.
...I'M FEELING GREAT TODAY.
I WISH I COULD SHARE...
...MY GOOD FEELINGS WITH YOU.

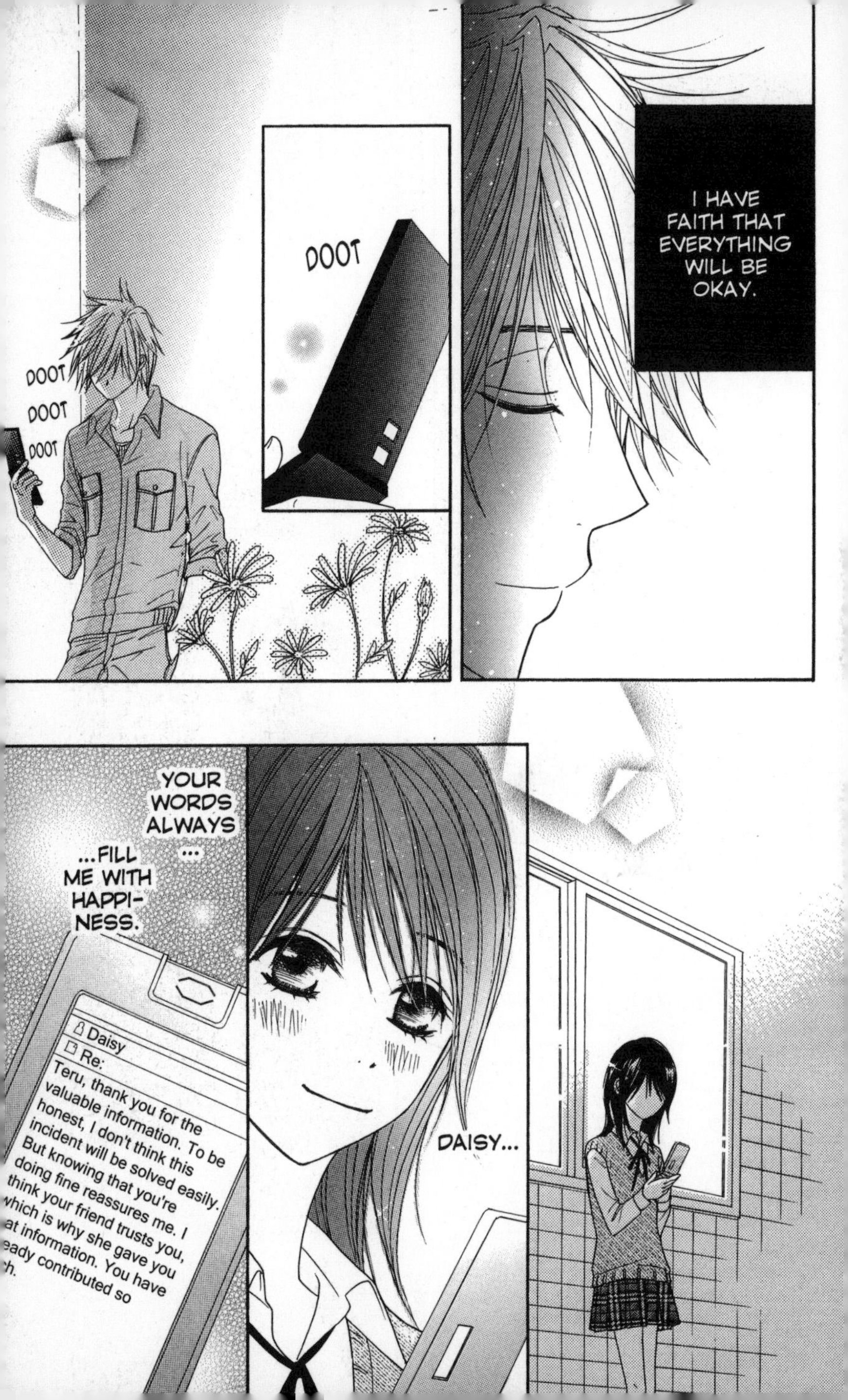
I HAVE FAITH THAT EVERYTHING WILL BE OKAY.
DOOT
DOOT
DOOT
DOOT
DAISY...
YOUR WORDS ALWAYS...
...FILL ME WITH HAPPI-NESS.
Daisy
Re:
Teru, thank you for the
valuable information. To be
honest, I don't think this
incident will be solved easily.
But knowing that you're
doing fine reassures me. I
think your friend trusts you,
which is why she gave you
at information. You have
eady contributed so
ch.

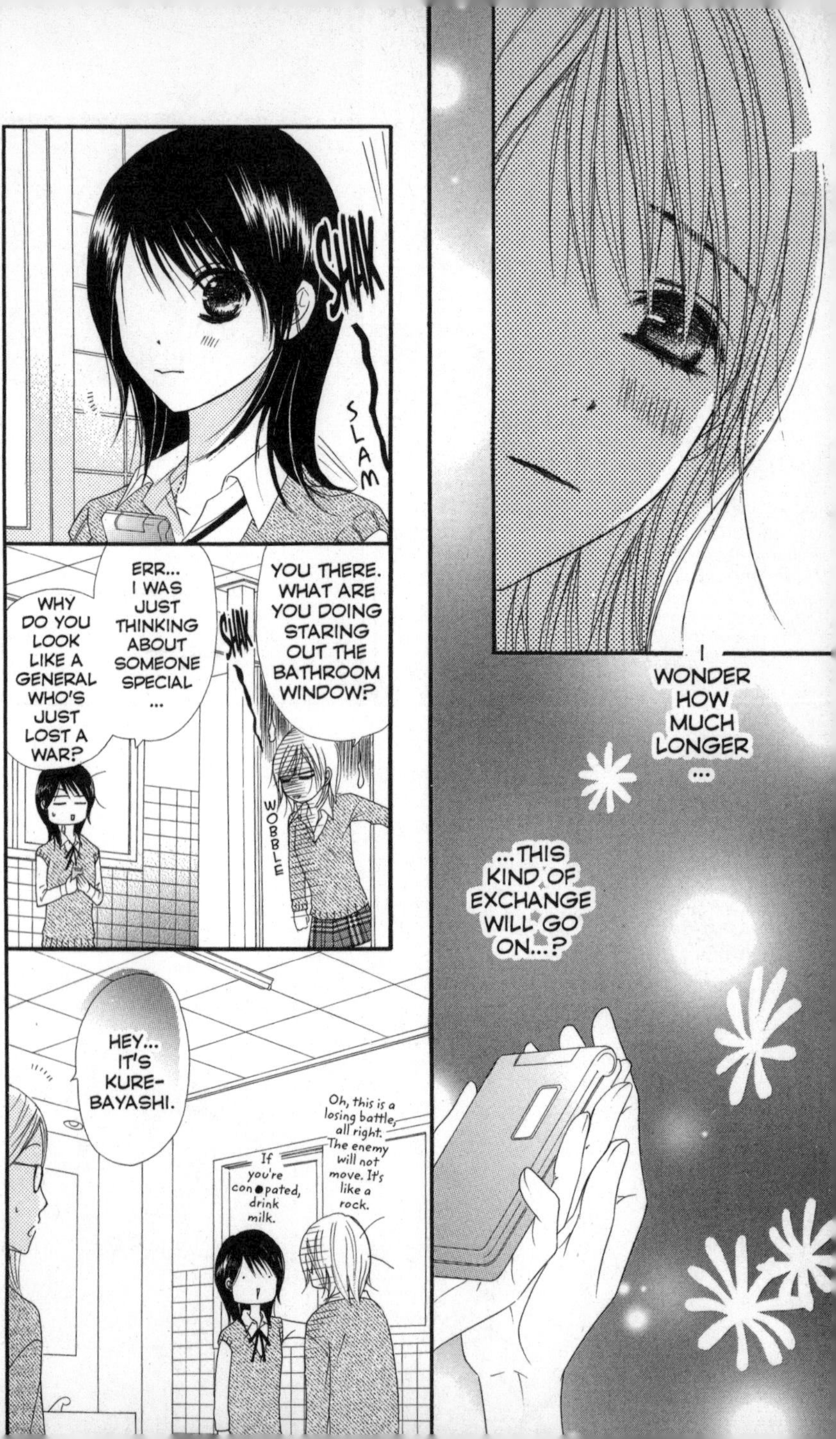
I WONDER HOW MUCH LONGER...
...THIS KIND OF EXCHANGE WILL GO ON...?
SHAK
SLAM
SHAK
YOU THERE. WHAT ARE YOU DOING STARING OUT THE BATHROOM WINDOW?
ERR... I WAS JUST THINKING ABOUT SOMEONE SPECIAL...
WHY DO YOU LOOK LIKE A GENERAL WHO'S JUST LOST A WAR?
WOBBLE
HEY... IT'S KURE-BAYASHI.
Oh, this is a losing battle, all right. The enemy will not move. It's like a rock.
If you're constipated, drink milk.

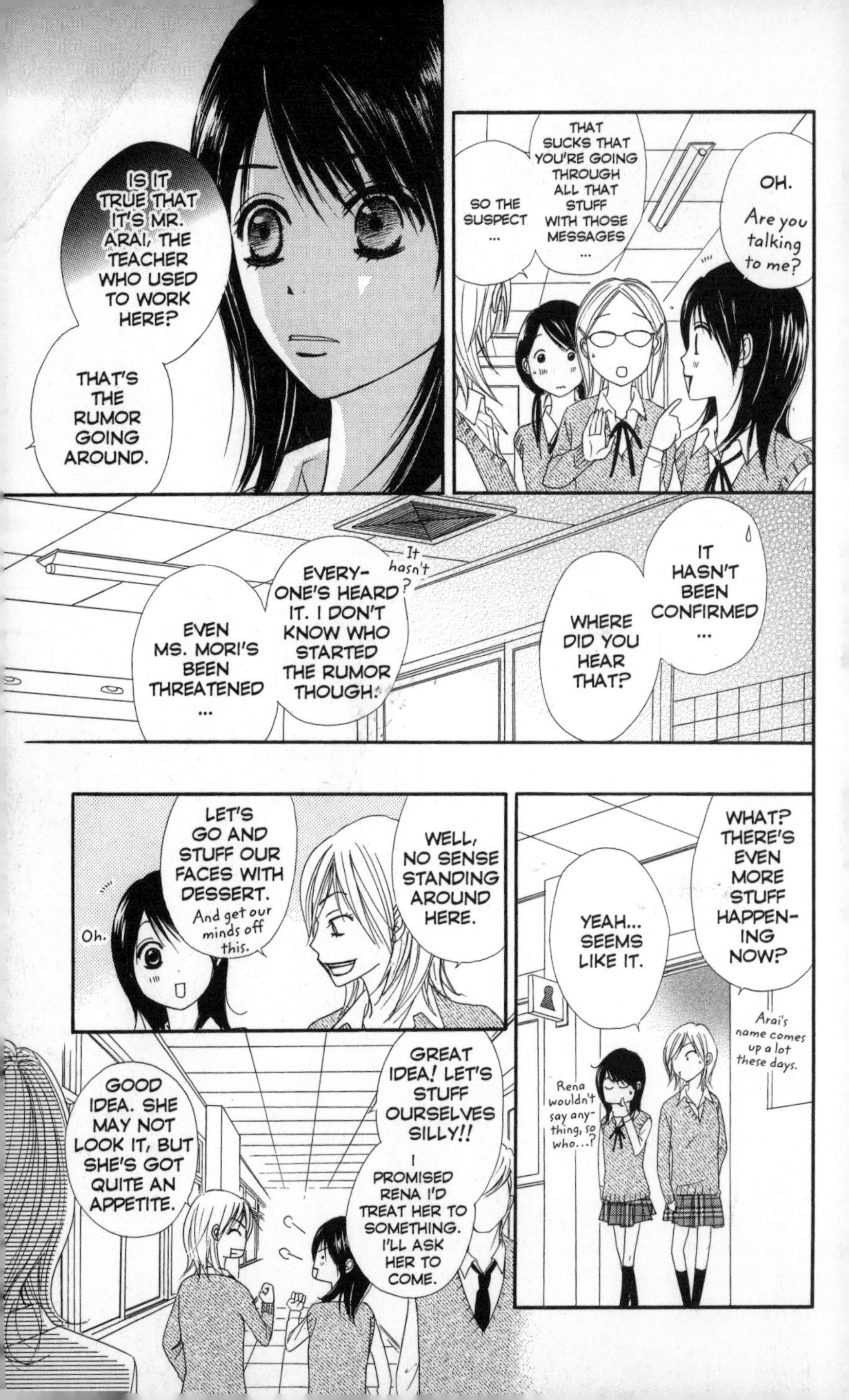
OH.
Are you talking to me?
THAT SUCKS THAT YOU'RE GOING THROUGH ALL THAT STUFF WITH THOSE MESSAGES...
SO THE SUSPECT...
IS IT TRUE THAT IT'S MR. ARAI, THE TEACHER WHO USED TO WORK HERE?
THAT'S THE RUMOR GOING AROUND.
IT HASN'T BEEN CONFIRMED...
WHERE DID YOU HEAR THAT?
It hasn't?
EVERYONE'S HEARD IT. I DON'T KNOW WHO STARTED THE RUMOR THOUGH.
EVEN MS. MORI'S BEEN THREATENED...
WHAT? THERE'S EVEN MORE STUFF HAPPENING NOW?
YEAH... SEEMS LIKE IT.
Arai's name comes up a lot these days.
Rena wouldn't say anything, so who...?
WELL, NO SENSE STANDING AROUND HERE.
LET'S GO AND STUFF OUR FACES WITH DESSERT.
And get our minds off this.
Oh.
GREAT IDEA! LET'S STUFF OURSELVES SILLY!!
I PROMISED RENA I'D TREAT HER TO SOMETHING. I'LL ASK HER TO COME.
GOOD IDEA. SHE MAY NOT LOOK IT, BUT SHE'S GOT QUITE AN APPETITE.

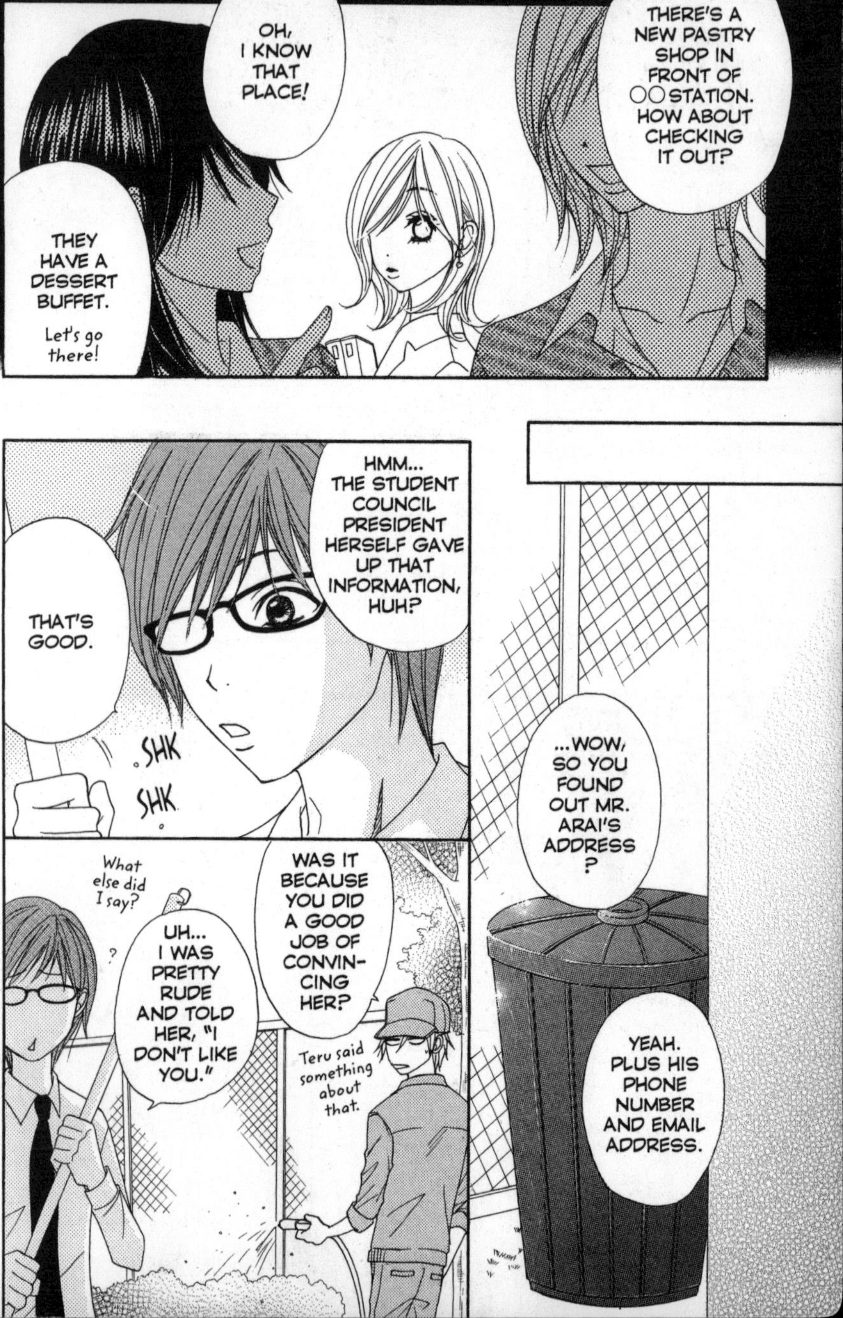
THERE'S A NEW PASTRY SHOP IN FRONT OF ○○STATION. HOW ABOUT CHECKING IT OUT?
OH, I KNOW THAT PLACE!
THEY HAVE A DESSERT BUFFET.
Let's go there!
...WOW, SO YOU FOUND OUT MR. ARAI'S ADDRESS?
YEAH. PLUS HIS PHONE NUMBER AND EMAIL ADDRESS.
HMM... THE STUDENT COUNCIL PRESIDENT HERSELF GAVE UP THAT INFORMATION, HUH?
THAT'S GOOD.
SHK
SHK
WAS IT BECAUSE YOU DID A GOOD JOB OF CONVIN-CING HER?
Teru said something about that.
UH... I WAS PRETTY RUDE AND TOLD HER, "I DON'T LIKE YOU."
What else did I say?
?

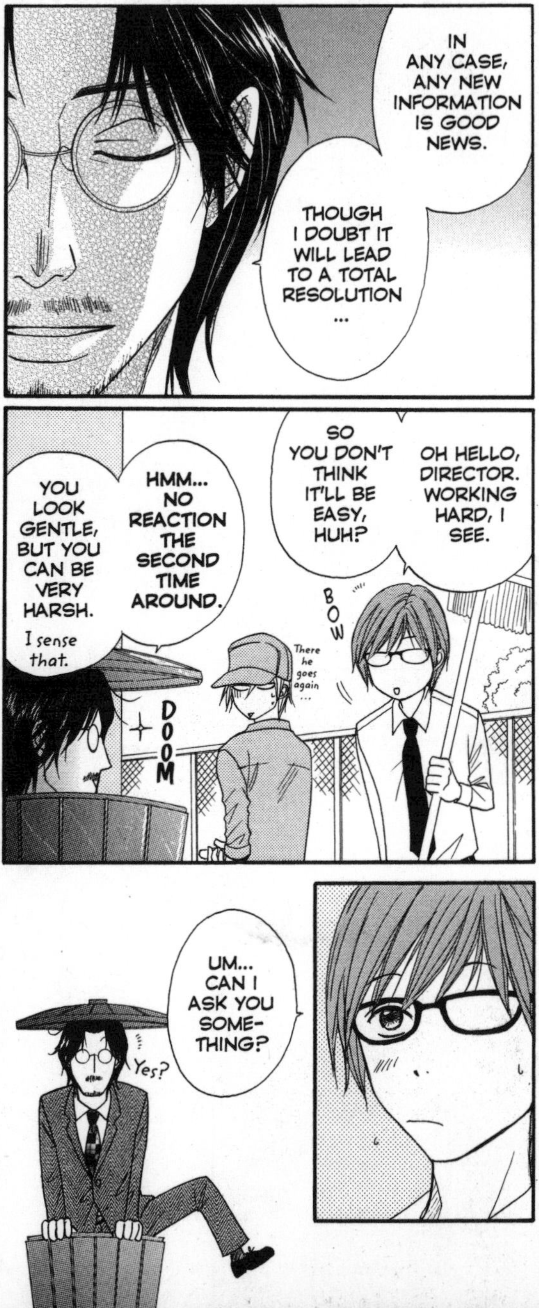
IN ANY CASE, ANY NEW INFORMATION IS GOOD NEWS.
THOUGH I DOUBT IT WILL LEAD TO A TOTAL RESOLUTION ...
OH HELLO, DIRECTOR. WORKING HARD, I SEE.
BOW
SO YOU DON'T THINK IT'LL BE EASY, HUH?
There he goes again ...
HMM... NO REACTION THE SECOND TIME AROUND.
YOU LOOK GENTLE, BUT YOU CAN BE VERY HARSH.
I sense that.
DOOM
UM... CAN I ASK YOU SOMETHING?
Yes?

DENGEKI DAISY QUESTION CORNER

BALDLY ASK!! ④

Q.
I'D LIKE TO KNOW IF TERU OR RIKO HAVE DEADLY OR LETHAL MOVES. SOMETHING THAT MIGHT PLEASE KUROSAKI AND EVEN SOICHIRO.

(H.W., MIYAGI PREFECTURE)

A.
RIGHT NOW, TERU'S ONLY SPECIAL MOVES ARE HAIR-PULLING AND SNEAKING PUNCHES. HOWEVER, THESE MOVES ARE ONLY EFFECTIVE WHEN THE OPPONENT ISN'T LOOKING. PLUS, SHE'S IN TRAINING TO IMPROVE HER SKILLS.
AS FOR RIKO, IT'S A HIGH KICK OR A TWO-STEP KICK WITH HER RIGHT LEG. NOW THIS IS A HIGH-PRECISION MOVE, CAPABLE OF SERIOUSLY INJURING AN OPPONENT, EVEN THOUGH IT'S NOT VERY FLASHY.
...OH. YOU'RE NOT TALKING ABOUT THIS KIND OF MOVE? SORRY. BUT I'M SURE KUROSAKI AND SOICHIRO HAVE BEEN ON THE RECEIVING END AND ARE QUITE PLEASED WITH THESE MOVES. PROBABLY. THEY'RE PERVERTED, AFTER ALL.

Q.
KUROSAKI IS BLOOD TYPE AB. DOES HE HAVE A HARD TIME GETTING OUT OF BED? I'M ALSO AB. I AM VERY LOW-SPIRITED ↓↓↓ IN THE MORNING.

(R.I., FUKUSHIMA PREFECTURE)

A.
YES. KUROSAKI IS NOTORIOUSLY BAD AT WAKING UP IN THE MORNING. THE AUTHOR IS BLOOD TYPE O, BUT SHE, TOO, IS LIKE A MORNING ZOMBIE.

GO TO ▶⑤

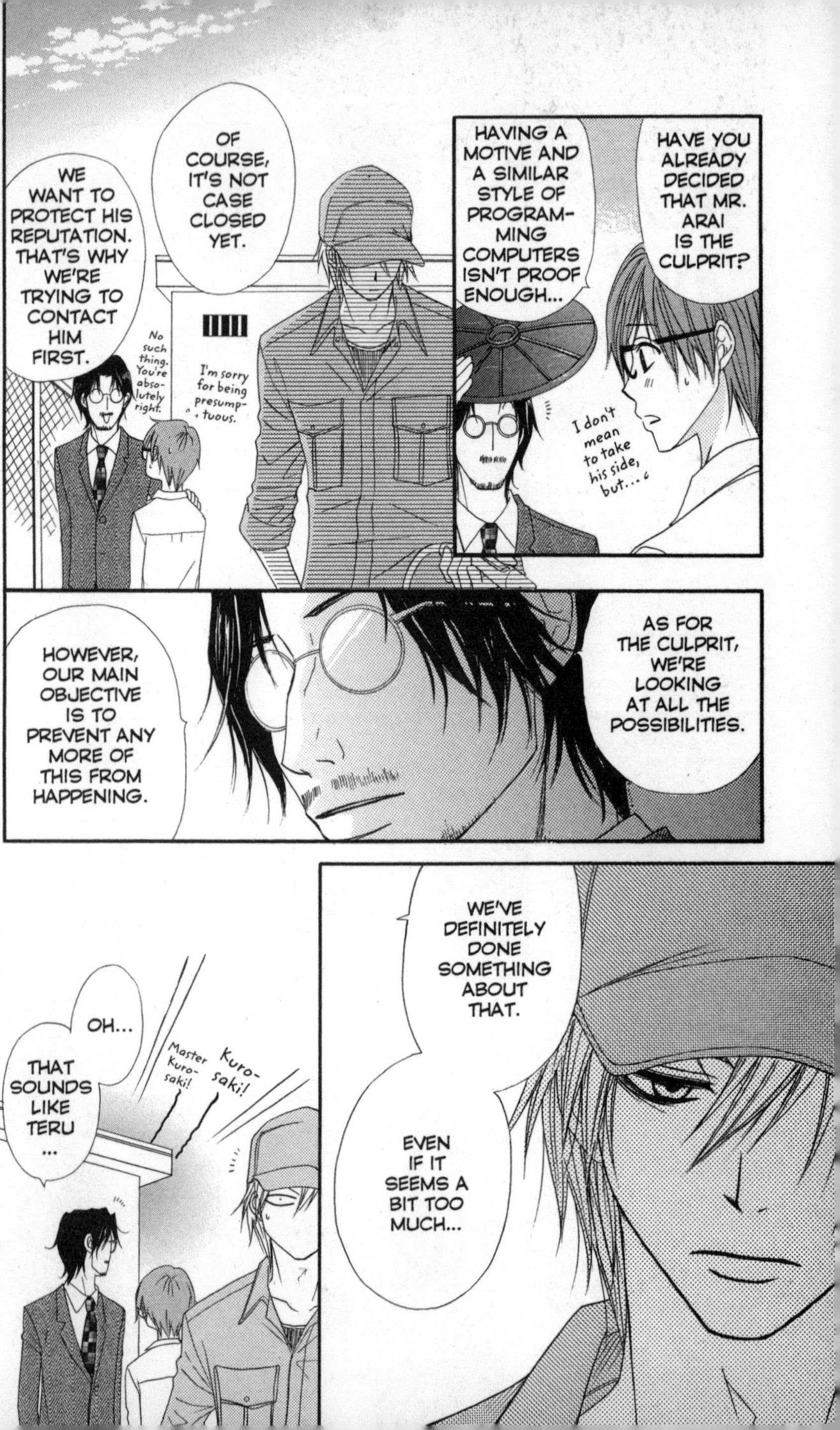
HAVE YOU ALREADY DECIDED THAT MR. ARAI IS THE CULPRIT?
HAVING A MOTIVE AND A SIMILAR STYLE OF PROGRAM-MING COMPUTERS ISN'T PROOF ENOUGH...
I don't mean to take his side, but...
OF COURSE, IT'S NOT CASE CLOSED YET.
I'm sorry for being presump-tuous.
WE WANT TO PROTECT HIS REPUTATION. THAT'S WHY WE'RE TRYING TO CONTACT HIM FIRST.
No such thing. You're abso-lutely right.
AS FOR THE CULPRIT, WE'RE LOOKING AT ALL THE POSSIBILITIES.
HOWEVER, OUR MAIN OBJECTIVE IS TO PREVENT ANY MORE OF THIS FROM HAPPENING.
WE'VE DEFINITELY DONE SOMETHING ABOUT THAT.
EVEN IF IT SEEMS A BIT TOO MUCH...
Kuro-saki!
Master Kuro-saki!
OH...
THAT SOUNDS LIKE TERU ...

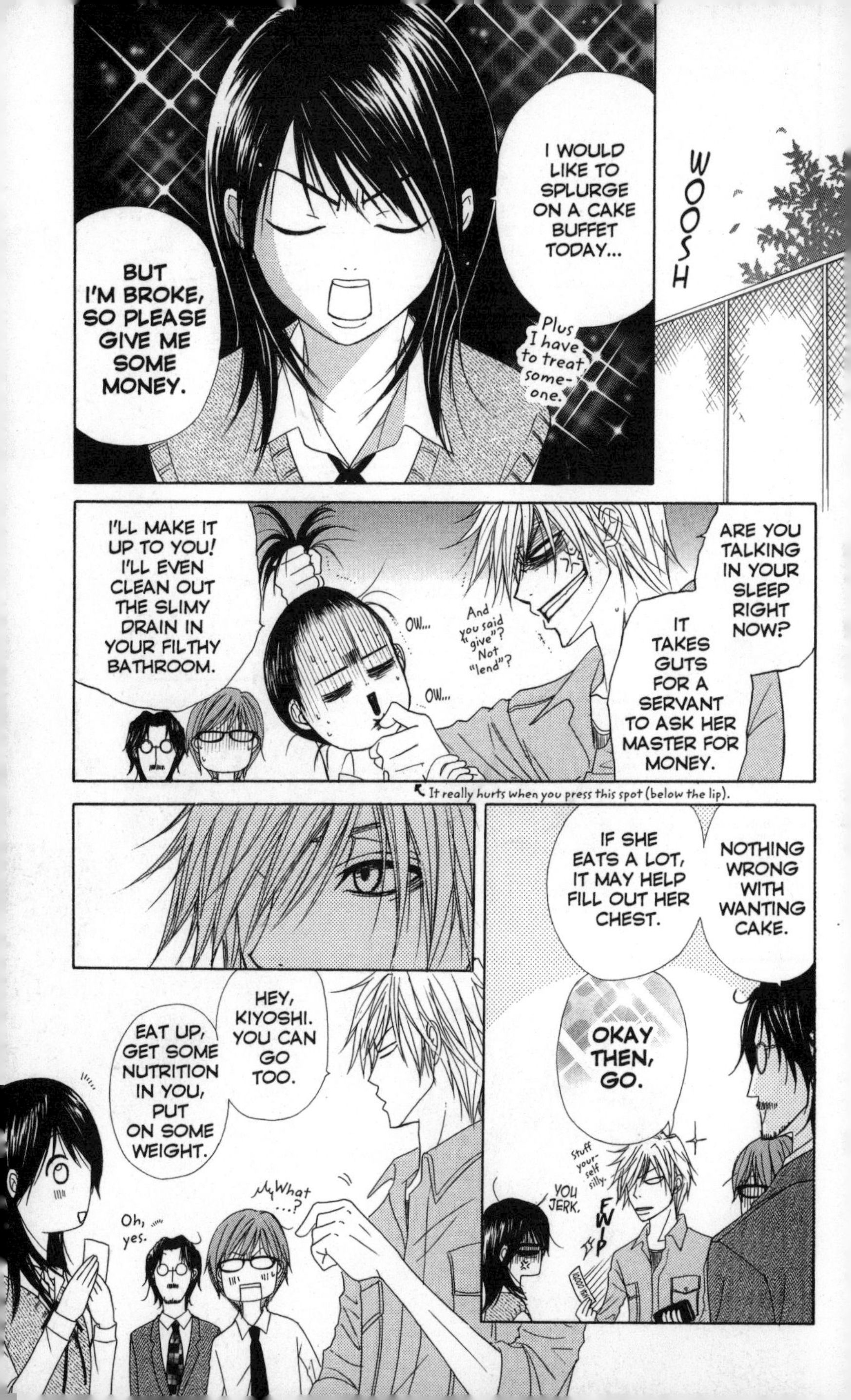
WOOSH
I WOULD LIKE TO SPLURGE ON A CAKE BUFFET TODAY...
Plus I have to treat someone.
BUT I'M BROKE, SO PLEASE GIVE ME SOME MONEY.
ARE YOU TALKING IN YOUR SLEEP RIGHT NOW?
IT TAKES GUTS FOR A SERVANT TO ASK HER MASTER FOR MONEY.
And you said "give"? Not "lend"?
OW...
OW...
I'LL MAKE IT UP TO YOU! I'LL EVEN CLEAN OUT THE SLIMY DRAIN IN YOUR FILTHY BATHROOM.
It really hurts when you press this spot (below the lip).
NOTHING WRONG WITH WANTING CAKE.
IF SHE EATS A LOT, IT MAY HELP FILL OUT HER CHEST.
OKAY THEN, GO.
Stuff yourself silly.
FWIP
YOU JERK.
HEY, KIYOSHI. YOU CAN GO TOO.
EAT UP, GET SOME NUTRITION IN YOU, PUT ON SOME WEIGHT.
What...?
Oh, yes.

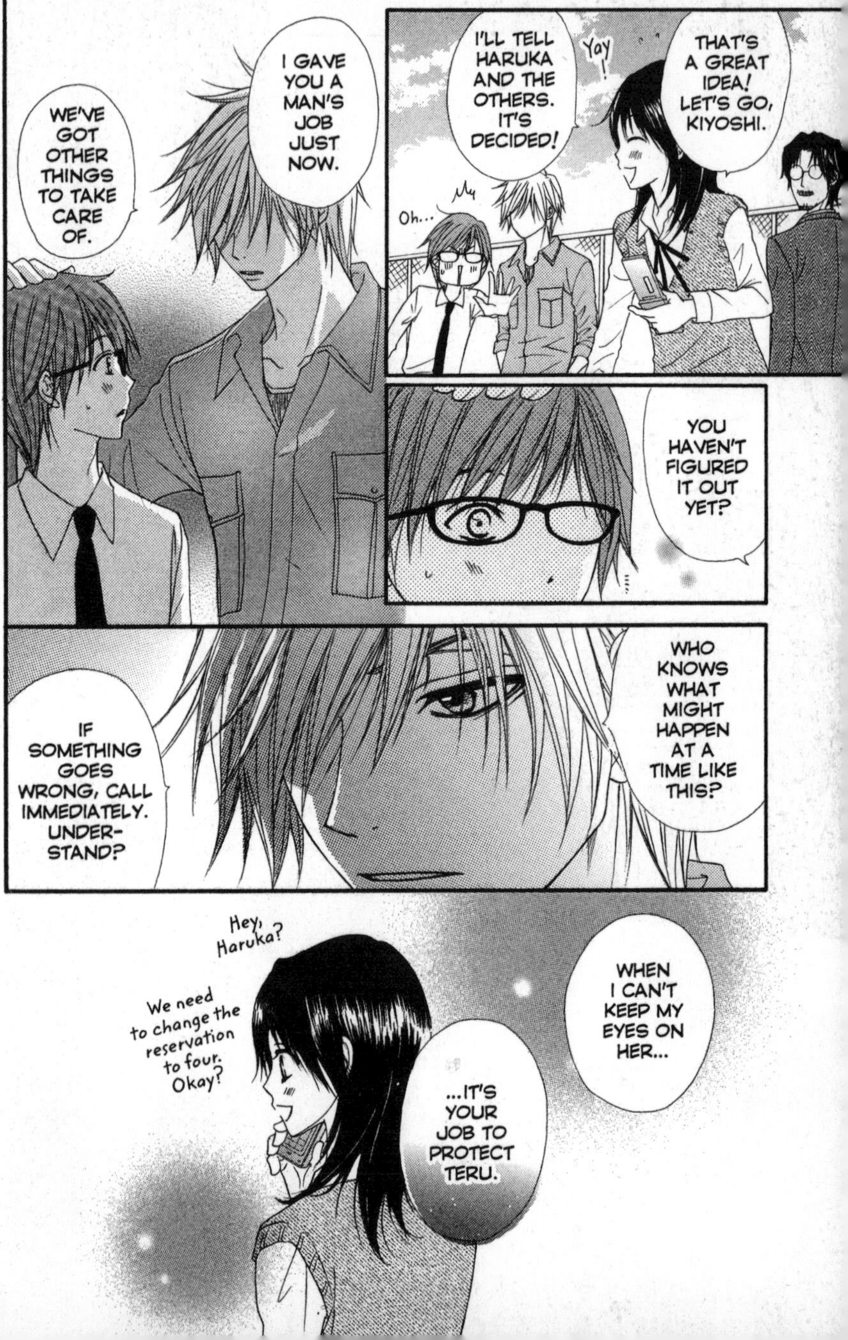

THAT'S A GREAT IDEA! LET'S GO, KIYOSHI.
I'LL TELL HARUKA AND THE OTHERS. IT'S DECIDED!
Yay!
Mu
Oh...
YOU HAVEN'T FIGURED IT OUT YET?
I GAVE YOU A MAN'S JOB JUST NOW.
WE'VE GOT OTHER THINGS TO TAKE CARE OF.
WHO KNOWS WHAT MIGHT HAPPEN AT A TIME LIKE THIS?
IF SOMETHING GOES WRONG, CALL IMMEDIATELY. UNDER-STAND?
WHEN I CAN'T KEEP MY EYES ON HER...
...IT'S YOUR JOB TO PROTECT TERU.
Hey, Haruka?
We need to change the reservation to four. Okay?

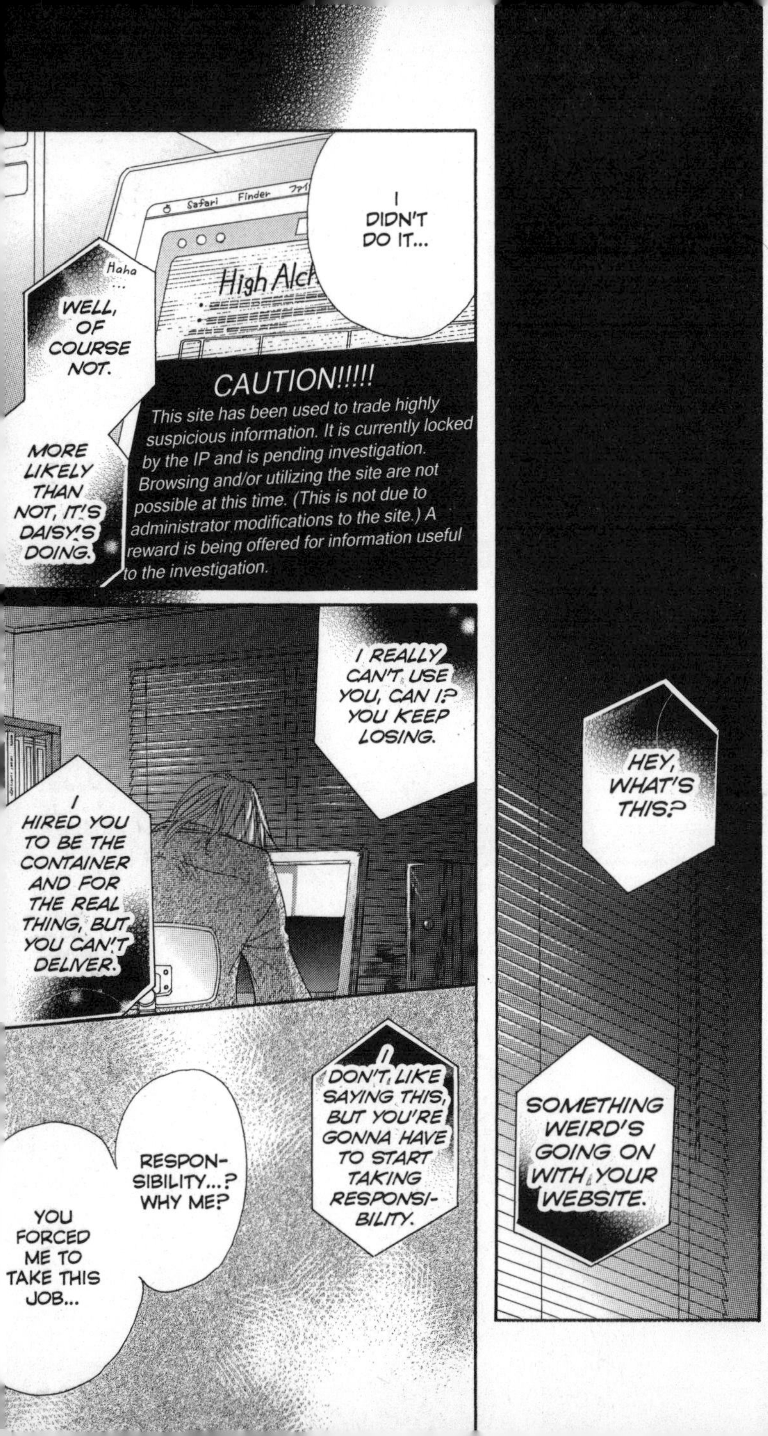
HEY, WHAT'S THIS?
SOMETHING WEIRD'S GOING ON WITH YOUR WEBSITE.
I DIDN'T DO IT...
Haha... WELL, OF COURSE NOT.
CAUTION!!!!!
This site has been used to trade highly suspicious information. It is currently locked by the IP and is pending investigation. Browsing and/or utilizing the site are not possible at this time. (This is not due to administrator modifications to the site.) A reward is being offered for information useful to the investigation.
MORE LIKELY THAN NOT, IT'S DAISY'S DOING.
I REALLY CAN'T USE YOU, CAN I? YOU KEEP LOSING.
I HIRED YOU TO BE THE CONTAINER AND FOR THE REAL THING, BUT YOU CAN'T DELIVER.
I DON'T LIKE SAYING THIS, BUT YOU'RE GONNA HAVE TO START TAKING RESPONSI-BILITY.
RESPON-SIBILITY...? WHY ME?
YOU FORCED ME TO TAKE THIS JOB...

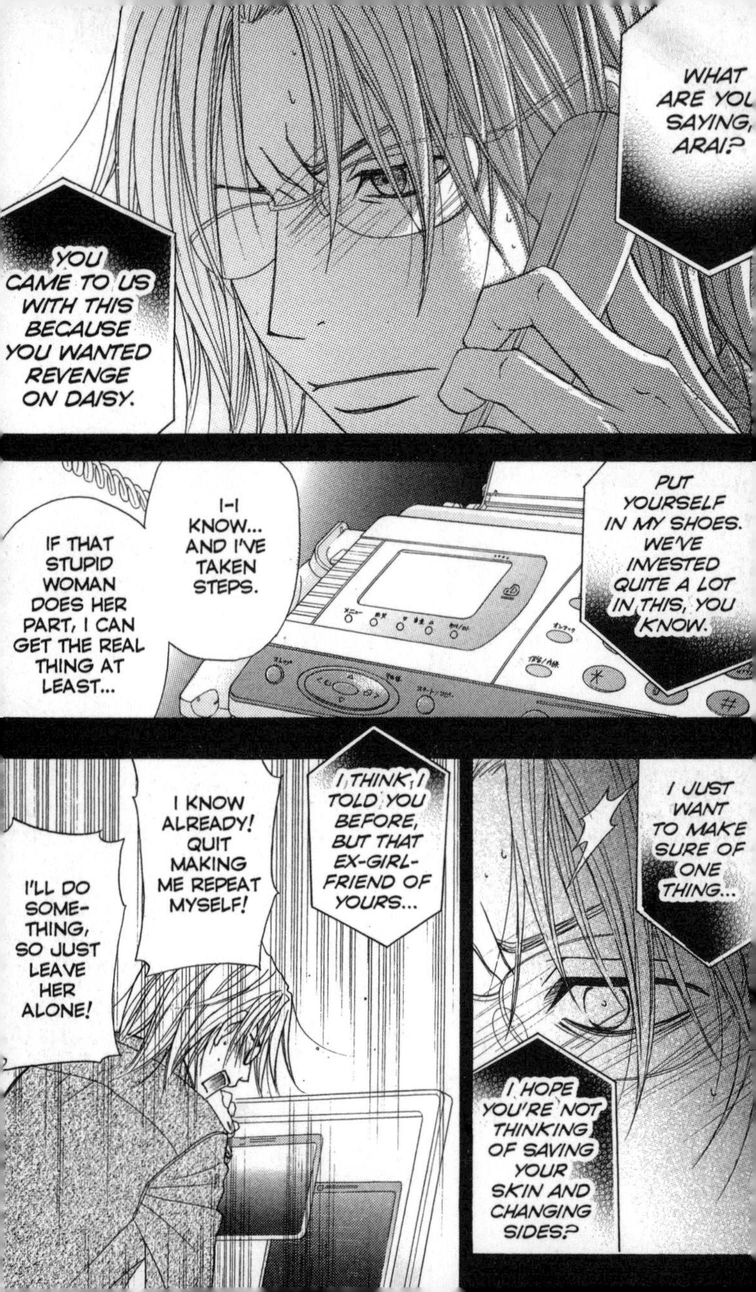
WHAT ARE YOU SAYING, ARAI?
YOU CAME TO US WITH THIS BECAUSE YOU WANTED REVENGE ON DAISY.
PUT YOURSELF IN MY SHOES. WE'VE INVESTED QUITE A LOT IN THIS, YOU KNOW.
I-I KNOW... AND I'VE TAKEN STEPS.
IF THAT STUPID WOMAN DOES HER PART, I CAN GET THE REAL THING AT LEAST...
I JUST WANT TO MAKE SURE OF ONE THING...
I HOPE YOU'RE NOT THINKING OF SAVING YOUR SKIN AND CHANGING SIDES?
I THINK I TOLD YOU BEFORE, BUT THAT EX-GIRLFRIEND OF YOURS...
I KNOW ALREADY! QUIT MAKING ME REPEAT MYSELF!
I'LL DO SOMETHING, SO JUST LEAVE HER ALONE!

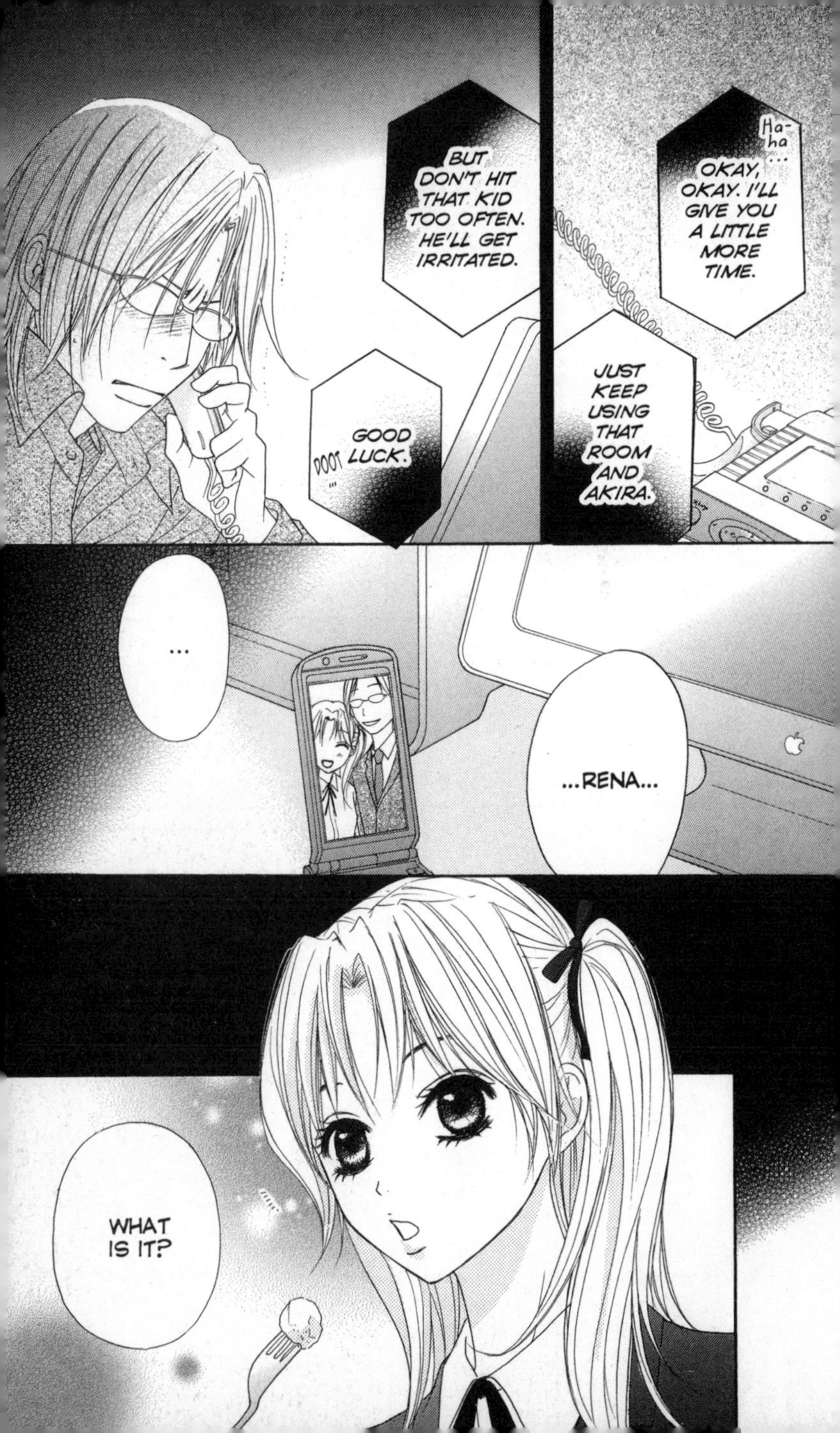
Ha-ha...
OKAY, OKAY. I'LL GIVE YOU A LITTLE MORE TIME.
JUST KEEP USING THAT ROOM AND AKIRA.
BUT DON'T HIT THAT KID TOO OFTEN. HE'LL GET IRRITATED.
GOOD LUCK.
DOOT...
...RENA...
...
WHAT IS IT?

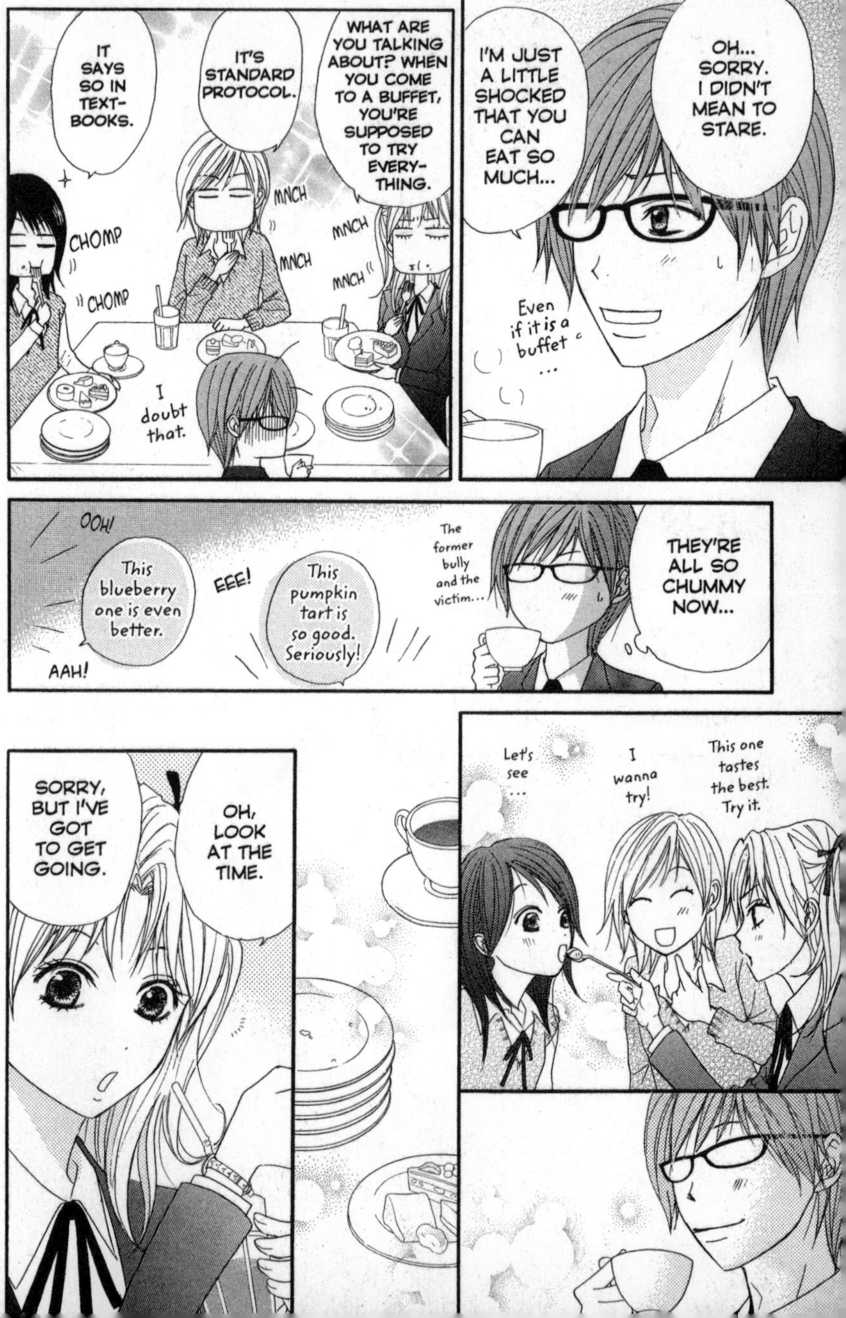
OH... SORRY. I DIDN'T MEAN TO STARE.
I'M JUST A LITTLE SHOCKED THAT YOU CAN EAT SO MUCH...
Even if it is a buffet...
WHAT ARE YOU TALKING ABOUT? WHEN YOU COME TO A BUFFET, YOU'RE SUPPOSED TO TRY EVERY-THING.
MNCH
MNCH
MNCH
IT'S STANDARD PROTOCOL.
MNCH
IT SAYS SO IN TEXT-BOOKS.
CHOMP
CHOMP
I doubt that.
THEY'RE ALL SO CHUMMY NOW...
The former bully and the victim...
This pumpkin tart is so good. Seriously!
EEE!
This blueberry one is even better.
OOH!
AAH!
This one tastes the best. Try it.
I wanna try!
Let's see...
OH, LOOK AT THE TIME.
SORRY, BUT I'VE GOT TO GET GOING.

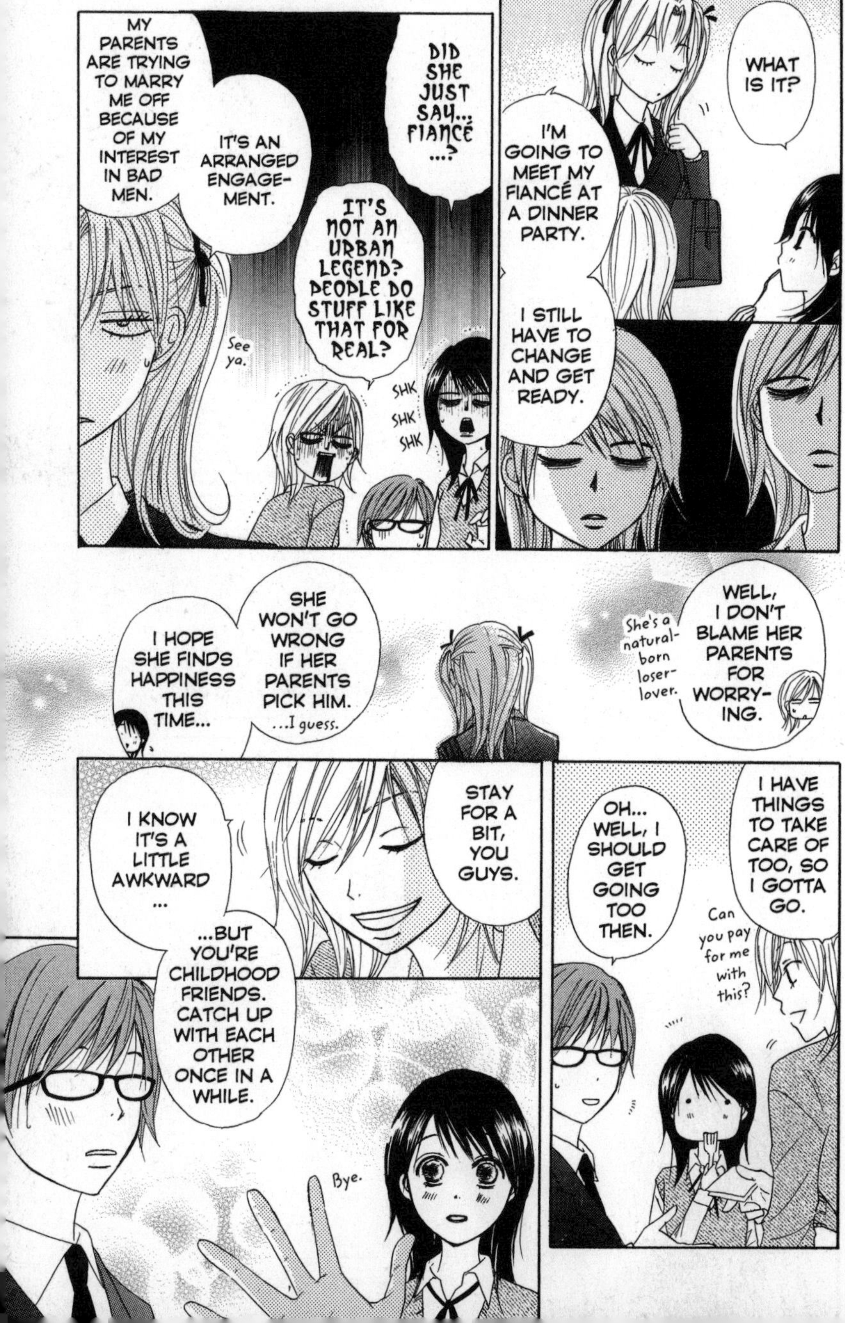
WHAT IS IT?
I'M GOING TO MEET MY FIANCÉ AT A DINNER PARTY.
I STILL HAVE TO CHANGE AND GET READY.
DID SHE JUST SAY... FIANCÉ ...?
IT'S AN ARRANGED ENGAGEMENT.
MY PARENTS ARE TRYING TO MARRY ME OFF BECAUSE OF MY INTEREST IN BAD MEN.
See ya.
IT'S NOT AN URBAN LEGEND? PEOPLE DO STUFF LIKE THAT FOR REAL?
SHK
SHK
SHK
WELL, I DON'T BLAME HER PARENTS FOR WORRYING.
She's a natural-born loser-lover.
SHE WON'T GO WRONG IF HER PARENTS PICK HIM.
...I guess.
I HOPE SHE FINDS HAPPINESS THIS TIME...
I HAVE THINGS TO TAKE CARE OF TOO, SO I GOTTA GO.
Can you pay for me with this?
OH... WELL, I SHOULD GET GOING TOO THEN.
STAY FOR A BIT, YOU GUYS.
I KNOW IT'S A LITTLE AWKWARD...
...BUT YOU'RE CHILDHOOD FRIENDS. CATCH UP WITH EACH OTHER ONCE IN A WHILE.
Bye.

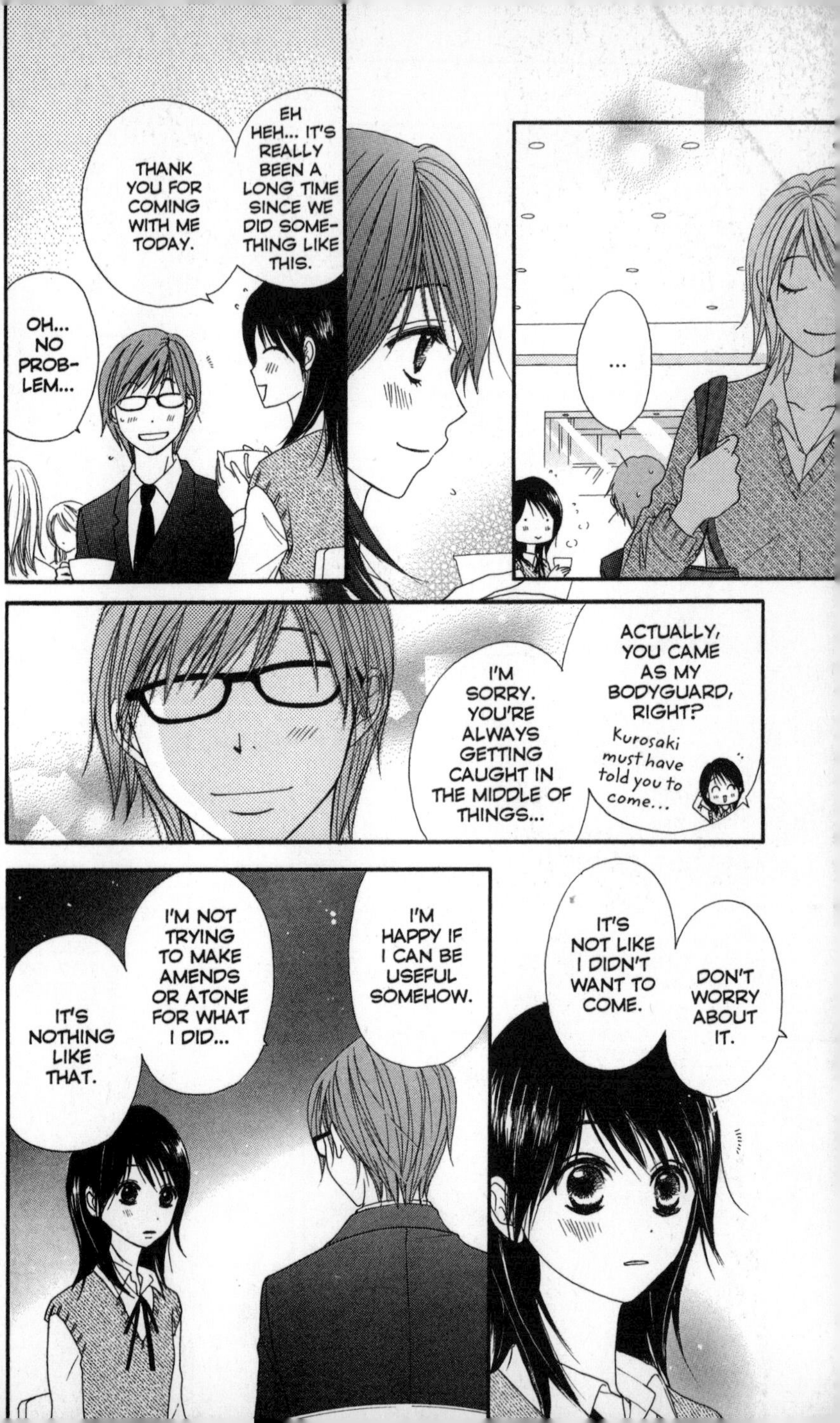
...
EH HEH... IT'S REALLY BEEN A LONG TIME SINCE WE DID SOME-THING LIKE THIS.
THANK YOU FOR COMING WITH ME TODAY.
OH... NO PROB-LEM...
ACTUALLY, YOU CAME AS MY BODYGUARD, RIGHT?
Kurosaki must have told you to come...
I'M SORRY. YOU'RE ALWAYS GETTING CAUGHT IN THE MIDDLE OF THINGS...
DON'T WORRY ABOUT IT.
IT'S NOT LIKE I DIDN'T WANT TO COME.
I'M HAPPY IF I CAN BE USEFUL SOMEHOW.
I'M NOT TRYING TO MAKE AMENDS OR ATONE FOR WHAT I DID...
IT'S NOTHING LIKE THAT.

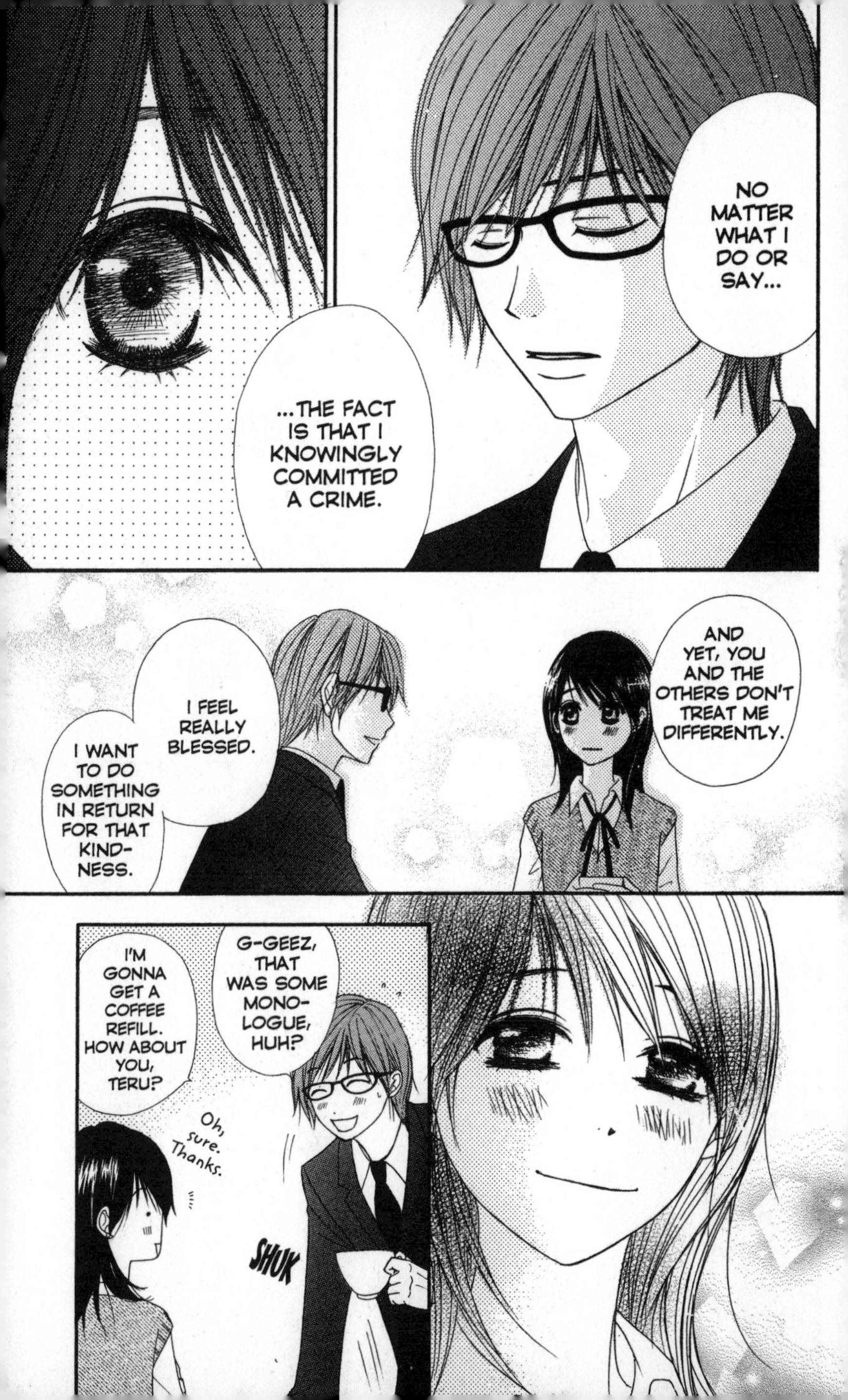
NO MATTER WHAT I DO OR SAY...
...THE FACT IS THAT I KNOWINGLY COMMITTED A CRIME.
AND YET, YOU AND THE OTHERS DON'T TREAT ME DIFFERENTLY.
I FEEL REALLY BLESSED.
I WANT TO DO SOMETHING IN RETURN FOR THAT KINDNESS.
G-GEEZ, THAT WAS SOME MONOLOGUE, HUH?
I'M GONNA GET A COFFEE REFILL. HOW ABOUT YOU, TERU?
Oh, sure. Thanks.
SHUK

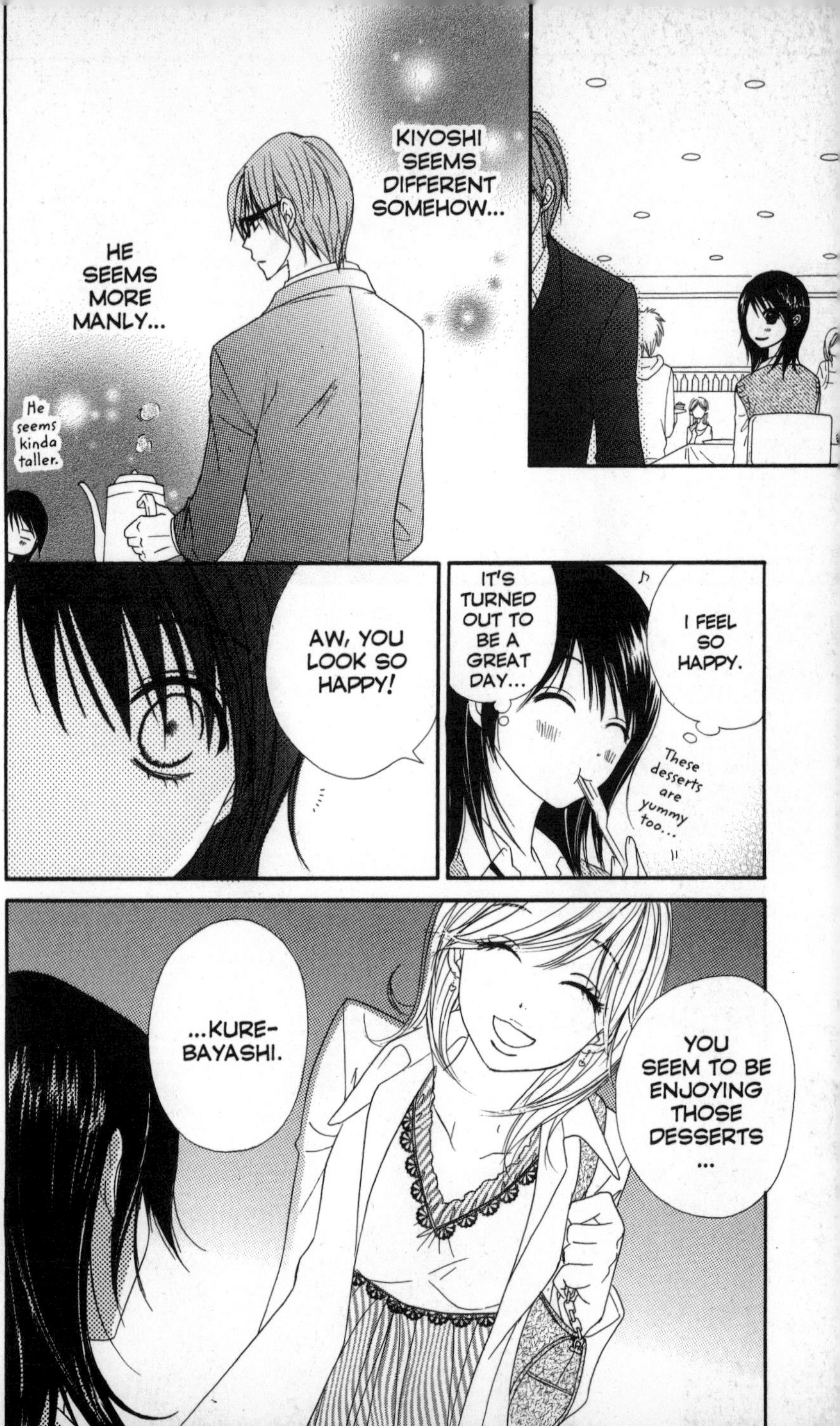
KIYOSHI SEEMS DIFFERENT SOMEHOW...
HE SEEMS MORE MANLY...
He seems kinda taller.
IT'S TURNED OUT TO BE A GREAT DAY...
I FEEL SO HAPPY.
These desserts are yummy too...
AW, YOU LOOK SO HAPPY!
YOU SEEM TO BE ENJOYING THOSE DESSERTS...
...KURE-BAYASHI.

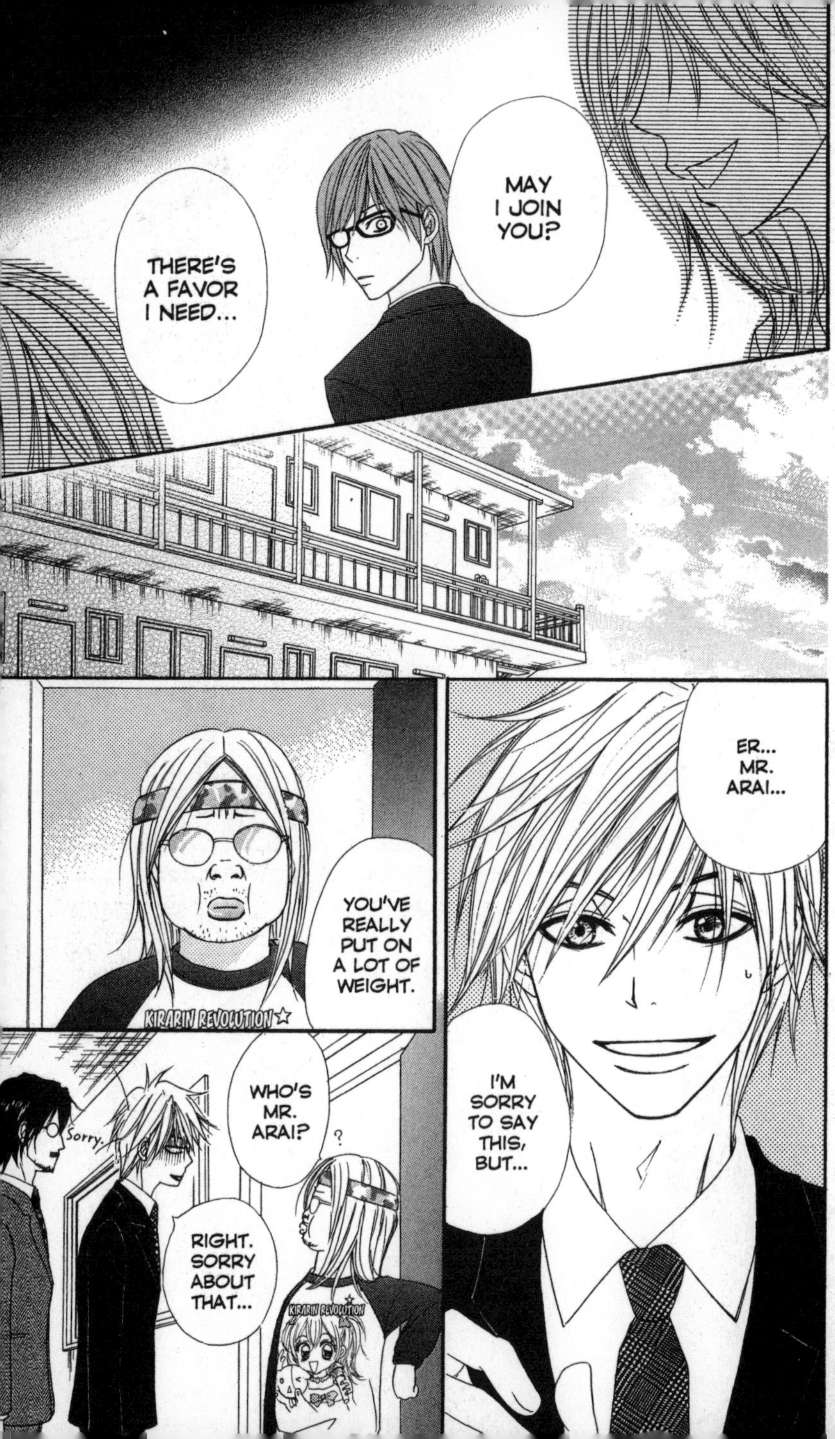
MAY I JOIN YOU?
THERE'S A FAVOR I NEED...
ER... MR. ARAI...
I'M SORRY TO SAY THIS, BUT...
YOU'VE REALLY PUT ON A LOT OF WEIGHT.
KIRARIN REVOLUTION☆
WHO'S MR. ARAI?
?
Sorry.
RIGHT. SORRY ABOUT THAT...
KIRARIN REVOLUTION

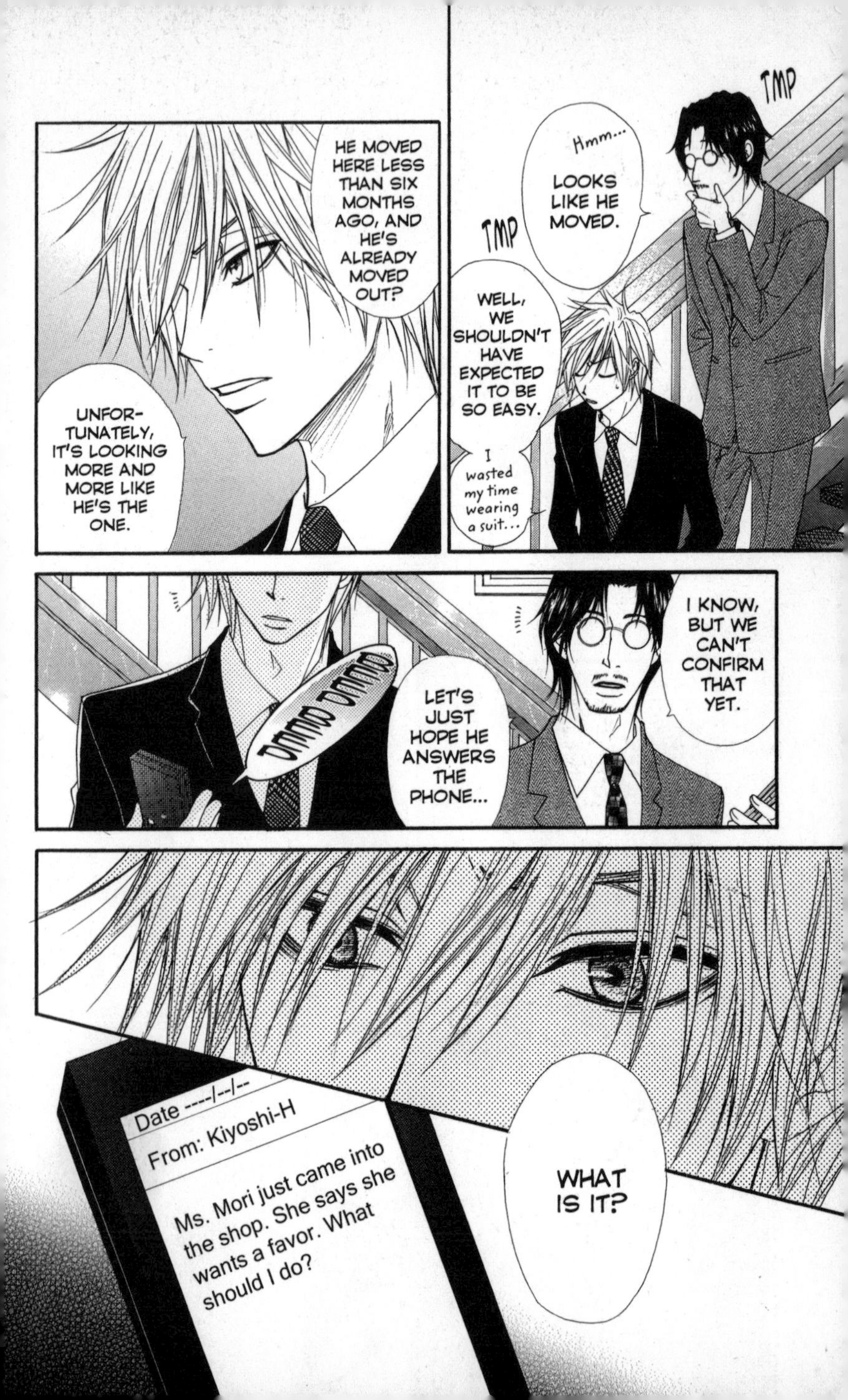
TMP
Hmm...
LOOKS LIKE HE MOVED.
TMP
WELL, WE SHOULDN'T HAVE EXPECTED IT TO BE SO EASY.
I wasted my time wearing a suit...
HE MOVED HERE LESS THAN SIX MONTHS AGO, AND HE'S ALREADY MOVED OUT?
UNFORTUNATELY, IT'S LOOKING MORE AND MORE LIKE HE'S THE ONE.
I KNOW, BUT WE CAN'T CONFIRM THAT YET.
LET'S JUST HOPE HE ANSWERS THE PHONE...
WHAT IS IT?
Date ----/--/--
From: Kiyoshi-H
Ms. Mori just came into the shop. She says she wants a favor. What should I do?

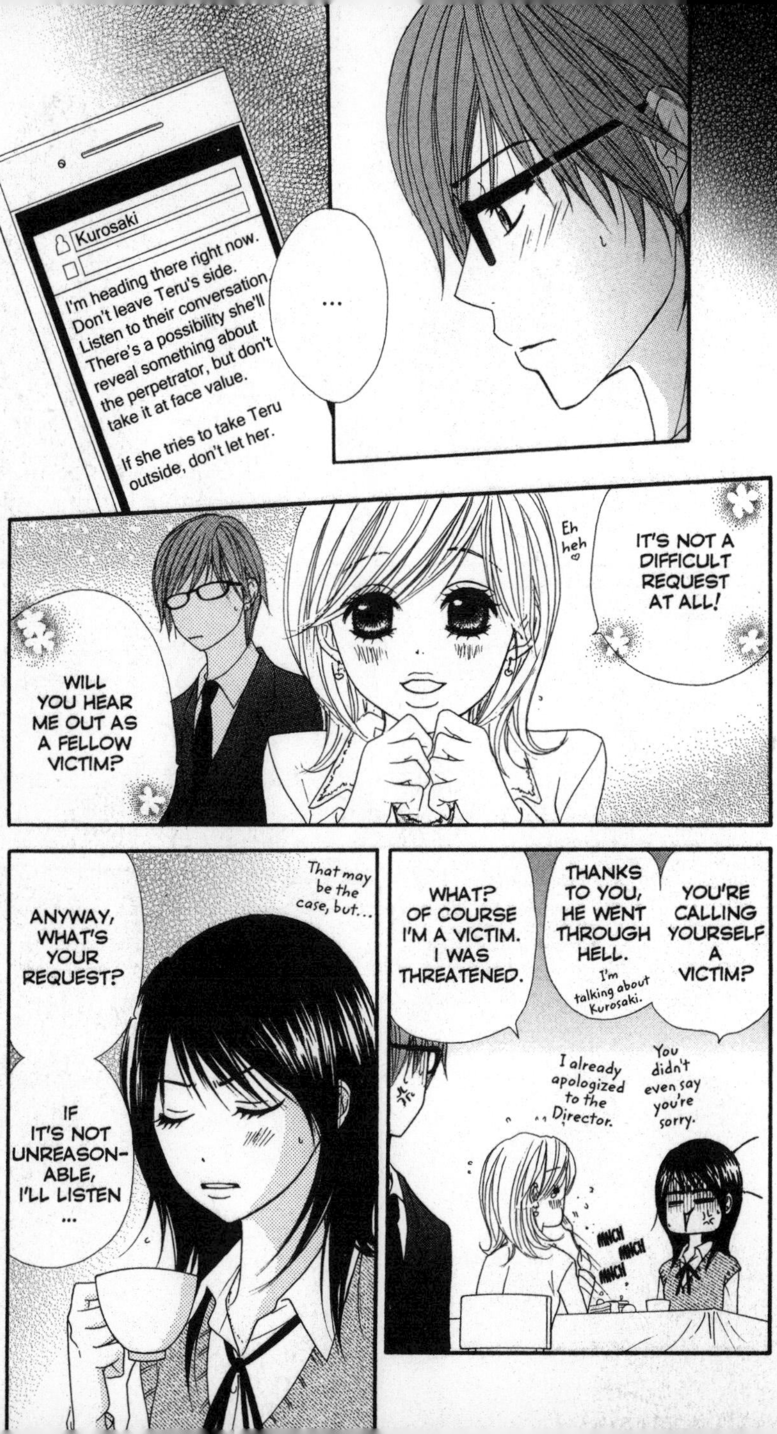
...
Kurosaki
I'm heading there right now. Don't leave Teru's side. Listen to their conversation. There's a possibility she'll reveal something about the perpetrator, but don't take it at face value.
If she tries to take Teru outside, don't let her.
Eh heh
IT'S NOT A DIFFICULT REQUEST AT ALL!
WILL YOU HEAR ME OUT AS A FELLOW VICTIM?
YOU'RE CALLING YOURSELF A VICTIM?
THANKS TO YOU, HE WENT THROUGH HELL.
I'm talking about Kurosaki.
WHAT? OF COURSE I'M A VICTIM. I WAS THREATENED.
You didn't even say you're sorry.
I already apologized to the Director.
MNCH MNCH MNCH
That may be the case, but...
ANYWAY, WHAT'S YOUR REQUEST?
IF IT'S NOT UNREASONABLE, I'LL LISTEN...

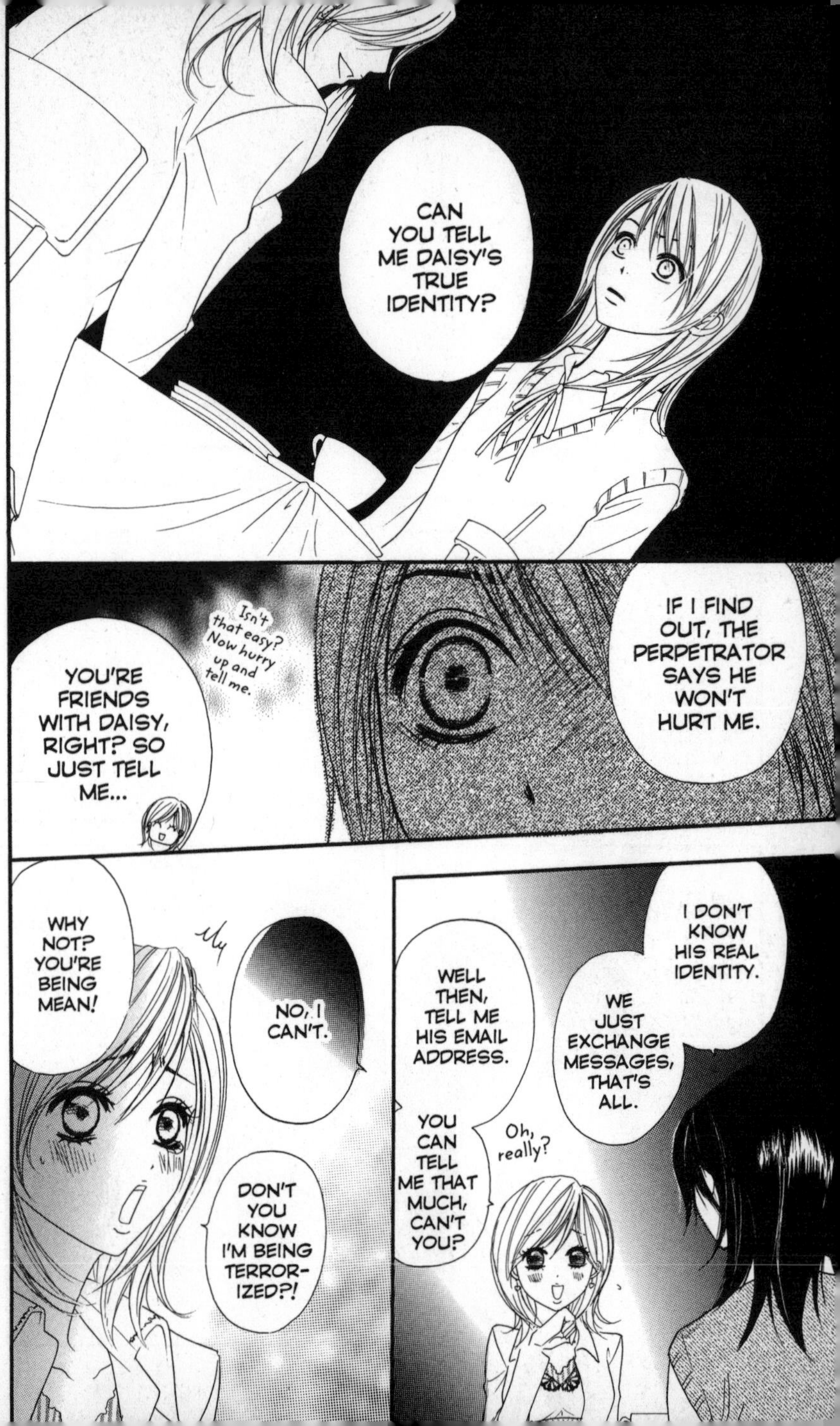
CAN YOU TELL ME DAISY'S TRUE IDENTITY?
IF I FIND OUT, THE PERPETRATOR SAYS HE WON'T HURT ME.
YOU'RE FRIENDS WITH DAISY, RIGHT? SO JUST TELL ME...
Isn't that easy? Now hurry up and tell me.
I DON'T KNOW HIS REAL IDENTITY.
WE JUST EXCHANGE MESSAGES, THAT'S ALL.
Oh, really?
WELL THEN, TELL ME HIS EMAIL ADDRESS.
YOU CAN TELL ME THAT MUCH, CAN'T YOU?
NO, I CAN'T.
WHY NOT? YOU'RE BEING MEAN!
DON'T YOU KNOW I'M BEING TERROR-IZED?!

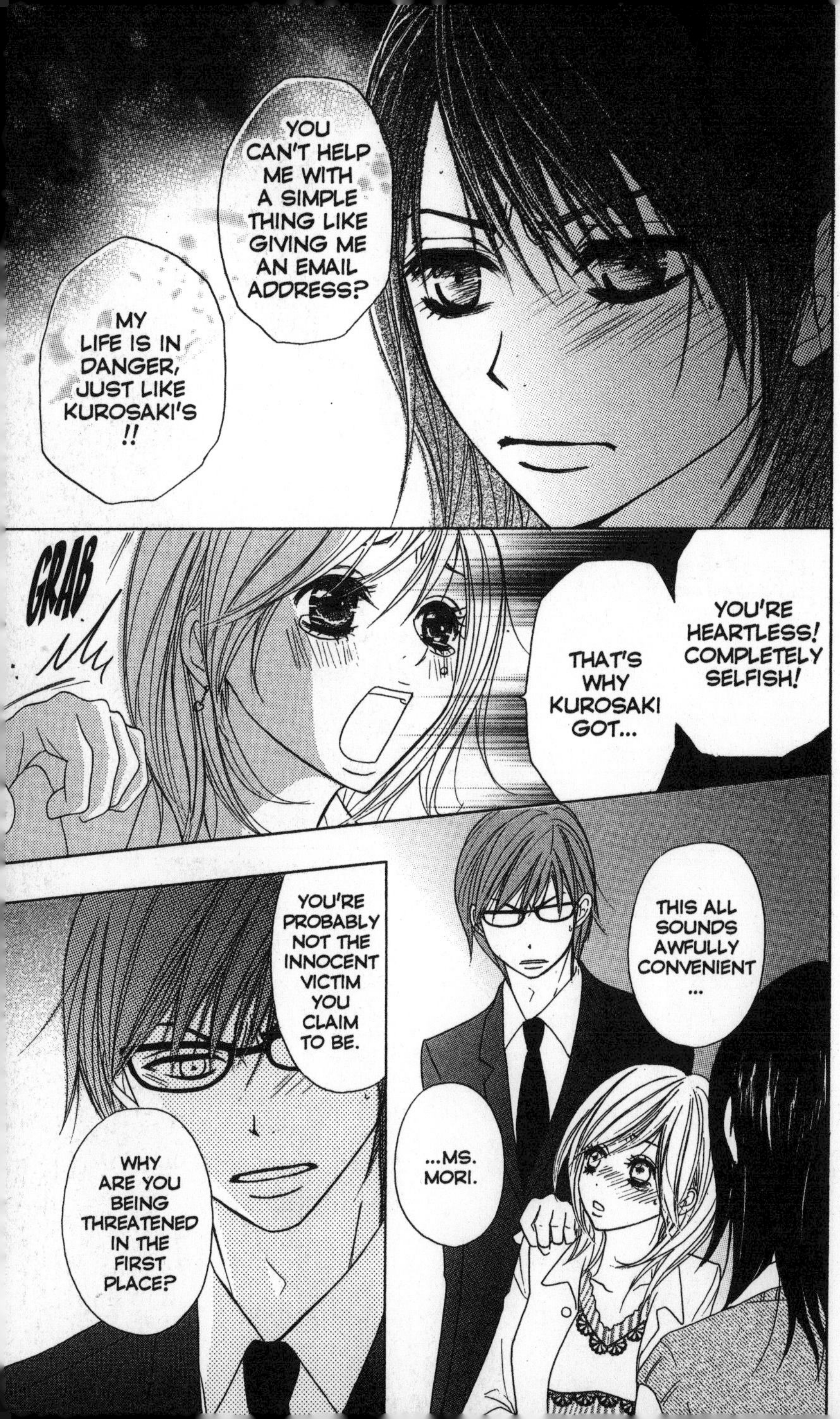
YOU CAN'T HELP ME WITH A SIMPLE THING LIKE GIVING ME AN EMAIL ADDRESS?
MY LIFE IS IN DANGER, JUST LIKE KUROSAKI'S !!
YOU'RE HEARTLESS! COMPLETELY SELFISH!
THAT'S WHY KUROSAKI GOT...
GRAB
THIS ALL SOUNDS AWFULLY CONVENIENT ...
...MS. MORI.
YOU'RE PROBABLY NOT THE INNOCENT VICTIM YOU CLAIM TO BE.
WHY ARE YOU BEING THREATENED IN THE FIRST PLACE?

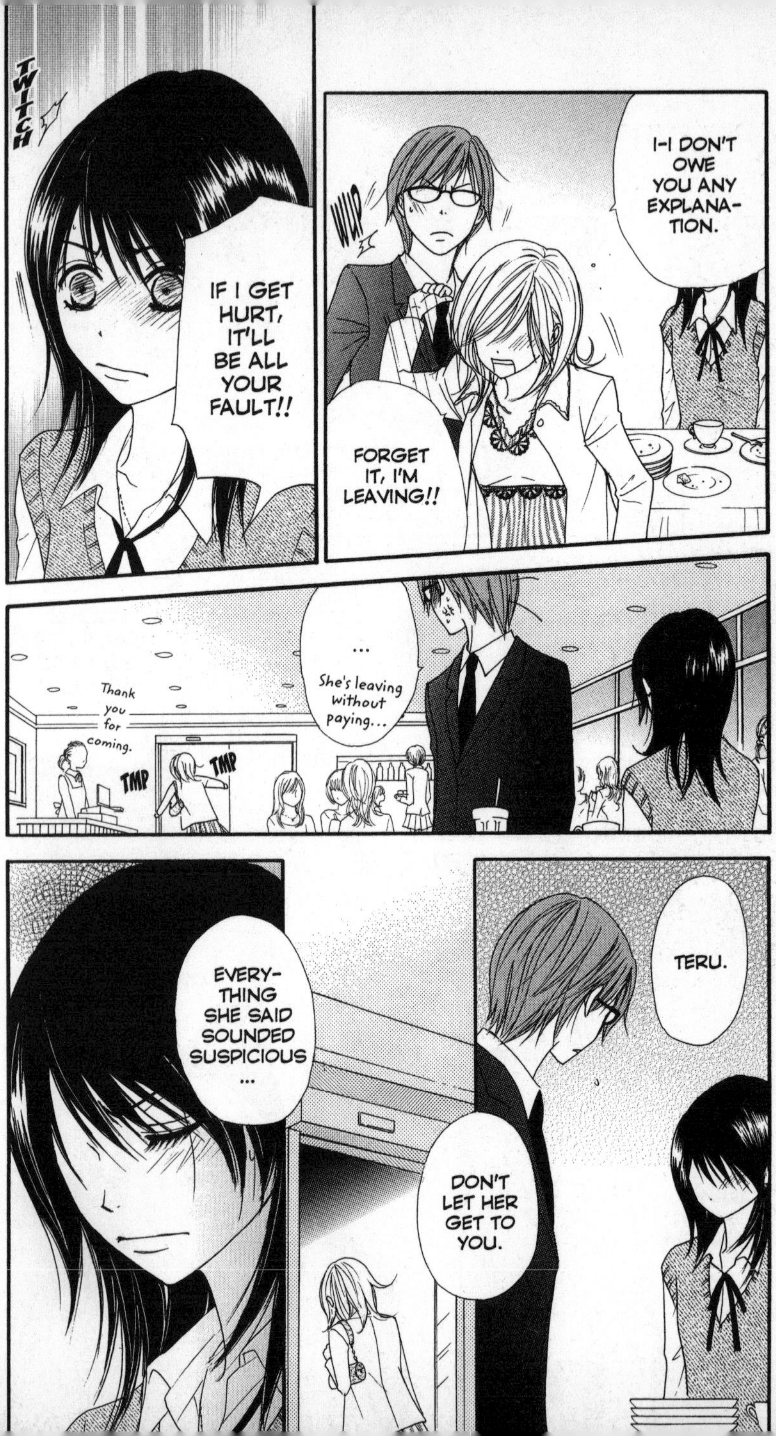
I-I DON'T OWE YOU ANY EXPLANA-TION.
WUP
FORGET IT, I'M LEAVING!!
TWITCH
IF I GET HURT, IT'LL BE ALL YOUR FAULT!!
...
She's leaving without paying...
Thank you for coming.
TMP
TMP
TERU.
DON'T LET HER GET TO YOU.
EVERY-THING SHE SAID SOUNDED SUSPICIOUS ...

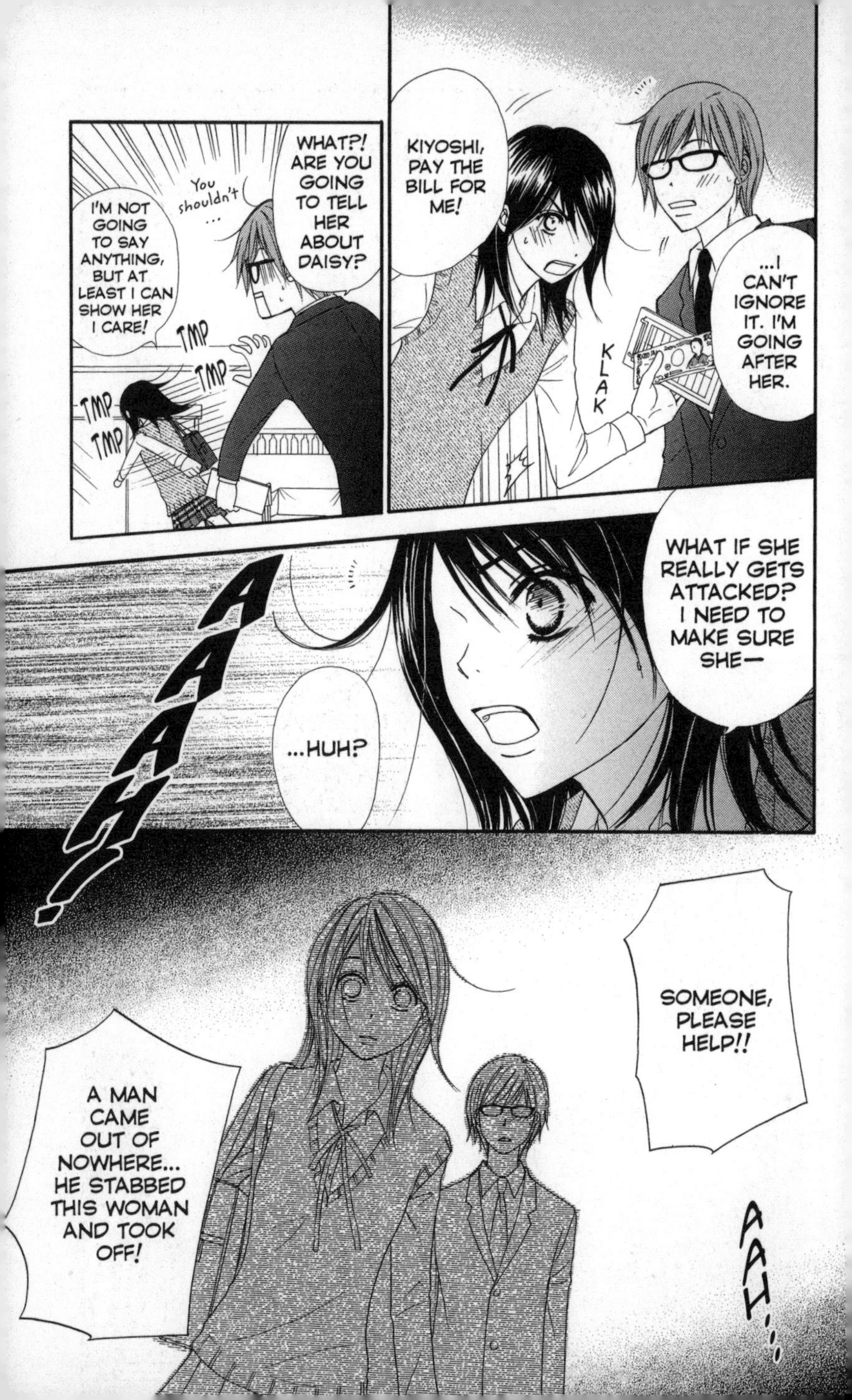
...I CAN'T IGNORE IT. I'M GOING AFTER HER.
KIYOSHI, PAY THE BILL FOR ME!
KLAK
WHAT?! ARE YOU GOING TO TELL HER ABOUT DAISY?
You shouldn't ...
I'M NOT GOING TO SAY ANYTHING, BUT AT LEAST I CAN SHOW HER I CARE!
TMP
TMP
TMP
TMP
WHAT IF SHE REALLY GETS ATTACKED? I NEED TO MAKE SURE SHE—
...HUH?
AAAAH!
SOMEONE, PLEASE HELP!!
AAH...
A MAN CAME OUT OF NOWHERE... HE STABBED THIS WOMAN AND TOOK OFF!

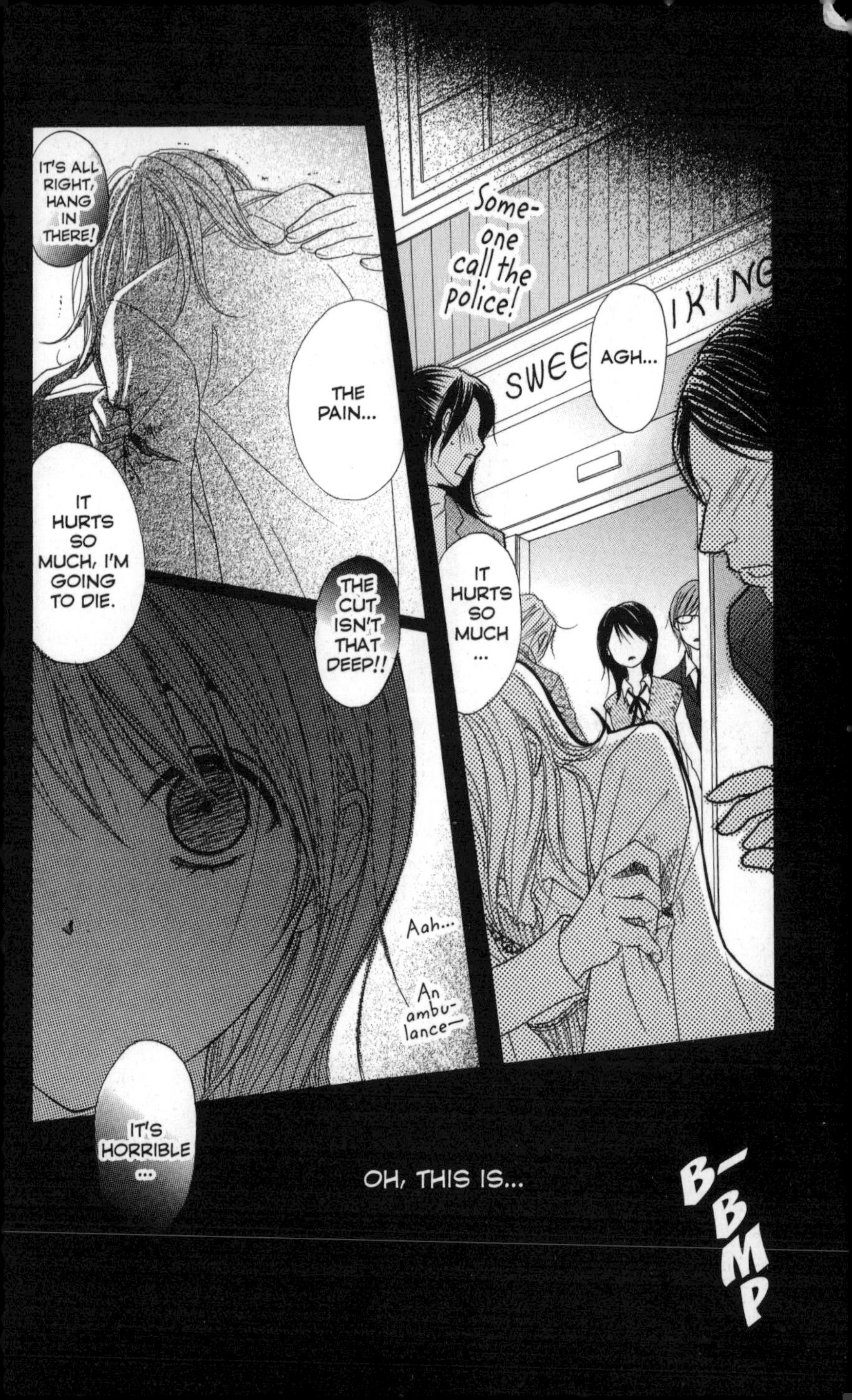
Some-one call the police!
AGH...
IT HURTS SO MUCH...
Aah...
An ambu-lance—
IT'S ALL RIGHT, HANG IN THERE!
THE PAIN...
IT HURTS SO MUCH, I'M GOING TO DIE.
THE CUT ISN'T THAT DEEP!!
IT'S HORRIBLE...
OH, THIS IS...
B-BMP
SWEE
IKING

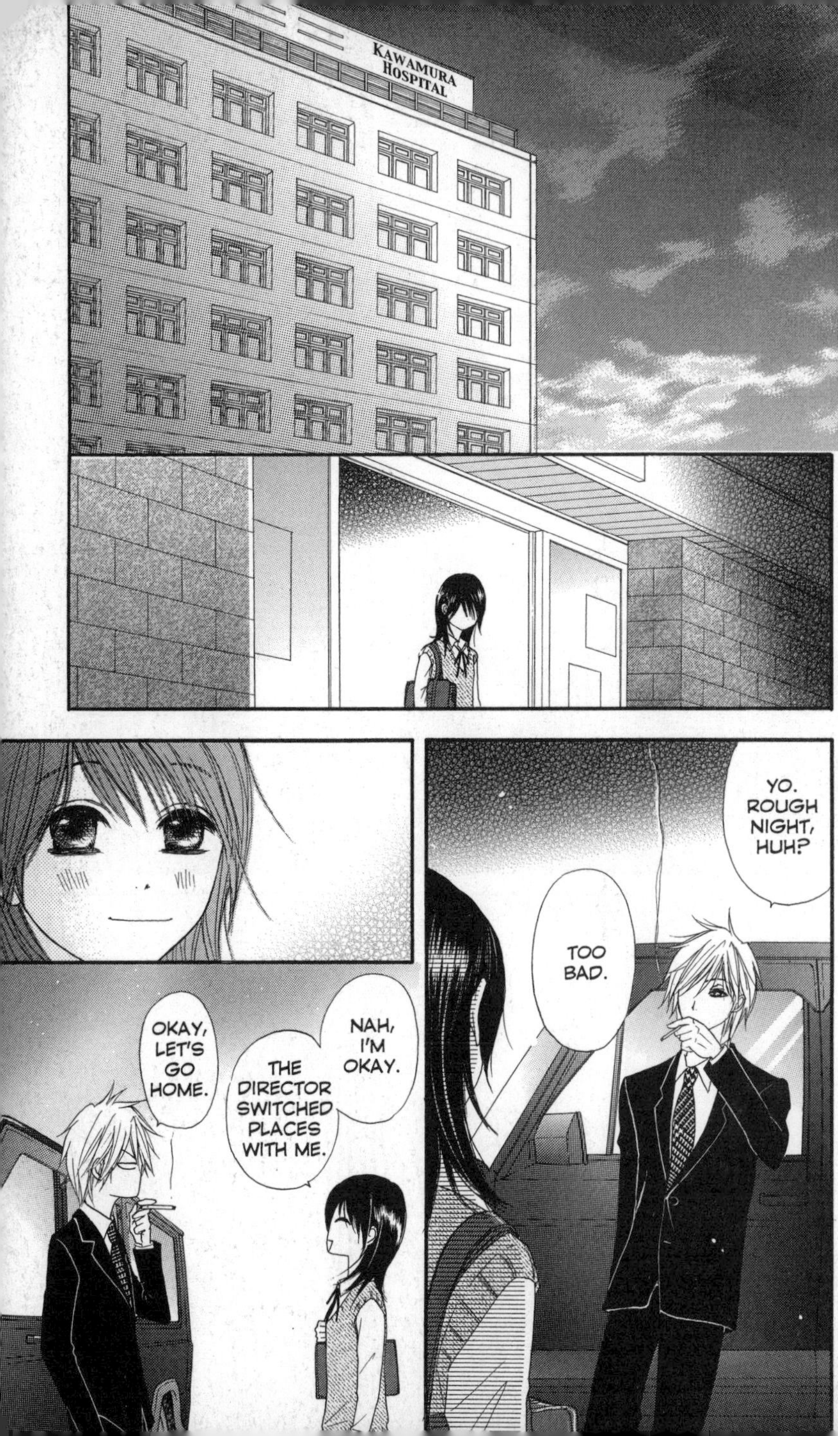
KAWAMURA HOSPITAL
YO. ROUGH NIGHT, HUH?
TOO BAD.
NAH, I'M OKAY.
THE DIRECTOR SWITCHED PLACES WITH ME.
OKAY, LET'S GO HOME.

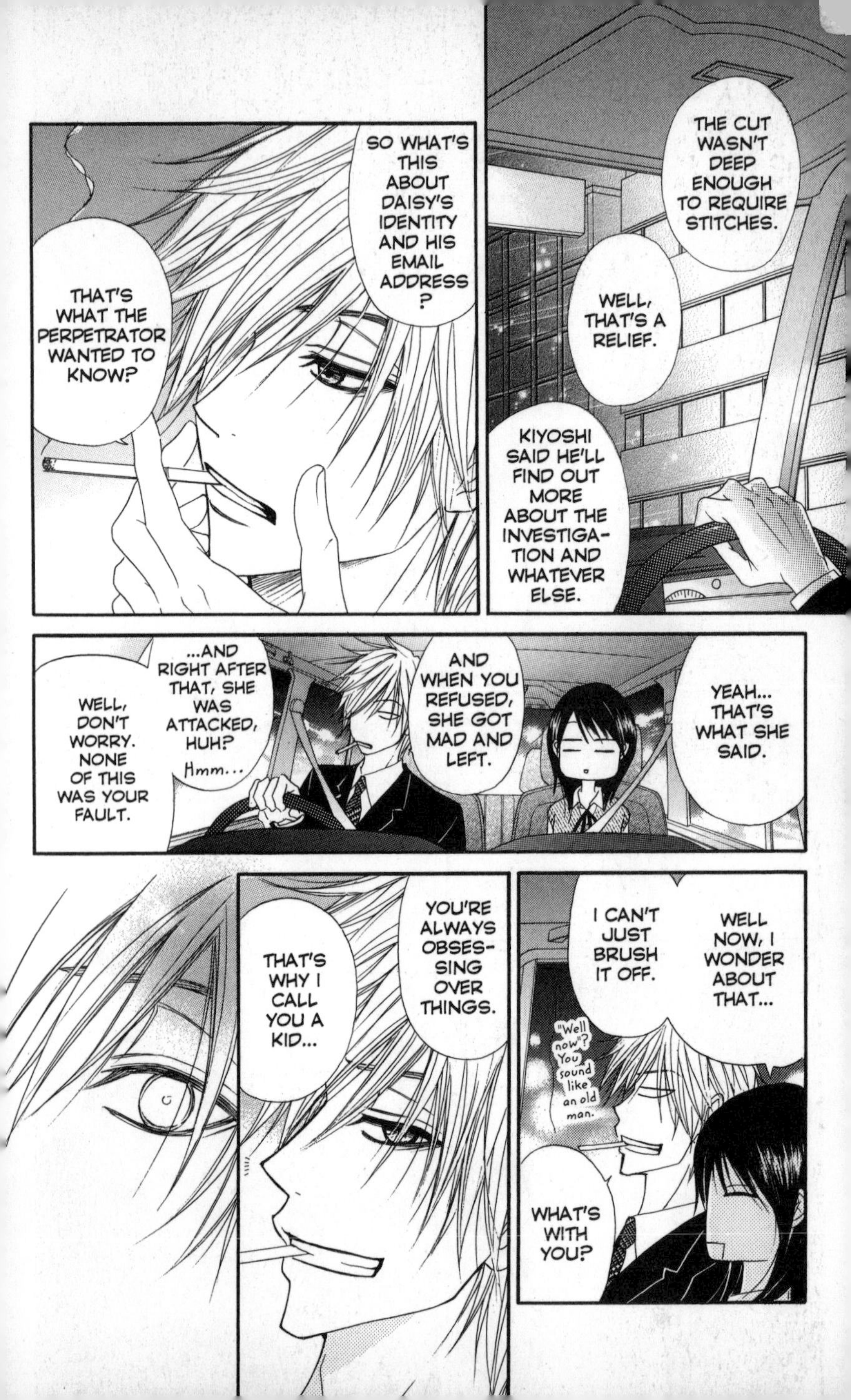
THE CUT WASN'T DEEP ENOUGH TO REQUIRE STITCHES.
WELL, THAT'S A RELIEF.
KIYOSHI SAID HE'LL FIND OUT MORE ABOUT THE INVESTIGA-TION AND WHATEVER ELSE.
SO WHAT'S THIS ABOUT DAISY'S IDENTITY AND HIS EMAIL ADDRESS?
THAT'S WHAT THE PERPETRATOR WANTED TO KNOW?
YEAH... THAT'S WHAT SHE SAID.
AND WHEN YOU REFUSED, SHE GOT MAD AND LEFT.
...AND RIGHT AFTER THAT, SHE WAS ATTACKED, HUH?
Hmm...
WELL, DON'T WORRY. NONE OF THIS WAS YOUR FAULT.
WELL NOW, I WONDER ABOUT THAT...
I CAN'T JUST BRUSH IT OFF.
"Well now"? You sound like an old man.
WHAT'S WITH YOU?
YOU'RE ALWAYS OBSES-SING OVER THINGS.
THAT'S WHY I CALL YOU A KID...

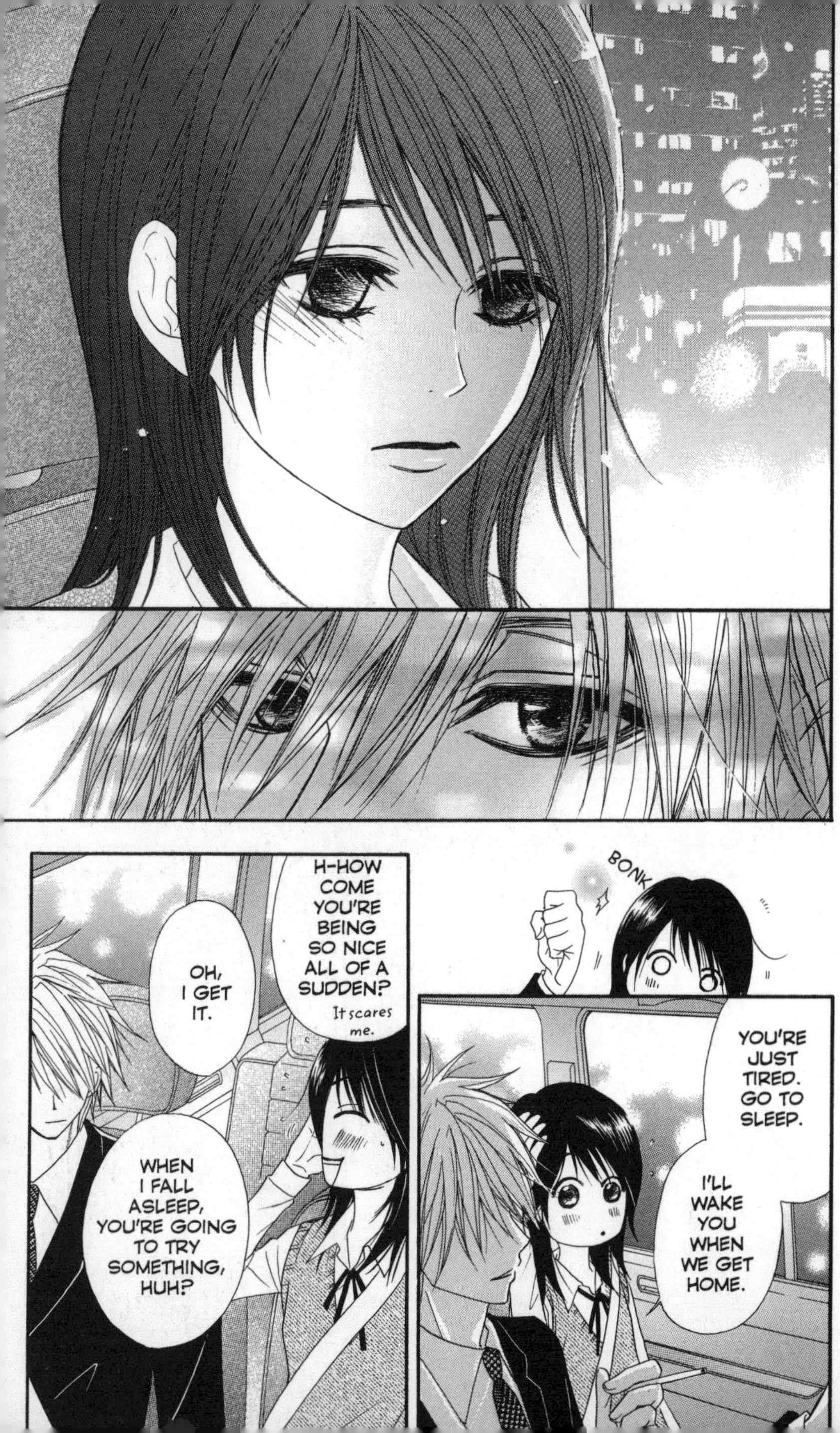
BONK
YOU'RE JUST TIRED. GO TO SLEEP.
I'LL WAKE YOU WHEN WE GET HOME.
H-HOW COME YOU'RE BEING SO NICE ALL OF A SUDDEN?
It scares me.
OH, I GET IT.
WHEN I FALL ASLEEP, YOU'RE GOING TO TRY SOMETHING, HUH?

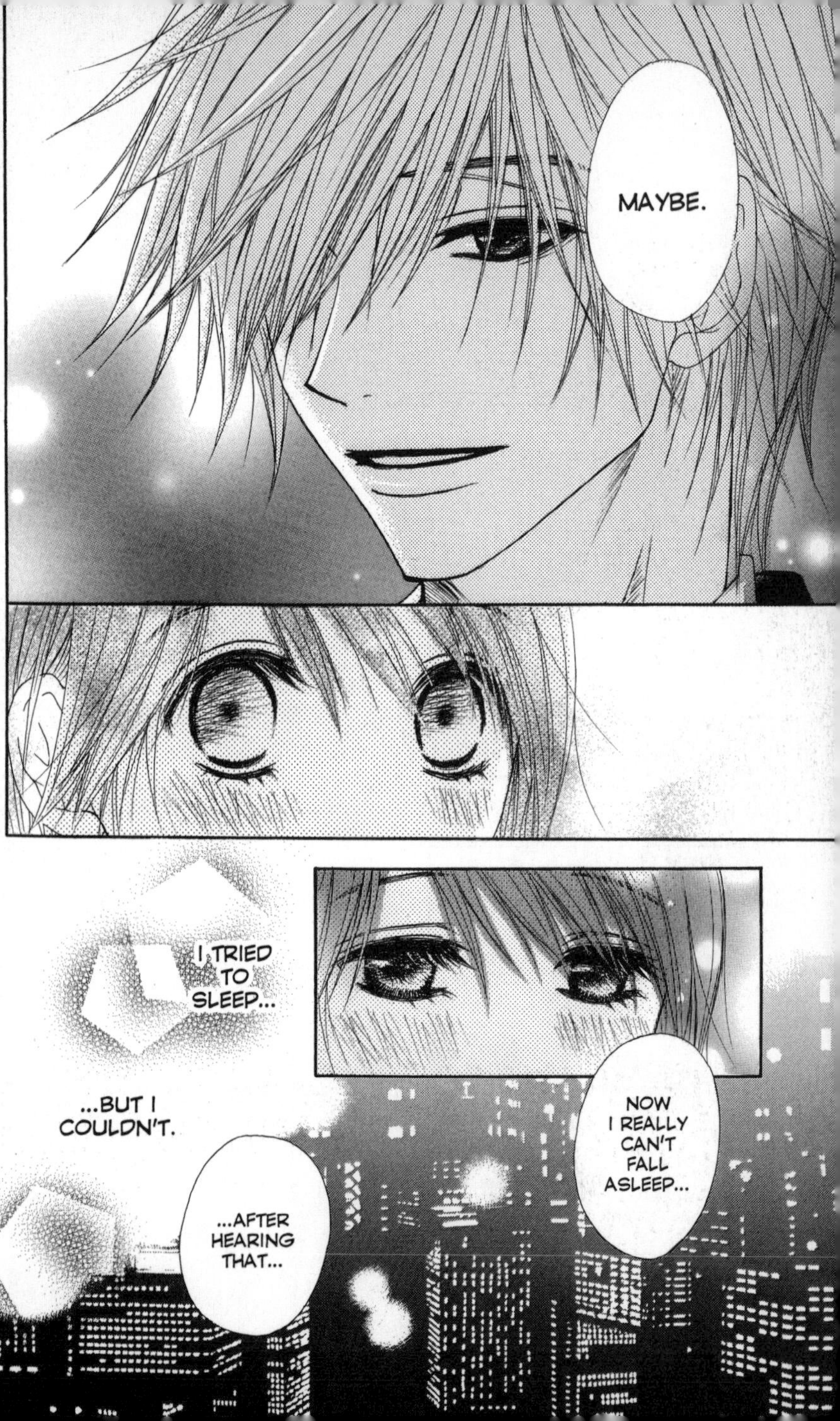
MAYBE.
NOW I REALLY CAN'T FALL ASLEEP...
...AFTER HEARING THAT...
I TRIED TO SLEEP...
...BUT I COULDN'T.

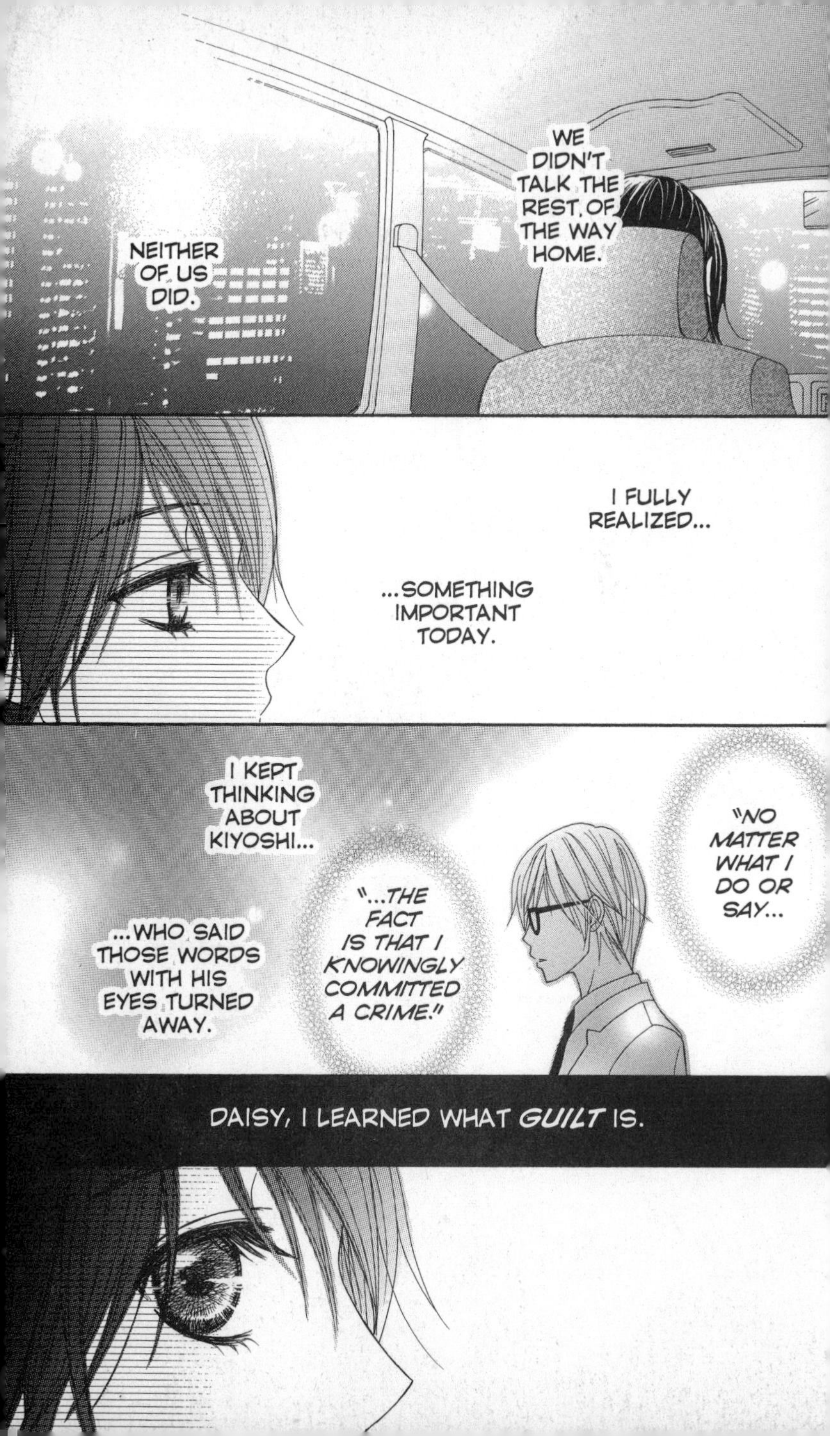

WE DIDN'T TALK THE REST OF THE WAY HOME.
NEITHER OF US DID.
I FULLY REALIZED...
...SOMETHING IMPORTANT TODAY.
"NO MATTER WHAT I DO OR SAY...
"...THE FACT IS THAT I KNOWINGLY COMMITTED A CRIME."
I KEPT THINKING ABOUT KIYOSHI...
...WHO SAID THOSE WORDS WITH HIS EYES TURNED AWAY.
DAISY, I LEARNED WHAT *GUILT* IS.

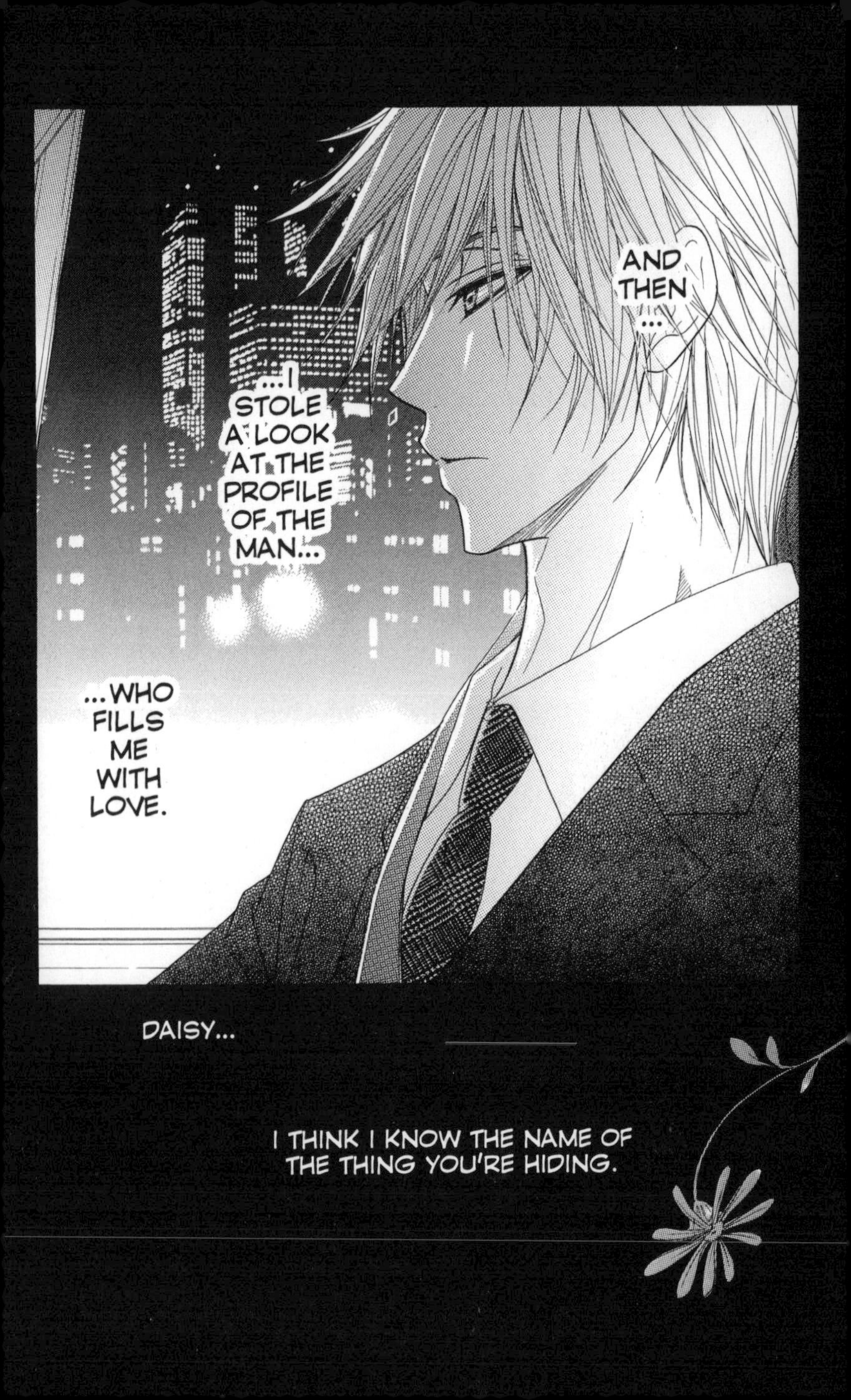
AND THEN ...
...I STOLE A LOOK AT THE PROFILE OF THE MAN...
...WHO FILLS ME WITH LOVE.

DAISY...

I THINK I KNOW THE NAME OF THE THING YOU'RE HIDING.

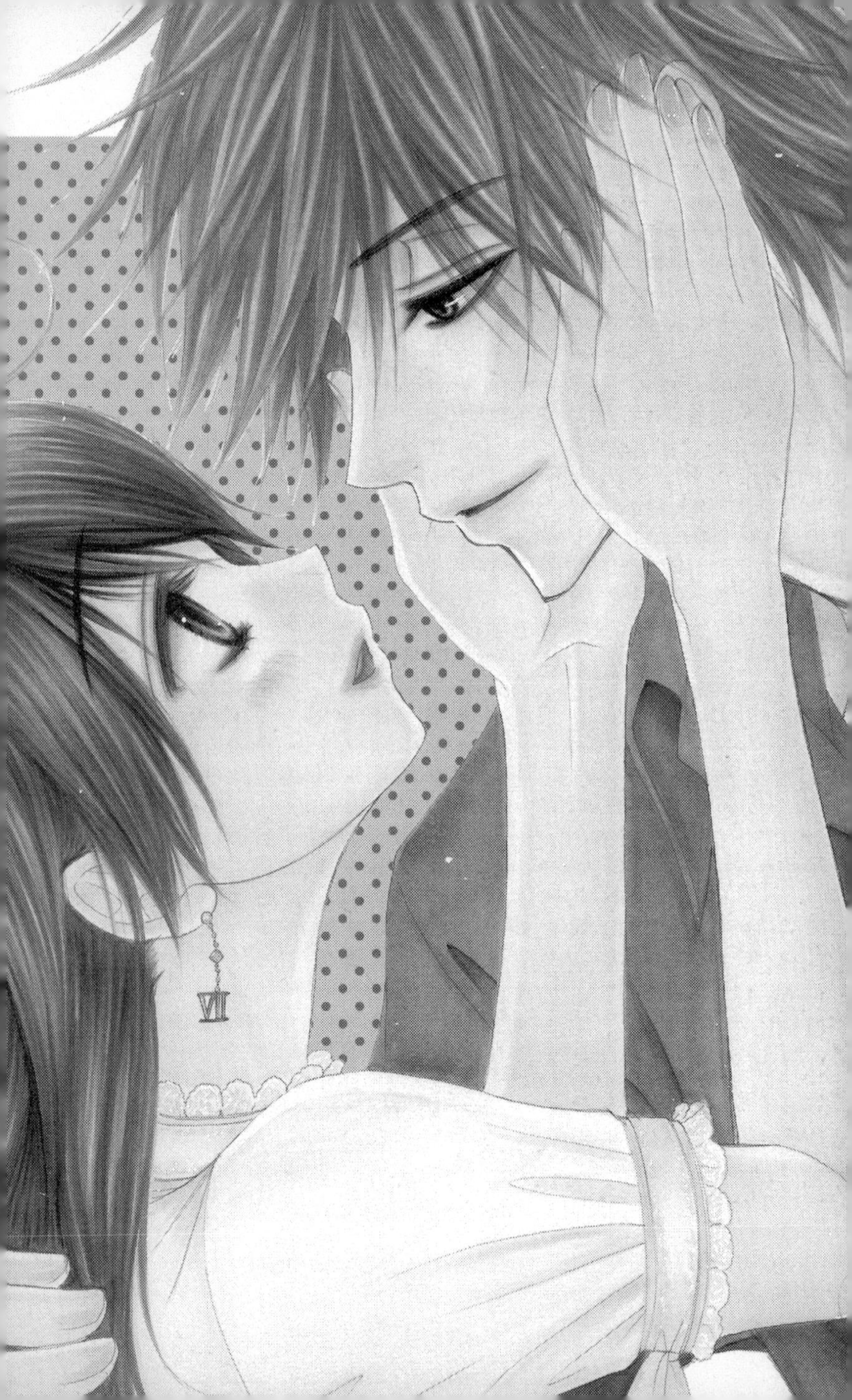

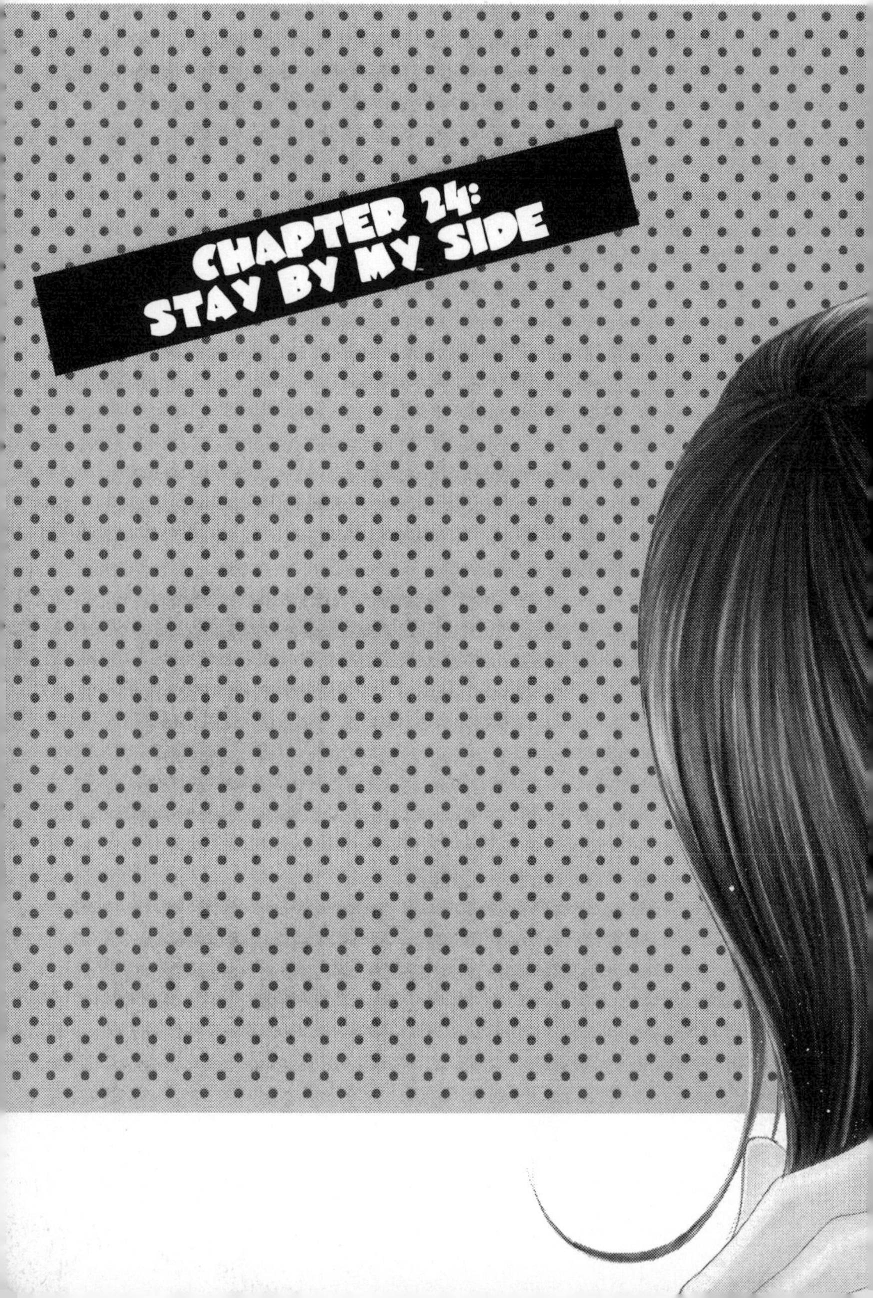
CHAPTER 24:
STAY BY MY SIDE

AFTERWORD

Just a little bit is okay... feel... with every nerve on my back...

ZZZ ZZZ

THANK YOU VERY MUCH FOR YOUR WARM RECEPTION OF *DENGEKI DAISY* VOLUME 5.
(THANKS TO AN EXTRA PAGE, THE AFTERWORD ENDED UP HERE.)

AS THE NUMBER OF VOLUMES INCREASES, I REGRET THAT I FEEL LIKE MY SKILLS ARE LACKING. HOWEVER, IT'S DUE TO ALL OF YOU READERS THAT I'VE BEEN ABLE TO GET TO THIS POINT. MY HEART IS FILLED WITH GRATITUDE.

IT'S ALWAYS HECTIC, BUT I WILL CONTINUE TO DO MY BEST.

I'LL WORK HARD TO GET VOLUME 6 OUT!! PLEASE... LET ME GET VOLUME 6 OUT!!!

ANYWAY, UNTIL WE MEET AGAIN.

最富 キョウスケ
KYOUSUKE MOTOMI

DENGEKI DAISY
"BALDLY ASK!!" CORNER
C/O DENGEKI DAISY EDITOR
VIZ MEDIA
P.O. BOX 77010
SAN FRANCISCO, CA 94107

← PLEASE MAIL YOUR QUESTIONS TO THIS ADDRESS. PLEASE USE THE SAME ADDRESS FOR OTHER MAIL AS WELL... BUT PLEASE CHANGE THE ADDRESSEE TO:

KYOUSUKE MOTOMI
C/O DENGEKI DAISY EDITOR

THANK YOU!

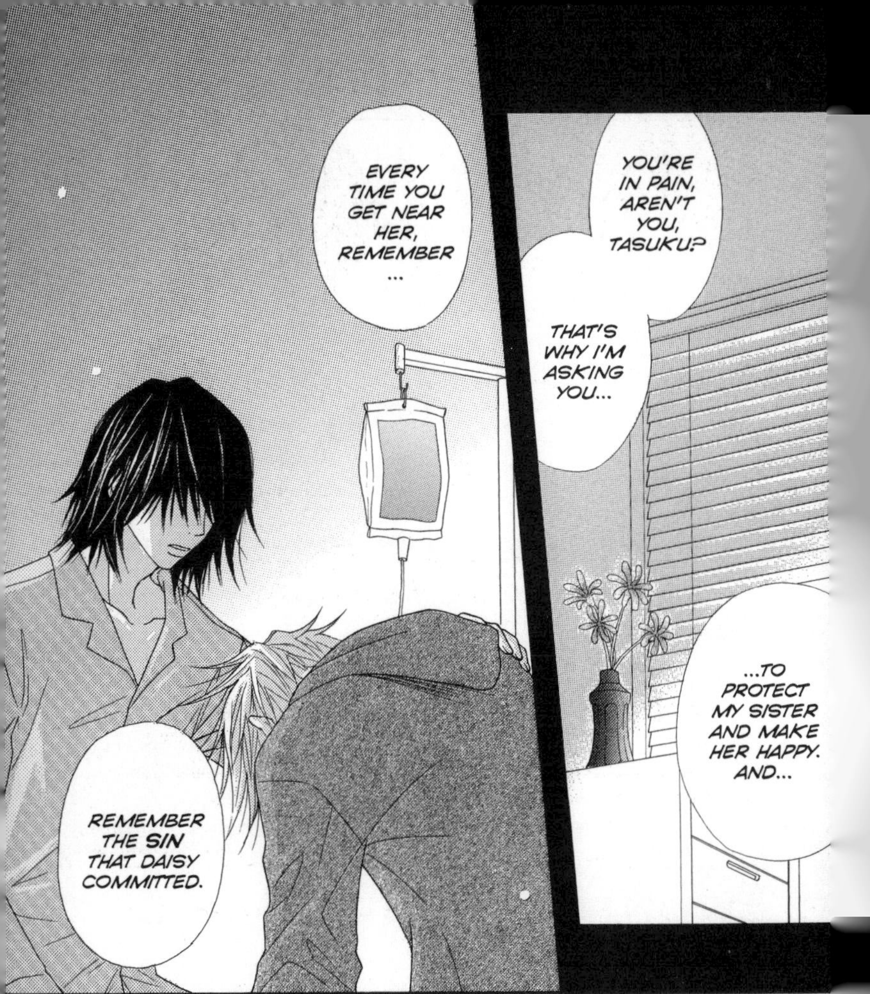
YOU'RE IN PAIN, AREN'T YOU, TASUKU?
THAT'S WHY I'M ASKING YOU...
...TO PROTECT MY SISTER AND MAKE HER HAPPY. AND...
EVERY TIME YOU GET NEAR HER, REMEMBER ...
REMEMBER THE SIN THAT DAISY COMMITTED.

THIS IS THE CURRENT DIFFERENCE IN HEIGHTS. BUT HEIGHT SEEMS TO BE INFLUENCED BY ONE'S PHYSICAL CONDITION AMONG OTHER THINGS (?).

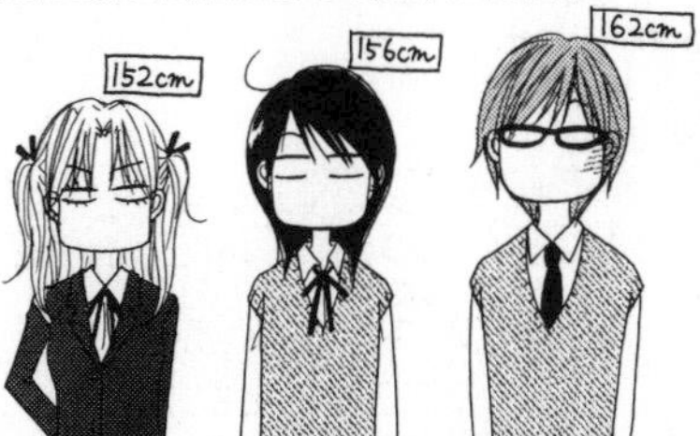
152cm
156cm
162cm

IN CHAPTER 23, TERU COMMENTS THAT KIYOSHI SEEMS TO HAVE GOTTEN TALLER. ACTUALLY, HE'S GROWN A LOT.

AT FIRST, WHEN HE USED TO WEAR THE FASHIONABLE GLASSES, HE WAS ABOUT THE SAME HEIGHT AS TERU, PERHAPS A BIT SHORTER. NOW HE WEARS REGULAR GLASSES, AND HE'S A LITTLE TALLER THAN TERU.

MAYBE IT'S BECAUSE HE ATE A LOT OF RICE DURING SUMMER BREAK. MAYBE HE'LL GROW EVEN TALLER. ALSO, RENA IS ACTUALLY A LITTLE SHORTER THAN TERU.

AMONG THESE THREE HALF-PINTS, TERU IS THE ONLY ONE WHO WANTS TO KEEP HER "PUNY" NICKNAME. WHAT AN UNFAIR WORLD.

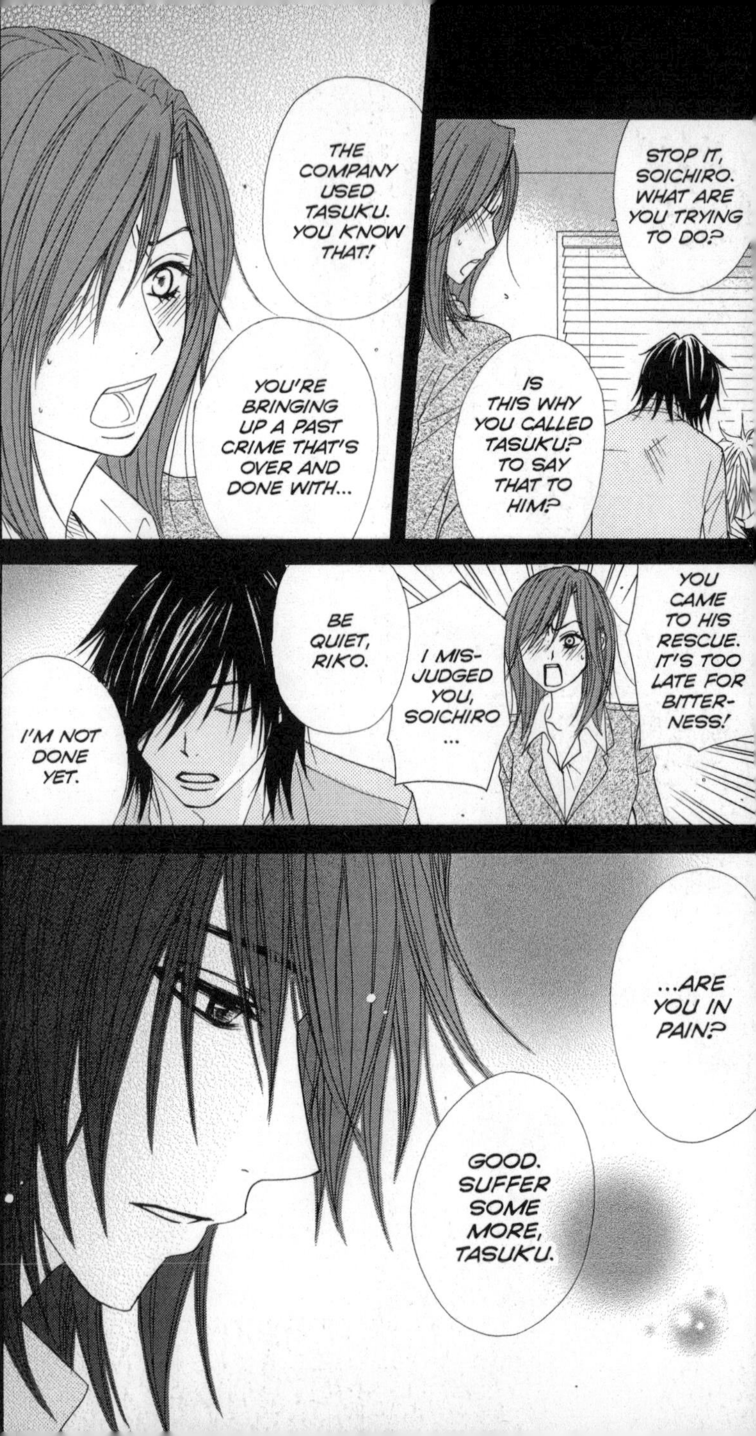
STOP IT, SOICHIRO. WHAT ARE YOU TRYING TO DO?
IS THIS WHY YOU CALLED TASUKU? TO SAY THAT TO HIM?
THE COMPANY USED TASUKU. YOU KNOW THAT!
YOU'RE BRINGING UP A PAST CRIME THAT'S OVER AND DONE WITH...
YOU CAME TO HIS RESCUE. IT'S TOO LATE FOR BITTERNESS!
I MIS-JUDGED YOU, SOICHIRO ...
BE QUIET, RIKO.
I'M NOT DONE YET.
...ARE YOU IN PAIN?
GOOD. SUFFER SOME MORE, TASUKU.

YOU WANTED TO FORGET THE CRIME YOU COMMITTED.
YOU WERE TOLD THAT THE CRIME WOULD BE FORGIVEN, AND YOU BELIEVED IT AND SOLD YOUR HEART.
THAT IS YOUR REAL SIN.
IN ORDER FOR YOU TO KEEP LIVING...
IN ORDER TO PROTECT THE THINGS THAT WILL BECOME DEAR TO YOU HEREAFTER...
...YOU MUST NEVER FORGET YOUR SIN OR THIS PAIN.

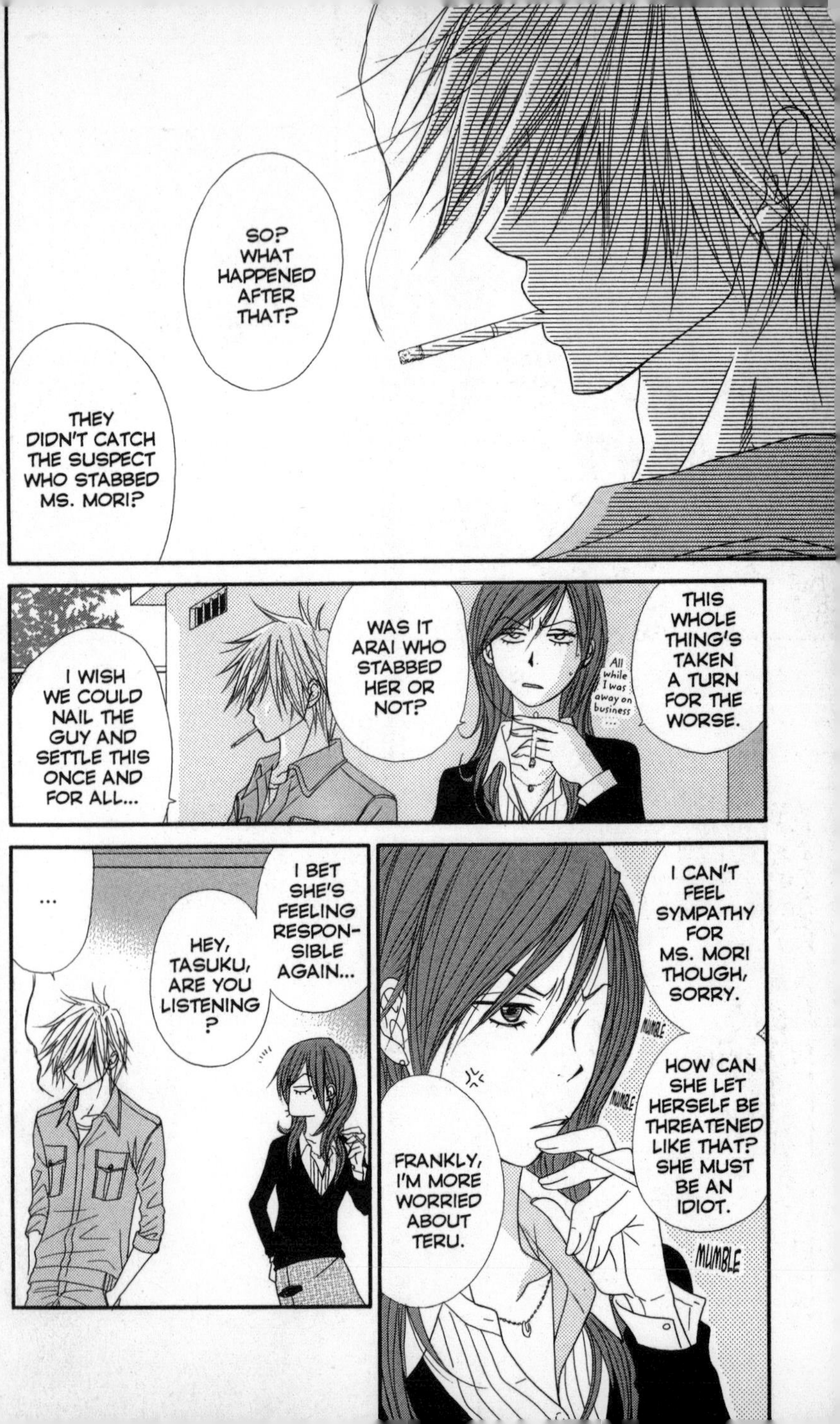
SO? WHAT HAPPENED AFTER THAT?
THEY DIDN'T CATCH THE SUSPECT WHO STABBED MS. MORI?
THIS WHOLE THING'S TAKEN A TURN FOR THE WORSE.
All while I was away on business...
WAS IT ARAI WHO STABBED HER OR NOT?
I WISH WE COULD NAIL THE GUY AND SETTLE THIS ONCE AND FOR ALL...
I CAN'T FEEL SYMPATHY FOR MS. MORI THOUGH, SORRY.
MUMBLE
HOW CAN SHE LET HERSELF BE THREATENED LIKE THAT? SHE MUST BE AN IDIOT.
MUMBLE
MUMBLE
FRANKLY, I'M MORE WORRIED ABOUT TERU.
I BET SHE'S FEELING RESPONSIBLE AGAIN...
HEY, TASUKU, ARE YOU LISTENING?
...

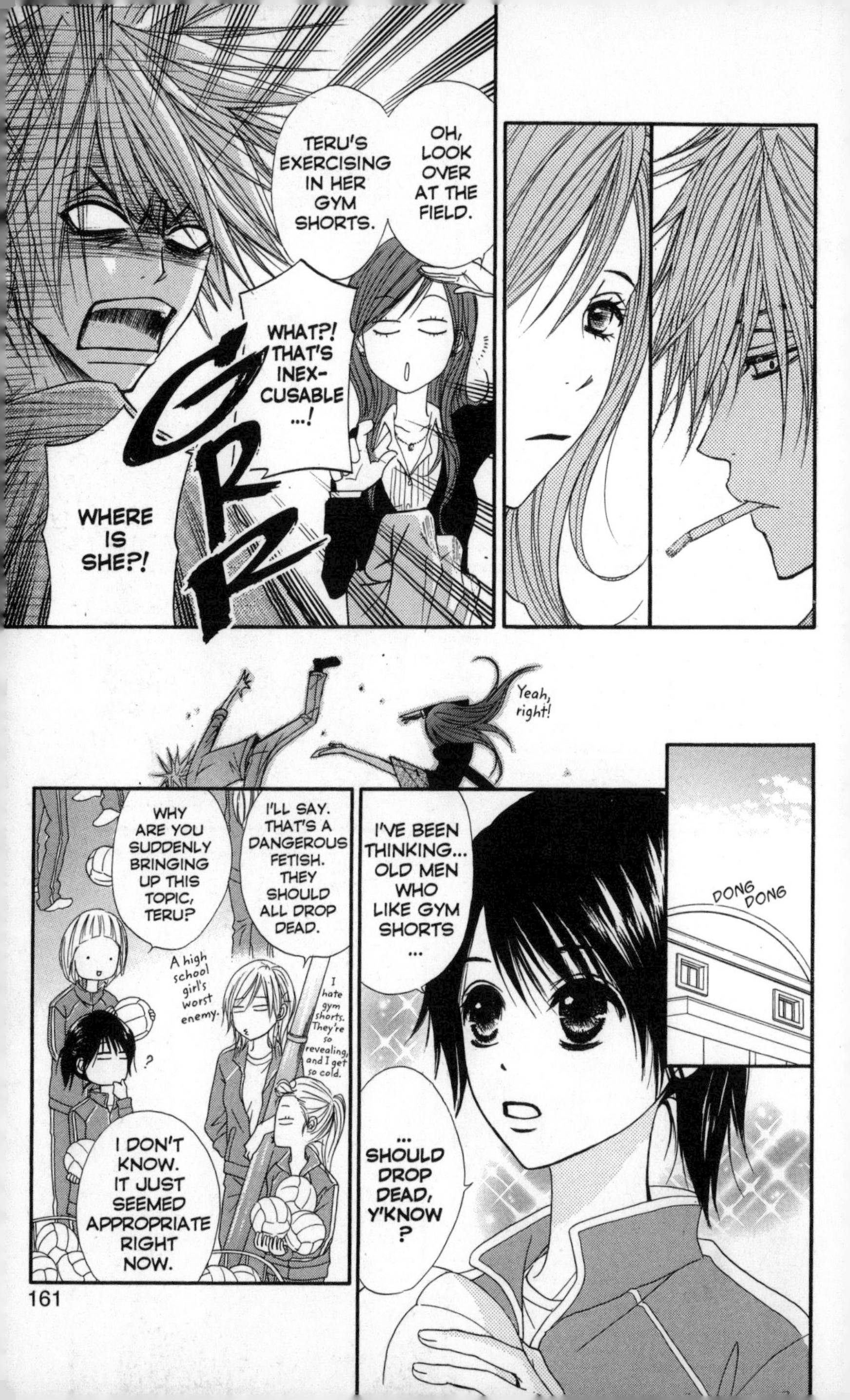
OH, LOOK OVER AT THE FIELD.
TERU'S EXERCISING IN HER GYM SHORTS.
WHAT?! THAT'S INEXCUSABLE ...!
GRR
WHERE IS SHE?!
Yeah, right!
DONG DONG
I'VE BEEN THINKING... OLD MEN WHO LIKE GYM SHORTS ...
... SHOULD DROP DEAD, Y'KNOW?
I'LL SAY. THAT'S A DANGEROUS FETISH. THEY SHOULD ALL DROP DEAD.
I hate gym shorts. They're so revealing, and I get so cold.
WHY ARE YOU SUDDENLY BRINGING UP THIS TOPIC, TERU?
A high school girl's worst enemy.
?
I DON'T KNOW. IT JUST SEEMED APPROPRIATE RIGHT NOW.

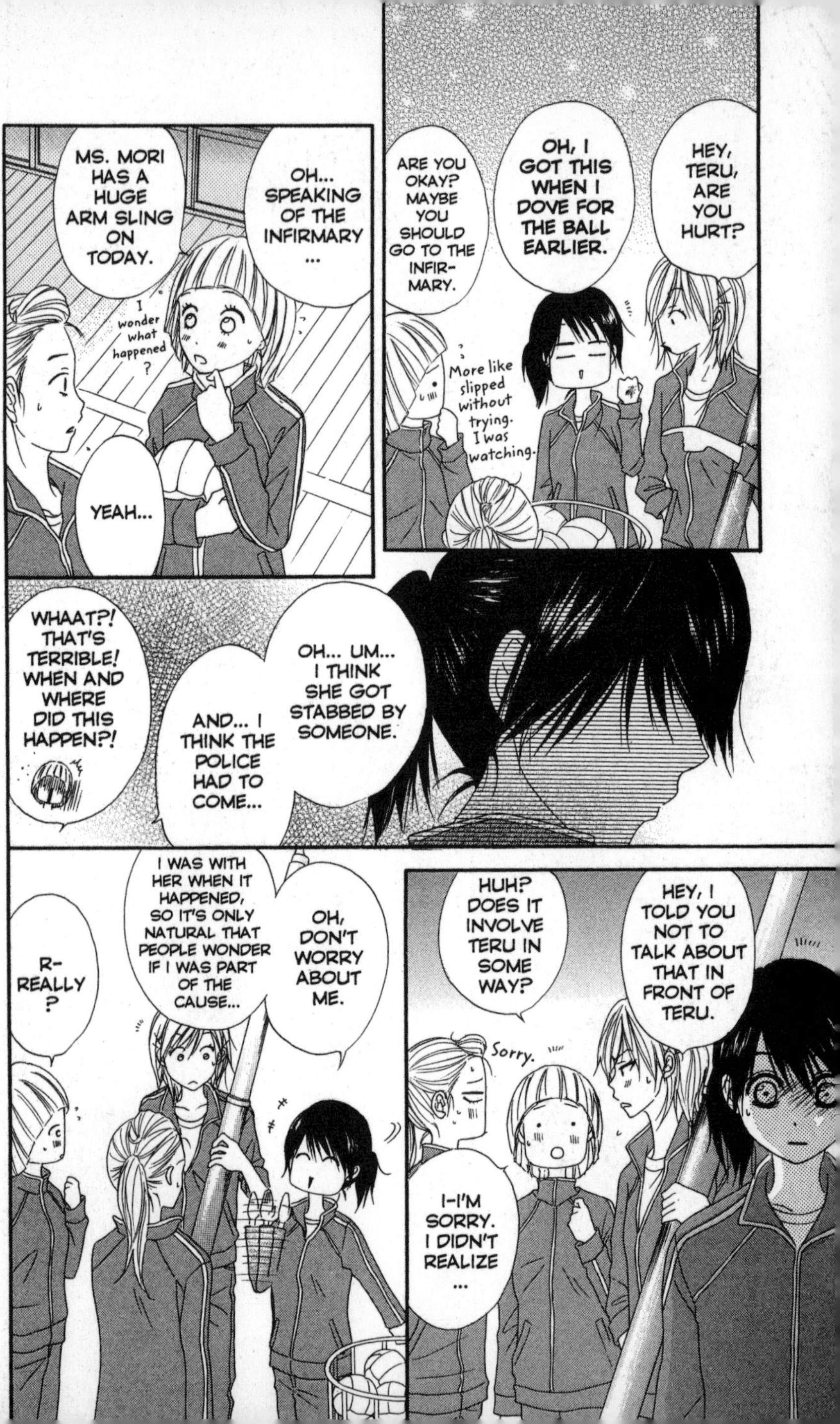
HEY, TERU, ARE YOU HURT?
OH, I GOT THIS WHEN I DOVE FOR THE BALL EARLIER.
ARE YOU OKAY? MAYBE YOU SHOULD GO TO THE INFIRMARY.
More like slipped without trying. I was watching.
OH... SPEAKING OF THE INFIRMARY...
MS. MORI HAS A HUGE ARM SLING ON TODAY.
I wonder what happened?
YEAH...
OH... UM... I THINK SHE GOT STABBED BY SOMEONE.
AND... I THINK THE POLICE HAD TO COME...
WHAAT?! THAT'S TERRIBLE! WHEN AND WHERE DID THIS HAPPEN?!
HEY, I TOLD YOU NOT TO TALK ABOUT THAT IN FRONT OF TERU.
HUH? DOES IT INVOLVE TERU IN SOME WAY?
Sorry.
I-I'M SORRY. I DIDN'T REALIZE...
OH, DON'T WORRY ABOUT ME.
I WAS WITH HER WHEN IT HAPPENED, SO IT'S ONLY NATURAL THAT PEOPLE WONDER IF I WAS PART OF THE CAUSE...
R-REALLY?

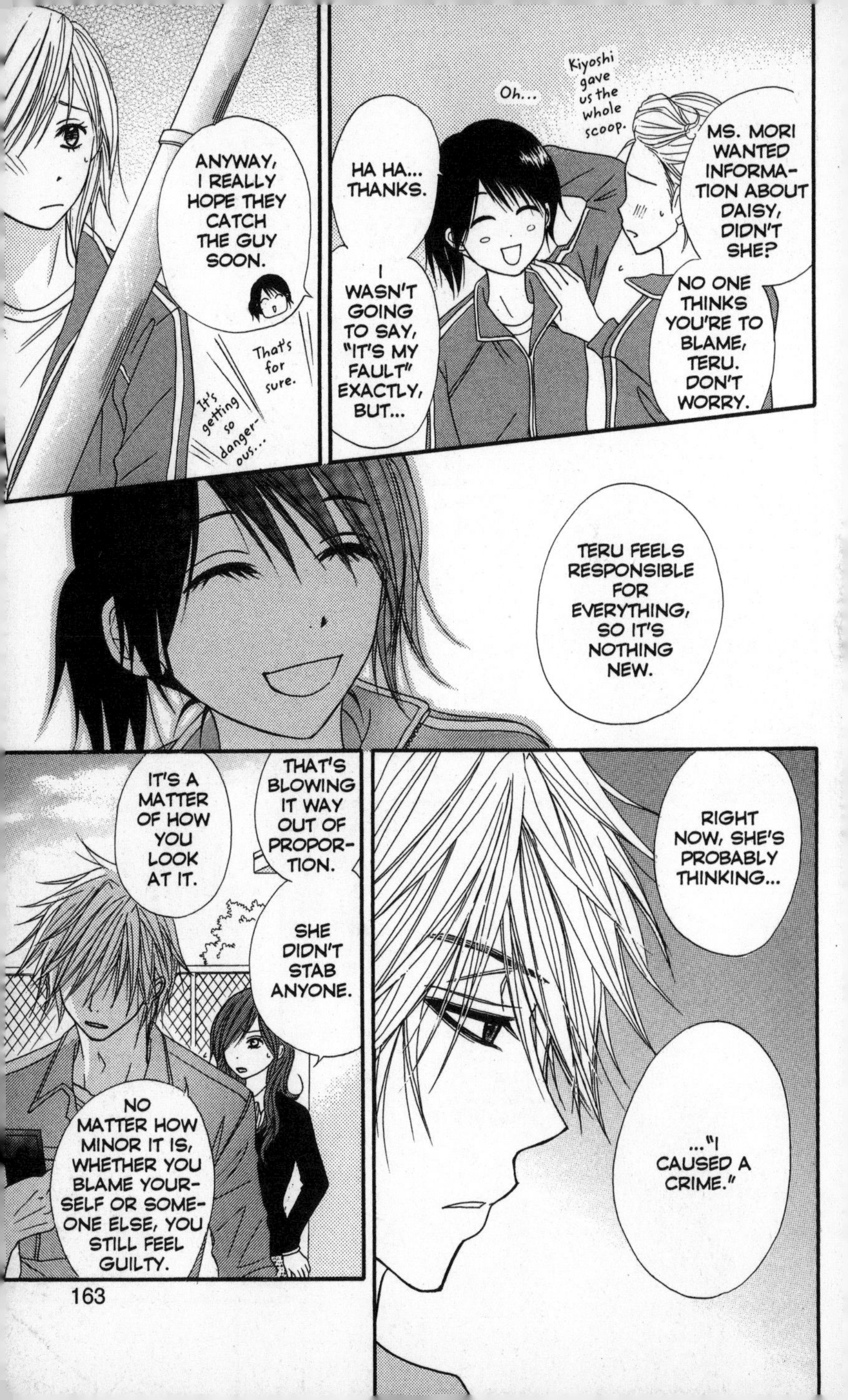
MS. MORI WANTED INFORMATION ABOUT DAISY, DIDN'T SHE?
Kiyoshi gave us the whole scoop.
Oh...
NO ONE THINKS YOU'RE TO BLAME, TERU. DON'T WORRY.
HA HA... THANKS.
I WASN'T GOING TO SAY, "IT'S MY FAULT" EXACTLY, BUT...
ANYWAY, I REALLY HOPE THEY CATCH THE GUY SOON.
That's for sure.
It's getting so danger-ous...
TERU FEELS RESPONSIBLE FOR EVERYTHING, SO IT'S NOTHING NEW.
RIGHT NOW, SHE'S PROBABLY THINKING...
..."I CAUSED A CRIME."
THAT'S BLOWING IT WAY OUT OF PROPORTION.
IT'S A MATTER OF HOW YOU LOOK AT IT.
SHE DIDN'T STAB ANYONE.
NO MATTER HOW MINOR IT IS, WHETHER YOU BLAME YOUR-SELF OR SOME-ONE ELSE, YOU STILL FEEL GUILTY.

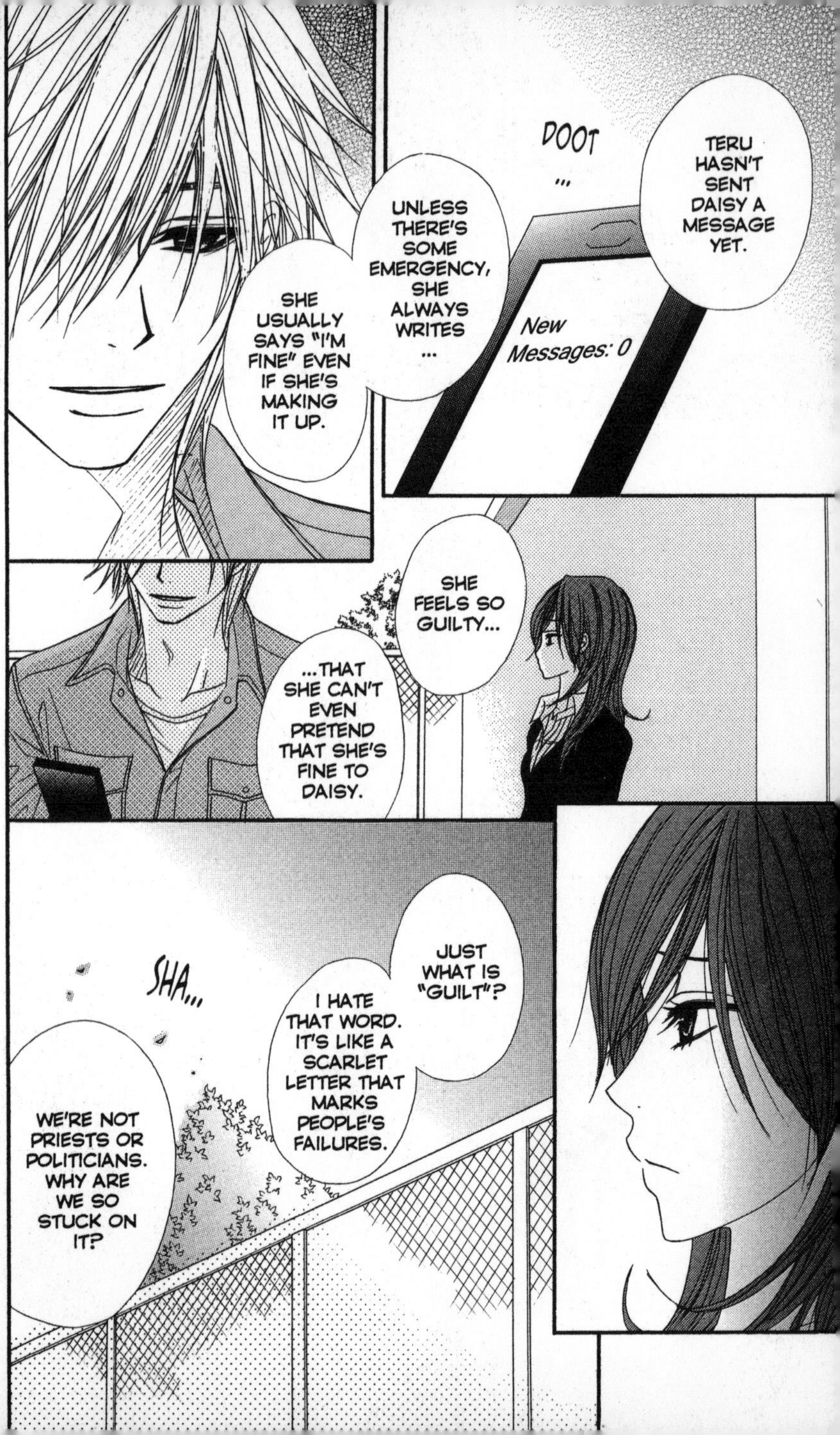
TERU HASN'T SENT DAISY A MESSAGE YET.
DOOT
...
New Messages: 0
UNLESS THERE'S SOME EMERGENCY, SHE ALWAYS WRITES...
SHE USUALLY SAYS "I'M FINE" EVEN IF SHE'S MAKING IT UP.
SHE FEELS SO GUILTY...
...THAT SHE CAN'T EVEN PRETEND THAT SHE'S FINE TO DAISY.
JUST WHAT IS "GUILT"?
SHA...
I HATE THAT WORD. IT'S LIKE A SCARLET LETTER THAT MARKS PEOPLE'S FAILURES.
WE'RE NOT PRIESTS OR POLITICIANS. WHY ARE WE SO STUCK ON IT?

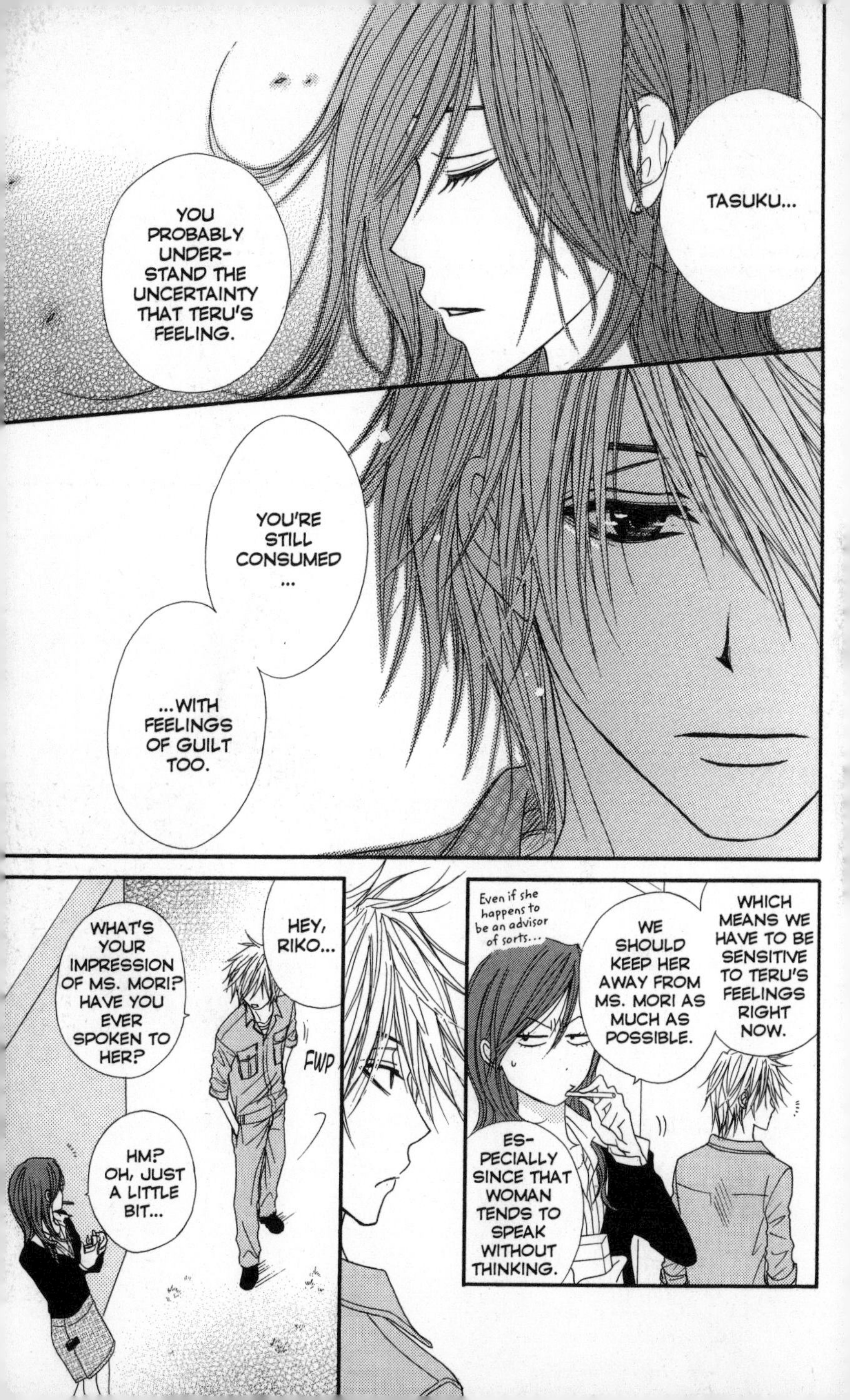
TASUKU...
YOU PROBABLY UNDER-STAND THE UNCERTAINTY THAT TERU'S FEELING.
YOU'RE STILL CONSUMED ...
...WITH FEELINGS OF GUILT TOO.
WHICH MEANS WE HAVE TO BE SENSITIVE TO TERU'S FEELINGS RIGHT NOW.
WE SHOULD KEEP HER AWAY FROM MS. MORI AS MUCH AS POSSIBLE.
Even if she happens to be an advisor of sorts...
ES-PECIALLY SINCE THAT WOMAN TENDS TO SPEAK WITHOUT THINKING.
HEY, RIKO...
FWP
WHAT'S YOUR IMPRESSION OF MS. MORI? HAVE YOU EVER SPOKEN TO HER?
HM? OH, JUST A LITTLE BIT...

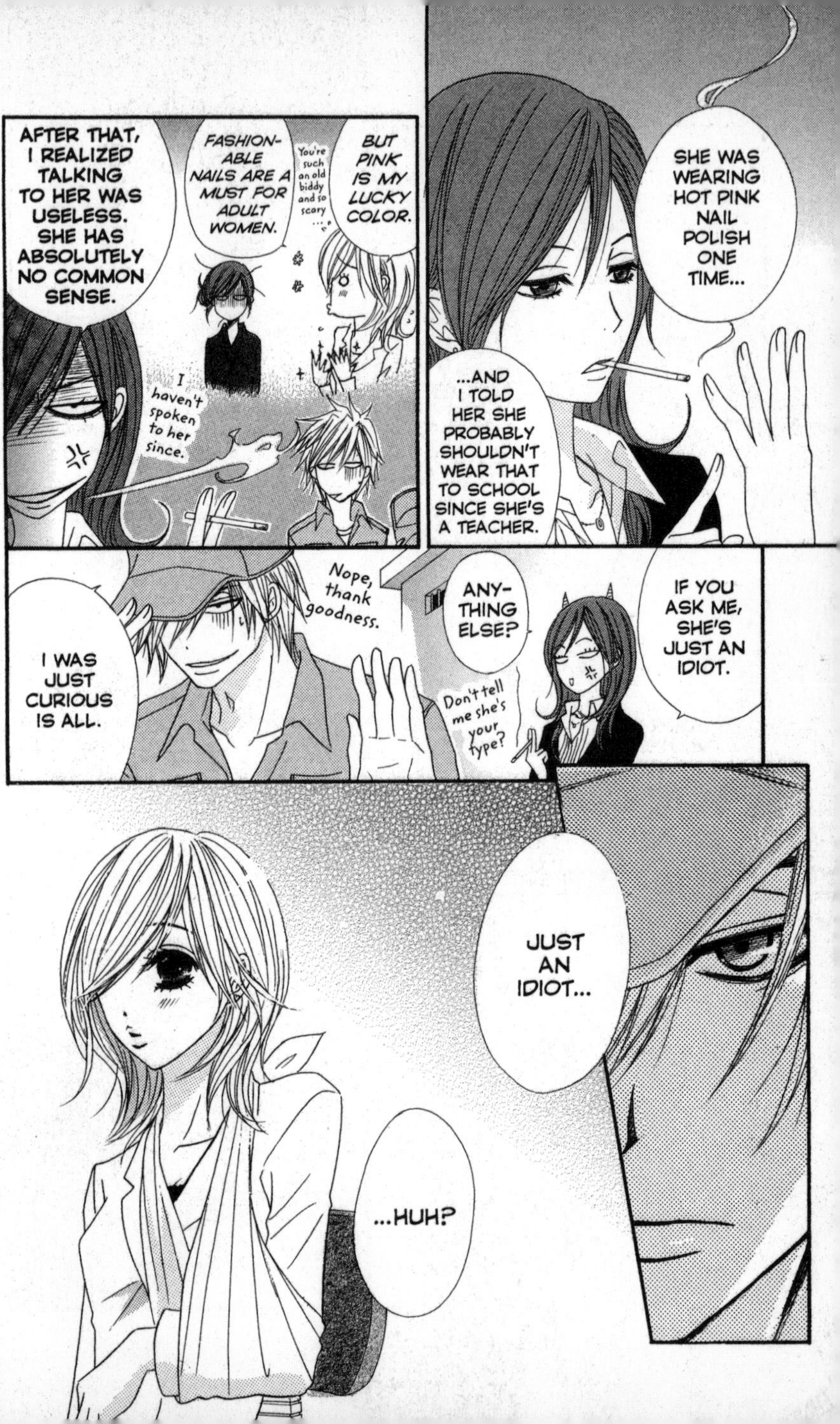
SHE WAS WEARING HOT PINK NAIL POLISH ONE TIME...
...AND I TOLD HER SHE PROBABLY SHOULDN'T WEAR THAT TO SCHOOL SINCE SHE'S A TEACHER.
BUT PINK IS MY LUCKY COLOR.
You're such an old biddy and so scary...
FASHION-ABLE NAILS ARE A MUST FOR ADULT WOMEN.
AFTER THAT, I REALIZED TALKING TO HER WAS USELESS. SHE HAS ABSOLUTELY NO COMMON SENSE.
I haven't spoken to her since.
IF YOU ASK ME, SHE'S JUST AN IDIOT.
ANY-THING ELSE?
Don't tell me she's your type?
Nope, thank goodness.
I WAS JUST CURIOUS IS ALL.
JUST AN IDIOT...
...HUH?

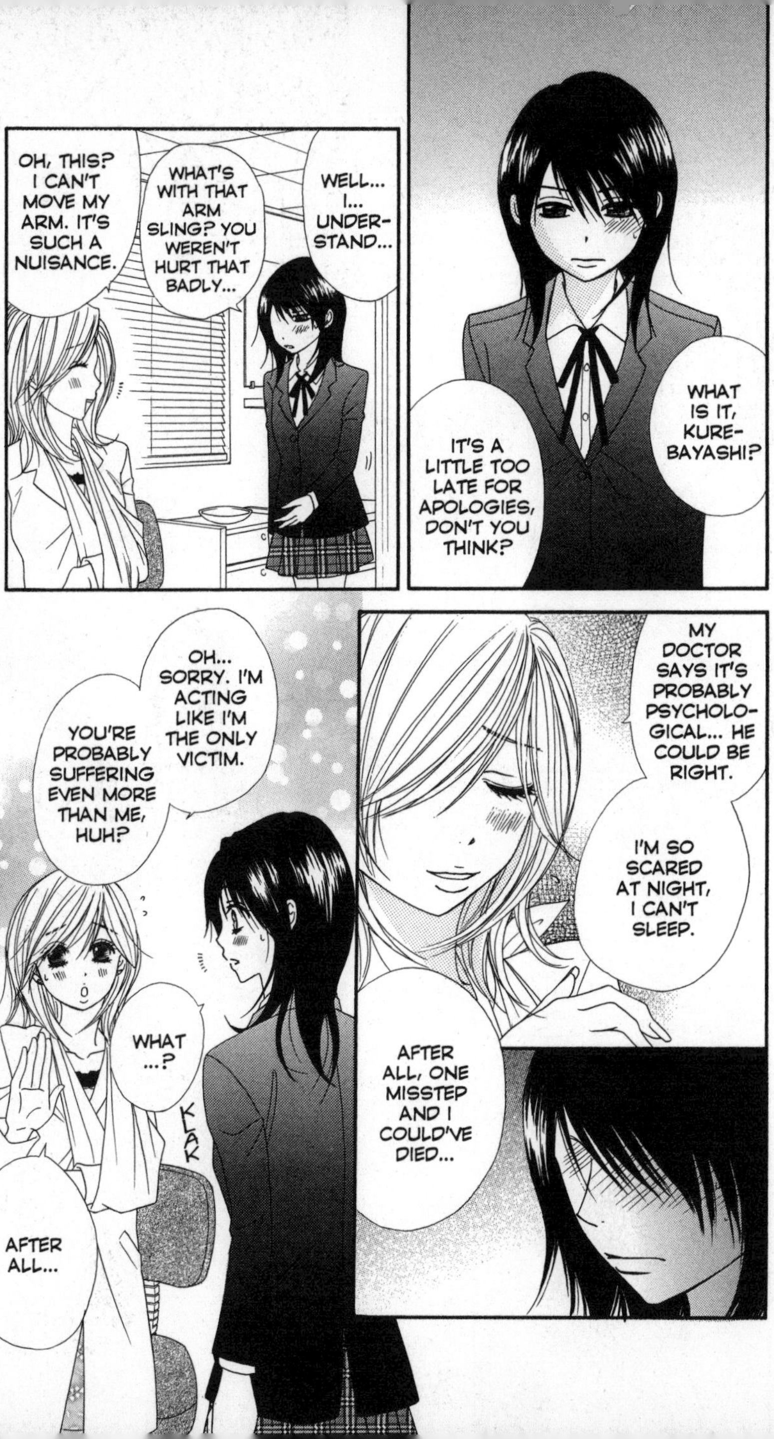
WHAT IS IT, KURE-BAYASHI?
IT'S A LITTLE TOO LATE FOR APOLOGIES, DON'T YOU THINK?
WELL... I... UNDER-STAND...
WHAT'S WITH THAT ARM SLING? YOU WEREN'T HURT THAT BADLY...
OH, THIS? I CAN'T MOVE MY ARM. IT'S SUCH A NUISANCE.
MY DOCTOR SAYS IT'S PROBABLY PSYCHOLO-GICAL... HE COULD BE RIGHT.
I'M SO SCARED AT NIGHT, I CAN'T SLEEP.
AFTER ALL, ONE MISSTEP AND I COULD'VE DIED...
OH... SORRY. I'M ACTING LIKE I'M THE ONLY VICTIM.
YOU'RE PROBABLY SUFFERING EVEN MORE THAN ME, HUH?
WHAT ...?
KLAK
AFTER ALL...

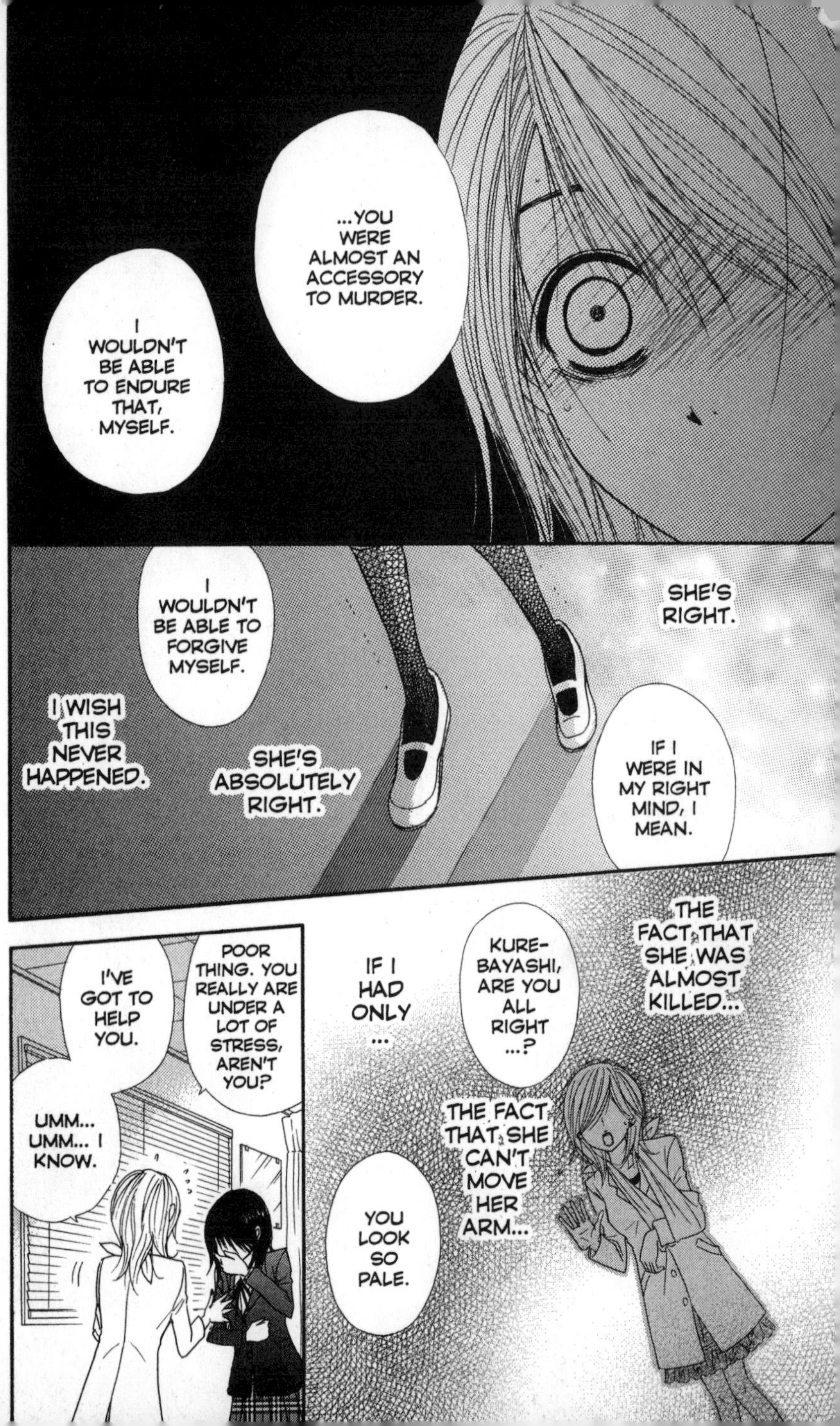
...YOU WERE ALMOST AN ACCESSORY TO MURDER.
I WOULDN'T BE ABLE TO ENDURE THAT, MYSELF.
SHE'S RIGHT.
IF I WERE IN MY RIGHT MIND, I MEAN.
I WOULDN'T BE ABLE TO FORGIVE MYSELF.
SHE'S ABSOLUTELY RIGHT.
I WISH THIS NEVER HAPPENED.
THE FACT THAT SHE WAS ALMOST KILLED...
KURE-BAYASHI, ARE YOU ALL RIGHT ...?
IF I HAD ONLY ...
THE FACT THAT SHE CAN'T MOVE HER ARM...
YOU LOOK SO PALE.
POOR THING. YOU REALLY ARE UNDER A LOT OF STRESS, AREN'T YOU?
I'VE GOT TO HELP YOU.
UMM... UMM... I KNOW.

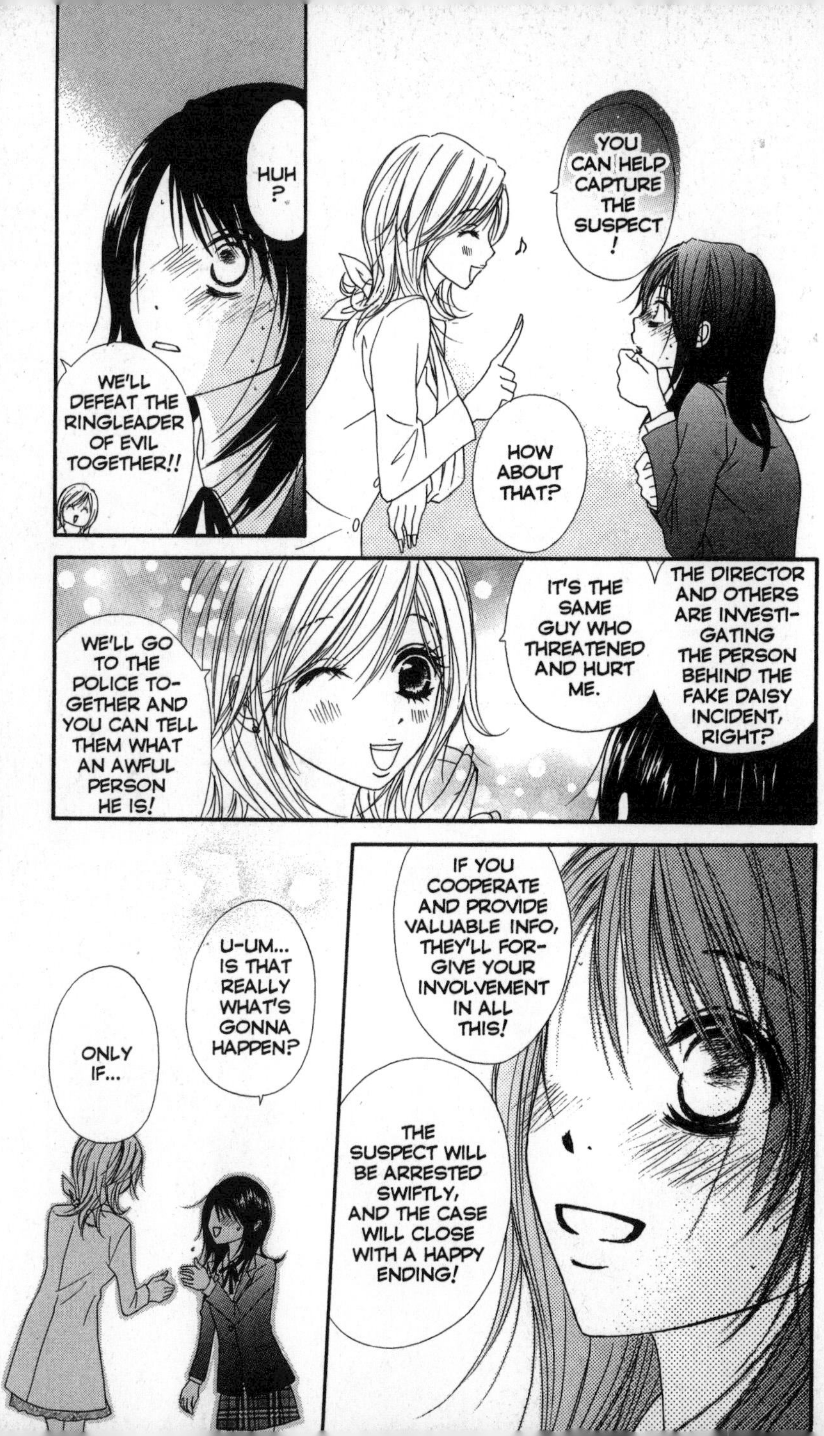
YOU CAN HELP CAPTURE THE SUSPECT!
HOW ABOUT THAT?
HUH?
WE'LL DEFEAT THE RINGLEADER OF EVIL TOGETHER!!
THE DIRECTOR AND OTHERS ARE INVESTI-GATING THE PERSON BEHIND THE FAKE DAISY INCIDENT, RIGHT?
IT'S THE SAME GUY WHO THREATENED AND HURT ME.
WE'LL GO TO THE POLICE TO-GETHER AND YOU CAN TELL THEM WHAT AN AWFUL PERSON HE IS!
IF YOU COOPERATE AND PROVIDE VALUABLE INFO, THEY'LL FOR-GIVE YOUR INVOLVEMENT IN ALL THIS!
THE SUSPECT WILL BE ARRESTED SWIFTLY, AND THE CASE WILL CLOSE WITH A HAPPY ENDING!
U-UM... IS THAT REALLY WHAT'S GONNA HAPPEN?
ONLY IF...

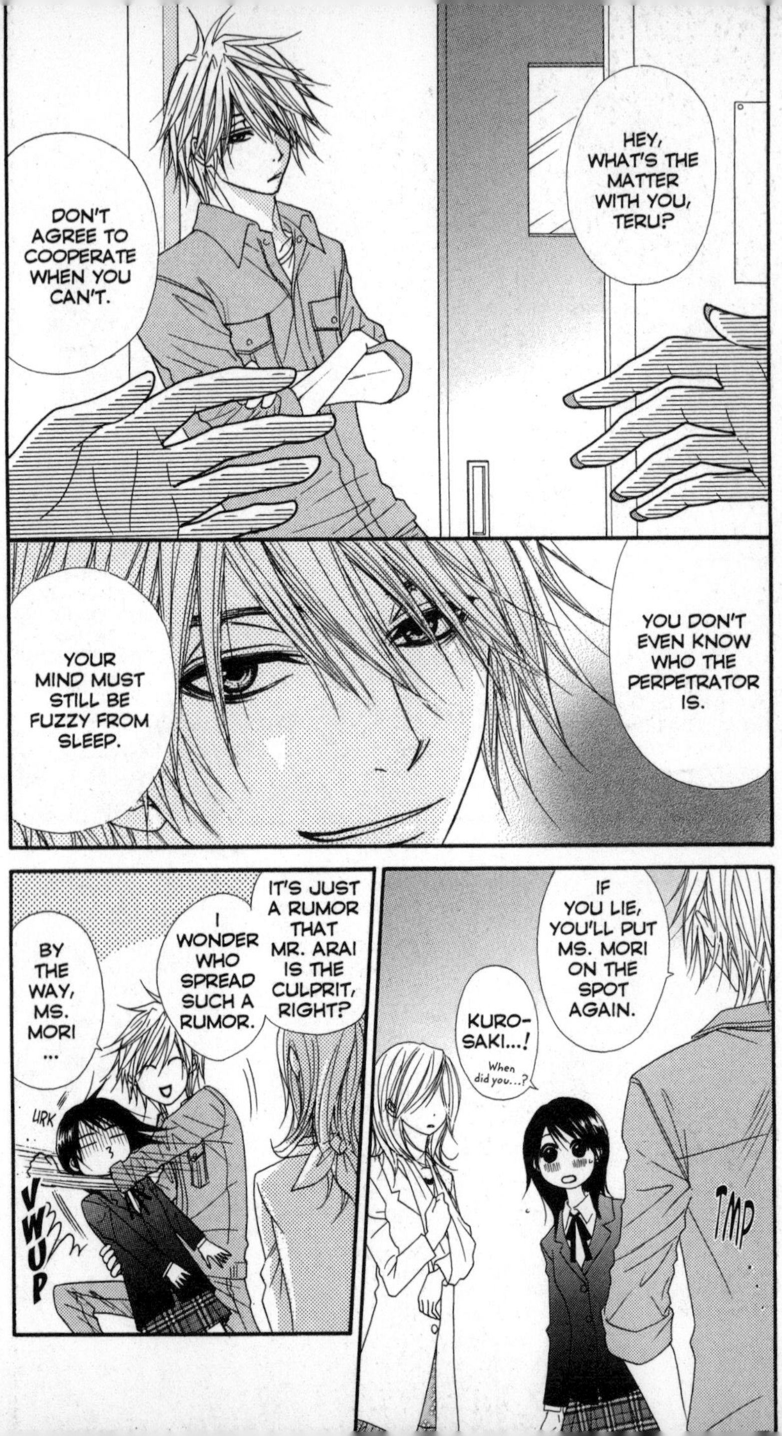
HEY, WHAT'S THE MATTER WITH YOU, TERU?
DON'T AGREE TO COOPERATE WHEN YOU CAN'T.
YOU DON'T EVEN KNOW WHO THE PERPETRATOR IS.
YOUR MIND MUST STILL BE FUZZY FROM SLEEP.
IF YOU LIE, YOU'LL PUT MS. MORI ON THE SPOT AGAIN.
KURO-SAKI...!
When did you...?
TMP
IT'S JUST A RUMOR THAT MR. ARAI IS THE CULPRIT, RIGHT?
I WONDER WHO SPREAD SUCH A RUMOR.
BY THE WAY, MS. MORI ...
URK
VWUP

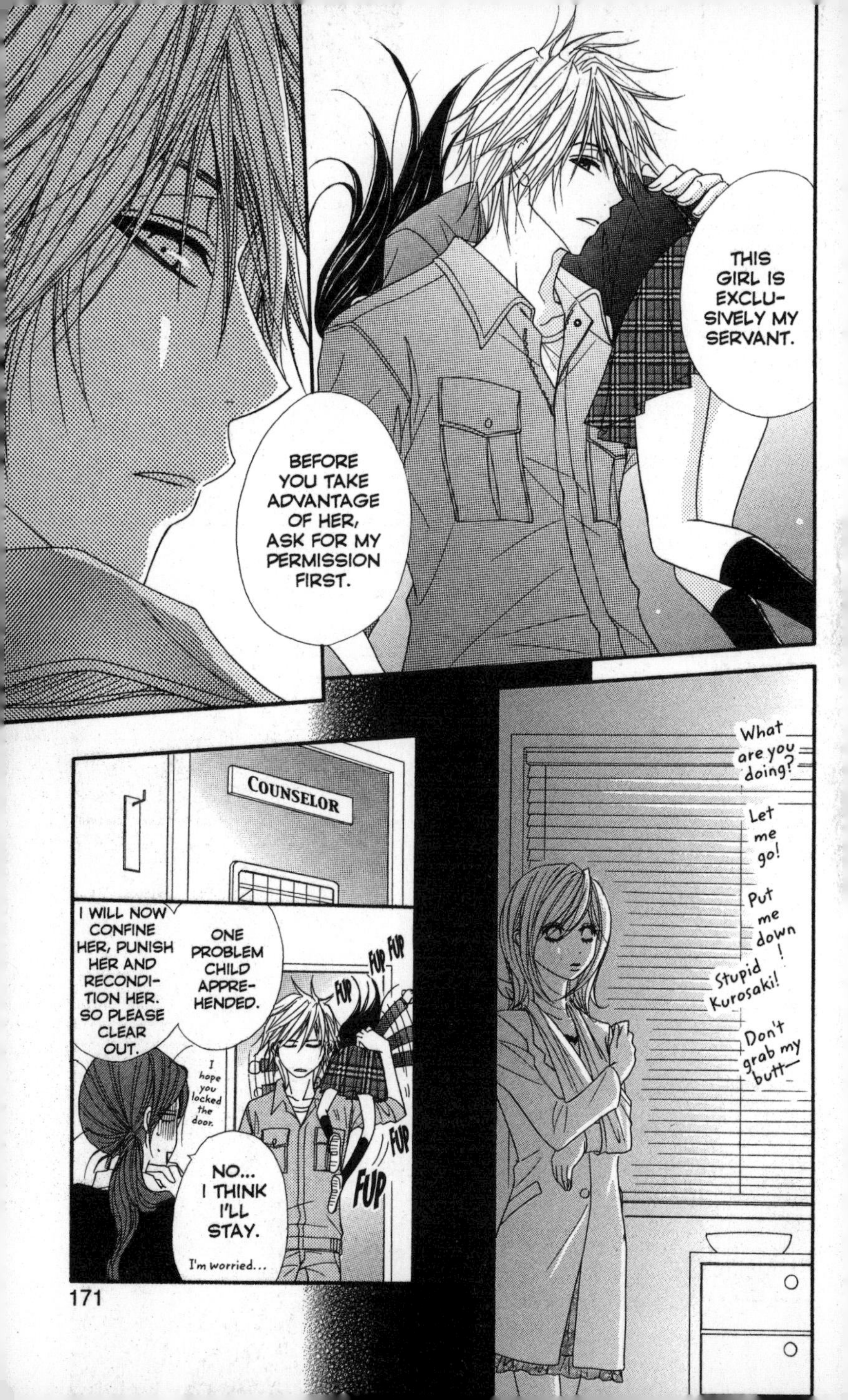
THIS GIRL IS EXCLU- SIVELY MY SERVANT.
BEFORE YOU TAKE ADVANTAGE OF HER, ASK FOR MY PERMISSION FIRST.
What are you doing?
Let me go!
Put me down!
Stupid Kurosaki!
Don't grab my butt—
COUNSELOR
ONE PROBLEM CHILD APPRE- HENDED.
I WILL NOW CONFINE HER, PUNISH HER AND RECONDI- TION HER. SO PLEASE CLEAR OUT.
FUP FUP
FUP
FUP
FUP
FUP
I hope you locked the door.
NO... I THINK I'LL STAY.
I'm worried...

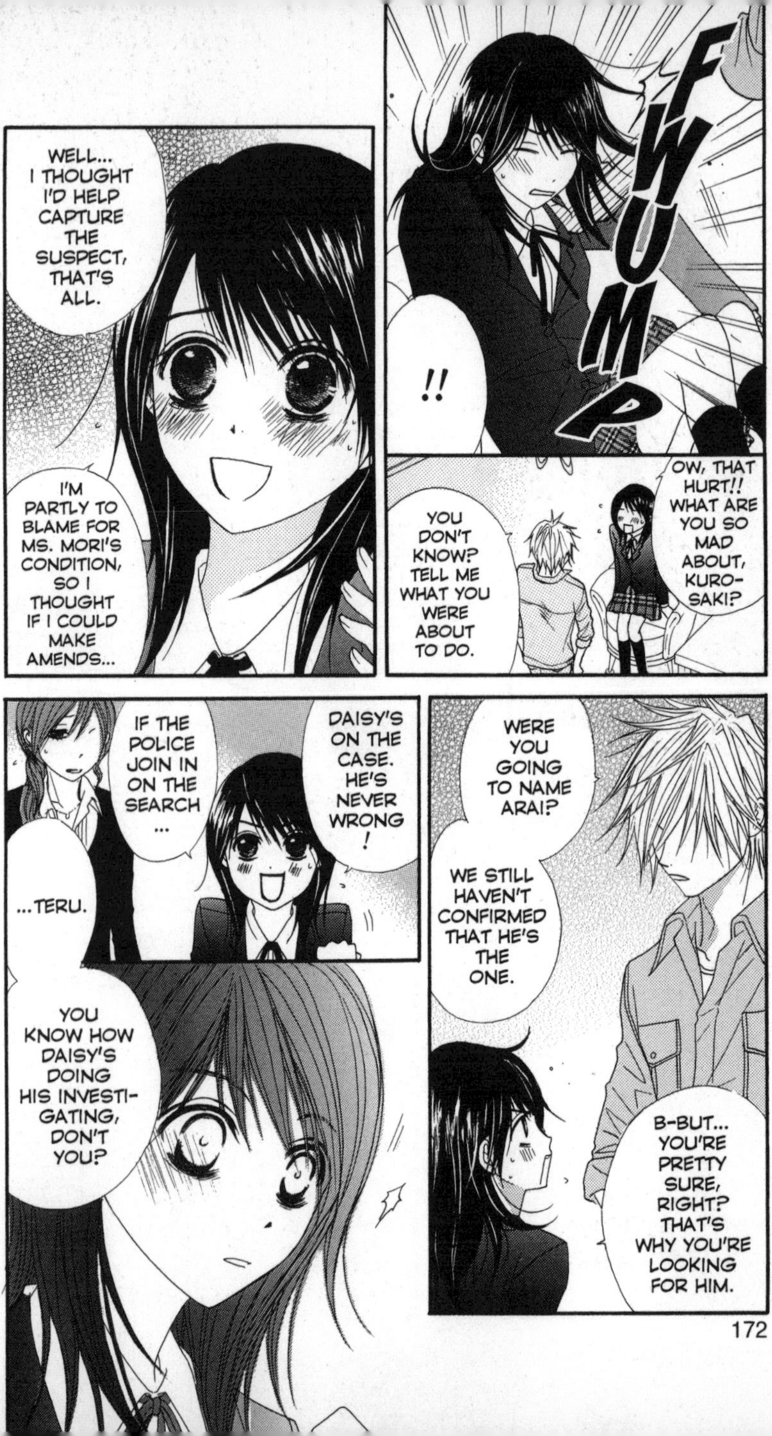
FWUMP
!!
OW, THAT HURT!! WHAT ARE YOU SO MAD ABOUT, KUROSAKI?
YOU DON'T KNOW? TELL ME WHAT YOU WERE ABOUT TO DO.
WELL... I THOUGHT I'D HELP CAPTURE THE SUSPECT, THAT'S ALL.
I'M PARTLY TO BLAME FOR MS. MORI'S CONDITION, SO I THOUGHT IF I COULD MAKE AMENDS...
WERE YOU GOING TO NAME ARAI?
WE STILL HAVEN'T CONFIRMED THAT HE'S THE ONE.
B-BUT... YOU'RE PRETTY SURE, RIGHT? THAT'S WHY YOU'RE LOOKING FOR HIM.
DAISY'S ON THE CASE. HE'S NEVER WRONG!
IF THE POLICE JOIN IN ON THE SEARCH ...
...TERU.
YOU KNOW HOW DAISY'S DOING HIS INVESTIGATING, DON'T YOU?

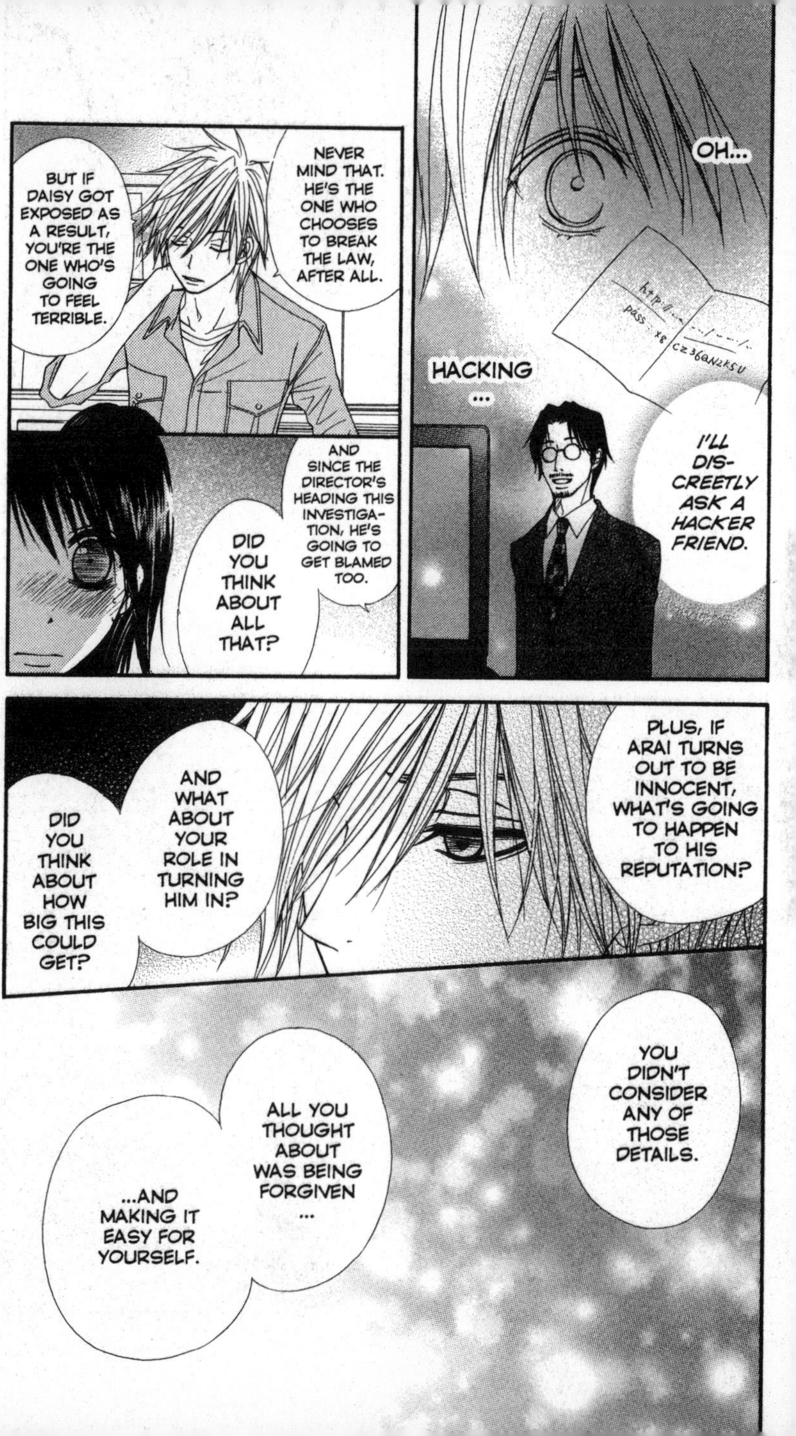
OH...
I'LL DIS-CREETLY ASK A HACKER FRIEND.
HACKING ...
NEVER MIND THAT. HE'S THE ONE WHO CHOOSES TO BREAK THE LAW, AFTER ALL.
BUT IF DAISY GOT EXPOSED AS A RESULT, YOU'RE THE ONE WHO'S GOING TO FEEL TERRIBLE.
AND SINCE THE DIRECTOR'S HEADING THIS INVESTIGA-TION, HE'S GOING TO GET BLAMED TOO.
DID YOU THINK ABOUT ALL THAT?
PLUS, IF ARAI TURNS OUT TO BE INNOCENT, WHAT'S GOING TO HAPPEN TO HIS REPUTATION?
AND WHAT ABOUT YOUR ROLE IN TURNING HIM IN?
DID YOU THINK ABOUT HOW BIG THIS COULD GET?
YOU DIDN'T CONSIDER ANY OF THOSE DETAILS.
ALL YOU THOUGHT ABOUT WAS BEING FORGIVEN ...
...AND MAKING IT EASY FOR YOURSELF.

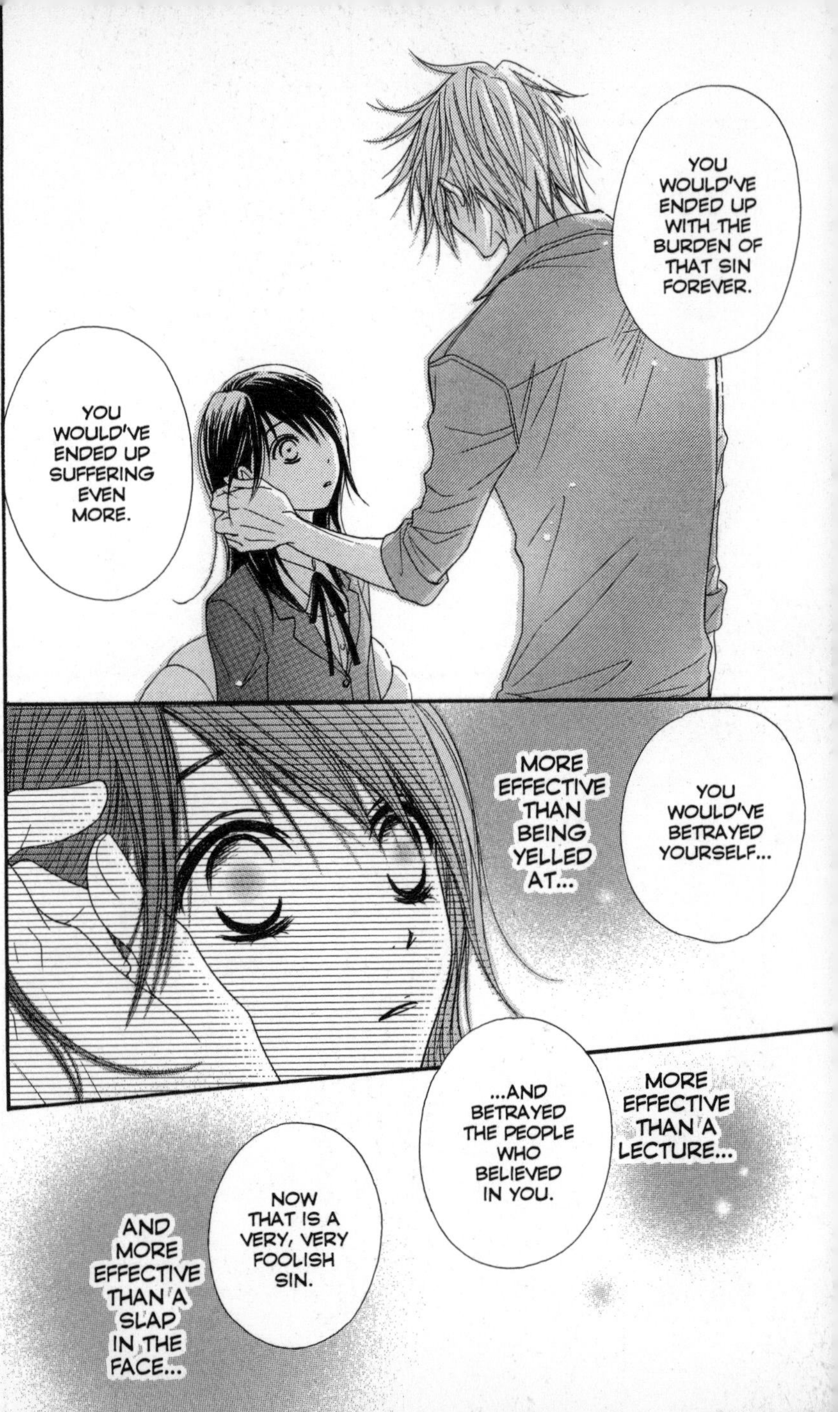
YOU WOULD'VE ENDED UP WITH THE BURDEN OF THAT SIN FOREVER.
YOU WOULD'VE ENDED UP SUFFERING EVEN MORE.
YOU WOULD'VE BETRAYED YOURSELF...
MORE EFFECTIVE THAN BEING YELLED AT...
MORE EFFECTIVE THAN A LECTURE...
...AND BETRAYED THE PEOPLE WHO BELIEVED IN YOU.
NOW THAT IS A VERY, VERY FOOLISH SIN.
AND MORE EFFECTIVE THAN A SLAP IN THE FACE...

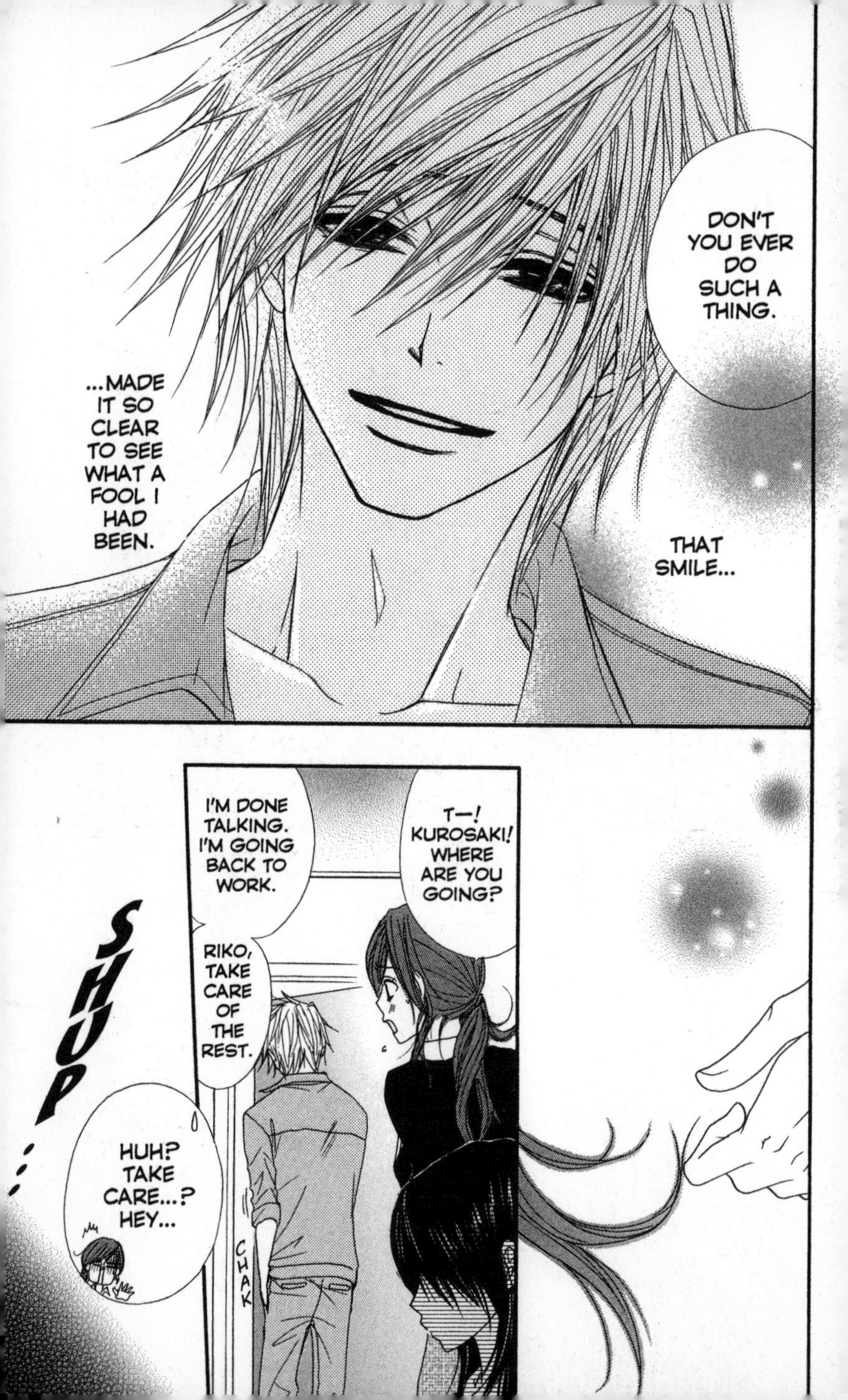
DON'T YOU EVER DO SUCH A THING.
THAT SMILE...
...MADE IT SO CLEAR TO SEE WHAT A FOOL I HAD BEEN.
T—! KUROSAKI! WHERE ARE YOU GOING?
I'M DONE TALKING. I'M GOING BACK TO WORK.
RIKO, TAKE CARE OF THE REST.
CHAK
SHUP...
HUH? TAKE CARE...? HEY...

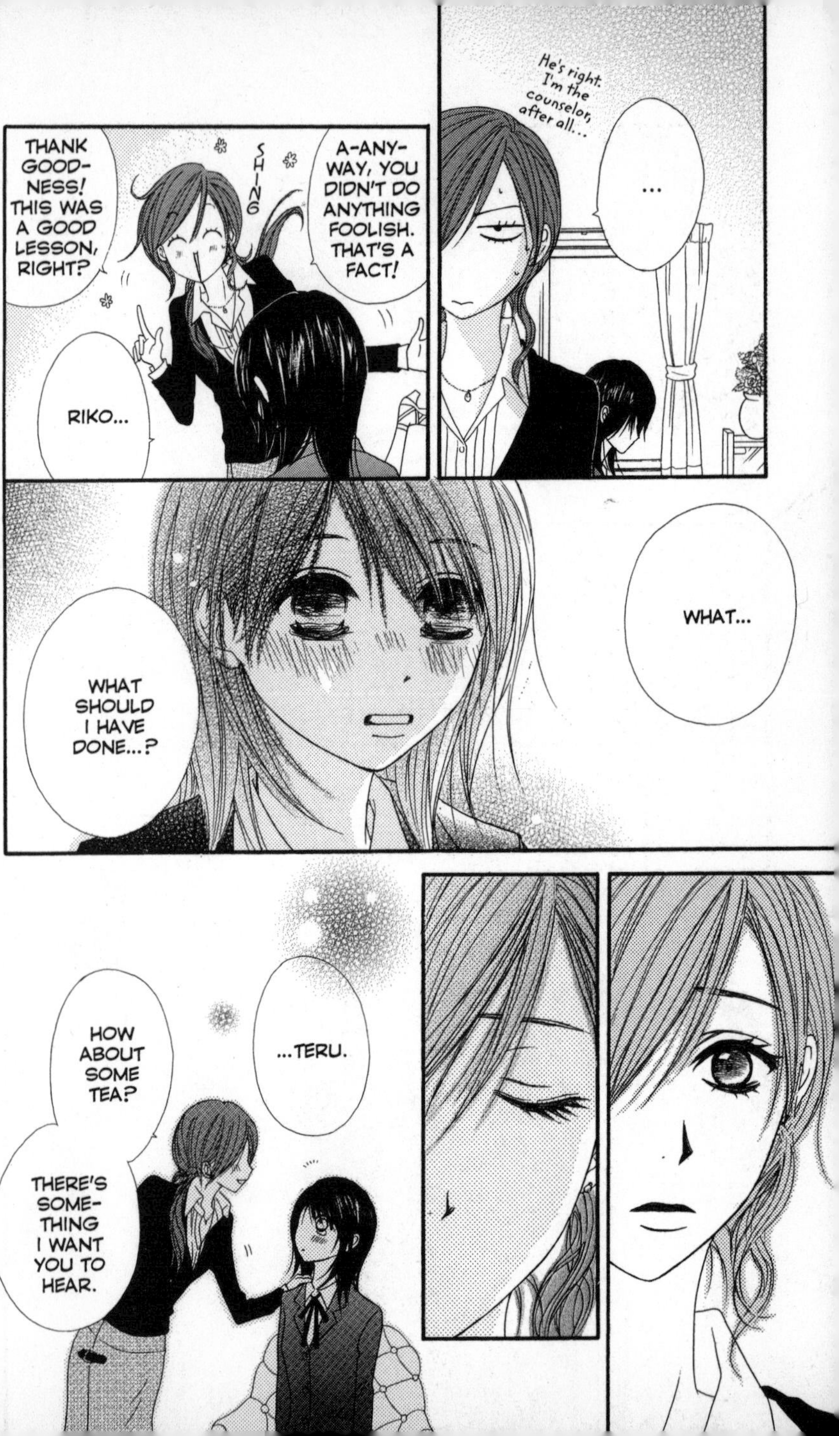
He's right. I'm the counselor, after all...
...
A-ANY-WAY, YOU DIDN'T DO ANYTHING FOOLISH. THAT'S A FACT!
SHING
THANK GOOD-NESS! THIS WAS A GOOD LESSON, RIGHT?
RIKO...
WHAT...
WHAT SHOULD I HAVE DONE...?
...TERU.
HOW ABOUT SOME TEA?
THERE'S SOME-THING I WANT YOU TO HEAR.

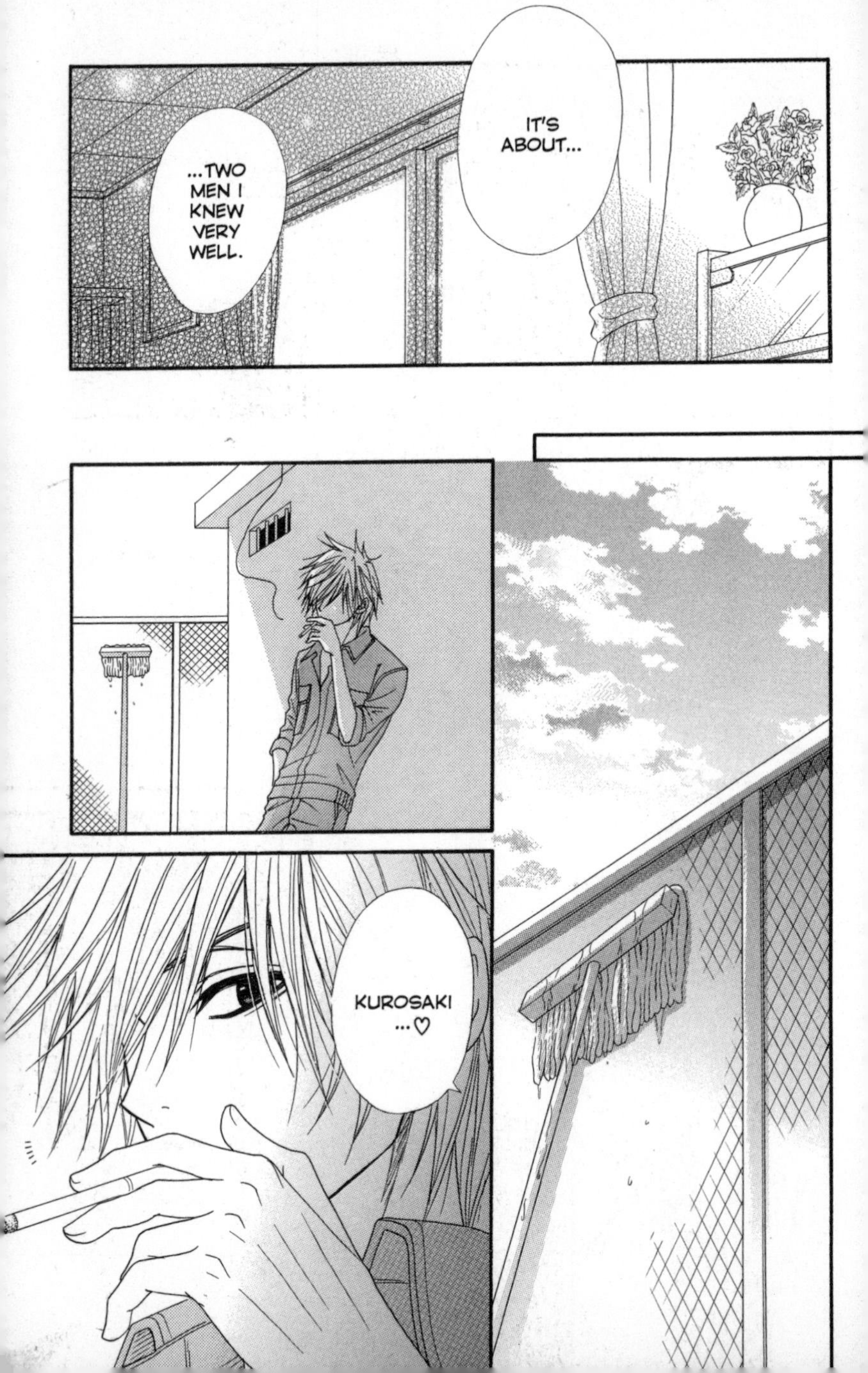
IT'S ABOUT...
...TWO MEN I KNEW VERY WELL.
KUROSAKI ...♡

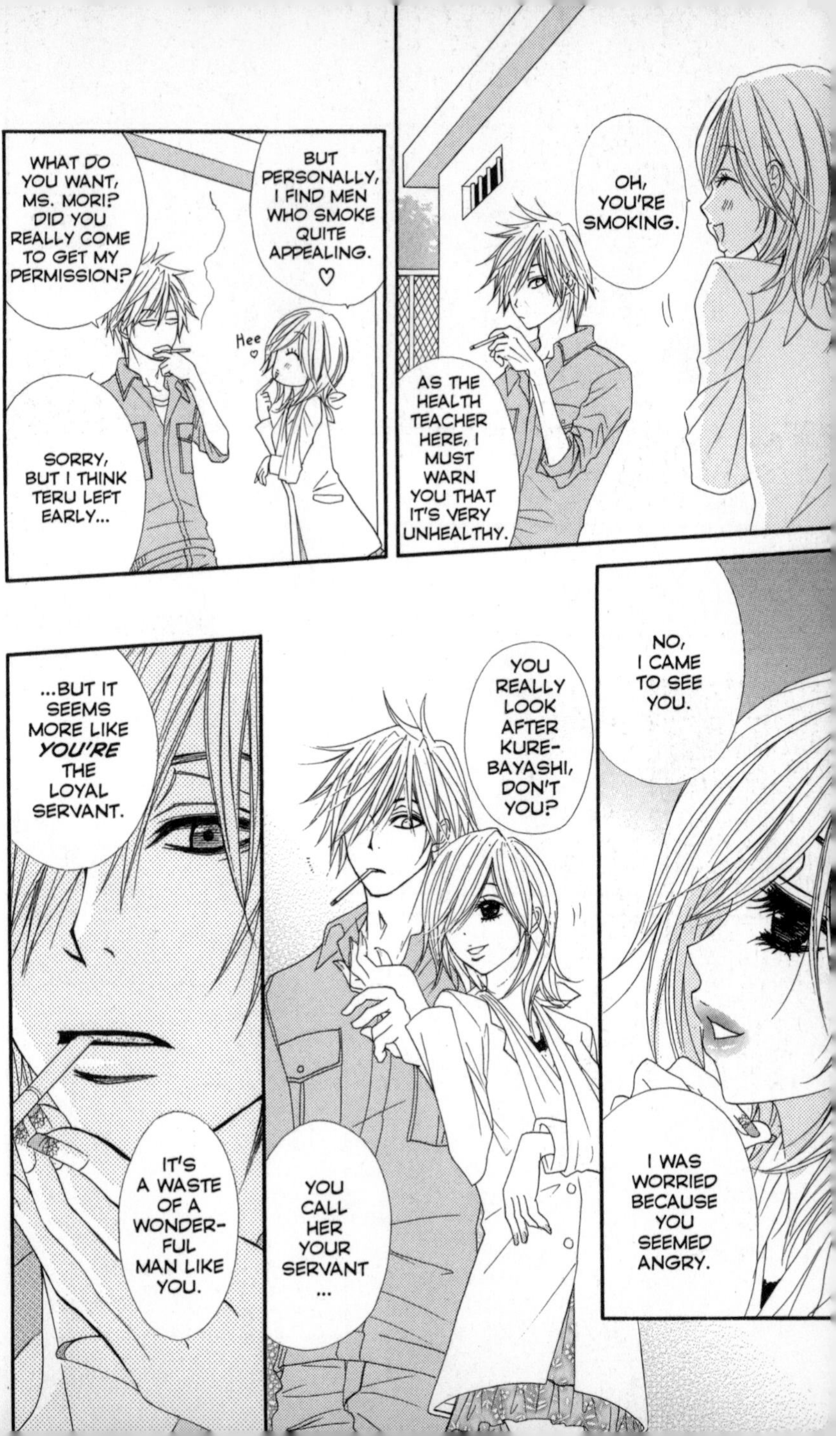
OH, YOU'RE SMOKING.
AS THE HEALTH TEACHER HERE, I MUST WARN YOU THAT IT'S VERY UNHEALTHY.
BUT PERSONALLY, I FIND MEN WHO SMOKE QUITE APPEALING. ♡
WHAT DO YOU WANT, MS. MORI? DID YOU REALLY COME TO GET MY PERMISSION?
Hee ♡
SORRY, BUT I THINK TERU LEFT EARLY...
NO, I CAME TO SEE YOU.
I WAS WORRIED BECAUSE YOU SEEMED ANGRY.
YOU REALLY LOOK AFTER KURE-BAYASHI, DON'T YOU?
YOU CALL HER YOUR SERVANT...
...BUT IT SEEMS MORE LIKE *YOU'RE* THE LOYAL SERVANT.
IT'S A WASTE OF A WONDERFUL MAN LIKE YOU.

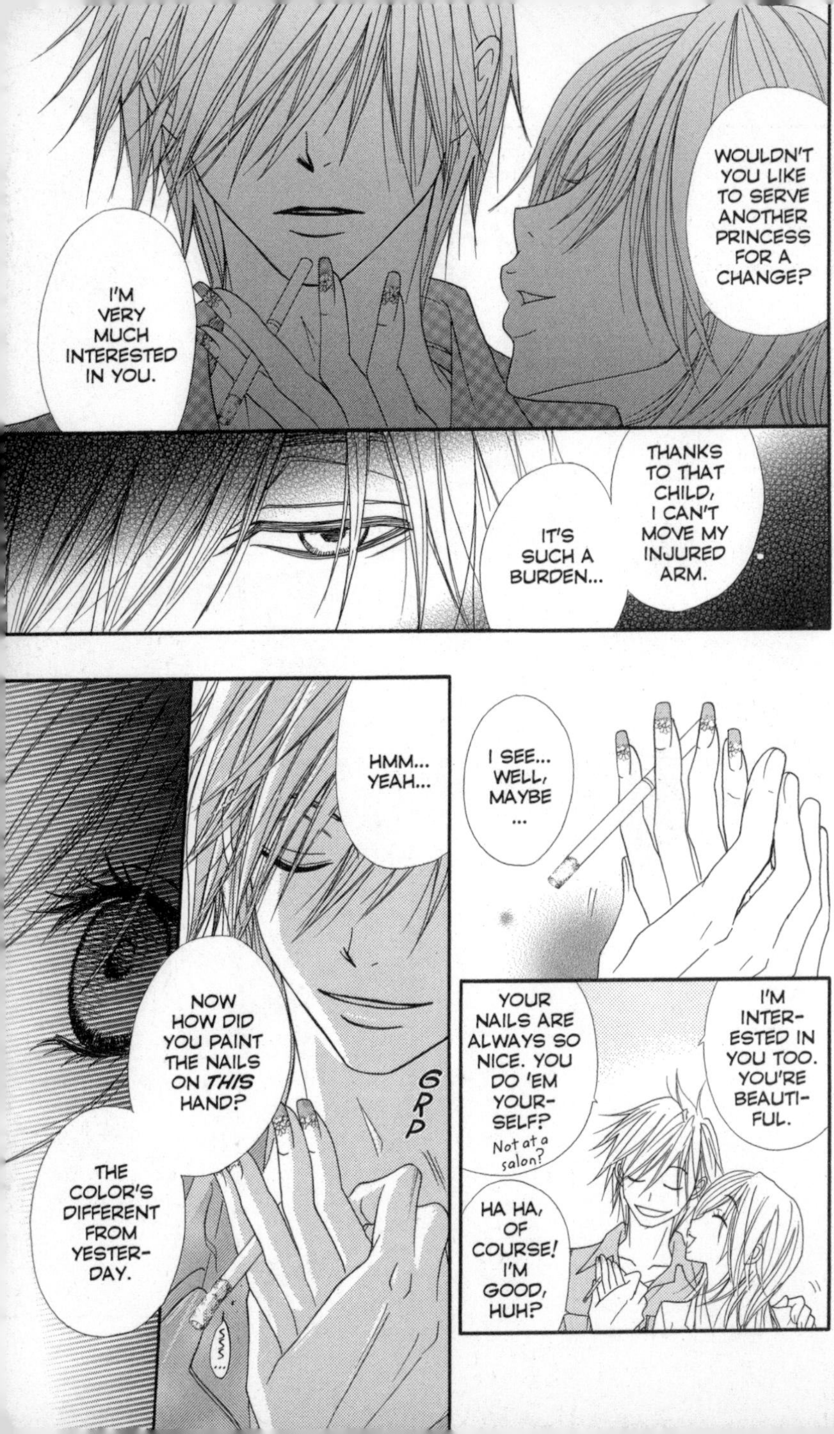
WOULDN'T YOU LIKE TO SERVE ANOTHER PRINCESS FOR A CHANGE?
I'M VERY MUCH INTERESTED IN YOU.
THANKS TO THAT CHILD, I CAN'T MOVE MY INJURED ARM.
IT'S SUCH A BURDEN...
I SEE... WELL, MAYBE ...
I'M INTER-ESTED IN YOU TOO. YOU'RE BEAUTI-FUL.
YOUR NAILS ARE ALWAYS SO NICE. YOU DO 'EM YOUR-SELF?
Not at a salon?
HA HA, OF COURSE! I'M GOOD, HUH?
HMM... YEAH...
NOW HOW DID YOU PAINT THE NAILS ON *THIS* HAND?
GRP
THE COLOR'S DIFFERENT FROM YESTER-DAY.

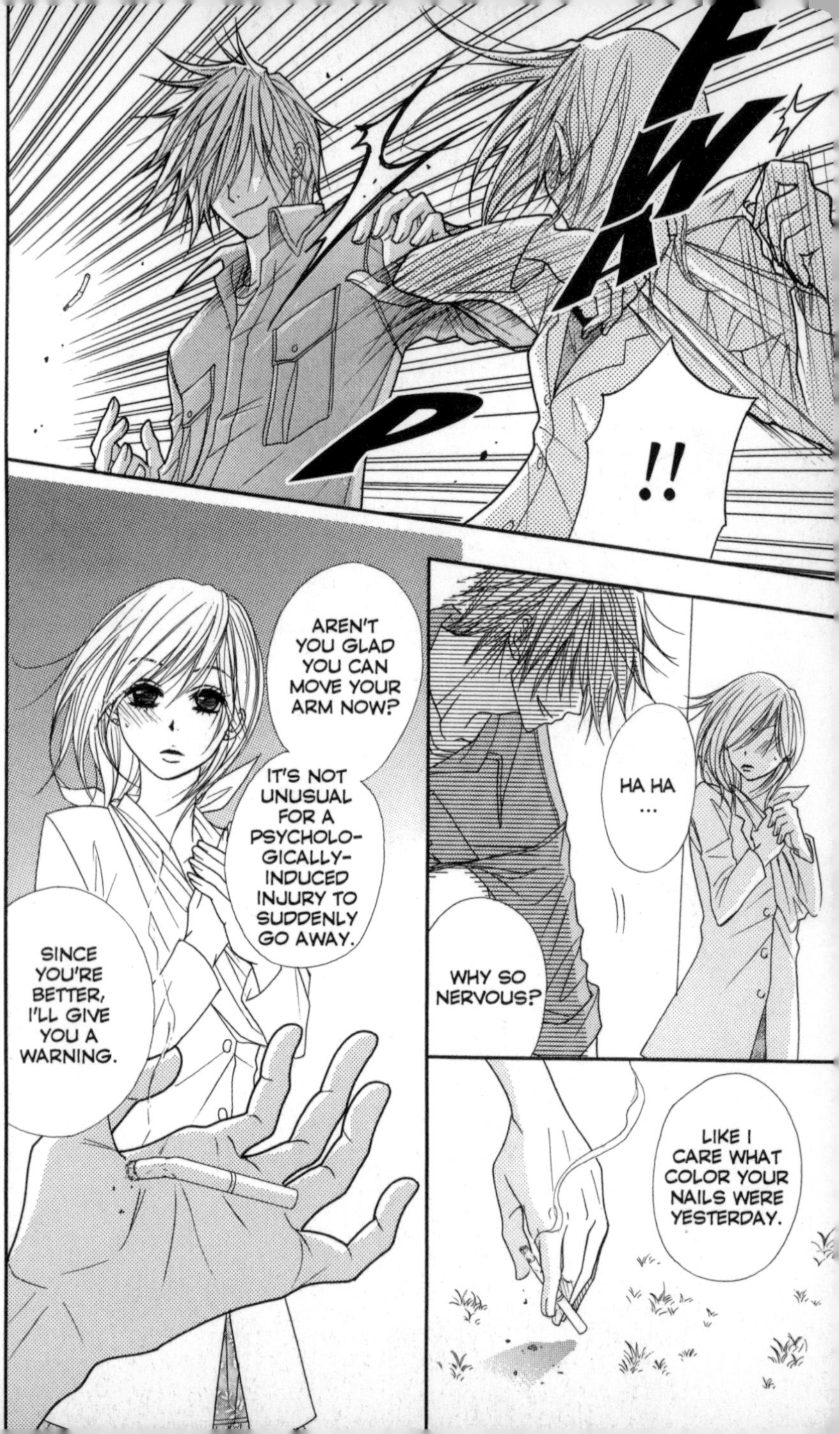
FWAP
!!
HA HA ...
WHY SO NERVOUS?
LIKE I CARE WHAT COLOR YOUR NAILS WERE YESTERDAY.
AREN'T YOU GLAD YOU CAN MOVE YOUR ARM NOW?
IT'S NOT UNUSUAL FOR A PSYCHOLO-GICALLY-INDUCED INJURY TO SUDDENLY GO AWAY.
SINCE YOU'RE BETTER, I'LL GIVE YOU A WARNING.

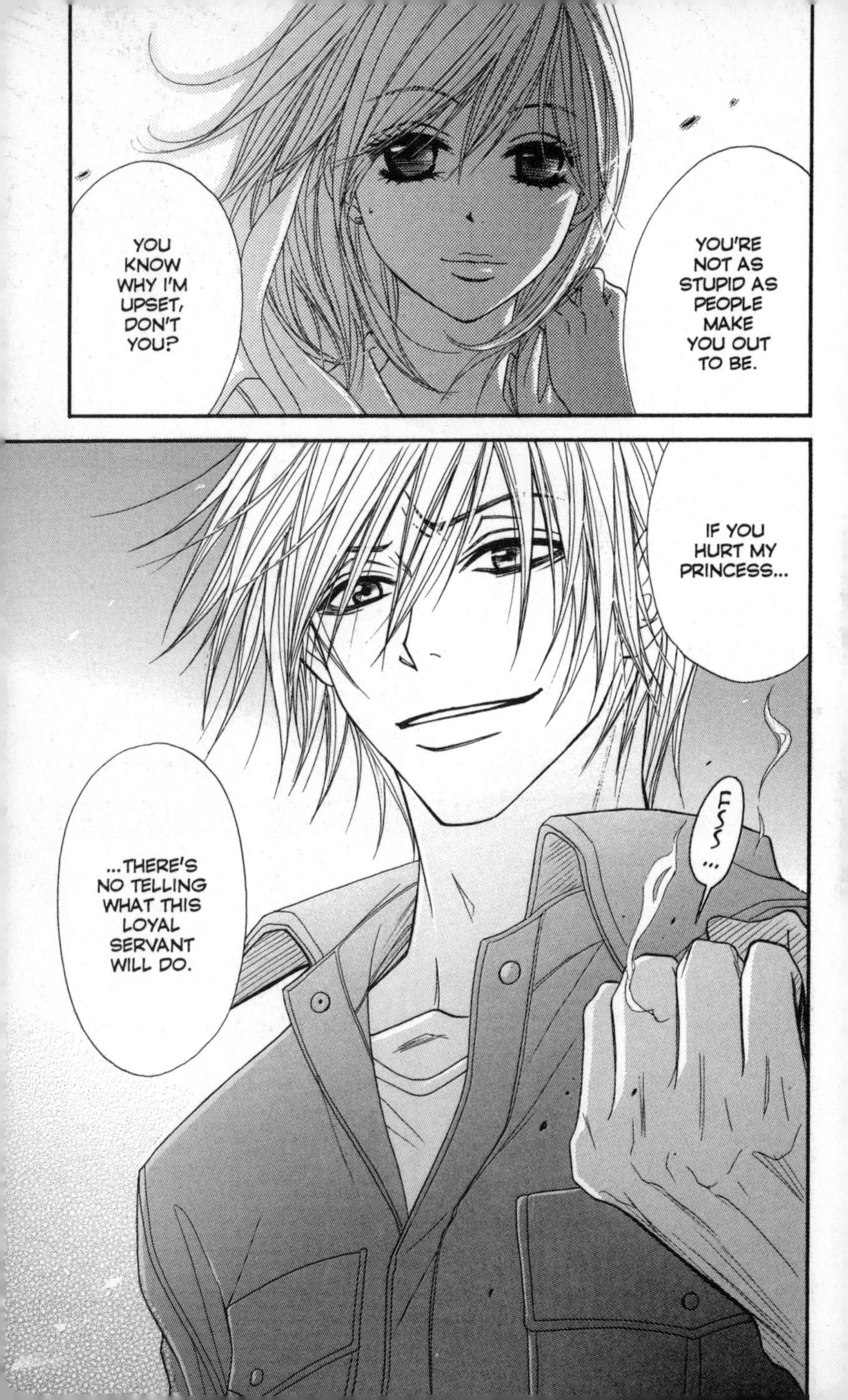
YOU'RE NOT AS STUPID AS PEOPLE MAKE YOU OUT TO BE.
YOU KNOW WHY I'M UPSET, DON'T YOU?
IF YOU HURT MY PRINCESS...
Fss...
...THERE'S NO TELLING WHAT THIS LOYAL SERVANT WILL DO.

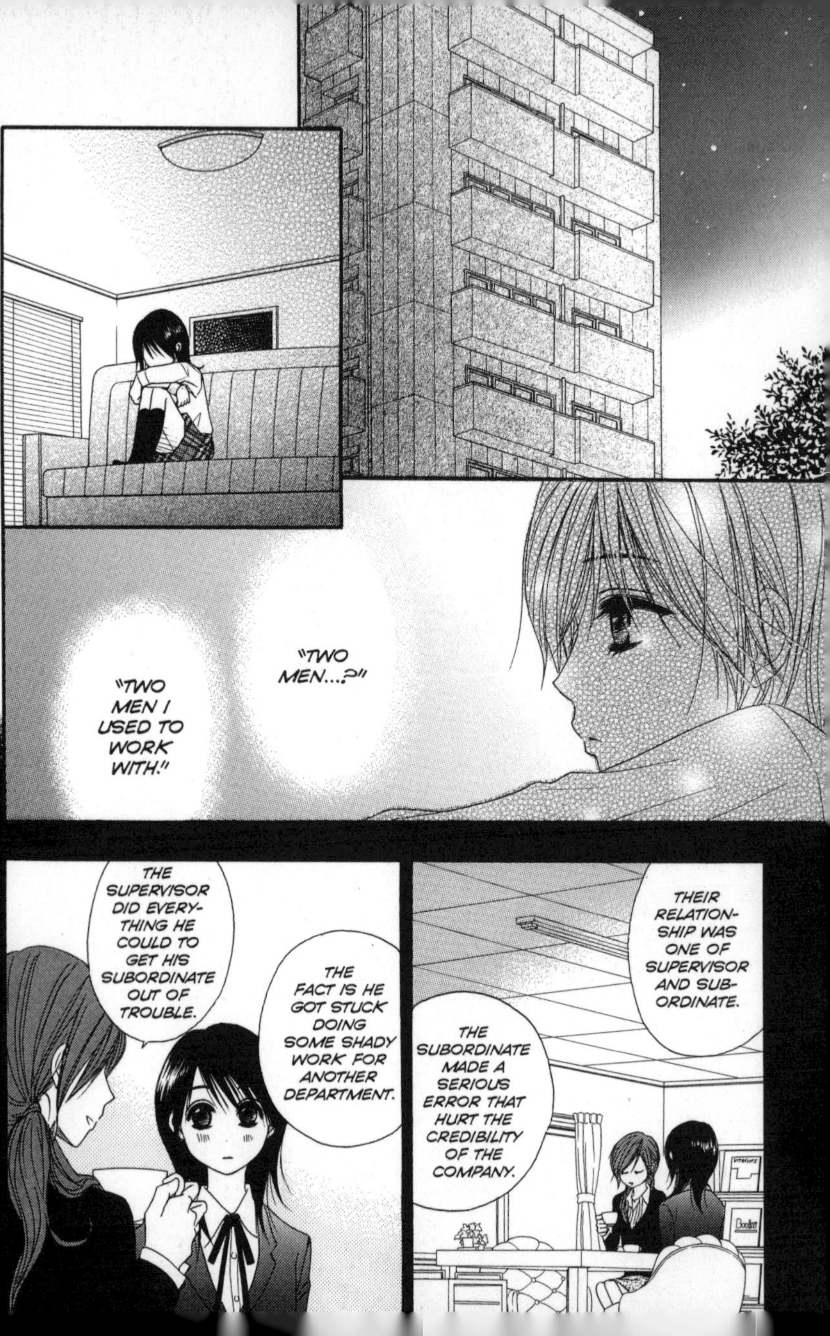

"TWO MEN...?"
"TWO MEN I USED TO WORK WITH."
THEIR RELATIONSHIP WAS ONE OF SUPERVISOR AND SUBORDINATE.
THE SUBORDINATE MADE A SERIOUS ERROR THAT HURT THE CREDIBILITY OF THE COMPANY.
THE SUPERVISOR DID EVERYTHING HE COULD TO GET HIS SUBORDINATE OUT OF TROUBLE.
THE FACT IS HE GOT STUCK DOING SOME SHADY WORK FOR ANOTHER DEPARTMENT.

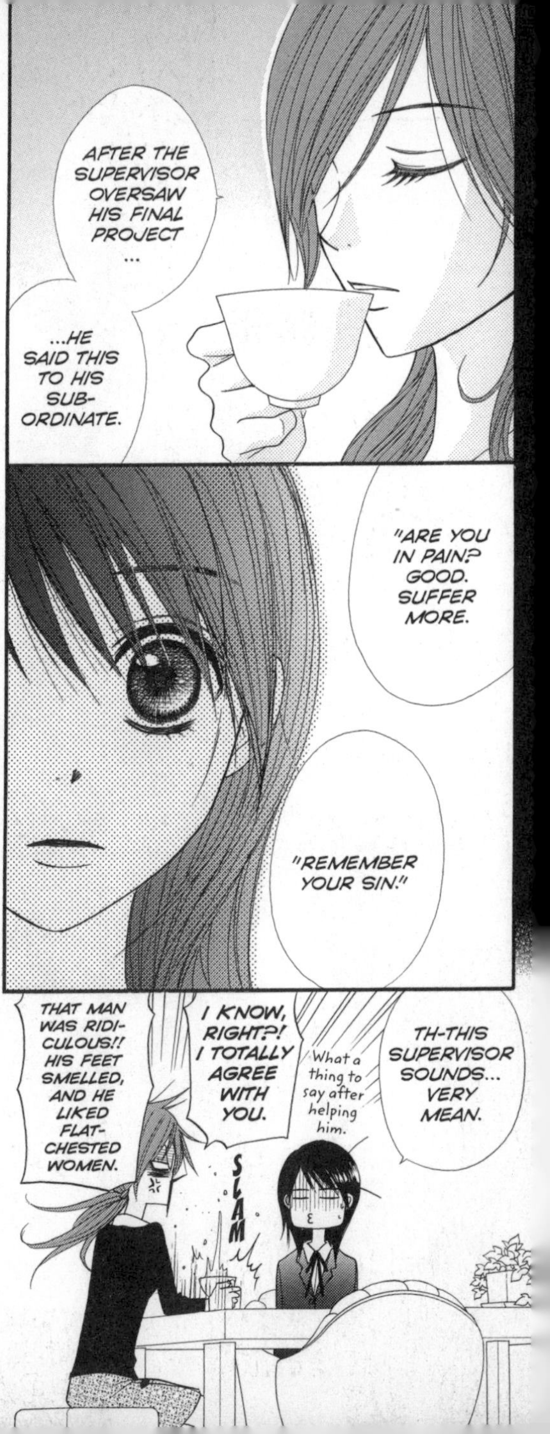
AFTER THE SUPERVISOR OVERSAW HIS FINAL PROJECT ...
...HE SAID THIS TO HIS SUB-ORDINATE.
"ARE YOU IN PAIN? GOOD. SUFFER MORE.
"REMEMBER YOUR SIN."
TH-THIS SUPERVISOR SOUNDS... VERY MEAN.
What a thing to say after helping him.
I KNOW, RIGHT?! I TOTALLY AGREE WITH YOU.
THAT MAN WAS RIDI-CULOUS!! HIS FEET SMELLED, AND HE LIKED FLAT-CHESTED WOMEN.
SLAM

DENGEKI DAISY QUESTION CORNER

BALDLY ASK!!

⑤

Q.
HERE IS A QUESTION FOR KUROSAKI AND THE OTHERS. DO YOU EAT TAIYAKI* FROM THE HEAD OR TAIL?

(UZUKI, HOKKAIDO)

A. HERE ARE THEIR ANSWERS AND REASONS.

(HEAD FIRST FACTION) KUROSAKI, KIYOSHI, HARUKA, BOSS
"THIS IS THE RIGHT WAY TO EAT IT."
"IT'S RUDE TO ATTACK FROM THE BACK."
"THAT'S EATING IT NORMALLY."
"NOTHING'S WRONG WITH EATING IT NORMALLY."

(TAIL FIRST FACTION) TERU, RIKO, ANDY, YOSHI
"I LIKE TO LEAVE THE BEST PART FOR LAST."
"NO, THE TAIL IS THE BEST PART."
"SOMETHING AS UNIQUE AS A TAIYAKI HEAD SHOULD BE RESPECTED AND SAVED FOR LAST. OTHERWISE, IT'S JUST AN IMAGAWAYAKI.**"
"I LIKE IT FROM THE BACK."

(THE REMAINDER)
RENA: "I'VE NEVER EATEN ONE."
SOICHIRO: "FIRST, MAKE A HOLE IN THE BUTT. THEN SUCK OUT ALL THE RED BEAN PASTE IN ONE INTAKE OF BREATH. THEN SLOWL—" (EDITED)

THAT'S ALL FOR THIS VOLUME. THANK YOU TO EVERYONE WHO SENT IN QUESTIONS. IF THERE AREN'T ANY REALLY UPSET READERS, WE'LL CONTINUE IN VOLUME 6!!!

*A fish-shaped cake that's filled with red bean paste and grilled on a waffle iron

**Round-shaped cake with filling inside that is made using a round iron mold.

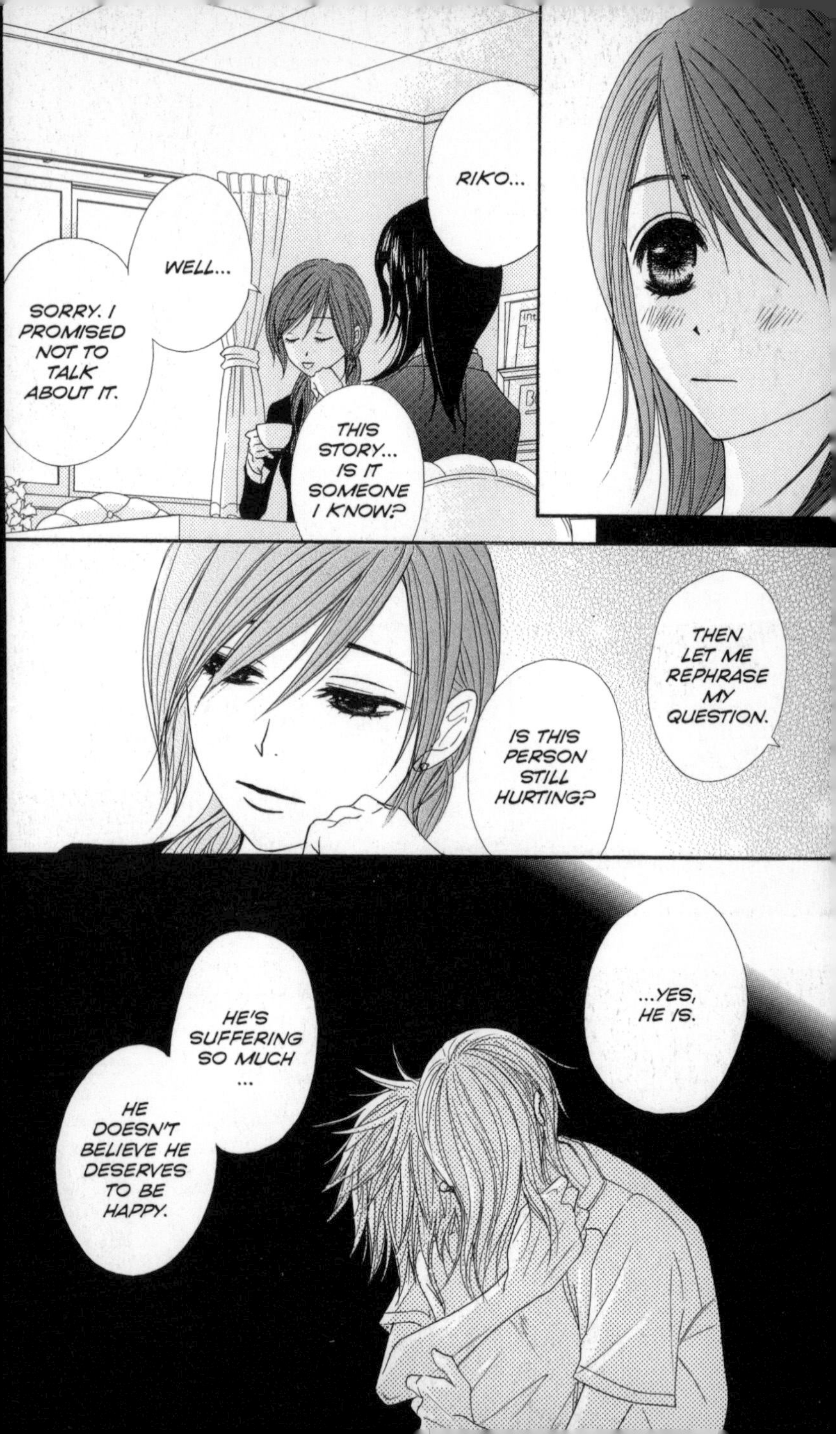
RIKO...
THIS STORY... IS IT SOMEONE I KNOW?
WELL...
SORRY. I PROMISED NOT TO TALK ABOUT IT.
THEN LET ME REPHRASE MY QUESTION.
IS THIS PERSON STILL HURTING?
...YES, HE IS.
HE'S SUFFERING SO MUCH...
HE DOESN'T BELIEVE HE DESERVES TO BE HAPPY.

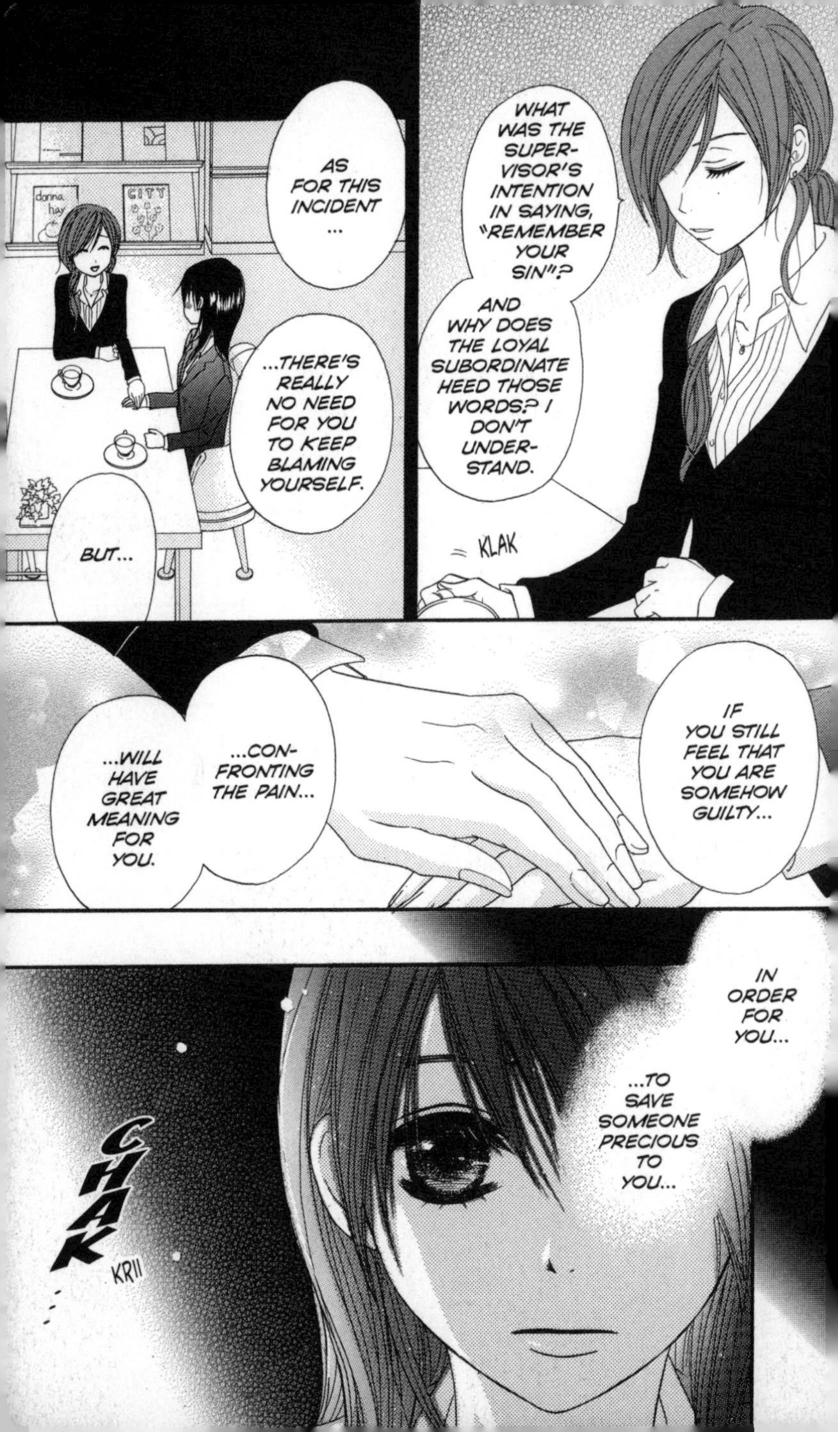
WHAT WAS THE SUPER-VISOR'S INTENTION IN SAYING, "REMEMBER YOUR SIN"?
AND WHY DOES THE LOYAL SUBORDINATE HEED THOSE WORDS? I DON'T UNDER-STAND.
KLAK
AS FOR THIS INCIDENT...
...THERE'S REALLY NO NEED FOR YOU TO KEEP BLAMING YOURSELF.
BUT...
IF YOU STILL FEEL THAT YOU ARE SOMEHOW GUILTY...
...CON-FRONTING THE PAIN...
...WILL HAVE GREAT MEANING FOR YOU.
IN ORDER FOR YOU...
...TO SAVE SOMEONE PRECIOUS TO YOU...
CHAK
KRII

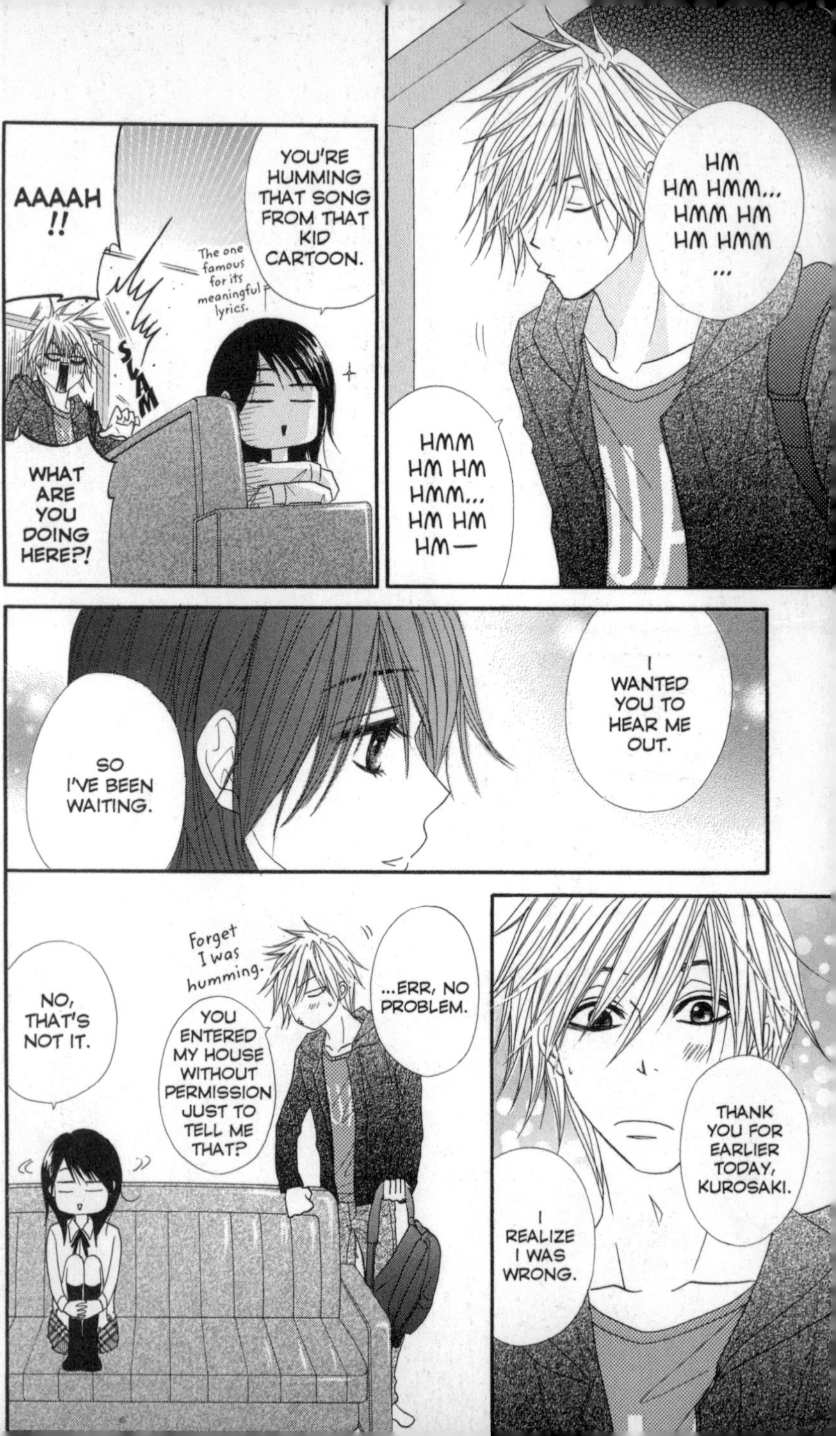
HM HM HMM... HMM HM HM HMM ...
HMM HM HM HMM... HM HM HM—
YOU'RE HUMMING THAT SONG FROM THAT KID CARTOON.
The one famous for its meaningful lyrics.
AAAAH !!
SLAM
WHAT ARE YOU DOING HERE?!
I WANTED YOU TO HEAR ME OUT.
SO I'VE BEEN WAITING.
THANK YOU FOR EARLIER TODAY, KUROSAKI.
I REALIZE I WAS WRONG.
...ERR, NO PROBLEM.
Forget I was humming.
YOU ENTERED MY HOUSE WITHOUT PERMISSION JUST TO TELL ME THAT?
NO, THAT'S NOT IT.

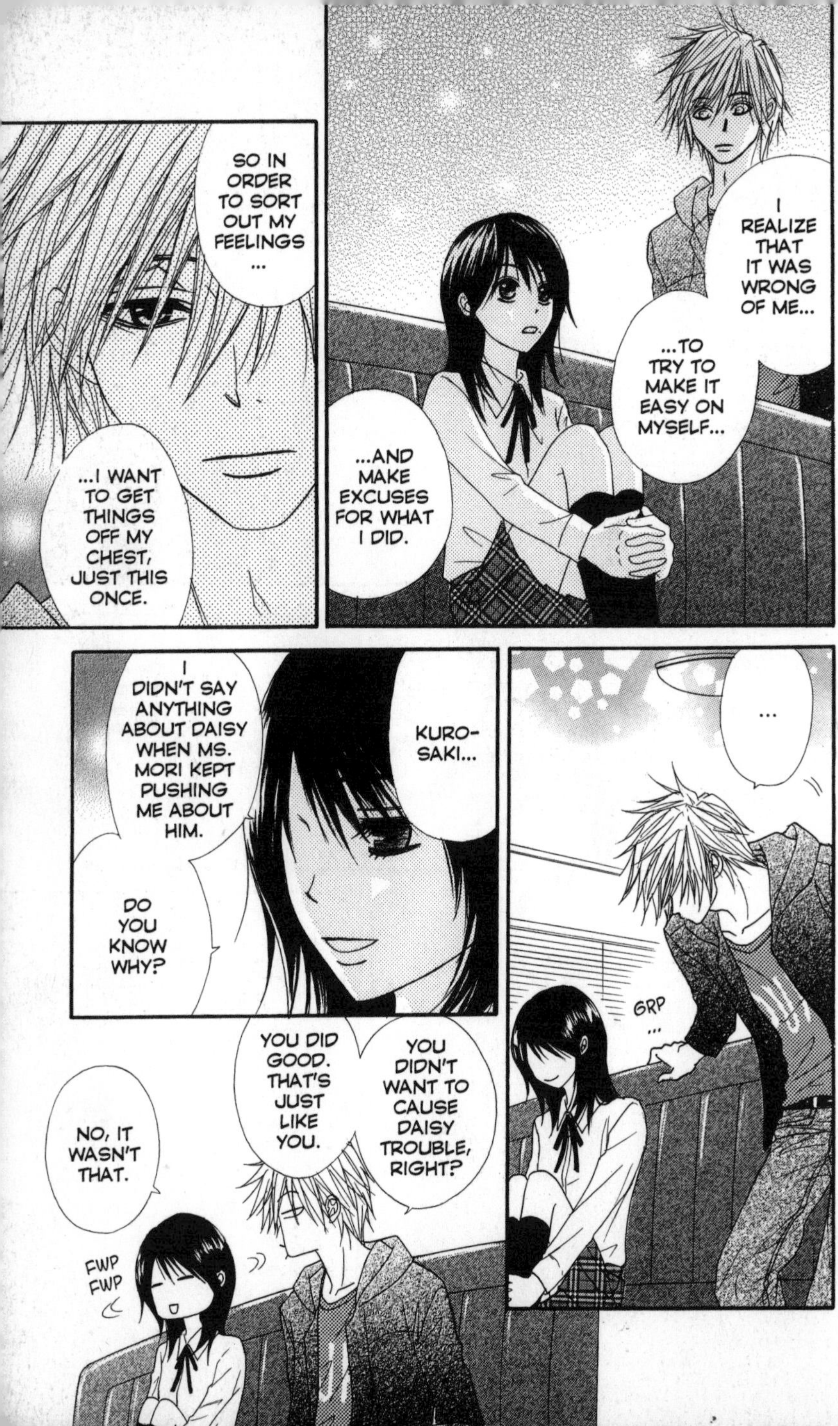
I REALIZE THAT IT WAS WRONG OF ME...
...TO TRY TO MAKE IT EASY ON MYSELF...
...AND MAKE EXCUSES FOR WHAT I DID.
SO IN ORDER TO SORT OUT MY FEELINGS...
...I WANT TO GET THINGS OFF MY CHEST, JUST THIS ONCE.
...
GRP...
KURO-SAKI...
I DIDN'T SAY ANYTHING ABOUT DAISY WHEN MS. MORI KEPT PUSHING ME ABOUT HIM.
DO YOU KNOW WHY?
YOU DIDN'T WANT TO CAUSE DAISY TROUBLE, RIGHT?
YOU DID GOOD. THAT'S JUST LIKE YOU.
NO, IT WASN'T THAT.
FWP FWP

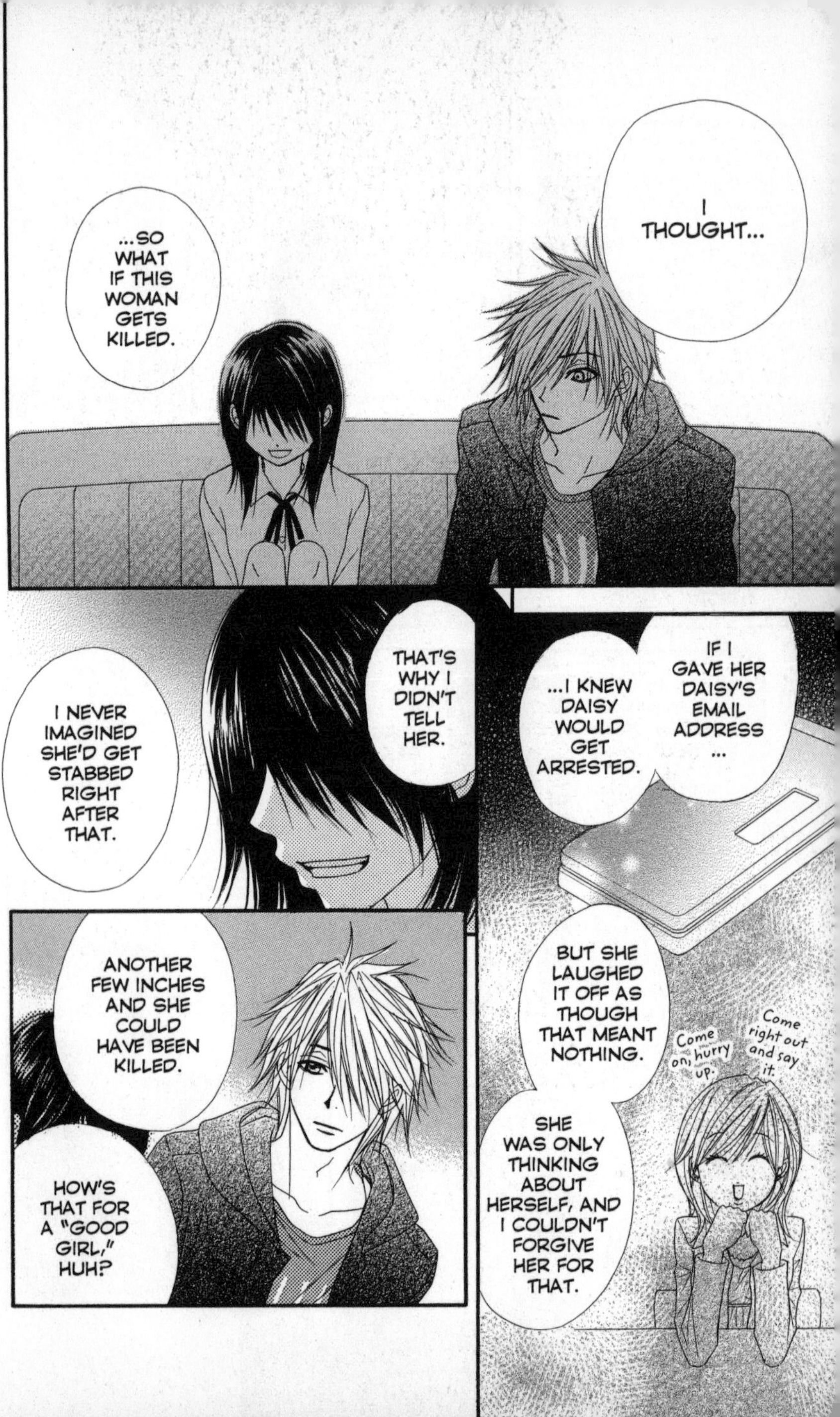
I THOUGHT...
...SO WHAT IF THIS WOMAN GETS KILLED.
IF I GAVE HER DAISY'S EMAIL ADDRESS ...
...I KNEW DAISY WOULD GET ARRESTED.
BUT SHE LAUGHED IT OFF AS THOUGH THAT MEANT NOTHING.
Come right out and say it.
Come on, hurry up.
SHE WAS ONLY THINKING ABOUT HERSELF, AND I COULDN'T FORGIVE HER FOR THAT.
THAT'S WHY I DIDN'T TELL HER.
I NEVER IMAGINED SHE'D GET STABBED RIGHT AFTER THAT.
ANOTHER FEW INCHES AND SHE COULD HAVE BEEN KILLED.
HOW'S THAT FOR A "GOOD GIRL," HUH?

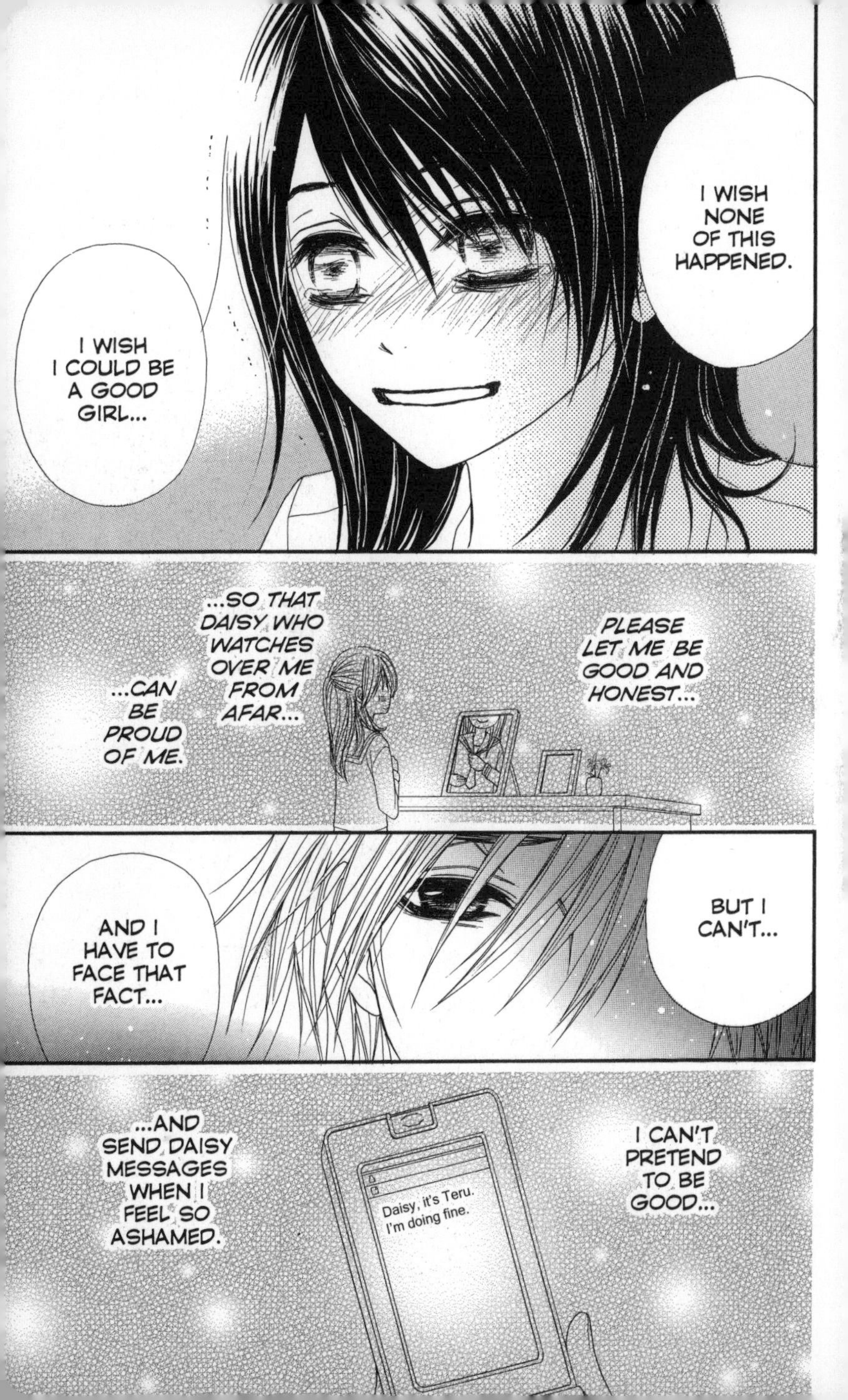
I WISH NONE OF THIS HAPPENED.
I WISH I COULD BE A GOOD GIRL...
PLEASE LET ME BE GOOD AND HONEST...
...SO THAT DAISY WHO WATCHES OVER ME FROM AFAR...
...CAN BE PROUD OF ME.
BUT I CAN'T...
AND I HAVE TO FACE THAT FACT...
I CAN'T PRETEND TO BE GOOD...
...AND SEND DAISY MESSAGES WHEN I FEEL SO ASHAMED.
Daisy, it's Teru. I'm doing fine.

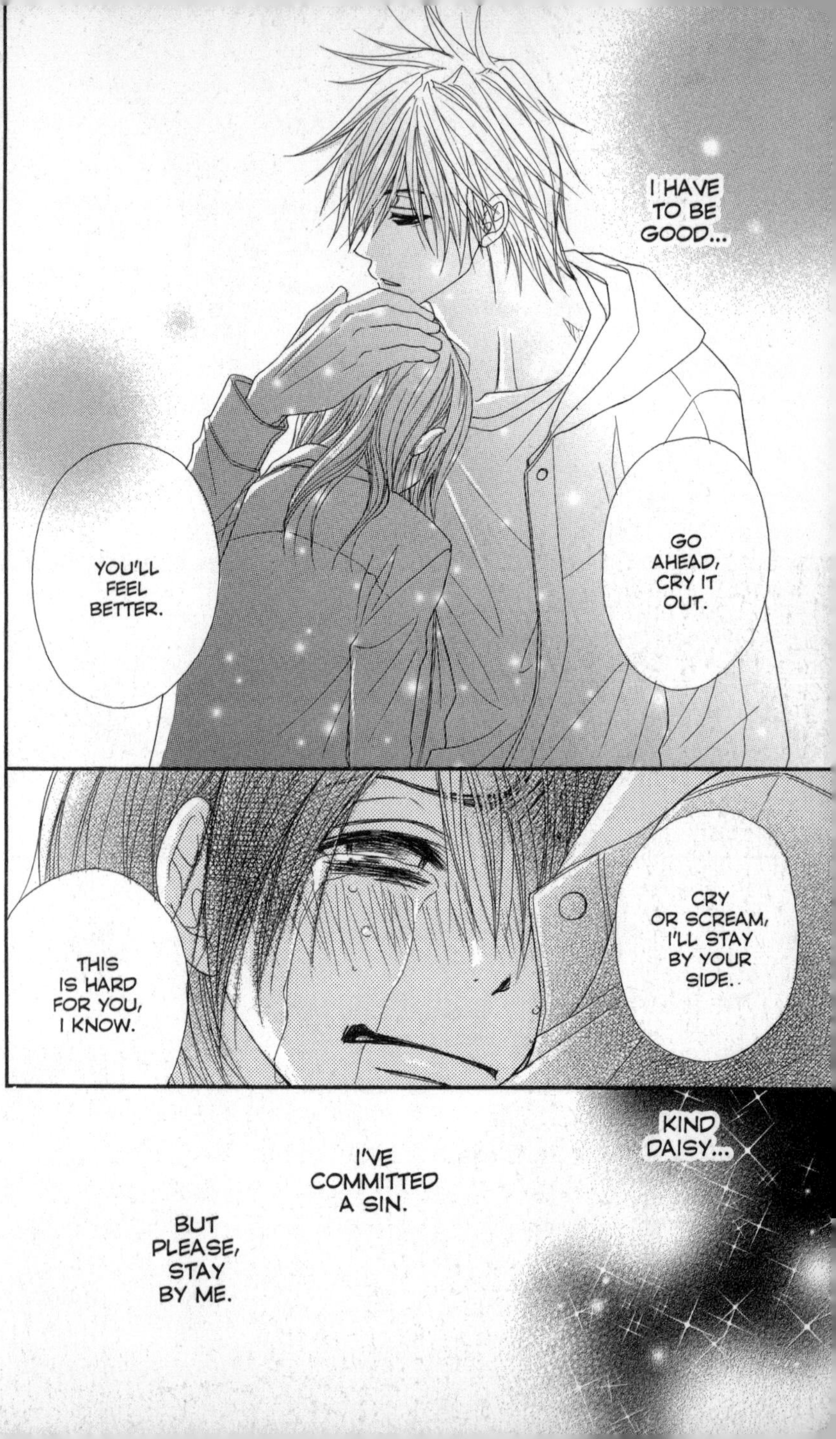
I HAVE TO BE GOOD...
GO AHEAD, CRY IT OUT.
YOU'LL FEEL BETTER.
CRY OR SCREAM, I'LL STAY BY YOUR SIDE.
THIS IS HARD FOR YOU, I KNOW.
KIND DAISY...
I'VE COMMITTED A SIN.
BUT PLEASE, STAY BY ME.

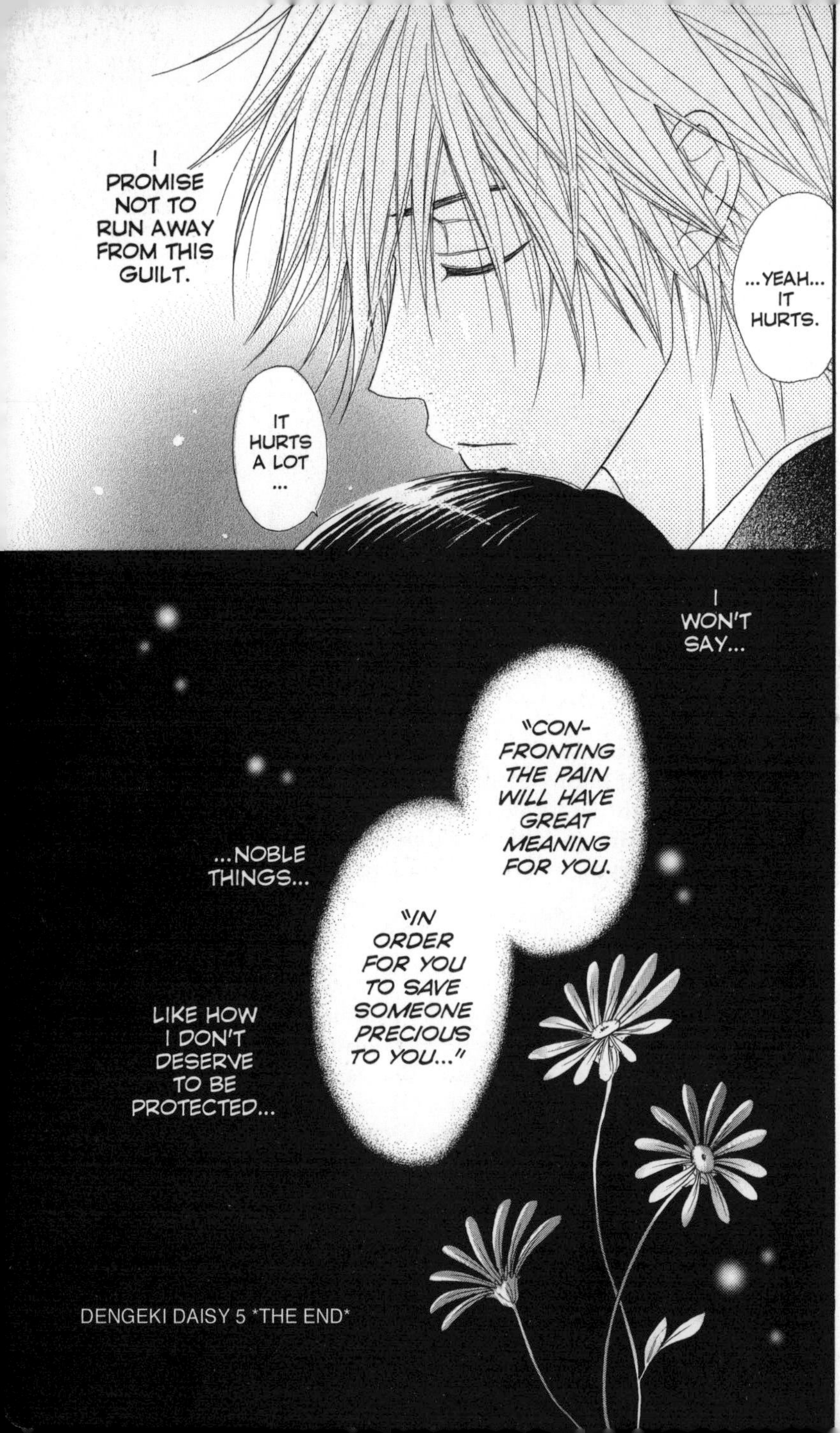
...YEAH... IT HURTS.
IT HURTS A LOT ...
I PROMISE NOT TO RUN AWAY FROM THIS GUILT.
I WON'T SAY...
"CON-FRONTING THE PAIN WILL HAVE GREAT MEANING FOR YOU.
"IN ORDER FOR YOU TO SAVE SOMEONE PRECIOUS TO YOU..."
...NOBLE THINGS...
LIKE HOW I DON'T DESERVE TO BE PROTECTED...
DENGEKI DAISY 5 *THE END*

I GO TO SLEEP BEFORE NOON. WHEN I GET UP, SOMETIMES THE SUN HAS ALREADY SET. WHAT A FAILURE I AM AS A HUMAN BEING, I THINK.

My life is out of sync. For the first time, I'm seriously thinking that this isn't good. Go to bed at night and wake up in the morning. This basic premise of living as a human being is what I've been trying to recapture lately.

-Kyousuke Motomi

Born on August 1, Kyousuke Motomi debuted in *Deluxe Betsucomi* with *Hetakuso Kyupiddo* (No-Good Cupid) in 2002. She is the creator of *Otokomae! Biizu Kurabu* (Handsome! Beads Club), and her latest work, *Dengeki Daisy*, is currently being serialized in *Betsucomi*. Motomi enjoys sleeping, tea ceremonies and reading Haruki Murakami.

DENGEKI DAISY
VOL. 5
Shojo Beat Edition

STORY AND ART BY
KYOUSUKE MOTOMI

© 2007 Kyousuke MOTOMI/Shogakukan
All rights reserved.
Original Japanese edition "DENGEKI DAISY"
published by SHOGAKUKAN Inc.

Translation & Adaptation/JN Productions
Touch-up Art & Lettering/Rina Mapa
Cover Design/Yukiko Whitley
Interior Design/Nozomi Akashi
Editor/Amy Yu

Printed in the U.S.A.

Published by VIZ Media, LLC
P.O. Box 77010
San Francisco, CA 94107

10 9 8 7 6 5 4 3 2 1
First printing, July 2011

www.viz.com   www.shojobeat.com

Story and Art by Miki Aihara | Creator of *Honey Hunt* and *Tokyo Boys & Girls*

Three volumes of
the original manga
combined into a
larger format with an
exclusive cover design
and bonus content

Full-length novel with
an alternate ending
and a bonus manga
episode

Hot Gimmick

If you think being a teenager is hard, be glad your name isn't Hatsumi Narita

With scandals that would make any gossip girl blush and more triangles than you can throw a geometry book at, this girl may never figure out the game of love!

LAND OF *Fantasy*

MIAKA YÛKI IS AN ORDINARY JUNIOR-HIGH STUDENT WHO IS SUDDENLY WHISKED AWAY INTO THE WORLD OF A BOOK, *THE UNIVERSE OF THE FOUR GODS*. WILL THE BEAUTIFUL CELESTIAL BEINGS SHE ENCOUNTERS AND THE CHANCE TO BECOME A PRIESTESS DIVERT MIAKA FROM EVER RETURNING HOME?

THREE VOLUMES OF THE ORIGINAL *FUSHIGI YÛGI* SERIES COMBINED INTO A LARGER FORMAT WITH AN EXCLUSIVE COVER DESIGN AND BONUS CONTENT

EXPERIENCE THE BEAUTY OF *FUSHIGI YÛGI* WITH THE HARDCOVER ART BOOK

ALSO AVAILABLE: THE *FUSHIGI YÛGI: GENBU KAIDEN* MANGA, THE EIGHT VOLUME PREQUEL TO THIS BEST-SELLING FANTASY SERIES

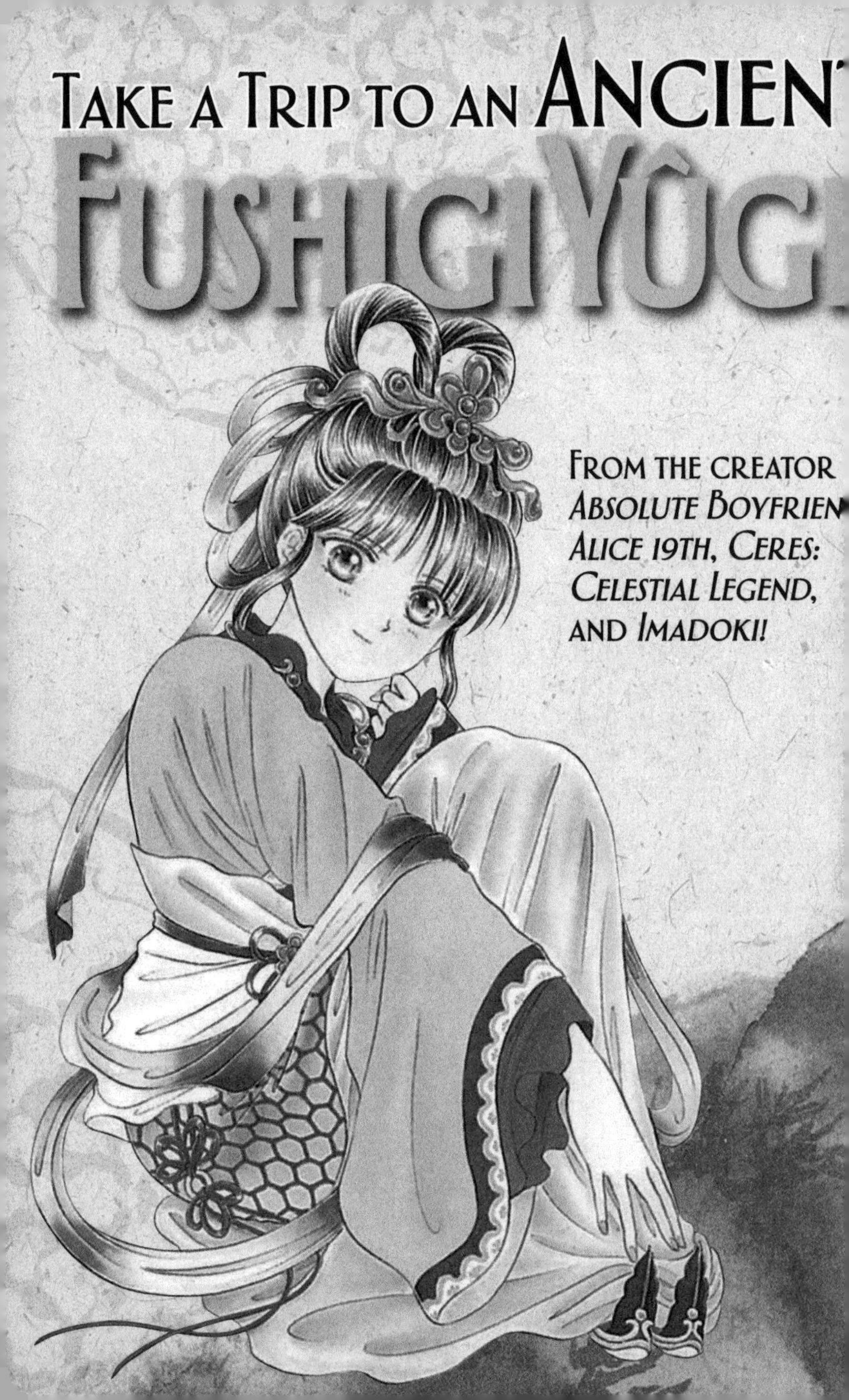
TAKE A TRIP TO AN ANCIEN
FUSHIGI YÛGI
FROM THE CREATOR
ABSOLUTE BOYFRIEN
ALICE 19TH, CERES:
CELESTIAL LEGEND,
AND IMADOKI!

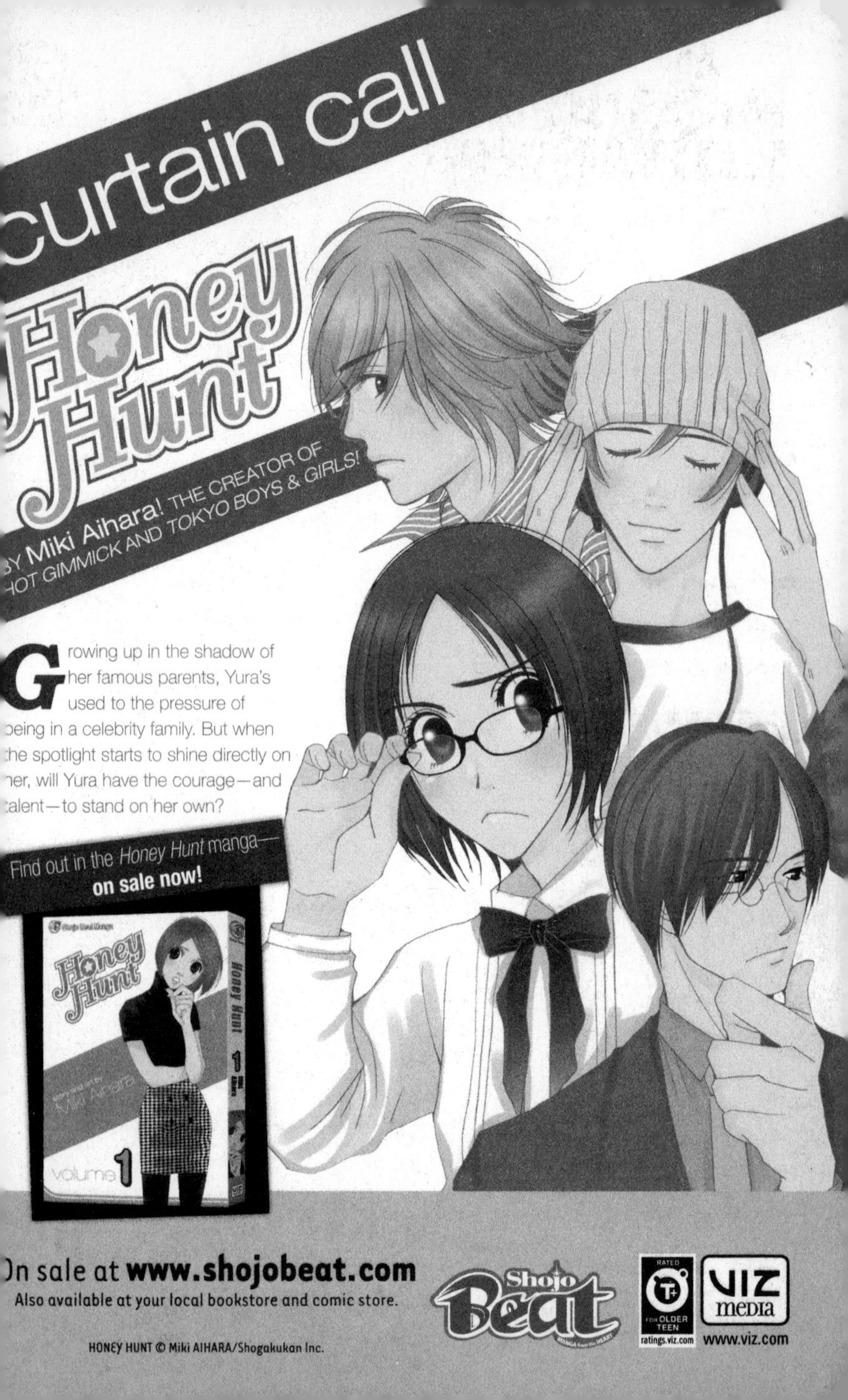